STRESS MANAGEMENT
PSYCHOLOGICAL
FOUNDATIONS

STRESS MANAGEMENT
PSYCHOLOGICAL
FOUNDATIONS

Stephen M. Auerbach
Virginia Commonwealth University

Sandra E. Gramling
Virginia Commonwealth University

Prentice Hall, Upper Saddle River, New Jersey 07458

Library of Congress Cataloging-in-Publication Data

Auerbach, Stephen M.
    Stress management: psychological foundations / Stephen M.
    Auerbach, Sandra E. Gramling.
        p.   cm.
    Includes bibliographical references and index.
    ISBN 0-13-722281-5
    1. Stress (Psychology) 2. Stress management. I. Gramling,
Sandra E., 1958– . II. Title.
BF575.S75A84 1998
155.9'042—dc21   97–5294
                                                    CIP

Editor in chief: Nancy Roberts
Acquisitions editor: Bill Webber
Assistant editor: Jennifer Hood
Managing editor: Mary Rottino
Production liaison: Fran Russello
Project manager: Marianne Hutchinson (Pine Tree Composition, Inc.)
Prepress and manufacturing buyer: Lynn Pearlman
Cover design: Bruce Kenselaar
Cover art: Tony Stone Images/Hugh Sitton
Director, Image Resource Center: Lori Morris-Nantz
Photo reseach supervisor: Melinda Lee Reo
Image permission supervisor: Kay Dellosa
Photo researcher: Rona Tuccillo
Marketing manager: Mike Alread

This book was set in 10/12 Novarese Book by Pine Tree Composition, Inc.
Text and covers printed and bound by Banta Company.

 © 1998 by Prentice-Hall, Inc.
Simon & Schuster/A Viacom Company
Upper Saddle River, New Jersey 07458

Printed in the United States of America
10 9 8 7 6 5 4 3 2

ISBN: 0-13-722281-5

PRENTICE-HALL INTERNATIONAL (UK) LIMITED, *London*
PRENTICE-HALL OF AUSTRALIA PTY. LIMITED, *Sydney*
PRENTICE-HALL CANADA INC., *Toronto*
PRENTICE-HALL HISPANOAMERICANA, S.A., *Mexico*
PRENTICE-HALL OF INDIA PRIVATE LIMITED, *New Delhi*
PRENTICE-HALL OF JAPAN, INC., *Tokyo*
SIMON & SCHUSTER ASIA PTE. INC., *Singapore*
EDITORA PRENTICE-HALL DO BRASIL, LTDA., *Rio de Janeiro*

Contents

CHAPTER 3
MODELS OF LEARNING: RELATION TO STRESS MANAGEMENT   51

PART II
PHYSIOLOGICAL FOUNDATIONS   71

CHAPTER 4
PHYSIOLOGY OF STRESS   71

CHAPTER 11
STRESS AND THE WORKPLACE   209

Preface

Stress management is an enormously popular topic with the lay public. This fact is reflected in the hundreds of popular books that have been published on the subject and in the frequency with which it is a prime topic on TV talk shows. It is also very popular with college students. At Virginia Commonwealth University, approximately six hundred students enroll in our undergraduate course in Stress Management each academic year. The course has two broad aims: (a) to explain the historical, theoretical, experimental, and physiological foundations of the stress concept and to show how these have provided the framework for the development and application of a wide range of stress management procedures; and (b) to teach students (in laboratory sections) when and how to use particular interventions to deal with specific stress-related problems. It has been our experience that none of the stress management books currently available are suitable as a text for the didactic aspect of the course. Some adequate generic skills management workbooks are available, but they do not dovetail optimally with the foundations material presented in class, and they do not emphasize a skills acquisition approach. We have therefore written two books that are designed to be used in tandem that cover these respective content areas.

Our aim in the present volume is fourfold: (a) to describe the theoretical and conceptual foundations of stress and stress management as they derive from the science of psychology, (b) to give an overview of the current status and developments in the field, (c) to delineate the basic elements of the major stress management intervention techniques and how to use them, and (d) to provide guidelines for when it is most appropriate to use particular techniques. This organization flows from our conviction that although stress management is based in psychology, and as a field has emerged from psychology, it has not heretofore been coherently conceptualized as such. In particular, research and theory by personality and social psychologists on stress and related concepts (such as anxiety and coping) has progressed along with work on the development of stress management techniques, but the two have not intersected with nor strongly influenced each other. Many of the most frequently used interventions, which are based in learning theory and research, are rarely tied to or conceptualized in terms of contemporary theory and research on stress and coping. In particular, though two broad ways of coping with stress are recognized and have been empirically validated by personality psychologists—trying to change the circumstances that are producing the stress versus trying directly to moderate the emotional arousal—stress management has been largely equated with the latter by the layperson and by many professionals. In this text, we distinguish between these two types of coping strategies using Lazarus & Folkman's (1984) widely embraced distinction between problem-focused and emotion-focused coping. We further attempt to characterize stress management interventions in terms of the extent to which they are useful in promoting one or the other of these types of strategies. For some interventions, this is an admittedly speculative enterprise at this point; but we believe that it is an important starting point for beginning to understand the mechanisms underlying how interventions work and when they can be best used, given the coping demands posed by different stressors. For each intervention described, we summarize the current status of the research on the effectiveness of that intervention.

In Part I of the book (Psychological Foundations) we review the historical, theoretical, and experimental foundations of the concepts of stress, fear, anxiety, and coping and then attempt to show how developments along these lines have provided the underpinnings for the evolution of the stress management procedures that are currently widely used. Two major theoretical approaches are introduced: Richard Lazarus's cognitive appraisal model and traditional learning theory (classical and operant conditioning). These two theoretical approaches serve as the foundation for virtually every procedure that falls under the rubric "stress management." In Chapter 2 (Coping) we spell out and exemplify Lazarus and Folkman's distinction between problem- and emotion-focused coping and adopt Lazarus's focus on the need to think in terms of active coping strategies in order to understand best how people are dealing with stressors at a given moment in time. Relatively stable coping-related traits are also considered in terms of their potential role in influencing coping effectiveness (coping outcome).

Part II (Physiological Foundations) deals with the physiological effects of exposure to stressors, emphasizing the role of cogntive appraisal as the starting point in the physiological as well as the psychological components of the stress response. Focus is on the nervous system, the immune system, and the endocrine system—the three most important body systems involved in the stress response. We think that we have provided more detailed coverage of the basic physiology of stress than other currently available stess management books, and that this detailed review sets the stage for the comprehensive coverage of stress-illness relationships that is provided, as well as for Chapter 10 on the use of drugs in stress management.

In Part III we deal directly with stress management procedures, detailing their origins, the way that they are implemented, and their current status in terms of overall effectiveness and relative utility for ameliorating particular types of stress-related problems. We divide stress management procedures into three categories: "Basic Techniques," "Prevention," and "Postvention." These categories and the techniques that they subsume reflect the wide range of procedures that may be included under "stress management." "Basic Techniques" covers the popular emotion-focused interventions (Progressive Muscle Relaxation, Meditation, Autogenics, Biofeedback) that many people associate with stress management to the exclusion of anything else, along with general problem-solving approaches, including examples of their applications to social skills and assertiveness training. The remaining two chapters in this section exemplify the concept, noted in the first chapter, that stress is "in the past, the present, and the future." That is, we are sometimes attempting to cope with a potential stressor, with one that is clearly impending, with one that is currently on the table, with the aftereffects of one that has just occurred, or with the long-term effects of a stressor that occurred many years ago. In these chapters we show how the interventions that are most appropriate and effective in "Prevention" situations are usually very different from those that are most useful in "Postvention" situations. Where appropriate, we have emphasized the self-management applications of the interventions discussed.

The last part contains two "Special Topics" chapters that address areas in which there is currently great interest (drugs, and stress and the workplace).

This book is most appropriate for an undergraduate course in stress management for students who have had a course in introductory psychology. Although we believe that the book may be used alone as a text for a strictly didactic lecture class, we have found it most effective to combine lecture with a laboratory experience in which students develop and implement a "self-change project" oriented around problematic stressors of their choice. Our companion volume (Gramling & Auerbach, *Stress Management Workbook: Techniques and Self-Assessment Procedures*) is designed to be used in conjunction with the present text as a laboratory manual, and is strongly recommended.

We would like to thank reviewers Tom Lombardo, Tom Ollendick, and Joy Clingman, our VCU colleagues Wendy Kliewer and Randy Sleeth, graduate students Laura Bayer and Dave Streicher, as well as the hundreds of undergraduate students who have passed through our Stress Management class in recent years for their constructive comments on earlier versions of the manuscript.

Stephen M. Auerbach

Sandra E. Gramling

STRESS MANAGEMENT
PSYCHOLOGICAL
FOUNDATIONS

CHAPTER 1
Stress

I was sitting in the last row of the Boeing 707 as the plane gradually ascended to its cruising altitude of 30,000 feet. The weather was beautiful as we departed San Diego, and we all looked forward to a leisurely flight to Dallas. Suddenly, a bearded man dressed in combat fatigues emerged from the rest room just behind me waving a revolver and screaming orders to the passengers. "Hands over your heads, head down in your lap, no talking!" "You (he pointed to one passenger), get to the front, lie down on your stomach, keep quiet!" "You (he pointed to another), tie him up—faster, faster!"—Passengers are blindfolded, most are tied up, but the terrorist and his accomplice who has emerged from the cockpit are not satisfied. Six of the passengers are forced to their knees, blindfolded, heads bowed. The other twenty or so passengers are told that they must vote for the person who must die. Things are not moving fast enough for the wild-eyed terrorists. The bearded one screams, "First one who screws up will get his goddamn head blown off." Suddenly, shots ring out! A blindfolded passenger slumps, bleeding, to the floor. His lifeless body, trailing blood, is dragged to the rear of the plane by one of the terrorists. "I told you not to screw up!" screams the bearded terrorist as he grabs a blindfolded and bound female passenger by the neck and kicks her viciously about the head and the body.—This is only the beginning of nearly ten hours of terror for the passengers and crew of Flight 222——.

Most people in this situation would become extremely anxious and even begin to panic. Their pulse would begin to race, their hands sweat and perhaps begin to tremble, and they might develop a sickening sensation that would spread through their digestive system and perhaps down into their bowels. They would simultaneously be rapidly assessing the extent of the danger, trying to get their stress levels under control ("this isn't happening," "it'll be over in a minute"), and attempting to figure out how they could minimize actual harm to themselves.

But I (the first author) experienced none of these changes. I became somewhat aroused when the bearded terrorist initially burst out of the rest room, and I maintained a state of alertness and interest during this initial period when the terrorists took control of the passengers and the plane. However, this situation did not threaten me. Why? Because I knew when the terrorists would attack, what they would do to the passengers, and all of the major events that would occur during the trip. Furthermore, I knew that I would not be harassed because I was designated a "Controller" (I wore a blue windbreaker with "FBI" emblazoned in large, gold letters across the front and back), my job being to monitor hostages for extreme stress reactions and to pull them out of the situation if necessary—in a carefully orchestrated simulation (see Figure 1–1).

The "hostages" were airline employees (stewards, stewardesses, and a few pilots), who also knew that this was a simulation and that they would not actually be harmed. Yet, talking with them after we had landed in Atlantic City, New Jersey—they had been "rescued" by an FBI SWAT team that had burst onto the plane unannounced after the "negotiations" with the "terrorists" had broken down—revealed that some of them had nonetheless **cognitively appraised** aspects of the situation as stressful; thus, for them, it was a **stressor.** But others had been no more fazed by the situation than I.

In other situations (e.g., waiting to see the dentist), some people approach a state of panic, whereas others casually read a novel. Yet some of these same people who freeze at the thought of the dentist's chair will consider parachuting from the open door of a moving airplane with excited anticipation, whereas most people find the prospect of doing this extremely stressful. How can such differences be ex-

Figure 1–1

Scene from a simulated hostage situation. (By permission of George Bradford and Dr. Thomas Strentz.)

plained? What exactly is stress, and how is it different from fear and anxiety? Where does it come from? Why do we experience stress in some situations and not in others? Why do some people experience stress in situations that others find neutral or even pleasurable? Is there anything good about stress? Can it drive you crazy? What is meant by *coping*, and how do we learn to deal with everyday stressors as well as with unexpected crises?

The rest of this chapter is devoted to providing preliminary answers to some of these basic questions. Because most of these questions will require more detailed treatment, they will be addressed in later chapters. First, we will consider some definitions of basic terms that you will be seeing throughout this book.

SOME BASIC DEFINITIONS

Stress, Stressors, and Cognitive Appraisal

The term *stress* is derived from the Latin "strictus" and the Old French "etrace." In the past the term has been used to designate both a stimulus (a force or pressure that causes distress) and a response to that stimulus (adversity, affliction) (Keefe, 1988). Currently, it is usually used to denote a set of changes that people undergo in situations that they appraise as threatening to their well-being. These changes involve physiological arousal, subjective feelings of discomfort, and overt behaviors. The circumstances that induce stress responses are designated **stressors.** Stressors have a number of important aspects that are related to the passage of time. Exposure to them may be relatively brief with a clear starting and stopping point (**acute** stressors), or exposure may persist for extended periods without clear demarcation (**chronic** stressors). Stressors impinge on us at different points in our life cycle, sometimes occurring "off-time" (incompatible with personal and societal expectations as to when they should occur) or at a "bad time" (e.g., concurrent with other stressors). Finally, stress may be induced by the anticipation of harmful circumstances that one thinks he or she is likely to confront, by an ongoing stressor, or by the harmful effects of stressors already encountered. All of these factors affect how we interpret stressful events, how we deal with them, and how effective we are in managing them.

Coping responses refer to attempts to do something about the stressors or to adjust to or manage the emotional upset that they are producing. Coping is a key concept in the study of the stress process, and we will have much more to say about it later in this book.

Though there are some situations that almost everyone responds to with high levels of stress, there are individual differences in how people respond to every situation. Thus, though most of us cringe at the thought of having to parachute from an airplane a substantial minority find this an exciting, challenging adventure. Most people avoid contact with snakes, yet others keep them as pets. On the other hand, whereas most people find automobiles, birds, and people with deep voices to be largely neutral objects, for others they provoke a stress reaction that may verge on panic.

The key concept here is **cognitive appraisal.** Situations become stressors for an individual only if they are construed as threatening or dangerous by that individual. As demonstrated in a study by Fenz & Epstein (1967) with parachuters, stress appraisals can change markedly over the course of exposure to a stressor, and patterns of stress arousal differ as a function of experience with the stressor. As Figure 1–2 shows, fear levels of veteran jumpers (as evaluated by a self-report measure) were highest the morning before the jump, declined continuously to the moment of the jump, and then increased slightly until after landing. The curve for novice jumpers,

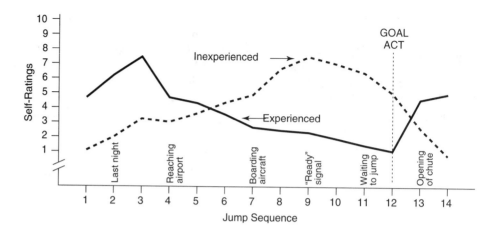

Figure 1–2

Changes in self-reported anxiety in experienced and inexperienced parachutists before and after a parachute jump.
(From Fenz, W. D. and Epstein, S., 1967. By permission of Williams and Wilkins.)

in contrast, increased up to a point shortly before the jump and then decreased continuously. For both groups, the peak of stress occurred somewhere during the anticipatory period rather than at the point of greatest objective danger (the act of jumping). This is not an unusual finding. Psychiatrist Peter Bourne similarly observed greater stress levels among draftees who were undergoing basic training than in airmen who were in the process of flying on dangerous missions in Vietnam. Situations with which we have had little experience are more unpredictable and tend to be viewed as less controllable. Such situations are often perceived as more stressful than those that are clearly more dangerous but also more familiar.

Anxiety and Fear

Stress seems to have supplanted "anxiety" and "fear" in everyday usage to indicate what we experience when we appraise circumstances as straining our ability to cope with them. Thus, whereas several decades ago the twentieth century was branded the "century of fear" by writer Albert Camus and the "Age of Anxiety" by poet W. H. Auden (Spielberger, 1972), from the perspective of the 1980s and the 1990s, it might be more popularly dubbed the "century of stress." As we approach the twenty-first century the word for stress is spreading rapidly throughout the world, and it is being increasingly incorporated into non-English languages. For example, a Japanese housewife might complain: "Shujin wa *stress* (pronounced "su-tor-es-u") ga tamura to okorippoku naru ("My husband becomes irritable when stress builds up"); in Russia, one might exclaim: V sostoyanii *stress* (pronounced "stress-a") u menya vsyo valitsya iz ruk ("In this state of stress I can't do anything right") (Shweder, 1997).

Historically, the word *fear*, which is derived from the Old English *fær*, meaning "sudden calamity or danger," has generally been used when the source of stress can be readily identified. The word *anxious*, in contrast, is derived from the Latin *anxius*, meaning "troubled in mind about some *uncertain* event," and is related to the Greek root meaning "to press tight or strangle" (Marks, 1978). Anxiety has long been considered to be a fundamental though very complex emotion, and the term continues to be used widely in the psychological literature.

Historically, two influential conceptions of anxiety are those of Sigmund Freud and those of existential philosophers and psychologists. Freud viewed the capacity for anxiety as an innate part of a person's self-preservative instinct. His (Freud, 1936) major distinction between types of anxiety (objective versus neurotic) was based primarily on their source (external events versus internal conflicts) and on whether the anxiety reaction was proportional to the actual magnitude of the external danger. Objective anxiety (equated with fear) was conceptualized as a realistic reaction that mobilized the individual to deal with danger. In contrast, neurotic anxiety was viewed as a response to unpleasant childhood experiences that a particular event might symbolize to the individual, rather than as a direct response to the immediate dangers posed by the event. It was thus viewed both as a disrupter of rational thought and effective action, and as a potential contributor to psychopathology.

For existentialists, anxiety is an ontological characteristic of people (part of the essence of human existence), a profound emotion that strikes at the "center core of our self-esteem" (May, 1958, p. 50). It is the reaction that we experience when, for example, someone whom we respect passes us on the street without speaking—a feeling that often lingers and affects our sense of self-worth. The term that some existentialists use for anxiety is the German *angst* (derived from the Latin equivalent of *anguish* and often translated as "dread"). Fear, in contrast, is what we experience when we are confronting a more objective physical threat, such as a trip to the dentist. The affect experienced in a fear reaction may be more intense than that in an anxiety response; but the threat is more peripheral to our sense of self and is viewed by existentialists as having minimal effect on our basic sense of who we are (May, 1950; 1958).

Current conceptions, rather than focusing on the types of qualitative differentiations made by Freud or the existentialists, emphasize distinguishing between anxiety as a momentary state (*state anxiety*) and as a personality trait (*trait anxiety*). The term *state anxiety*, along with the terms *fear* and *stress*, denote a transitory reaction to a situation or set of circumstances that are appraised as dangerous or threatening. When the stressor either is removed, changes so that it is no longer viewed as posing a threat, or is coped with effectively the reaction diminishes and our attention shifts to other aspects of our environment. This definition of state anxiety simply designates a response state. It does not imply anything about the nature or source of the events that are evoking the reaction, or whether the reaction seems to be a realistic one given the situation that is evoking it. Though subtle distinctions have been made among the terms *stress, fear,* and *state anxiety,* they will be used interchangeably in this way throughout this volume.

Stress, fear, and state anxiety are distinguished from trait anxiety, which is conceptualized as a relatively stable personality disposition or trait. People high in trait or "chronic" anxiety appraise a greater number of situations as dangerous or threatening than do low trait-anxious people, and they respond to the situations with more intense stress (state anxiety) reactions (Spielberger, 1972). Instruments that measure trait anxiety ask people to characterize how they *usually* feel, and thus they measure how people *characteristically* respond to situations. Some of the items from a widely used trait anxiety measure (the Trait Anxiety scale of the State-Trait Anxiety Inventory-STAI) are presented in Table 1–1. Whereas trait anxiety is usually mea-

---

TABLE 1–1. SAMPLE ITEMS FROM THE TRAIT ANXIETY SCALE OF THE STATE-TRAIT ANXIETY INVENTORY

Directions: For each statement, circle the response that describes how you *generally* feel.

	Almost Never	Sometimes	Often	Almost Always
1. I feel pleasant.	*	*	*	*
2. I am happy.	*	*	*	*
3. I feel like a failure.	*	*	*	*
4. I feel inadequate.	*	*	*	*

sured by using self-report instruments, state anxiety is evaluated in several different ways, which are described in the next section.

MEASURING STRESS REACTIONS

How do we know whether we are experiencing a stress reaction? How can we detect whether others are under stress? Stress reactions are measured in three broad ways: (a) self-reports, (b) behavioral observations, and (c) psychophysiological measures.

Self-Report

Self-report is the technique most commonly used by behavioral scientists to evaluate subjective stress levels. Among the most frequently used self-report measures of state anxiety are Walk's (1956) Fear Thermometer and the State Anxiety Scale of the STAI. Some of the items from the STAI State Anxiety Scale are presented in Table 1–2. It may be noted that in contrast to the Trait Anxiety Scale of the STAI, which asks how you usually feel, the State Anxiety Scale asks how you feel *right now*.

Self-report state anxiety scales may be administered and scored easily and quickly. Furthermore, as illustrated in Figure 1–1, they may be administered repeatedly and still provide valid measures of momentary changes in stress levels. However, they have been criticized by some because they are face valid (i.e., their intent is clear), so that people motivated to disguise their stress level can readily do so.

Behavioral Observations

Overt behavioral measures of stress include direct and indirect observational measures (Bernstein, Borkovec, & Coles, 1986; Nietzel, Bernstein, & Russell, 1988). Direct measures focus on behaviors associated with stress-related physiological arousal, including heavy breathing, tremors, perspiration, self-manipulations such as nail biting, eyeblinks, postural orientation, and body movement such as pacing. That we are sometimes unaware of such behaviors is illustrated by this comment from a novice jumper in the Fenz & Epstein (1967) study: "I was not afraid at all until I looked down and saw my knees trembling. Then I realized how really scared I was" (Fenz, 1975, p. 313).

TABLE 1–2.   SAMPLE ITEMS FROM THE STATE ANXIETY SCALE OF THE STATE-TRAIT ANXIETY INVENTORY

Directions: For each statement circle the response that describes how you feel *right now*, that is, *at this moment*.

	Not at All	Somewhat	Moderately So	Very Much So
1. I am tense.	*	*	*	*
2. I feel at ease.	*	*	*	*
3. I am jittery.	*	*	*	*
4. I feel confused.	*	*	*	*

Although speech disturbances, including both verbal (e.g., repetitions, omissions, incomplete sentences, slips of the tongue) and nonverbal indicants (e.g., change in rate, pauses, hand movements) have been analyzed intensively, no single measure or pattern has emerged as a reliable indicant of stress (Siegman, 1982; Spence, 1982). Another way in which we commonly express fear reactions and assess them in others is through facial expressions. This area has been studied by Ekman and Friesen (1975), who concluded that the facial features that take on the most distinctive appearance during fear are the eyebrows (raised and drawn together), eyes (open, lower lids tensed), and the lips (stretched back) (see Figure 1–3).

Indirect observational measures involve evaluating the degree to which people avoid feared objects. For example, in the behavioral avoidance test (BAT), an individual is instructed to approach a feared stimulus (such as a snake) and engage in increasingly intimate interactions with it (e.g., look at a caged snake from a distance, approach it, touch it, hold it). The rationale is that the higher the level of fear elicited, the earlier in the sequence the person will try to avoid the feared stimulus (Nietzel et al., 1988). Other examples include asking claustrophobics (people fearful of being closed in) to remain in a closed chamber as long as they can or asking acrophobics (people with fear of heights) to climb a ladder and then assessing their progress (Bernstein et al., 1986).

Psychophysiological Measures

Physiological arousal is an integral component of the stress response. The most frequently monitored response systems are cardiovascular responses (measures such as heart rate and blood pressure), electrodermal responses (measures of the electrical conductance of the skin), and muscular tension. These measures are important in their own right as independent indicants of stress level, and in particular as indices of stress-related diseases (see Chapter 5).

Before leaving this topic it should be noted that despite the availability of a number of different types of reasonably valid stress measures, the area is not as precise as it might appear. A major problem is that only a moderate degree of agreement or "synchrony" is obtained when stress is measured simultaneously using two or more of the three major measurement modes. This less-than-perfect correspondence is in part due to sources of error in obtaining the measures themselves. These source errors include subjects' misrepresenting their actual feelings on self-report measures, extraneous sources of variance on physiological measures (such as the physical condition of the subject), and poor agreement among observers on some behavioral measures. But current researchers underscore the notion that stress is a complex multidimensional state, and the fact that each type of measure represents parallel but interacting response systems that may contribute independently as well as influence the other systems, depending upon the individual and his or her circumstances. If possible, therefore, it is best to obtain at least two and possibly all three types of measures and then identify the manner and the extent to which each response component contributes to an individual's stress reaction.

Individual Differences: Is There Evidence for a Stress-Prone Personality?

Psychologists have long been interested in developing tests that would predict how people will behave and respond emotionally in a wide range of situations. An example is the STAI Trait Anxiety Scale (described previously), which assumes that people may be characterized by a pervasive dispositional tendency to respond to situations with elevated (or diminished) stress levels, and that this disposition or trait can be reliably

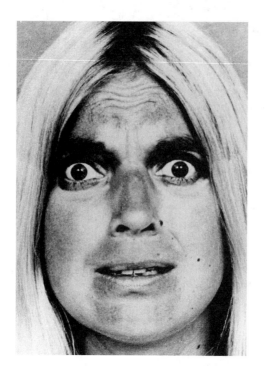
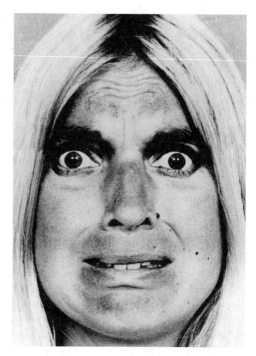

Figure 1-3

Facial expressions showing fear. (Reproduced by permission of Dr. Paul Ekman, Human Interaction Laboratory and Consulting Psychologists Press, Inc.)

measured. Are such measures useful? Yes, to an extent. For example, we know that most people have some fear of snakes. This fact is not surprising, since snakes pose a realistic threat. But not everyone fears snakes to the same degree. Are people who have an extreme fear of snakes *generally* fearful people? Are people who are extremely fearful of the dark, of the dentist, or of vacuum cleaners generally fearful people? No. Level of general trait anxiety, as measured by tests like the STAI Trait Anxiety Scale, *is* predictive of how fearful or how stressed a person will get in situations in which there is a threat to self-esteem or a threat of failure (Auerbach, 1973a). However, common phobias or fears of specific situations, especially when the perceived threat has a strong physical component, is not related to general trait anxiety level.

Measures of general trait anxiety are therefore not good predictors of people's fearfulness when confronted by snakes (Mellstrom, Cicala, & Zuckerman, 1976), impending surgery (Auerbach, 1973b; Martinez-Urrutia, 1975), tooth extraction (Auerbach, Kendall, Cuttler, & Levitt, 1976), electric shock (Hodges & Spielberger, 1966), viewing a film depicting physically painful accidents (Lushene, 1970), or an exploding balloon (Lamb, 1969). But such fears can be predicted by scales designed to evaluate proneness to experience fear in these particular situations (e.g., Snake Questionnaire, Fear of Surgery Questionnaire, Dental Anxiety Scale). Examples of items from some *situation-specific* trait anxiety (also called *specific fear*) inventories are presented in Table 1–3.

Whereas some of us find certain situations, often those involving physical threats, particularly stressful, there are people at the other end of the continuum who actively seek out risky situations (such as skydiving and scuba diving) because they find these experiences stimulating and exciting. Such persons, who have a need for varied, novel, and complex sensations, are said to be "sensation seekers." High sensation seekers, particularly those who score high on the Thrill and Adventure Seeking subscale of the Sensation Seeking Scale, report less fear in situations involving potential physical harm (Zuckerman, 1979). Yet, though we may think of the sensation seeker as being the polar opposite of the chronically anxious neurotic person, Zuckerman has found that sensation seeking is unrelated to general trait anxiety. Furthermore, though people who are more prone to take risks are often thought to be nonconforming and to engage in antisocial behavior, it has been shown by Levenson (1990) that these traits characterize only one group of risk takers (exempli-

---

TABLE 1–3.   SAMPLE ITEMS FROM THREE SPECIFIC FEAR INVENTORIES

Test	Key	Item
SNAQ	True	I avoid going to parks or on camping trips because there may be snakes about.
	False	I enjoy reading articles about snakes and other reptiles.
SPQ	True	I dislike looking at pictures of spiders in a magazine.
	False	I have no fear of nonpoisonous spiders.
MQ	True	I feel sick or faint at the sight of blood.
	False	Blood and gore upset me no more than the average person.

SNAQ: Snake Questionnaire.
SPQ: Spider Questionnaire.
MQ: Mutilation Questionnaire.

Source: Reproduced from Klorman, Weerts, Hastings, Melamed, & Lang, 1974, Table 1, p. 202. Copyright 1974 by the Association for the Advancement of Behavior Therapy. Reprinted by permission of the publisher.

TABLE 1–4.   SAMPLE ITEMS FROM THE SENSATION SEEKING SCALE—FORM V.

Directions: For each pair of statements circle the one that best describes your interests or preferences.

1. A. I like "wild," uninhibited parties.
   B. I prefer quiet parties with good conversation.
2. A. I often wish I could be a mountain climber.
   B. I can't understand people who risk their necks climbing mountains.
3. A. I have tried marijuana or would like to.
   B. I would never smoke marijuana.
4. A. I like to date members of the opposite sex who are physically exciting.
   B. I like to date members of the opposite sex who share my values.

Source: Zuckerman, 1979, pp. 397–398. By permission of Marvin Zuckerman and L. Erlbaum Publishing Co.

---

fied by drug users). Other risk takers (exemplified by rock climbers) actually score higher in sensation seeking than antisocial risk takers but show no antisocial inclination; and a third group of "prosocial" risk takers (exemplified by police officers and firefighters decorated for bravery) are actually below average in sensation seeking.

Examples of items from the Sensation Seeking Scale are presented in Table 1–4. The exhilaration produced by unfamiliar sensations is reflected in the faces of the people depicted in Figure 1–4, who are in the process of taking the "5-story plunge"

Figure 1–4

Individual differences in sensation seeking.

at Disneyworld's Splash Mountain ride. The withdrawn expression on the face of the individual in the third row (a clinical psychologist well known to the authors of this book) illustrates that, as with other personality traits, there are wide individual differences in sensation seeking.

In trying to explain why some people are more prone to be sensation seekers than others, Konner (1990) poses an interesting question: if sensation seeking results in risky and often life-threatening behavior, given that the behavior has a substantial genetic component (Zuckerman, Buchsbaum, & Murphy, 1980), why hasn't this seemingly maladaptive trait eventually disappeared? Konner's answer is that thrill seekers not only court more physical danger but also engage in more promiscuous and more unusual sexual practices, and do so more frequently. Thus, "sexy sensation seekers perpetuate their genes" (p. 135). Furthermore, seemingly fearless, heroic behavior is encouraged and reinforced by others. Throughout our evolutionary past, we have all gained from "having a minority of sensation seekers in the ranks—people who wouldn't hesitate to snatch a child from a pack of wild dogs or to fight an approaching grass fire with a counterfire (p. 137)." As a species, Konner points out, we are not built to be completely rational. The fact that there is fun in taking risks is not incidental; we have been designed emotionally for survival and reproduction, not for perfect safety. "The more reckless among us," he notes, "may have something to teach the careful about the sort of immortality that comes from living fully every day (p. 139)."

STRESS: LEARNED OR INNATE?

Are we *born* afraid of some things, or are we a *tabula rasa* (blank slate) at birth and learn to fear things as a result of negative experiences with them?

The Learning Model

John B. Watson, an early learning theorist, thought that there were three stimuli that innately (without learning) produced fear reactions: stimuli capable of producing pain, sudden loss of support, and noise. He thought that all other fears were learned by a classical conditioning process through which stimuli came to elicit a fear response by being associated with an aversive or a painful stimulus. In a famous experiment, he demonstrated learning of fear with Little Albert, an eleven-month-old infant who was conditioned or "taught" to fear furry objects. Albert was first evaluated and shown to have no particular fear of animals. He was then given a white rat together with a loud noise that was produced by striking a steel bar. After several pairings of the noise and the rat, Albert showed signs of extreme fear (crying, avoidance) at the sight of the rat. In the terminology of classical conditioning, the loud noise was an unconditioned stimulus (UCS) that innately elicited a fear response. As a result of its being paired with this UCS, the white rat (a previously neutral stimulus for Albert) came to be a conditioned stimulus (CS) for a fear response. Furthermore, Albert's fear response generalized to other furry objects (a fur coat, a dog, a rabbit), which also elicited a fear reaction in him when he encountered them.

The classical conditioning model of fear acquisition, based by Watson on the earlier work of the Russian physiologist Ivan Pavlov, has served as the foundation for the development of many important stress management techniques. Furthermore, it is consistent with common experience. Feelings of stress and anxiety are not easy for people to control. The racing of the heart, the queasy feeling in the pit of the stomach, and the other physiological changes that accompany fear are *not voluntary* responses in the same way as are standing or talking. They are *respondents* that are *elicited*, sometimes unexpectedly, by things that we encounter, and often we cannot control them regardless of how hard we try.

Thus, fear is not an *operant* behavior (like walking, talking, and eating) that is voluntarily emitted and directly influenced by the consequences that it produces (rewards, punishments). Therefore, offering a young man who becomes apprehensive in the presence of red-headed women a large monetary reward if he will not feel anxious in their presence will not help diminish his stress level. His fear of redheads is probably the result of a series of unpleasant encounters with redheads, such that the very sight of them has become a conditioned fear stimulus. Reducing his stress level in this situation involves disrupting the connections between the key elements responsible for the elicitation and maintenance of the stress response. Additional details on the classical and operant learning models and information on stress management techniques that are based on them are presented in Chapters 3 and 9.

Unlearned Fears

Gray (1987) and others (McNally, 1987; Seligman, 1971) argue that Watson's theory was too simple. Stimuli other than loud noise, sudden loss of support, and pain-producing situations are capable of eliciting intense fear reactions, without having to be repeatedly associated with an unconditioned fear stimulus. Darkness, dead or mutilated bodies, and snakes are examples of "special evolutionary dangers"; these are things that we are biologically prepared to learn to fear, and therefore that are "easier" to develop fear reactions to, because they have been associated with the threat to survival of our species throughout its history. Because these predispositions to fear dangerous stimuli were adaptive, they evolved through natural selection. (Similar unlearned fears have been identified in animals: for example, in some birds, the shadow of a hawk; in monkeys, the decapitated head of another monkey; in rats, being placed in a large open field; Kimble, 1961).

It has also been found that the ease with which we learn certain fears varies over the life cycle, and this variation seems to be determined by evolutionary factors. For example, animal fears tend to be acquired early in childhood. It is conjectured that children are particularly predisposed to acquire such fears because they have always been especially vulnerable to predators and dependent on adults for protection. Social fears, on the other hand, which are usually established during puberty and adolescence, seem to be related to the struggle for dominance that has occurred historically within all primate social hierarchies during this period (Ohman, 1986). Though learning explanations may plausibly account for these findings, other studies support an "innate predisposition" explanation. For example, it has been found that fear responses to pictures of monkeys displaying threatening expressions are obtained from monkeys which have been reared in social isolation and that these responses become more pronounced as the monkeys mature (peaking at three months of age) (Gray, 1987). Gray (1987, pp. 17–18) concludes that "it is much easier to transfer fear (by an apparent classical conditioning procedure) to some stimuli (e.g., caterpillars) than to others (e.g., opera glasses); given what we know (but Watson did not) about the maturation of certain fears, especially of animals, it is easy to accept (the) conclusion that certain stimuli may elicit a 'lurking fear in the background' (owing to innate factors) so that an added disturbance can bring out a full-blown fear reaction."

Other problems with a strict classical conditioning approach to the etiology of fears have been noted. In classical conditioning the conditioned response is never exactly the same as the unconditioned response, but it should at least be very similar to it. Yet many animals, when presented with a signal (conditioned stimulus) that they are about to be shocked, become immobile or "frozen with fear." This is a much different response from the frantic increase in activity that they exhibit when they are actually shocked (unconditioned stimulus). Though these behaviors may represent differentially adaptive coping responses in the two situations, nonetheless their presence poses some problems for the standard classical conditioning model (Bailey, 1987; Gray, 1987). In addition, McNally (1987) points out (a) that some phobias are established after a single occurrence of a traumatic event (rather than through repeated association of the conditioned stimulus with the unconditioned stimulus) and that these are often "unprepared" fears such as fear of the dentist or of automobiles; (b) that phobics rarely report experiencing painful unconditioned stimuli in conjunction with the object they have come to fear; and (c) that conditioned fear responses can be established through instructions and modeling (in both humans and primates) as well as through direct CS-UCS pairings.

The Role of Cognitive Appraisal

The last two points are of extreme practical importance. We often have no actual experience of harm or unpleasantness with things that we come to fear greatly. For example, most of us are at least somewhat uneasy about flying on airplanes or about the prospect of having a nuclear power plant located near us, though few of us have personally experienced harm resulting from these situations. Nevertheless, though we all pride ourselves on how logical we are, we are often not very rational in appraising how dangerous or risky different events actually are. (See Figure 1–5.) As noted by Allman (1985), the general public's

> concern for the safety of nuclear reactors—which have claimed a total of three deaths over the previous 30 years—brought the industry to a virtual standstill. It's the same general public that smokes billions of cigarettes a year while banning an artificial sweetener because of a one-in-a-million chance that it might cause cancer; the same public that eats meals full of fat, flocks to cities prone to earthquakes, and goes hang gliding while it frets about pesticides in foods, avoids the ocean for fear of sharks, and breaks into a cold sweat on airline flights (pp. 31–32).

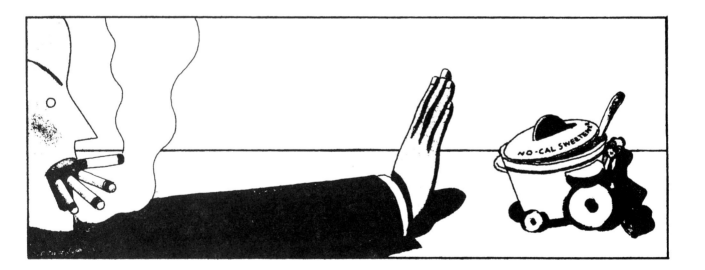

Figure 1–5

Cartoon reproduced from Allman, 1985, pp. 32–33. (By permission of Steven Guarnaccia.)

Events that we most overestimate and most underestimate in terms of the frequency with which they result in death are presented in Table 1–5. Events for which we overestimate the actual danger tend to be dramatic and sensational, and comprise situations that we are constantly exposed to through newspapers and broadcast media. For example, as a result of a steady barrage of publicity through the media, the prospect of exposure to asbestos particles for even a brief period engenders fear and dread in most people. This reaction occurs despite the fact that the death rates attributed to smoking, drowning, airplane crashes, or even playing high school football are 100 to more than 1000 times as great as that resulting from asbestos exposure in buildings (Lemonick & Dorfman, 1990; Mossman, Bignon, Corn, Seaton, & Gee, 1990). Situations that we underestimate tend to be unspectacular both because they usually claim just one victim at a time and because they often are common in nonfatal form, so that we tend not to associate them with aversive outcomes.

If the chances of an activity or event resulting in death are not the sole factor in determining perceptions of its riskiness, what does determine perceptions of dangerousness? Slovic, Fischoff, & Lichenstein (1979) found that it was the degree to which an event was perceived as involuntary (versus voluntary), delayed (versus immediate), unknown to science (versus known), unfamiliar, potentially catastrophic (versus chronic), and dreaded. These were the risk characteristics that differentiated people's perceptions of nuclear power (which was rated as highly risky and dreaded) and their ratings of X rays and nonnuclear electrical power (whose risks were judged to be much lower). Electric power, in fact, results in more than one hundred times the number of fatalities, and X rays more than twenty times the number of fatalities each year, as does nuclear power.

Conclusion

Is fear learned or innate? Clearly, some fears are much easier to learn than others because we are biologically prepared to acquire them as a result of evolutionary influences. But learning via classical conditioning accounts for how we come to expe-

TABLE 1–5. BIAS IN JUDGED FREQUENCY OF DEATH	
Most Overestimated	**Most Underestimated**
All accidents	Smallpox vaccination
Motor vehicle accidents	Diabetes
Pregnancy, childbirth, and abortion	Stomach cancer
Tornadoes	Lightning
Floods	Stroke
Botulism	Tuberculosis
All cancer	Asthma
Fire and flames	Emphysema
Venomous bites or stings	
Homicide	

Reproduced from Slovic, Fischoff, & Lichenstein (1979), p. 16. *Environment*, 21(3), 14–20, 36–39. Reprinted with permission of the Helen Dwight Reid Educational Foundation. Published by Heldref Publications, 1319 Eighteenth Street, NW, Washington, DC 20036–1802. Copyright © 1979.

rience stress in many situations, and this model has served as the basis for the development of several important stress management techniques. However, we do not learn most fears simply by experiencing a previously neutral event contiguously with an unconditioned fear stimulus. Cognition plays a very important role. We draw conclusions about how threatening an event is on the basis of our observations and of information from diverse sources. Sometimes we develop firmly held beliefs about how dangerous things are even though they are not based in fact. Because cognition plays such a crucial role in stress perception, many stress management techniques are oriented around changing erroneous belief systems. These techniques are discussed in Chapters 6, 7, 8, and 9.

STRESS: IS IT ALL BAD?

Most of us try to avoid stressful situations. The experience of anxiety is unpleasant. It portends pain and is a reflection of the knowledge that pain or death can be experienced at any time. But hard as we may try, we can never completely predict or control the occurrence of aversive events, and the knowledge of our inevitable death is universal. Stress, then, if not always in the forefront of our thinking and feeling, is still our constant companion. For many of us, it is an ongoing source or a by-product of unhappiness, unproductivity, and unmet goals. As a result, physicians receive more complaints about stress than about common cold symptoms, and tranquilizers are among the most widely used drugs in the world (Barlow, 1988). The spiraling drug and alcohol abuse crisis is often viewed as a product of peoples' desire to block out sources of stress or to anesthetize the painful feelings associated with it. Everyone seems to be involved in some form of stress management program, either a program derived from the increasing number of popular self-help books, one supervised by a professional, or perhaps one provided at work. It would seem that if somehow stress and anxiety could be completely eliminated, life would be an unbroken stream of pleasant experiences.

But though we devote so much of our energy and thinking to avoiding stress, there is evidence from studies with both animals and humans that exposure to stress has beneficial effects. Rats handled as infants are less fearful, more exploratory, faster learners, and have more robust immune systems later in life. In humans, physical stature as adults is greater in cultures that expose children to stress (e.g., circumcision, scarification, sleeping apart from parents) than those that are careful to prevent stress exposure, even controlling for nutrition, climate, and other relevant variables (Aldwin & Stokols, 1988). Though failure experiences in dealing with stressful circumstances can inhibit future ability to function under stress, success experiences enable learning of important coping and problem-solving skills that are then used to deal effectively with future stressful encounters. Furthermore, such success experiences promote a positive self-concept and induce a generalized sense of self-efficacy, which in turn enhance persistence in coping with future stressors. This notion is captured in the old adage "good mariners are not made by calm seas." (See Chapter 2 for a more detailed treatment of this topic.)

More generally, stress is at the very root of what makes us uniquely human (May, 1950). In the real world of mortal humans, stress signals danger and thus protects us. It is essential for survival and growth, and for the very evolution of our species. It motivates us to achieve and fuels creativity. Without fear, there would be no courage; without anxiety and apprehension would we ever experience the pleasure and relief that accompany triumph over great obstacles? Stress is thus an enigma, with both good and bad effects. It is subjectively unpleasant and can lead to serious adjustment problems if not managed appropriately. Yet it guides us, energizes us, and is the very "shadow of intelligence" (Liddell, 1949; cited in Barlow, 1988). In other ways, stress and anxiety are paradoxical constructs with seemingly contradictory characteristics. These inconsistencies are reviewed in the next section. They will be referred to and covered in more detail throughout this book as we seek to unravel the mysteries of stress.

THE PARADOXES OF STRESS

1. Stress is both *rational* and *irrational*. Stress *makes sense*. We *should* be afraid of things that pose realistic threats and should learn how to deal with or avoid contact with them. Thus, we are careful about engaging in physical activities that may be dangerous or harmful, we try to do things that will lower the probability of disease, and we are usually quick to seek treatment if we are ill. In addition, when we express fear, this action communicates to others who may not be attending to the source of threat that there is danger looming, thus enabling them also to deal with the situation. Indeed, much of our time is spent weighing probabilities, trying to maximize our chances of achieving our goals and enjoying ourselves while keeping alert for signs of potential threats. But sometimes there doesn't appear to be a rational explanation for why we experience anxiety. Sometimes we experience a vague sense of dread or foreboding that doesn't seem to be attached to any particular situation or problem ("free floating anxiety"). When we do face a dangerous situation, our fear reactions are often not proportional to the actual likelihood of being harmed. For example, although most of us experience at least some uneasiness when boarding a commercial airplane, few of us think twice about getting into our cars. Yet riding in a car is many times more risky than flying (Bryson, 1989). Some of us develop phobias of particular things or situations (e.g., open spaces, red-headed women) that pose very little real threat.

2. Stress is both *normal* and *abnormal*. This attribute is related to the rational/irrational paradox. Stress is a normal, adaptive reaction to threat, which signals danger and prepares us to take defensive action. Over time we learn which coping strategies are successful for us in particular situations. This learning is part of the normal process of personal growth and maturation. But stress can cause psychological problems if the demands posed by stressors overwhelm our coping capabilities at that time. If a sense of being overwhelmed and unable to control events persists over a period of time, our stress signaling system ceases to work in an adaptive way. We misread and overinterpret the actual degree of threat posed by situations, we make poor decisions as to what coping strategies to use, we realize that we are coping inefficiently, and a cycle of increasing distress and ineffective coping may result. Some people who have experienced high-level stress for extended periods or who are attempting to deal with the aftereffects of traumatic stressors may become extremely socially withdrawn and show other signs of severe emotional dysfunction. (See box entitled Psychopathology on page 18, for an overview of the psychopathological conditions in which anxiety and stress play a central motivational role). This is true on a physiological as well as on a psychological level. If the complex physiological changes (e.g., activation of the cardiovascular system, suppression of immune functioning) that are adaptive in helping us cope with an emergency are repeatedly triggered over time, the changes themselves may become extremely damaging or may make us more susceptible to disease (see Chapters 4 and 5).

Stress management interventions are designed to short-circuit cycles of ineffective coping by teaching more accurate situation assessment, effective coping strategies, and when and how to apply them to particular problematic stressors.

3. *Everyday hassles* as well as events requiring *major readjustments* can be very stressful. The media focuses our attention on disasters such as plane crashes, earth-

quakes, and epidemics that suddenly disrupt the lives of many people or on particularly gruesome crimes or other happenings likely to attract attention. But for most of us, much of the stress in our lives results from having to deal with ongoing problems pertaining to our jobs, personal relationships, and everyday living circumstances. The extent of exposure to such daily hassles not only is strongly predictive of our daily mood (Stone, 1987) and of our future experience of physical and psychological symptoms (Stone, Reed, & Neale, 1987), but also is actually more predictive of negative health outcomes than is the frequency of exposure to major life events (Lazarus & Folkman, 1984).

4. The experience of stress is *universal*. Fear "is a basic, fundamental, discrete emotion that is universally present across all ages, cultures, races, and species" (Barlow, 1988, p. 44). But there are individual differences in the things that evoke fear responses in people and in the way that fear is experienced, not only as a result of personal learning experiences but also as a function of *cultural differences*. (See Figure 1–6.) For example, as described by Barlow (1988), in 1967 a wave of anxiety swept Singapore. Reactions among males—especially those from the ethnic Chinese population—were characterized by an overwhelming fear that their sexual organs were retracting into their abdomens. They believed that when the organ totally retracted, death would result. The disorder (*koro*) occurs periodically in that population, and it usually stems from guilt pertaining to past sexual conduct. In contrast, in many Latin American cultures, intense anxiety symptoms that are associated with fear of black magic and the "evil eye" may occasionally result in "voodoo" death. Such a death is the result of sudden increases in autonomic activity accompanied by the victim's perception of having little opportunity to alter the situation, eventually resulting in internal organ damage and death (Barlow, 1988).

Evolutionary psychologists argue that the universality of anxiety results from the fact that it is part of our genetic heritage. Because anxiety signals danger, it helped our ancestors get their genes transmitted to the next generation by maximizing their survival, and also motivated them to protect their offspring and add to their resources even in times of plenty. Another factor is the "mismatch" between the demands of our ancestral environment and those of our modern environment. Our species initially evolved, biologically and behaviorally, to adapt to the requirements of our ancestral "hunter-gatherer" environment. Though the demands of modern so-

Figure 1–6

By permission of Doug Marlette and Creators Syndicate.

$\mathscr{P}$SYCHOPATHOLOGY

Stress can be painful psychologically and can produce strong physiological sensations. Sometimes when intense stress is experienced or when it seems to be experienced much of the time, we may begin to ask, "Is this what it's like to go crazy?" Or we may wonder if this is how we are going to feel forever: "Have I changed permanently?"

Just what is the dividing line between normal stress reactions and those that are considered to be maladaptive and indicative of psychopathology? This is not an easy question to answer. Though psychologists and psychiatrists have labored hard to develop precise behavioral guidelines for recognizing mental disturbance in its many forms, there is still considerable subjectivity involved in making this determination. For disorders in which anxiety is the primary feature, one major criterion is whether the stress reaction seems to be proportional to the actual degree of danger that the individual is confronting. In other words, is the individual's response a reasonable one given the situation that he or she is in? A second consideration is whether the anxiety experienced is used in constructive ways. When a stress response is functional, attention is directed to the external environment, and concentration and appropriate problem-solving activity increase. Dysfunctional stress reactions are characterized by "anxious apprehension" (Barlow, 1988). Attention turns inward, and there is preoccupation with thoughts of failure, there is a sense of lack of control, and problem-solving becomes increasingly ineffective. When disproportionate stress reactions are sustained over long periods of time and when negative thoughts focusing on past or anticipated dangers become the center of attention rather than important ongoing activities, mental health professionals begin to consider whether the behavior fits one of the categories that describe different forms of psychopathology.

Psychopathological conditions in which anxiety plays a central role and in which the individual is considered to be "in good contact with reality" were previously termed neuroses. The present version of the Diagnostic and Statistical Manual of Mental Disorders (American Psychiatric Association, 1994) uses the term **anxiety disorders.** Many of the techniques used to manage everyday stressors and subclinical stress-related problems were developed in work with people diagnosed as having one of the anxiety disorders; in subsequent chapters we will be referring to some of these diagnostic conditions in describing these techniques.

The distinctive features of the major anxiety disorders are described in the following sections; stress-related physical disorders are described in Chapter 5.

Generalized Anxiety Disorder (GAD). The essential feature of GAD is excessive, continual, and unrealistic worry that the individual finds difficult to control. This chronic apprehension is oriented around a number of events and activities rather than a specific situation or circumstance. Major areas of worry involve family, money, work, and illness. Compared with other anxiety disorders, there is also excessive worry about "minor things" (Barlow, 1988). GAD has been characterized as "the basic anxiety disorder—almost as an expression of 'pure' high trait anxiety" (Rapee & Barlow, 1993, p. 109).

Phobia. Phobias are marked by persistent fears of specific, clearly defined objects or situations. **Social phobias** refer to the experience of persistent fear and/or avoidance of situations in which an individual is required to perform some task while knowing that others will be watching and evaluating him or her. Common social phobias include public speaking, eating in public places, and, for males, urinating in a crowded lavatory. Social phobics sometimes also have more general problems socializing and mixing with others (Barlow, 1988). Social phobias are distinguished from **specific (or simple) phobias** in which the focus of the fear and avoidance reaction is a wide range of nonsocial specific objects and situations. Among the most prevalent sources of specific phobia are illness/injury, storms, and animals. Snakes, heights, and flying produce the greatest frequency of intense fears. However, they are not classified as phobias for most persons because their ease of successful avoidance does not produce extended periods of disability (Barlow, 1988; citing Agras, Sylvester, & Oliveau, 1969). Among the most debilitating of the specific phobias is agoraphobia (fear of open spaces or being alone in situations from which escape might be difficult), as illustrated in the following first person account:

> Many a time I have slunk in alleys instead of keeping on the broad streets, and often have walked long distances—perhaps a mile—to avoid crossing some pasture or open square, even when it was a matter of moment to me to save all the time possible. The dominating impulse is to always have something within reach to steady myself by in case of giddiness. This feeling is at times so strong that even when on a steamboat or a vessel, I cannot bear to look across any wide expanse of water, feeling almost impelled to jump in out of sheer desperation. This malady has throttled all ambition, and killed all personal pride, spoiled every pleasure. Over this the will seems to have no control. The malady is always present. I am conscious of it during every hour that I am awake. (Adapted from Marks, 1978, pp. 80–81.)

Panic Disorder. This condition is characterized by recurrent, unexpected panic attacks. A panic attack is defined as "a discrete period in which there is sudden onset of intense apprehension, fearfulness, or terror, often associated with feelings of impending doom" (American Psychiatric Association, 1994, p. 393). Accompanying this are various physiological changes such as breathing difficulty and choking sensations, palpitations, and chest pain. Panic attacks also occur in the context of other anxiety disorders. Panic disorder is closely linked to agoraphobia; it is thought that underlying agoraphobia is the fear of having a panic attack in a public place where no help is available. Almost all patients diagnosed with panic disorder display some degree of agoraphobic avoidance (Rapee & Barlow, 1993).

Obsessive-Compulsive Disorder (OCD). This condition is characterized by persistent ideas, thoughts, impulses, or images (obsessions) that cause anxiety and are viewed by the individual as being uncontrollable, and compulsive repetitive behaviors (e.g., handwashing) whose goal is to reduce anxiety. At some point the individual has recognized that the obsessions or compulsions are unreasonable (American Psychiatric Association, 1994). OCD is a disorder in which individuals resort to magic and rituals to establish a foothold of control over dangerous events in their lives. Because the dangerous events that must be avoided are thoughts, images, or impulses rather than well-defined stimuli (as in a phobia), the ritualistic behaviors can severely interfere with everyday functioning and the disorder can be very difficult to treat successfully (Barlow, 1988).

Posttraumatic Stress Disorder (PTSD). The identification of PTSD as an emotional disorder was primarily based on observations of soldiers' short- and long-term reactions to combat. Previous terms used to describe the postexposure symptoms of combat veterans include shell shock, war neurosis, and acute combat reaction. Presently, the development of a distinctive cluster of symptoms following personal exposure to any extremely traumatic stressor involving death, serious injury, or threat of physical harm is classified under PTSD. These symptoms include (a) recurrent **reexperiencing** of the traumatic event through dreams, waking imagery, or flashbacks, and the experience of intense distress on exposure to situations that resemble some aspect of the traumatic event; (b) persistent **avoidance** of thoughts, feelings, and activities associated with the trauma; and (c) increased **arousal** as reflected in sleeping problems, anger outbursts, and difficulty concentrating (American Psychiatric Association, 1994). In some cases, symptoms do not appear until months or years after exposure to the traumatic event. PTSD is the only anxiety disorder in which the stressor(s) eliciting the stress reaction can unequivocally be identified.

That the experience of severe psychological trauma can continue to take its toll long after the traumatic events are experienced is exemplified by World War II concentration camp survivors for whom "the pain is as raw today as it was fifty years ago." "Some survivors can't look at or listen to trains, pass smokestacks, or wait on lines. Others can't tolerate tardiness or the waste of food. They wolf their meals. The sound of spoken German makes them physically ill . . . many still jump when the phone rings, their voices prickly with dread when they answer. Who could it be? What do they want?" (Brecher, 1994, pp. xxiv, xxi).

ciety (which feature far greater social isolation, less intimacy and stability, and the need for more complex cognitive coping strategies) are drastically different from those of our ancestral environment, our species largely ceased to evolve 40,000 years ago. Differences in stress levels and overall levels of maladjustment in different modern societies are viewed as being proportional to the extent of mismatch between current environmental demands and those of the early "environments of evolutionary adaptation" in those societies (Bailey, 1995). Differences in the manner in which anxiety is expressed are due to different belief systems that have evolved in each culture.

5. Stress may enhance as well as hinder performance. For example, on learning and performance tasks, high levels of stress result in reduced levels of working memory capacity and clearly interfere with performance of tasks that require rapid detection, sustained attention, or attention to multiple sources of input (Evans & Cohen, 1987). On less complex tasks, and as learning progresses, high stress levels may facilitate performance (Spielberger, 1966).

The classic view of the relationship between stress and performance is represented in the Yerkes-Dodson inverted-U model, which posits that both low and high levels of arousal decrease performance, whereas intermediate levels enhance performance. While this model has not been unequivocally validated and while there are many other factors that may affect the relationship between stress and task performance (e.g., intelligence, what is being measured), it seems to be at least partially correct (Levine, 1971). For example, Janis (1958) found that surgical patients with moderate preoperative fear levels adjusted better after surgery than those with low or high preoperative fear. He reasoned that patients with moderate fear levels realistically appraised the situation and planned for how they would deal with the stressful aspects of the recovery period, and thus were better able to tolerate those stressors. Patients low in preoperative fear engaged in unrealistic denial and thus were unprepared for the demands of the postoperative period, whereas those high in preoperative fear got overly anxious and carried their inappropriately high stress levels over to the recovery period, where it continued to inhibit them from realistically dealing with the demands of the situation.

The negative effect of unrealistically low fear levels is also exemplified in Fenz & Epstein's (1967) description of two first-time sky divers who surprised everyone with their apparent total lack of concern during training and on the morning of their first jump. But their reactions changed dramatically once they entered the aircraft. "One began vomiting, and the other developed a coarse tremor. Both pleaded for the aircraft to be turned back. Upon leaving, they stated that they were giving up jumping" (Fenz & Epstein, 1967, pp. 49–50).

6. Interpersonally, stress brings out both the "worst" and the "best" in us. A greater incidence of negative social behaviors, including less altruism and cooperation and more aggression, have generally been observed in stressful circumstances (Evans & Cohen, 1987). In addition to any learning influences, these behaviors may result from the fact that stress signals real or imagined threats to survival and is therefore a potent elicitor of regressive, self-serving survival behaviors (Bailey, 1987). The highly publicized murder of Kitty Genovese, witnessed by thirty-eight people who watched from the safety of their apartments and who ignored her pleas for help (Latane & Rodin, 1977), and the more recent beating and death of a Detroit woman while forty people watched and did nothing (Fields-Meyer, 1995) exemplify this tendency, as does the behavior during World War II of many thousands of "ordinary" Germans who were either actively involved in the persecution of Jews and other minorities or who conveniently turned their heads (Elkins, 1971; Goldhagen, 1996). On the other hand, we are all aware of selfless acts of individual valor by seemingly ordinary people who, in emergency situations, rise to the occasion and

risk their own lives to save others. Even in Hitler-dominated Europe, there were a few who "had the courage to care" and risked great harm to themselves and their families in order to save others (Gross, 1988; Oliner & Oliner, 1988). These included people like German industrialist Oskar Schindler (Keneally, 1982), Chiune Sugihara ("Japan's Schindler"; Watanabe, 1995), and Swedish diplomat Raoul Wallenberg (Bierman, 1981), whose heroic behavior was seemingly driven by great conviction rather than by mere momentary reaction and who sustained their heroism in the face of continuous stress. In stressful circumstances in which cooperation and altruism have survival value for all concerned, as in the wake of a natural disaster, helping-oriented activities and resource-sharing are among the most common short-term reactions (Perry & Lindell, 1978).

7. Sometimes the best way to deal with stress is to *do something* about the situation that is causing the stress ("fight or flight"). In situations over which we have little direct control, however, it is better *to directly lower our stress response* without trying to modify the stressor ("grin and bear it"). Some stress management techniques teach emotional control, whereas others teach problem-solving skills. The nature of the stressor that you are dealing with, as well as your own capabilities, determines which techniques or combination of techniques you should use to deal with that stimulus. Ways of coping, how we develop coping skills, and how we teach others to cope are discussed in detail in Chapter 2 and Chapters 6 through 9.

8. Stress is in the *past*, the *present*, and the *future*. The prospect of an impending threatening encounter (e.g., a school exam) may evoke high-level stress in us, but we also experience stress when reflecting back on past unpleasant or humiliating experiences or when dealing with an immediate, ongoing danger. This temporal relationship is an important aspect of stressors that helps determine which stress management techniques and coping strategies are the most effective ways of dealing with them. In Chapters 6 through 9 we detail how different stress management and crisis intervention procedures are applied to aid coping with past, ongoing, and anticipated future stressors.

 UMMARY

1. The term *stress* is used to designate an individual's response to circumstances that he or she appraises as dangerous or threatening. Stress reactions have three major components: subjective feelings of discomfort that are measured by self-report instruments; behavioral changes; and physiological arousal. The term *stressor* is used to designate the circumstances or the stimuli that elicit the stress response.

2. The terms *state anxiety* and *fear*—like stress—denote a response state, and are to be distinguished from *trait anxiety*, which is a measure of relatively stable individual differences in state anxiety proneness.

3. People high in trait anxiety are especially fearful in interpersonal situations involving threat to self-esteem or threat of failure; however, trait anxiety differences are not good predictors of how people will respond to physically threatening situations that are best predicted by situation-specific measures. Some people (*sensation seekers*) seek out physically dangerous and other risky situations.

4. Learning (via classical conditioning) plays a strong role in fear acquisition. However, fears of some stimuli are innate. Other stimuli ("special evolutionary

dangers") are easier to develop fear reactions to because they have historically been threats to the survival of our species. Observational learning and cognitive factors also play important roles in fear acquisition.

5. Stress is far from being simply a destructive experience that needs to be avoided. It has many positive aspects, as well as paradoxical effects that vary as a function of the individual and his or her circumstances.

KEY TERMS

anxiety disorders   Psychopathological conditions in which anxiety plays a central role. They include Generalized Anxiety Disorder (characterized by chronic apprehension), Phobia (persistent fear of a particular object or situation), Panic Disorder (recurrent unexpected panic attacks), Obsessive-Compulsive Disorder (persistent intrusive thoughts and images that seem uncontrollable, along with repetitive behaviors designed to reduce anxiety), and Posttraumatic Stress Disorder (a cluster of symptoms following exposure to a traumatic event, including reexperiencing of the event, avoidance of trauma-related thoughts, and chronic emotional arousal).

behavioral measures of stress   Overt behaviors (e.g., facial expressions, speech hesitations, avoidance of a stimulus) that may be indicative of a stress reaction.

classical conditioning   Also called Pavlovian or respondent conditioning this is learning that results from the pairing of previously neutral stimuli with stimuli that elicit responses (respondents) automatically and without prior learning.

cognitive appraisal   Process by which an event is evaluated in terms of its personal significance for the individual. Events appraised as threatening or dangerous elicit a stress reaction.

daily hassles   Seemingly minor annoyances that occur on an ongoing basis and that may contribute to chronically high levels of stress.

fear   Stress response to a specific identifiable stimulus.

operant conditioning   Also called Skinnerian conditioning, this is learning that involves voluntarily emitted behaviors (operants) that are controlled by the consequences that follow them (reinforcers, punishers).

physiological measures of stress   Bodily changes (e.g., cardiovascular arousal, increased muscle tension) that most persons experience when exposed to a stimulus that they appraise as stressful.

reinforcer   In operant conditioning, any stimulus that, when made contingent upon a response, increases the rate of that response. Money or the approval of others are positive reinforcers that most people will work for. Negative reinforcers are unpleasant stimuli (e.g., a feared situation) that people learn to avoid.

self-report measures of stress   Questionnaires (e.g., the State Anxiety scale of the STAI) that ask people to report how they are currently feeling in terms of their stress level.

sensation seeking   Personality trait that identifies people who have a need to be exposed to novel, risky situations and who actively seek out such situations.

state anxiety   Stress or anxiety level at a given moment in time.

stress   Response experienced when one appraises a situation or stimulus as threatening or harmful.

stressor   Stimulus that is appraised as threatening or harmful and that therefore elicits a stress reaction.

trait anxiety   Personality trait that identifies chronically anxious people who are especially prone to experience state anxiety in situations involving a threat to self-esteem or a threat of failure.

unlearned fears   Stimuli that do not require prior learning to elicit a fear reaction (e.g., loud noise, loss of support, pain producers in children) or stimuli that we are predisposed to fear because they have historically posed threats to human survival (e.g., snakes).

CHAPTER 2
Coping

Writer Norman Cousins suddenly became ill and soon found it difficult to move his neck, arm, hands, fingers, and legs. After being hospitalized, he was told by doctors that he had a disease called ankylosing spondylitis and that his chances of full recovery were one in five hundred. He decided to take matters into his own hands. He was determined to live! He did his own research on his illness and developed his own treatment program. He was grateful that his personal physician did not try to discourage him from proceeding. Though he was in great pain, he decided that pain-killers and anti-inflammatory drugs were doing more harm than good to his overall condition, so he stopped taking them. He decided to take massive doses of vitamin C and to use laughter (induced by old Candid Camera TV episodes and humorous books) to enhance his overall body chemistry and to act as a pain-killer. Cousins had to leave the hospital when his laughter began to disturb the other patients. Eventually he completely recovered from his illness.

(Adapted from Cousins, 1976)

It was 1939. Ruth Thomas was an attractive Jewish woman in her late twenties, who resided in Berlin, Germany. She was living a nightmare that would continue for six years. At first she adjusted to the persecutions of the Nazis and the continuous threat of death and torture through her "capacity to see the world not as it was but as she wished it to be." She dealt with her unacceptable reality by pretending that it didn't exist. This seemingly impractical approach nevertheless "reinforced her unquenchable will to survive and her conviction that she would survive despite the increasing odds against her." "We've been here one hundred and fifty years. Hitler is a parvenu. I shall survive him." Late in

1942 she was ordered to report to Gestapo headquarters. She knew that unless she took action, she would soon be on a train bound for a concentration camp. Thomas could no longer deny reality. She went "underground" and spent the rest of the war, sometimes on the edge of starvation, playing "cat and mouse" with the Gestapo. In 1945 she watched with her mother as Russian troops liberated Berlin.

(Adapted from Gross, 1988)

Captain David Cronin was making his next-to-last flight as a pilot after almost forty years of commercial and military flying. Shortly after his Boeing 747 (which was filled with passengers) took off from Honolulu, a cargo door and a section of the fuselage tore away. Nine people were missing, and twenty-seven others had been injured. Cronin had to find a way to safely land the damaged plane with only two of its four engines working. Describing his reaction, Cronin said, "After saying a brief prayer, I got back to business." During the 25-minute flight back to Honolulu, he made a number of split-second decisions and unconventional maneuvers, and then safely landed the quivering, shuddering plane.

Each of the people just described found themselves in stressful situations and used different strategies to cope with the stress that they were experiencing. Upon learning that he was ill, Norman Cousins took personal responsibility for improving his situation. He carefully assessed what was needed, put together a plan of action, and embarked on a program designed to modify the stimulus (his disease) that was causing him stress. He expended little energy bemoaning his fate, denying his situation, or fantasizing about how much better things could be. In contrast, one way that Ruth Thomas effectively coped with an intolerable situation was to temporarily block it out and to fantasize that things were really better than they were. But when circumstances demanded that she deal with reality, she took the actions necessary to insure her survival. David Cronin's situation left him little room for contemplation or reverie. He had to act quickly and decisively in the face of imminent death. Both he and his passengers survived because he was able to bring to bear specialized skills that he had acquired over a lifetime, despite the knowledge of the terrible consequences if he failed.

What exactly is meant by the term *coping*? How can we classify the major coping techniques (such as those used by these three people), and under what circumstances is each technique most effective? How do we learn to become effective (or ineffective) copers? How important are intelligence, personality traits, and past experience in determining how effectively people will cope with particular situations? Before we attempt to answer these and other basic questions about coping, let us consider more generally the role that coping plays in the stress/appraisal process.

STRESS, APPRAISAL, AND COPING

As noted in Chapter 1, cognitive appraisal is the process by which an event is evaluated as threatening or dangerous. Lazarus & Folkman (1984) have distinguished between two aspects of the appraisal process: primary appraisal and secondary appraisal. **Primary appraisal** refers to our initial assessment of an event in terms of how it might affect our well-being. An event may be construed as irrelevant, positive, or harmful. Harmful appraisals may involve anticipated threats, ongoing stressors, or past events that are producing negative evaluations of oneself. **Secondary appraisal** involves evaluations of the resources that we have at our disposal (coping options) that might be useful in escaping from or minimizing the stress in a harmful or potentially harmful situation. For example, on entering a crowded nightclub, you might appraise the situation as largely positive because of the anticipation of having a good time, but you might also experience some stress as you contemplate the possibility of a fire starting and being unable to escape (primary appraisal). Even though you do not appraise the situation as being immediately dangerous, you begin looking for exits and contemplating the best avenues of escape should this be necessary (secondary appraisal). You may or may not decide to use these coping strategies, depending on whether something happens (e.g., you smell smoke) to prompt you to reappraise the situation as one that is imminently threatening to your well-being.

It is important to note that in using the term *coping*, we adopt Lazarus & Folkman's (1984) convention of distinguishing between coping as a set of processes and coping outcomes. Coping processes refer to the different strategies or tactics that we use to deal with stressful situations and the emotions elicited by them. Coping outcomes refer to how effective these strategies are in dealing with environmental demands or damping stressful emotions.

Lazarus & Folkman (1984) emphasize that coping is a *transactional* process. We are continually appraising the meaning of situations to us (whether they remind us of past harms or signify future threat, signify a potential for gain, or are neutral or irrelevant). Events that need to be managed and that call for action prompt us to evaluate our coping options and engage in some form of coping behavior. This process is not mechanical or linear. We often deal with multiple events simultaneously, and our attention shifts as we reappraise the significance of events and as we assess how successfully we think that we have dealt with particular stressors. At a particular moment, one event may emerge as figure from ground because the outcome of the encounter with that event is particularly important. However, each encounter is appraised against the backdrop of other ongoing events, and it is also influenced by our knowledge of past triumphs and unsatisfactory outcomes, by the coping strategies that we used in those instances, and by anticipations of future challenges.

Lazarus and Folkman's (1984) appraisal model has at its center an aware individual who is constantly processing alternatives and making *conscious* choices. Stress levels and the other emotions that we experience are determined by these conscious decisions and by the effectiveness of the coping strategies that they lead to. But recently psychologists have begun once again to consider seriously the role of the *unconscious* in determining emotions, coping, and other behaviors (see box on page 28).

DIFFERENT WAYS OF COPING

Coping strategies are thoughts and actions that we use to deal with stressful situations and lower our stress levels. Lazarus & Folkman (1984) have distinguished between two broad types of coping techniques: problem-focused and emotion-focused. When using **problem-focused** coping, we attempt to short-circuit the negative emotions we are experiencing by doing something to modify, avoid, or minimize the situation that is threatening us. When using **emotion-focused** coping, we try to moderate or eliminate our unpleasant emotions by using mechanisms such as positive reappraisal, denial, and wishful thinking. In both cases, we are trying to **control** our stress level. In problem-focused coping, we do something to change or get away from the things that are causing us emotional upset. In emotion-focused coping, we try to minimize the stress reaction directly without confronting or trying

COPING: CONSCIOUS OR UNCONSCIOUS?

Sigmund Freud, M.D., was the first psychologist to systematically study coping. He developed a complex theory that emphasized the role of defense mechanisms such as repression in the coping process. These defense mechanisms are devices that we use to lower our stress level when our world becomes too anxiety-provoking (for Freud the anxiety almost always stemmed from conflicts involving sexual and aggressive impulses). For example, in repression we block from awareness thoughts and feelings that are making us anxious. According to Freud, defense mechanisms operate automatically and unconsciously. We are not aware of what defenses we are using, and we are not able to voluntarily stop using them (Janis, Mahl, Kagan, & Holt, 1969).

Though it had a significant impact on many people's thinking, Freud's concept of unconscious motivation and coping fell into disrepute with most behavioral scientists, who argued that the unconscious could not be studied scientifically and that there was no way to prove its viability. The studies that were conducted in the 1950s that seemed to show that people could be influenced to buy certain products because of subliminal messages ("Eat popcorn, Drink Coke") and the studies that seemed to show that unconscious repression interfered with the perception of "dirty" words ultimately were rejected because of methodological problems. Lazarus and Folkman's (1984) influential theory, which we highlight in this book and which represents the main thrust of current thinking, stresses the overriding importance of conscious cognitive activity in all phases of the stress appraisal and coping process.

But the unconscious seems to be making a comeback. For example, it has been pointed out that many of our everyday coping activities (e.g., avoidance maneuvers while driving) become habitual and automatic and that we engage in them without conscious awareness. Furthermore, current research supports the notion that under certain circumstances we analyze the meaning of events, reach conclusions about them, and act on them "without being able to articulate the reasoning by which they were reached" (Kihlstrom, 1987, p. 1447). Many leading scholars now accept the reality of unconscious processes; the question being studied now is just how "smart" or "dumb" unconscious processes are (Loftus & Klinger, 1992).

to do something about the cause of the stress. Examples of different emotion-focused and problem-focused coping strategies are presented in Table 2–1.

On the basis of statistical clustering analyses of items on the Ways of Coping Checklist (Folkman & Lazarus, 1985; Folkman, Lazarus, Dunkel-Schetter, DeLongis, & Gruen, 1986), it appears that coping strategies can be broken down into eight subcategories. Two of these categories (Confrontive Coping, Planful Problem-Solving) represent types of problem-focused coping. Confrontive Coping describes aggressive efforts to change the situation, including attempts involving risk taking. Planful Problem-Solving describes other kinds of efforts to alter the situation inducing the stress along with an analytic approach to solving the problem. Five categories (Distancing, Self-Control, Accepting Responsibility, Escape-Avoidance, Positive Reappraisal) represent types of emotion-focused coping; and one (Seeking Social Support) may be primarily emotion- or problem-focused. Distancing describes efforts to detach oneself from the stressor or to create a positive outlook. Self-control describes efforts to control one's feelings or actions. Accepting Responsibility acknowledges one's own role in the problem and includes the theme of trying to put things right. Escape-Avoidance describes wishful thinking and attempts to escape or avoid by engaging in other activities. Positive Reappraisal describes efforts to create positive meaning by focusing on personal growth and also includes items pertaining to prayer and religion. Social Support describes efforts to seek information about

---

TABLE 2–1. SAMPLE ITEMS FROM THE WAYS OF COPING CHECKLIST

Problem-Focused Coping Subscales

Confrontive Coping
   I stood my ground and fought for what I wanted.
   I tried to get the person responsible to change his or her mind.
   I took a big chance and did something very risky.
Planful Problem-Solving
   I made a plan of action and followed it.
   I came up with a couple of different solutions to the problem.
Seeking Social Support (Problem-Focused)
   I talked to someone who could do something concrete about the problem.

Emotion-Focused Coping Subscales

Distancing
   I went on as if nothing had happened.
   I looked for the silver lining—tried to look on the bright side of things.
Self-Control
   I tried to keep my feelings to myself.
   I tried not to burn my bridges, but leave things open somewhat.
Accepting Responsibility
   I realized I brought the problem on myself.
   I made a promise to myself that things would be different next time.
Escape-Avoidance
   I wished the situation would go away or somehow be over with.
   I tried to make myself feel better by eating, drinking, smoking, using drugs
   or medication, etc.
Positive Reappraisal
   I changed or grew as a person in a good way.
   I rediscovered what is important in life.
   I prayed.
Seeking Social Support (Emotion-Focused)
   I accepted sympathy and emotional support from someone.

Source: Folkman et al., 1986.

---

the stressor and to elicit tangible support (Problem-Focused) as well as emotional support (Emotion-Focused) from others.[1]

---

[1]The Lazarus & Folkman distinction between problem-focused and emotion-focused coping is the most widely accepted conceptualization of coping strategies, and it is one that we will continue to use throughout this book. However, it should be noted that other coping factors have been identified in analyzing data from the Ways of Coping Checklist and other coping questionnaires (see Endler & Parker, 1990; Holohan & Moos, 1987; Moos & Billings, 1982). Carver, Scheier, & Weintraub (1989) have developed a coping inventory (COPE) that is being used increasingly in research investigations. The COPE distinguishes among five subscales of problem-focused coping (active coping—"I take additional action to get rid of the problem," planning—"I try to come up with a strategy about what to do," suppression of competing activities—"I put aside other activities in order to concentrate on this," restraint coping—"I force myself to wait for the right time to do something," and seeking instrumental social support—"I ask people who have had similar experiences what they did"); and five subscales of emotion-focused coping (seeking emotional social support—"I talk to someone about how I feel," positive reinterpretation—"I look for something good in what is happening," acceptance—"I learn to live with it," denial—"I refuse to believe that it has happened," and turning to religion—"I seek God's help"); in addition to three other subscales (behavioral disengagement, mental disengagement, and alcohol-drug disengagement).

Effectiveness of Different Coping Strategies

A common assumption is that direct problem-solving is always a more effective way of dealing with stress than suppressing or directly moderating emotions. This is the "American way," a "can-do" philosophy that is instilled in us in early childhood that carries with it the need to view ourselves as competent and able to instrumentally control almost any situation. Consistent with this view, among mental health professionals, accurate reality testing is traditionally considered the "hallmark of mental health" (Lazarus, 1983), whereas coping strategies that involve suppression of anxiety and other unpleasant emotional states are considered immature and maladaptive. Clinical experience and research indicates that this conclusion is accurate as a broad generalization, and that effective problem-focused coping is indeed the prime contributor to a sense of self-worth or self-efficacy (Bandura, 1990). Norman Cousins's unhesitatingly confrontive approach to a situation that most others would have given up on exemplifies creative use of problem-focused coping.

But emotion-focused coping is also useful under certain circumstances. Though Norman Cousins apparently made little use of it, most of us engage in some emotion-focused coping under high-level stress in order to suppress disablingly high anxiety levels and to enable us to evaluate situational demands, plan appropriately, and perform more effectively (see Janis, 1958). Even in situations as complex as marital counseling, teaching couples emotion-focused strategies such as acceptance, tolerance, and the way to detach from problems using metaphor and humor is important in order to set the stage for effective problem-solving and active change approaches (Christensen, Jacobson, & Babcock, 1995; Walker, Johnson, Manion, & Cloutier, 1996). In general, emotion-focused coping is also useful as a short-term strategy and as a way of managing largely uncontrollable situations in contrast to the relative ineffectiveness of problem-focused coping in such situations (Forsythe & Compas, 1987; Strentz & Auerbach, 1988; Suls & Fletcher, 1985).

The utility of emotion-focused coping was demonstrated by Ruth Thomas, who initially dealt with the nightmarish world of Nazi persecution "by pretending it didn't exist." This helped both to reinforce her "will to survive" and to prepare her for the ordeal of "playing cat and mouse with the Gestapo" that followed. Extensive emotion-focused coping would have been counterproductive for Captain Cronin because of his need to act quickly, but even in the urgency of his situation he took a brief moment to "catch his breath" (say a prayer) before getting "back to business."

Strentz & Auerbach (1988) demonstrated the superiority of emotion-focused coping in a situation in which there were minimal opportunities to modify a stressful situation through problem-solving. In a research investigation conducted in conjunction with the FBI, airline flight attendants and pilots were abducted by "terrorists" and held hostage for four days in order to study their reactions to the stress of captivity. Great efforts were made to make the situation as realistic as possible. During the abduction the hostages were riding in a van on a city street when

Five terrorists (special agents of the FBI) took quick and complete control of the subjects with sufficient force and noise to ensure complete cooperation. The terrorists fired automatic weapons (blanks) but did not use blank firing adaptors, adding to the realism for hostages who might have been familiar with these weapons. Terrorists' faces were covered with a ski mask or kaffiyeh (a Middle Eastern headpiece). The terrorists exploded flash bangs (tactical hand grenades), creating noise and bright light but no fragmentation. The van's driver and his assistant were both wearing concealed blood bags. During the shooting they broke the bags by hand and allowed the blood to soak into their clothing as they turned to face the hostages and fell to the floor—The terrorists commanded the hostages to place their hands on top of their heads and to make no other moves until ordered. The terrorists told them that a violation of this order would result in their deaths. While some terrorists provided cover, two terrorists removed the hostages, one at a time, from the van and placed them on the ground, spread-eagled face down. The terrorists immediately searched them, handcuffed their hands behind them, and covered their heads with pillowcases (Strentz & Auerbach, 1988, pp. 654–655).

During the four days of captivity, the hostages were warned not to attempt to escape or communicate with anyone. They were detained in the same room but were isolated from each other visually by the pillowcases placed over their heads. Measures taken throughout the study indicated that the subjects experienced very high stress levels. Prior to the abduction, some of the subjects had received training in the use of emotion-focused coping strategies. They were taught to use techniques such as deep breathing and muscular relaxation to moderate their stress levels and to fantasize that they were somewhere else. Other subjects received problem-focused training. They were taught ways to communicate with each other nonverbally, how to manipulate their captors, and how to gather intelligence. The subjects who received emotion-focused training (and who actually used emotion-focused coping strategies to the greatest extent) had the lowest stress levels and adjusted best emotionally during captivity.

Anecdotal reports from actual former hostages who had been held for relatively short periods of time are consistent with these findings. For example, a federal-prison guard who was held hostage for nine days by prisoners (Cuban deportees) in a high security unit said, "I was trying to defend myself in the initial takeover—but when I realized it was a no-win situation I felt it was best to submit to whatever was coming because I knew I was caught and there was no way out—(we) passed the time praying together, reading and enduring fear ("Guard held," 1991).

Most of us never have the experience of being abducted and held hostage. But most of us at various times are exposed to short-term stressors over which we have little control. Perhaps the most frequently experienced type of these is painful or anxiety-inducing medical examinations or treatments. An example of a diagnostic procedure that is becoming increasingly common is Magnetic Resonance Imaging (MRI), which requires that the patient lie still in a tightly enclosed cylinder for up to an hour. Severe anxiety reactions and panic in patients are not uncommon (Brennan, Redd, et al., 1988). Short of refusing to undergo the procedure or demanding to be released from the imaging chamber, the patient has no problem-focused coping options. Patients who cope successfully use emotion-focused coping techniques like escape-avoidance and positive reappraisal to psychologically remove themselves from the situation for the relatively brief period of its occurrence.

But emotion-focused coping is not an effective strategy for dealing with stress on a sustained basis. For example, in the Nazi concentration camps, denial, emotional detachment, and passive submission were useful coping devices for inmates in dealing with the initial shock of suddenly having to adjust to a living nightmare; however, survival ultimately "depended upon an exquisite sensitivity to the mood of the guards and constant alertness to opportunities for gaining extra food or better work assignments" (Schmolling, 1984, p. 114). Inmates who never tried actively to do something about their situation, who believed the statements of the guards that they would never leave the camp alive . . . these people experienced "learned helplessness." They "stopped eating, sat mute and motionless in corners, and . . . died without apparent physical cause" (Seligman, 1975, p. 175).

Even in situations in which opportunities for actually changing crucial aspects of the situation are restricted, there is evidence that having a sense of some degree of control over the situation enhances adjustment. Many people who are institutionalized (e.g., nursing home residents, the chronically ill) live in environments that are stressful because they have little control. Seligman (1975) suggests that the stress levels of such patients can be lowered and their health improved if they are given maximum control over their everyday activities (such as choosing what they want for breakfast, what color they prefer for their curtains, or whether to sleep late or wake up early). Research findings have supported Seligman's suggestions. For example, psychologists Ellen Langer and Judith Rodin told one group of elderly nursing-home residents that they could decide what they wanted their rooms to look like, when they wanted to go to the movies, and whom they wanted to interact with. A second comparable group of elderly residents, who were randomly assigned to live on another floor, were told that the staff would care for them and would try to keep them happy. Residents in the first group became more active and reported feeling happier than those in the second group. They also became more alert and involved in different kinds of activities, such as movie attendance and socializing. Furthermore, during the eighteen-month period following the intervention, 15 percent of the subjects in the first group died, whereas 30 percent of the subjects in the second group died (Rodin, 1980).

The case of American news correspondent Terry Anderson also demonstrates the benefits of finding ways to exercise problem-focused control, even in the context of a seemingly hopeless situation. In 1985 Anderson was abducted and held hostage for more than six-and-one-half years in Lebanon. His life was one of "rigid rules enforced by brutal guards, a life in a small cell devoid of daylight—a life of chains and blindfolds—a sentence of unknown length, empty days evolving into years." Though there was virtually no opportunity for escape (another hostage who attempted escape was quickly recaptured and beaten savagely), Anderson found ways of manipulating his situation ("bullying and badgering" both captors and fellow hostages) to reduce its stressfulness and enhance his sense of control. He insisted that fellow hostages learn a sign language that he had half-invented, and he constantly demanded books and better treatment from his captors. Gradually the living conditions of the hostages improved. Anderson emerged from captivity "opinionated, eloquent, blunt, and confident," and with at least one new practical skill: during captivity he got another hostage to teach him French until he became fluent ("Forceful Hostage," 1991).

THE DEVELOPMENT OF COPING

In the preceding section we considered some of the mechanisms that we use to deal with the many different kinds of psychological stressors which we face in our everyday lives. We now take a step backward chronologically and consider the origins of coping. Let us begin by examining what we know about how infants learn to cope and then trace how coping develops throughout childhood and adolescence.

Coping in Infancy and Early Childhood

There is evidence that the coping process begins from the moment of conception. One of the first stressors experienced by the fetus is maternal anxiety. Unusually high fetal activity and later irritability have been found consistently when mothers have experienced high levels of pregnancy anxiety (Field, 1991). During the first three months of life, pain and physical discomfort are the primary sources of stress, but then the primary stressors begin to change. From the ages of four to twelve months unpredictable events, such as the appearance of adult strangers or sudden separation from the mother, are the main stressors, whereas during the second year of life parental restriction, punishment, and prolonged separation are the main sources of fear (Kagan, 1983).

One of the first coping mechanisms used by the infant is a "rudimentary, biologically rooted social behavior"—crying (Lipsitt, 1983). Because this very adaptive expression of distress typically attracts both the aid and the solace of others, it is typically the first strategy that infants learn for enlisting both problem-focused and emotion-focused coping assistance from others. Other infant behaviors, particularly self-soothing techniques, seem purely designed to modulate emotions. These behaviors include sucking on their hands or fingers or on an available object, clasping their hands together, and rocking. Older infants pacify themselves through thumb-sucking or physical contact with an attachment object such as a blanket or soft toy (Karraker & Lake, 1991). Infants also learn how to solicit emotion-focused coping assistance through crying or raising their arms to request being picked up or comforted. Generally the goal of these behaviors is to secure "proximity to the attachment figure and the concomitant security that accompanies this proximity" (Karraker & Lake, 1991, p. 94).

Karraker & Lake (1991, p. 94) also outline the range of problem-focused coping behaviors observed in infants. Much of the problem-focused coping observed in young infants involves using motor skills to escape from stressors (e.g., moving away from a frightening stranger or an alarming toy) or sometimes to confront and defuse a stressor (e.g., remove a barrier, push a peer away, turn off a noisy toy). Infants also learn "communicative actions that signal to adults that they want help in eliminating a stressor. Examples are infants in a strange environment pointing at the door, waving bye-bye or saying 'home' after the mother's return in order to get mother to remove them from the situation." Infants may also show "anticipatory" problem-focused coping. For example, "when they recognize that the babysitter has arrived and parents are planning to leave they may attempt to prevent their departure by crying, clinging to them, trying to get them to play a game, blocking the door, etc. Also, they may attempt to mitigate their own distress (emotion-focused coping) by getting their security blanket or ignoring their parents."

The importance of the infant's relationship to its primary caretakers or "attachment figures" (usually its parents) cannot be overestimated. It is in these relationships that the infant learns and rehearses the coping behaviors that will be used in dealing with future stressful occurrences. In Lipsitt's (1983) view, the attachment process has biological roots. It is "part of the evolutionary history that prepares human infants for defense against hostile interpersonal encounters long before they will be in need of such talent" (p. 164)—it is "a time for the practice and fine tuning of responses essential to survival, socialization and the preservation of self-esteem" (p. 187). The familiar infant games of pat-a-cake and peek-a-boo are seen as part of a natural proclivity on the part of the infant to increase tension and disequilibrium in order to provide, within the safe confines of the attachment relationship, a testing ground for various coping strategies that the infant will need later on.

Not only is the relationship with one's parents important in this developmental sense, but it also has been found to be the single most important factor in determining how well children cope with particular stressors. Children exposed to disasters and war cope better when their parents function effectively in the face of stress and when they are not separated from their parents (Garmezy & Rutter, 1985); children living in homes where there is severe marital conflict adjust better if there is a good relationship with one of the parents (Rutter, 1990). Congruent findings have been obtained in studies on monkeys. Monkeys reared from birth without mothers but with extensive peer contact function well in familiar and stable social settings, but they coped poorly with stress (such as brief social separation) later in life. In contrast, monkeys reared by nurturant foster mothers were able to cope effectively with such stressful challenges when they encountered them later on (Suomi, 1991).

Concerned parents provide emotional support and a secure base for exploration and practicing different strategies for dealing with frightening situations. They also foster the development of problem-focused coping skills through modeling effective behavior and by providing children concrete opportunities to experience mastery.

Furthermore, through persuasion and encouragement, such parents reinforce children's belief in themselves and their ability to apply their skills (Bandura, 1990).[2]

Coping in Older Children and Adolescents

The stressors of middle childhood have their own distinctive character that separates them from infancy, adolescence, and adulthood. These stressors are captured in descriptions by children of common experiences reported to psychologist Donald Wertlieb and colleagues in a study of stress and coping in children:

> Every time we have to chose up sides for a game, they never pick me, even last. They don't want me on the team.
>
> —9-year-old Tom

> He can't live with us anymore, my daddy, because he was mean to my mother and hitted us kids when we didn't even do anything. And I stayed at his new house and he didn't hit me and he gave me this doll.
>
> —7-year-old Michelle

> I can't never do the part with the take-away numbers. I did all the problems real fast and she put big red x's on them and said I wasn't trying. And I started crying inside but I couldn't because they would all see.
>
> —8-year-old Izzy
> (Reprinted from Wertlieb, Wiegel, & Feinstein, 1987, p. 548).

In trying to deal with stressors, children use a wide range of active problem-solving strategies as well as those designed directly to manage emotions. For example, Curry and Russ (1985) asked eight-, nine-, and ten-year-old children who had just undergone restorative dental treatment what they thought about, what they said to themselves, and what they wished for during the examination, and also observed their behavior in the dental chair. Though this was a largely uncontrollable situation, the responses included problem-oriented thoughts (e.g., "I told myself to be still") and behaviors (attempts to establish a supportive relationship with the dentist or to participate actively in the treatment process) designed to alter the situation, as well as behaviors designed to still their fears directly (e.g., "I said to myself, God is with you, so don't worry"; "I tried to concentrate on that Muppet Poster hanging on the wall").

Band & Weisz (1988) asked children to tell about a time when they felt "bad, unhappy, or scared" and then to "tell me all the things you did and thought," how those thoughts/actions "made things better," and whether each strategy worked (p. 248). They found that even children as young as six are sufficiently aware of stress and of the need to cope in their own lives to be able to identify stressors, to describe how they attempted to deal with them, and to assess how successful their efforts were. As children get older and mature, they tend to use a greater number and variety of cognitive coping strategies. Like adults, they are more likely to attempt to change stressful circumstances that they perceive as controllable (e.g., deal with school failure by trying to improve grades) and to try to deal with less controllable and less fa-

---

[2]As noted earlier in this chapter, the question of whether coping always involves making conscious choices is currently being debated by scholars. This question is especially salient when considering cognitive appraisal and coping processes in children. At birth and in early infancy, distress reactions and coping are clearly regulated by hard-wired (innate and unconscious) appraisals. Appraisals and coping reactions come under more conscious control—they become "more reflective, self-regulated, and internalized" as children mature through childhood, middle childhood, and adolescence (Skinner & Wellborn, 1994).

miliar situations by managing the emotions that they elicit (e.g., deal with the pain of "getting a shot" by thinking happy thoughts) Band & Weisz, 1988). Overall, however, across situations older children report greater use of emotion-control strategies. This finding is consistent with the idea that emotion-control strategies involve greater cognitive control and a higher level of abstraction and also an increased appreciation that certain manipulative strategies will not work in some situations (e.g., screaming in the doctor's office will not prevent a shot) (Band & Weisz, 1988; Curry & Russ, 1985; Wertlieb, Wiegel, & Feldstein, 1987).

The study of stress and coping among adolescents has become a very serious matter given the fact that suicide rates among adolescents are high and on the increase, as is the rate of substance abuse (Aneshensel & Gore, 1991). What are the predominant concerns of adolescents? The following 15 events (out of 125) were rated as most stressful (in descending order) by eleven- to fourteen-year-old, predominantly white children from largely middle and upper middle class backgrounds (Dise-Lewis, 1988):

1. One of your parents died.
2. A close family member (grandparent, brother, sister) died.
3. Your parents decided to get a divorce.
4. Your mom or dad was put in jail.
5. You were picked up by the police.
6. You were suspended from school.
7. Your mom or dad moved out of your home.
8. You got caught stealing something.
9. You had to move in with relatives or into a foster home.
10. Someone close to you (like a friend) died.
11. You were kept back in the same grade.
12. You got suspended from school.
13. A member of your family got in serious trouble with the police.
14. You've taken drugs.
15. One of your parents physically hit you.*

Wagner and Compas (1990) found that, overall, females report more stress during adolescence than do males, with females in junior and senior high school reporting particularly more interpersonal stressors than males. Different kinds of stressors were most strongly related to emotional and behavioral problems in different groups of adolescents: family stressors in junior high students, stressors pertaining to peer relations in senior high students, and academic stressors in college students.

Regarding coping-strategy use, Dise-Lewis (1988) found that adolescents use a wide range of problem-oriented and emotion-regulation coping techniques and that those techniques that provide a means of distraction from the stressor were most useful. The majority of studies indicate, however, that use of problem-focused and approach coping strategies is associated with better adjustment and less distress among adolescents, whereas use of avoidance and other forms of emotion-focused coping are, in general, less effective stress management strategies (Compas, Malcarne, & Fondacaro, 1988; Ebata & Moos, 1991, 1994; Glyshaw, Cohen, & Towbes, 1989; Hanson, Cigrang, et al., 1989; Kurdek & Sinclair, 1988). Consistent with this finding, retrospective studies have found that use of emotion-focused strategies

---

*From Dise-Lewis, J., 1988. The Life Events and Coping Inventory. *Psychosomatic Medicine*, 50, 484–499. By permission of Williams & Wilkins.

such as wishful thinking, avoidance, and substance abuse to deal with the stress of sexual abuse and incest during adolescence and childhood is associated with poorer adjustment as adults (Coffey, Leitenberg, Henning, Turner, & Bennet, 1996; Johnson & Kenkel, 1991; Leitenburg, Greenwald, & Cato, 1992).

COPING STYLE AS A PERSONALITY TRAIT

In Chapter 1 we distinguished between anxiety as a relatively stable personality trait (trait anxiety) and as an emotional state that fluctuates over time and across situations (state anxiety). Coping also may be conceptualized as a relatively stable tendency or style (personality trait) or as an active, ongoing process (state) that changes as a function of the situation which an individual finds himself or herself in. Consistent with the Lazarus-Folkman approach, we have emphasized that in order to best understand stress reactions and to modify them, we must be able to understand *ongoing coping strategies*. But there has been extensive work on classifying people in terms of the strategies that they *typically* use to deal with stress; also, there is evidence that though people adjust their coping strategies to the demands of situations they also develop predispositions to cope with stress in particular ways (Folkman & Lazarus, 1985; Lazarus & Folkman, 1984) and that these coping dispositions, like most other personality traits, remain fairly stable from the postadolescent years throughout adulthood (Costa & McCrae, 1986).

One older approach that has been used to measure general styles of coping is to present people with a series of sentence stems and to ask them to complete the sentences in terms of "your real feelings." This is an example of a projective test of personality (like the Rorschach Inkblot Test) that assumes that when people are presented with an unstructured stimulus and are asked to complete it or make sense out of it, they will do so in a way that reveals their underlying personality traits, attitudes, and dispositions. The Modified Coper-Avoider Sentence Completion Test (DeLong, 1970) classifies people as Copers or Avoiders on the basis of their responses to different sentence stems. Copers are people who, when faced with threats, tend to be very vigilant for ways to actively deal with the stress; they would be expected to initiate more problem-focused than emotion-focused coping strategies. Avoiders, in contrast, in situations that are arousing would be more prone to suppress their emotions by using avoidance or denial and would be less prone to actively seek out ways of defusing or moderating the stressor itself. Examples of items from the Modified Coper-Avoider Sentence Completion Test and the types of responses that would be indicative of a coping versus an avoidant coping style are presented in Table 2–2.

Many other coping disposition measures have been developed. Among the most widely used are the Repression-Sensitization Scale (Byrne, 1961), the Defense Mechanism Inventory (Gleser & Ihilevich, 1969), the Internal-External Locus of Control Scale (Rotter, 1966), and the Miller Behavioral Style Scale (MBSS; Miller, 1987). The MBSS assesses how people tend to deal with information about a stressful event when they are threatened with the event. On the basis of their responses to the MBSS, people are classified on two dimensions: monitoring (the extent to which they tend to seek out and scan for information about threat) and blunting (the extent to which they tend to distract themselves from and ignore threat-relevant information). Monitoring and blunting are assessed on the MBSS by having people imagine several different threatening situations and then indicate for each of the situations how they would deal with them. An example of one of these situations, as well as the types of responses that are classified as "monitoring" and "blunting," is presented in Table 2–3.

The Coper-Avoider Sentence Completion Test and the MBSS are examples of *global* coping style measures that are designed to assess how people are inclined to

---

TABLE 2–2. EXAMPLES OF ITEMS FROM THE MODIFIED COPER-AVOIDER SENTENCE COMPLETION TEST

Responses that are judged as indicating "intense, immediate, personalized involvement" are scored as Coper responses, whereas responses judged as indicating "denial, remoteness, and lack of personalized involvement" are scored as Avoider responses.

Stem: A crippling disease _____
    Examples of "Coper" responses: is a tragedy.
                                             is something I have lived with my
                                           whole life.
    Examples of "Avoider" responses: is God's will.
                                           I don't have any.

Stem: A man's body _____
    Examples of "Coper" responses: is great when it's the right man.
                                           is ugly.
    Examples of "Avoider" responses: should be left to science.
                                           is his own business.

Source: DeLong, 1970

---

cope with *most* stressful situations. Other measures have been developed that are designed to evaluate coping tendencies in specific situations. For example, the Krantz Health Opinion Survey (KHOS; Krantz, Baum, & Wideman, 1980) assesses the extent to which people prefer to have information or to be actively involved in their own treatment when they are in a stressful medical situation. Examples of items from the KHOS are presented in Table 2–4.

Measures of both general and situation-specific coping dispositions have shown to be useful in helping determine how best to prepare people who are about to confront stressful situations. For example, Miller and Mangan (1983) divided gynecologic patients to undergo a diagnostic evaluation for possible cervical cancer into monitors and blunters on the basis of their scores on the MBSS. Half of the patients in each MBSS group, prior to the examination, were given extensive information de-

---

TABLE 2–3. A SCENE AND SAMPLE ITEMS FROM THE MILLER BEHAVIORAL STYLE SCALE

Directions: Vividly imagine that you are on an airplane, thirty minutes from your destination, when the plane unexpectedly goes into a deep dive and then suddenly levels off. After a short time, the pilot announces that nothing is wrong, although the rest of the ride may be rough. You, however, are not convinced that all is well. Check *all* of the statements that might apply to you.

(M)   I would call for the stewardess and ask her exactly what the problem was.
(B)   I would order a drink or tranquilizer from the stewardess.
(B)   I would settle down and read a book or magazine or write a letter.
(M)   I would listen carefully to the engines for unusual noises and would watch the crew to see if their behavior was out of the ordinary.

(M—Monitoring response; B—Blunting response). By permission of Suzanne M. Miller

TABLE 2–4.   SAMPLE ITEMS FROM THE KRANTZ HEALTH OPINION SURVEY

Directions: Indicate whether you agree or disagree with each of the following statements.

1. I usually don't ask the doctor or nurse many questions about what they're doing during a medical exam.
2. Instead of waiting for them to tell me, I usually ask the doctor or nurse immediately after an exam about my health.
3. I'd rather have the doctors and nurses make the decisions about what's best than for them to give a me a whole lot of choices.
4. Learning how to cure some of your own illnesses without consulting a physician is a good idea.

Agreement with item 1 and disagreement with item 2 indicate a preference for information about one's own health care. Disagreement with item 3 and agreement with item 4 indicate a preference for active participation in one's own medical care.

Source: Krantz et al., 1980.

tailing the forthcoming procedure and the sensations that would be experienced. The remaining patients in each group received minimal information about the impending procedure. Patients responded to the two information conditions in a manner consistent with their coping styles. For blunters, having minimal information reduced anxiety, depression, discomfort, and psychophysiological arousal both before and after the procedure. Conversely, monitors showed a reduction in stress level when they were given extensive information. They had fewer signs of pain during the procedure and lowered psychophysiological arousal by the end of the procedure.

Martelli, Auerbach, Alexander, & Mercuri (1987) demonstrated the usefulness of the KHOS Information scale in helping determine how best to prepare patients to cope with a stressful dental procedure involving multiple tooth extractions that was performed under local anesthesia. (The almost universal dread experienced by people about to face the dentist is pithily captured by poet Ogden Nash: "Some tortures are physical and some are mental, the but one that's both is dental.") In this study, patients were divided into high and low information preference groups on the basis of their KHOS scores. Some of the patients in each group were prepared for the procedure with an intervention designed to promote *problem-focused* coping strategies. This intervention included information about the impending surgery, the instruments that the surgeon would use and the sensations that the patient would experience, and also instruction in how to discriminate among the different sensations, how to label them, and how to use self-statements to analyze incoming information. In addition, patients were given practice in the use of these strategies when the intervener pinched their cheek and told them to imagine that it was a sensation that they were experiencing during surgery. Other patients were prepared with an intervention designed to foster *emotion-focused* coping strategies. These patients were given instruction in the use of a brief relaxation procedure, practice in using calming self-statements (e.g., "I will just relax, and it will be over soon"), and attention redirection (e.g., imagining that surgery is over or is just a dream), as well as practice in the use of these strategies. A third group of patients received a *mixed-focus* intervention that included components of both the problem- and emotion-focused interventions in an abbreviated, combined format.

The results of the study are depicted in Figure 2–1. It can be seen that the mixed-focus intervention produced the best overall results on all of the outcome measures (dental surgeon's rating of patient adjustment, patient self-ratings of anxiety, pain, and satisfaction with the surgical procedure), and response to this intervention was unaffected by patient dispositional differences in preference for information. But for patients who received either the problem-focused or emotion-focused intervention, their preference for information was very important in determining their response. For example, patients who had a high preference for information and who received the emotion-focused intervention had the poorest adjustment, were the least satisfied, and experienced more pain than any other group of patients, whereas high preference patients who received the problem-focused intervention were the best adjusted and experienced the least pain and anxiety. In contrast, low preference for information patients responded better to the emotion-focused intervention.

The findings of this study, along with those of other recent investigations, demonstrate that the extent to which dispositional differences in coping style are important depends on the nature of the stressor that an individual is confronting. The stress situation that the patients in the Martelli, Auerbach, Alexander, & Mercuri (1987) study were facing involved a mix of both problem-focused and emotion-focused coping demands. These patients were under local anesthetic and awake during the two-hour surgery and therefore had to be reasonably alert to what was happening. They could interact with the surgeon and had to follow instructions. Thus, they likely felt they had some degree of instrumental control over what was happening to them. Yet they knew that their amount of control was limited, and for much of the time they had to "grin and bear" the pain and discomfort. Therefore, it makes sense that the mixed-focus intervention, which offered both problem-focused and emotion-focused coping strategies, was most effective and worked well with all patients regardless of their coping disposition. Patients could choose those aspects of the intervention that were congruent with their coping disposition and deemphasize those that weren't. Patients given either the problem-focused or the emotion-focused intervention were not given this choice, and when the intervention they received did not match their coping style, they responded poorly.

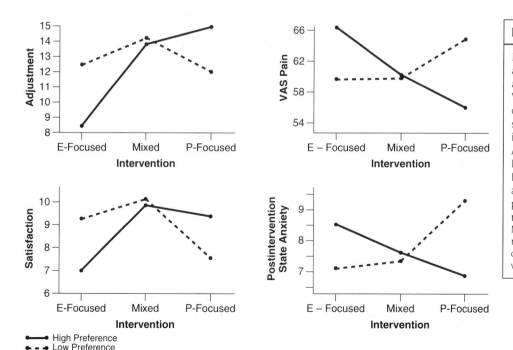

Figure 2–1

Mean postintervention state anxiety scores, adjustment and satisfaction ratings, and VAS pain scores for subjects differing in KHOS Information scale preference and type of intervention. (VAS = Visual Analogue Scale; P = problem, E = emotion; KHOS = Krantz Health Opinion Survey; High- and Low-Preference refer to preference for health care–related information.) (From Martelli, Auerbach, et al., Copyright 1987 by the American Psychological Association. Reprinted with permission.)

The findings of this study may be contrasted with those of the study described earlier in this chapter (Strentz & Auerbach, 1988) in which airline employees about to be abducted and held hostage were given either emotion-focused or problem-focused preparation. In this study, coping predispositions (measured by the Internal-External Locus of Control Scale) made relatively little difference. All subjects adjusted better when they had received the emotion-focused preparation. This result is not surprising given the nature of the stressor. In contrast to dental surgery, rather than presenting a mix of coping demands, hostage captivity presented the subjects no opportunity to control or alter the course of the situation. Emotion-focused coping was thus the only viable option; even those who were predisposed to using problem-focused coping could not use it effectively because there were very few opportunities to do so. Thus, coping dispositions are most useful in determining how to help people deal with a stressful encounter when the coping demands of the situation are ambiguous and contain a mix of emotion-focused and problem-focused elements. But when the situation is extreme and the coping demands are unambiguous, coping dispositions become less important.

TRAITS AND EXPERIENCES ASSOCIATED WITH EFFECTIVE COPING

We have just seen that under certain circumstances differences in coping predispositions can help determine how people will respond to stress management interventions and can indicate who will cope most effectively in different situations. Are there other traits or experiences of people that help them be more effective copers? In this section we review evidence on how intelligence, personality traits other than coping dispositions, and one's past experiences influence how effectively people cope with stress.

Intelligence

Are more intelligent people more effective copers? An initial reaction might be that more intelligent people should have more problem-focused coping skills at their disposal and should therefore be better able to size up situations and choose appropriate strategies for dealing with aversive events. However, we also know that coping has a strong emotional component and that persons of high intelligence seem to have as much trouble as anyone else in moderating their stress levels so that they can effectively use their skills.

Little systematic research is available that bears directly on the question of the relationship between coping and intelligence. Much of what is available comes from studies of children who demonstrate resiliency when exposed to continuing high-level stress. These studies indicate that intellectual ability is indeed an important predictor of effective coping. For example, Felsman and Vaillant (1987) found that the best predictor of good adult outcomes (emotional stability, maturity, social and interpersonal involvement and growth) among male children from "multiproblem" families (characterized by family discord, parental deviance, high crime neighborhood) was "boyhood competence" ("dexterity and intelligence in completion of serious tasks"). This relationship is probably so because more intellectually able children can more readily discern danger, find escape routes, and locate sources of help (Garmezy & Rutter, 1985). Studies of children of psychiatrically disturbed parents indicate that children who cope best are those who have the intellectual ability and creativity to obtain adult care and support from others, and who find other activities to keep them from becoming enmeshed in parental psychopathology (Cohler, 1987).

Personality Traits: Hardiness, Locus of Control Orientation, Learned Resourcefulness, and Optimism

Superior problem-solving ability and intellectual capability alone cannot explain why some people show great fortitude when confronted by highly stressful events, while others succumb. Behavioral scientists have recognized this phenomenon and have attempted to isolate and measure personal characteristics that account for individual differences in coping ability. Four personality traits in particular have received increasing attention from clinicians and researchers: hardiness, locus of control orientation, learned resourcefulness, and optimism.

Hardiness consists of three components—commitment, control, and challenge (Kobasa, 1982). That is, hardy people believe in what they are doing and are fully involved in their daily activities; they believe that life experiences are controllable; and they view change in a positive sense and as a normal occurrence rather than as an aversive event. Differences in hardiness seem to influence a person's initial evaluation of a stressful event (primary appraisal) and therefore influence coping indirectly. For example, high hardy people make more positive self-statements (Allred & Smith, 1989) and display more positive affect and higher frustration tolerance (Wiebe, 1991) when under stress, and they are generally more physically healthy (Orr & Westman, 1990) than those who are low in hardiness.

Locus of Control Orientation is a dispositional measure of one's beliefs about and expectations for control of events in one's life (Rotter, 1966). People characterized as "internals" believe that they have personal control over events and can directly influence what happens to them through their behavior. "Externals," in contrast, believe that the outcomes of events are largely determined by factors outside their personal control (such as powerful others or luck). Though research findings are not entirely consistent, in general internals tend to be more task-oriented and use more problem-focused coping in stressful situations than do externals, who use more emotion-focused coping strategies (Strentz & Auerbach, 1988). Internals in general seem to experience less distress and deal more effectively with stress than do externals (Cohen & Edwards, 1989; Parkes, 1984), though there is evidence that internals do particularly well and externals relatively poorly in situations where there is opportunity for control or the expectation that control should be exercised (Auerbach et al., 1976; Strentz & Auerbach, 1988).

Learned resourcefulness refers to problem solving and to emotion regulation self-control skills that contribute to the belief that one can deal with "manageable levels of stress" (Rosenbaum, 1990). People high in resourcefulness also score high on measures of self-confidence and self-perceived skill in social interaction, cope more effectively with depression (Lewinsohn & Alexander, 1990), and have been found to benefit more from therapeutic intervention (Biran, 1990) than do persons low in resourcefulness.

Because *optimism* is particularly relevant to coping and is generating increasing research, we will discuss it in some detail. Optimism has been defined as the extent to which people have the generalized expectancy that good things will happen (Scheier & Carver, 1985). Seligman (1991) suggests that the central characteristic of optimists is that they view defeats as temporary setbacks, whereas pessimists believe that negative events will last a long time. Defeats are viewed as challenges for optimists and stimulate greater effort to overcome adversity. An amusing anecdote concerning Seligman illustrates the rewards of maintaining an optimistic outlook (see box on page 42).

Janoff-Bulman (1989) has concluded that most of us tend to be overly optimistic. We maintain an "illusion of invulnerability"—we overestimate the likelihood that positive events will happen to us and underestimate the likelihood of negative events. It is important that we do this because these illusions allow us to maintain a

---

OPTIMISM PAYS

Bob Dell was forty-five years old with a wife and two kids and a mortgage. After twenty-five years with a meat-packing plant, he was suddenly without a job and had no immediate prospects. His formal education consisted of a high school diploma. About this time he was approached by an insurance agent who wanted to sell him a policy. He told the agent he was unemployed and couldn't afford anything. The agent told Bob that his insurance company was currently hiring salespeople and that he should apply. Bob had never sold anything, but being an optimist he decided to give it a try. Psychologist Martin Seligman, consulting for the insurance company, had persuaded the company to hire prospective salespeople who were low in aptitude but high in optimism. Bob Dell was one of 130 applicants identified as "optimists" on a measure that Seligman had developed which was included in the materials that job candidates had to fill out. In less than a year, Bob "went from sausage-stuffer to super salesman, earning twice what he'd made at the packing plant." When he learned from a magazine article about the experimental program that he'd participated in, "with characteristic optimism" he called Seligman, introduced himself, and sold him a retirement policy. (Adapted from Buckley, 1990)

---

sense of coherence and purpose and to compartmentalize the knowledge of our ultimate mortality (see Taylor & Brown, 1988). Though psychologically healthy and effective people maintain accurate perceptions and good contact with reality, there is evidence that maintaining overly positive beliefs about our own self-worth and our degree of personal control are associated with effective use of problem-focused coping and ability to adapt successfully to stressful events (Scheier, Mathews, et al. 1989; Scheier, Weintraub, & Carver, 1986; Taylor & Brown, 1988; Taylor, Kemeny, et al., 1992). For example, Scheier, Mathews, et al. (1989) found that among patients receiving coronary artery bypass surgery, optimists recovered faster during hospitalization and returned more quickly to their normal life activities after discharge. Optimism was measured by a twelve-item self-report scale (the Life Orientation Test, see Table 2–5). There is also evidence that optimistic people deal better with negative

---

TABLE 2–5.   SAMPLE ITEMS FROM THE LIFE ORIENTATION TASK (A MEASURE OF OPTIMISM)

Directions: Indicate whether you agree or disagree with each of the following statements.

1. In uncertain times I usually expect the best.
2. If something can go wrong for me, it will.
3. I always look on the bright side of things.
4. I hardly ever expect things to go my way.

Agreement with items 1 and 3 and disagreement with items 2 and 4 are indicative of an optimistic outlook.

Source: Reprinted by permission from the American Psychological Association and Michael F. Scheier, Scheier and Carver (1985), p. 225.

information that challenges their positive beliefs and make better use of the information to solve problems. They are better at reading environmental cues and selecting situations and tasks that they can control, and they also know when to quit situations that they cannot change (Janoff-Bulman, 1989).

Asserting that illusory beliefs enhance coping competence may seem to be inconsistent with the idea that the hallmark of effective coping is accurate appraisal of situational demands and development of realistic solutions to problems. Perhaps it is best to think of overly optimistic beliefs as an overlay or general set of cognitions that serves as an emotion-focused mechanism enabling us to persevere with problem-solving attempts in the face of stress. When we are actively dealing with *specific stressors*, however, it is counterproductive to overestimate (or underestimate) our capabilities. We need to be realistic and accurate about our actual resources and abilities to deal with particular situations as well as about the probable payoffs and negative consequences of different solutions. In some situations, if we are overly optimistic and misjudge our capabilities the consequences can be disastrous (as with the poor swimmer who miscalculates and drowns), whereas in others "he who hesitates is lost" (as in the situation in which a bully who would have been deterred by active resistance becomes even more aggressive when his victims are passive).

Maintaining an optimistic mindset seems to be especially important for people who have been victimized by uncontrollable traumatic events and who seem to have lost their will to live. Victims of traumatic events have had their basic assumptions about the world and themselves (that the world makes sense and is benevolent, that they are worthy and decent people and can control what happens to them) severely challenged, and they are faced with the task of rebuilding these basic assumptions. "One of the greatest threats of victimization is the possibility of an existence without any illusions" (Janoff-Bulman, 1989, p. 163). Some victims of traumatic stressors have reinstated their positive illusions by involving themselves in rebuilding activities that might be construed as meaningful and contributory to a belief that there is morality in the world. For example, parents whose children who have died of leukemia seem to have benefited from a "survivor mission" of supporting research that might prevent such tragedies in the future, antiwar Vietnam veterans "found their mission" in telling about the war (Lifton & Olson, 1976), and concentration camp survivors who "had lost all relation to life" and had become completely isolated later emigrated to Israel and found a dynamic community to build on and seemed to find both meaning and a sense of control through these activities (Eitinger, 1980). Some victims, even in seemingly hopeless situations, refuse to surrender and continue to try to change the circumstances that have transformed their lives, sometimes with startling results (Ruth Thomas, who survived persecution in Nazi Germany, is a sterling example). In contrast, people who continue to wallow in their misfortune and who are unable to regain their basic illusions of optimism and meaningfulness never fully recover from exposure to traumatic events.

The following account exemplifies the main elements of hardiness, learned resourcefulness, and optimism in action, as two parents cope with the knowledge that their young son will soon die of an incurable disease:

Until the age of 6 Lorenzo Odone was a normal, talented child. Then he was stricken with a rare genetic disease (adrenoleukodystrophy-ALD) that slowly paralyzes and then kills. Lorenzo's parents, Micheala and Augusto Odones, were told that ALD kills children an average of 2 to 3 years after diagnosis. There were no exceptions. The Odones refused to accept this. Though they had no scientific training, they did their own research, organized and financed a scientific conference on ALD, and found a potential dietary treatment for it—one that had been demonstrated by one researcher to work in the test tube only. After much work, they found a single company that manufactured an edible form of the olive oil that contained the acid that lowered the level of the fatty acid causing the neurological damage in ALD victims. After doing more research, they found another acid (erucic acid) that had similar action, combined the two, and administered the mixture to Lorenzo. It was a success! Within two weeks the level of the destructive fatty acid in Lorenzo's blood had dropped to normal. As a result of his parents' continued optimism and unwillingness to give in, Lorenzo is alive today (in 1991) at age 13. Most of the damage done to him by ALD (severely damaged motor skills including inability to speak, and impaired hearing) was irreversible since the protective myelin sheath insulating the body's nerve fibers that is destroyed by ALD does not regenerate. But the Odones still refuse to capitulate. They have developed a foundation whose goal is to promote research on repairing damaged myelin. They are *determined* to restore their son to full health.

(Adapted from Ryan, 1991)

The Odones would not have been successful had they not relentlessly pursued their goal despite seemingly insurmountable obstacles. It should be noted, however, that their experience was exceptional, and often endeavors such as theirs are not successful. But for some people just the act of making great efforts, despite lack of success, is beneficial. It allows them to say to themselves "at least I tried everything possible." Other victims and their loved ones, however, regardless of how extensive their efforts have been, are left with a sense of profound guilt because they tell themselves "I didn't try hard enough." It is thus important to recognize that sometimes particular circumstances are indeed unchangeable, that continued attempts to alter them are unrealistic, and that self-blame or blaming of victims by others can be very destructive. Under such circumstances it is wise to temper overly optimistic beliefs in the face of cold reality and to move on to other challenges.

Past Experience: Developing a Sense of Self-Efficacy

How do people become effective problem-solvers, such as people like the Odones who, in the most stressful situations, find a way to deal with adversity and are even able to turn misfortune into advantage? Bandura (1977) argues that effective copers develop a sense of *self-efficacy*, which he defines as "expectations of personal mastery—a conviction that one can successfully execute the behavior required to produce the (desired) outcomes" (p. 193). The most important way in which we develop expectations of self-efficacy is through successful personal mastery experiences. Success enhances confidence, and efficacy expectations tend to generalize to other situations (especially similar ones) where performance may have been previously debilitated by thoughts of personal incompetencies. Consistent with this notion Aldwin, Sutton, and Lachman (1996), in a study of more than 800 middle-aged and older men, found that over 80% said they had drawn on previous experience to help them deal with a current serious problem. One man who had received an unexpected battlefield promotion during World War II said that as a result he had learned that he could be an effective leader in dangerous situations, and that he often thought back to this experience to give him confidence when dealing with current work problems.

We may also be influenced by observing others (peers or those we admire) successfully mastering stressful situations, or through verbal persuasion that we can be successful. In these ways we acquire skills and refine them, learning where, when, and how they are useful in mastering stressors. As we do so, we develop a broadening sense of our competencies and capabilities and subsequently become optimistic about our ability to influence events that affect our lives. If this belief is not unrealistically exaggerated, and if it is appropriately tempered by realistic appraisals of our coping capabilities and resources as we contend with specific stressors, it fosters greater accomplishments and better stress-coping ability. (See Figure 2–2).

> **Efficacy**
>
> Yesterday, I thought helplessness was here to stay.
> There was nothing I could do or say,
> From snakes and bugs I ran away.
>
> Then you see, I took a course in guided mastery.
> It beat all my years of therapy.
> I finally learned self-efficacy.
>
> Finally, now rejection means nothing to me.
> Now, I choose and try persistently.
> I really do believe in me.

Figure 2–2

Sung to the tune of "Yesterday" with apologies to Lennon and McCartney. (From O'Leary, Ozer, Parker, & Wiedenfeld. Copyright 1994 by the Association for Advancement of Behavior Therapy. Reprinted by permission of the publisher.)

It is important to emphasize that whereas coping ability is very much a function of past experience, a history of effective coping does not necessarily produce someone who is a superior coper. That is, success in dealing with stress does not *automatically* result in a sense of self-efficacy and increasing mastery of a wider and wider range of situations. Two crucial factors need to be considered. They are (a) the causal attributions we make to ourselves regarding *why* we were able to cope with a stressor, and (b) whether we appropriately generalize the coping skills that we learned in dealing with a particular stressor when new stressors are encountered.

Both of these factors can be illustrated by examining the survivors of the Nazi concentration camps (Auerbach, 1986). If successful coping always enhances future coping ability, then we would expect that dealing with the stresses of everyday life after being released would have been a "piece of cake" for the few who survived the extreme stresses of the camps. But in fact the majority of survivors were greatly debilitated psychologically, suffering from a continuing "persecution syndrome" that persisted for the rest of their lives (Eitinger, 1980). This outcome was due to two major factors. First, most of the survivors, rather than attributing their success to their superior ability to control their environment, concluded that sheer luck was the most important factor (Benner, Roskies, & Lazarus, 1980). In addition, many survivors experienced severe guilt over compromises made to ensure their survival or over the very fact of their survival while so many others perished (Chodoff, 1974), rather than experiencing the heightened sense of self-efficacy that should have resulted from triumph over a great obstacle.

Further diminishing the survivors' ability to adjust to a "normal" existence was the fact that the coping strategies that they used effectively in the nightmare world of the camps (depersonalization, intense vigilance for danger cues, focus on getting food, and suppressing hunger cues) were inappropriately generalized to the post-camp environment, where those strategies not only were not useful but also were seen as deviant by others. These strategies, which had kept them alive in the brutal world of the concentration camps, had become habitual, and most former inmates were unable to give them up and adjust to a new environment with new coping demands. (For an exception, see box on page 46).

On a larger scale, another example of the disastrous consequences of inappropriately maintaining a once-effective coping strategy in a new situation involved the European Jews in the period preceding and during the Nazi holocaust (Auerbach, 1986). For the most part, the Jews as a group attempted to deal with Nazi aggression intellectually, through written and oral appeals and petitions. This coping strategy was an established tradition. Jews had survived as a unit through two thousand

---

$\mathscr{R}$OMAN FERBER: A CONCENTRATION-CAMP SURVIVOR WHO PROSPERED

Roman Ferber was one of the thousand-odd concentration-camp prisoners helped by Oskar Schindler, whose exploits were made famous in Thomas Keneally's (1982) book and Steven Spielberg's subsequent film *Schindler's List*. According to Brecher (1994), who interviewed many of the Schindler's List survivors, most of them credited God and luck, in addition to Schindler, for their endurance. Ferber said, however, "I'm not one of those who attribute survival to God. Some of us had much better intuition, survival instincts, tenacity. I happen to be one that fit that picture very well. My survival is based on being very opportunistic. I took many more chances. I was the product of the environment. I adapted, adjusted, took the opportunity that was there. I look at myself and think, 'How come I'm here and so many others are not?' Sheer guts, stamina, cunning, Actually, I did very well at Auschwitz. I had a lot of bread. I was an expert at stealing" (Brecher, 1994, p. 160). The tenacity and other coping skills that Ferber honed at Auschwitz apparently served him well in his long and successful career as a high level bureaucrat in New York City government. Rather than harboring feelings of guilt over having survived or of hatred for Germans (like many other survivors), he took the view that living in the past was bound to be destructive, and that in comparison to the camps "everything that followed was relatively easy in life." (Brecher, 1994, p. 177)

---

years of repression in this way, while making minimal use of physical retaliation. During the World War II period, this response persisted despite its blatant lack of success (Hilberg, 1980). The current policy of the state of Israel always to meet aggression with counteraggression largely stems from the desire to "never again" make the same mistake. Some have argued that because this aggressive stance has been so successful in recent years in repelling enemies, it has become a somewhat overgeneralized response on the other end of the continuum, and that a more effective coping strategy for dealing with Israel's current problems would include more of the elements of negotiation that historically were the hallmark of the Jewish response to aggression. As of this writing, Israel has, in fact, with the cooperation of its Arab neighbors, moved in this direction, and the prospects of a positive outcome for all are promising.

The Environment: Social Support as a Coping Aid and Stress Buffer

In addition to personality traits like hardiness and optimism, and learning to use acquired skills appropriately to deal with new problems, a third factor that has a powerful impact on our ability to cope effectively with stressors is the availability of others to support and aid us. As the Beatles sang, "a little help from my friends" goes a long way in assisting us to "get by" in times of trouble. Social support systems are said to provide emotional sustenance, tangible resources and aid, and information when we are in need (Caplan, 1974). As previously noted, concerned, supportive parents are the single most important factor in determining how well children cope under stress, and numerous studies with adults have linked social support to good health and superior ability to cope with stress (e.g., Andrews, Tennant, Hewson, & Schonell, 1979; Auerbach, Martelli, & Mercuri, 1983; Gore, 1978). Consistent with the cognitive appraisal model, it has been found that it is the *perception* of the availability of interpersonal resources, rather than the actual amount that is provided or the actual extensiveness of one's social network, that is most closely related to how well people deal with health-related and other stressors (Cohen & Wills, 1985; Sarason, Sarason, & Pierce, 1990).

Some research indicates, however, that there are circumstances under which attempts at social support may not produce positive effects. For example, many support persons, when confronted with victims of life crisis situations, as a result of their own heightened anxieties and feelings of vulnerability and their misconceptions about the recovery process, make support attempts that are judged as unhelpful by the recipient. Such support persons often discourage victims from discussing their feelings and instead focus on giving advice and encouraging recovery. However, research with people grieving over lost loved ones indicates that the opportunity to vent feelings is one of the most helpful kinds of support and that giving advice and encouraging recovery is unhelpful (Lehman, Ellard, & Wortman, 1986; Wortman & Lehman, 1985). In this vein, though social support generally enhances the emotional adjustment and quality of life of cancer patients, when friends or support groups dwell on the negative side of the disease or dismiss patients' psychological problems once treatment ends, the result is often increased anger and anxiety (Meyerowitz, 1996).

Also, providing emotional and material support to people under stress without requiring problem-solving activity on their part may provide short-term relief, but it does little to defuse feelings of loss of control or foster feelings of independence and ability to influence long-term outcomes. In this regard, it has been observed that survivors of catastrophic events often fare best when they get involved in projects in which they have an *active* role in building on, and thereby deriving a sense of meaning from, their experiences. For example, some survivors of the Hiroshima atomic bomb blast during World War II derived solace from talking about their horrifying experiences in the belief that this might help prevent future use of nuclear weapons (Lifton & Olson, 1976). Similarly, Eitinger (1980) found that many of the Jewish concentration-camp survivors who showed the best adjustment were those who emigrated to Israel and became involved in an environment that was supportive but that also made demands on them for cooperation, effort, and building the community.

$\mathcal{S}$UMMARY

1. Coping processes refer to the strategies that we use to deal with stressors and with the dysphoric emotions elicited by them.

2. Two broad types of coping strategies may be distinguished. In problem-focused coping, we attempt to modify, avoid, or diminish the situation that is threatening us. In emotion-focused coping, we attempt to moderate our stressful emotions directly.

3. Problem-focused coping is the most effective strategy for dealing with stressful situations when there are realistic opportunities for altering crucial aspects of those situations. Even in situations in which such opportunities are limited, having an illusion of control may enhance adjustment.

4. Emotion-focused coping is useful as a short-term strategy for dealing with highly stressful situations in which there are few problem-focused coping options.

5. Even very young infants display both problem-focused and emotion-focused coping behaviors. The infant's relationship to its primary caretakers ("attachment figures") is crucial for the learning and development of coping behaviors that the infant will use in dealing with future stressors. Parental relationships also serve as an important buffer against stress and as an important source of the learning of coping skills for older children.

6. Though people tend to adjust their coping strategies to the demands of the situations that they are dealing with, people do develop predispositions to cope with stress in particular ways.

7. These coping dispositions or traits appear to be most useful in determining how to help people deal with a stressful encounter when the coping demands of the situation contain a mix of emotion-focused and problem-focused elements.

8. Intelligence and the personality traits of hardiness, internal locus of control, learned resourcefulness, and optimism are associated with good coping ability.

9. Effective copers develop a sense of self-efficacy, largely through personal mastery experiences in which they attribute their success to their ability to exert control over their environment. It is also crucial that the coping strategies learned in one setting be appropriately generalized when new stressors are encountered.

10. The availability of supportive people who are perceived to be responsive to the coping needs elicited by stressors, provides an important stress buffer that enhances coping ability.

𝒦EY TERMS

coping dispositions   Relatively stable tendencies of people to employ particular types of coping strategies irrespective of the nature of the stressor that is being confronted.

coping strategies   Ways in which an individual copes with a stressor or the stress elicited by a stressor at a particular moment in time.

emotion-focused coping   Coping strategies whose aim is to moderate the emotional distress produced by exposure to a stressor.

hardiness   Personality trait associated with more positive self-views, better frustration tolerance, and physical health.

learned helplessness   Response produced when people (or animals) are repeatedly exposed to aversive situations over which they have no control; its three major components are loss of motivation to respond, diminished learning ability, and emotional disturbance (primarily depression and anxiety).

learned resourcefulness   Personality trait associated with higher levels of self-confidence and effective coping skills.

locus of control orientation   Personality trait involving expectancies for control. Internals view themselves as having a high degree of personal control over important outcomes in their lives, whereas externals perceive these outcomes as largely being outside their personal control and subject to external factors such as chance. In general, internals are more effective copers than externals.

optimism Personality trait reflecting the expectancy that good things will happen; high optimism is associated with more effective coping ability and adaptation to stressors.

primary appraisal Initial appraisal of the meaning of a situation to an individual (i.e., irrelevant, positive, harmful).

problem-focused coping Coping strategies whose aim is to modify or instrumentally escape from or avoid a stressor that is producing a stress reaction.

secondary appraisal Evaluation of coping resources that are available to deal with a potential stressor.

self-efficacy Expectation that one can successfully master a particular problem or situation; it may be situation-specific or refer to a more general sense of competence.

social support Aid provided by others that often serves as an effective stress buffer; it can involve material resources and/or emotional support.

CHAPTER 3
Models of Learning: Relation to Stress Management

The cognitive appraisal model of stress and coping that we have presented in this book has been of great heuristic value. This model has generated a great deal of research by personality and social psychologists, so that we have been able to learn much about the factors that induce stress in people and about the dynamics of the coping process. There has also been a great deal of research on, and many volumes have been published about, stress management interventions—the way to do them and the circumstances under which they are most effective. But most of these techniques that have been developed by clinical and other applied psychologists are based on learning models developed largely by experimental psychologists (derived from the principles of classical, operant conditioning, and cognitive-behavioral models of learning). Thus, stress and coping theory on the one hand, and stress management interventions that are designed to enhance coping effectiveness on the other, have evolved from different subdisciplines within the behavioral sciences that use their own terminology and sometimes have conflicting viewpoints. As a result, there has been little communication between the two camps, and it has therefore not been well established from a theoretical standpoint *how* interventions produce effective coping.

In this chapter we attempt to bridge these gaps by integrating the basic concepts relevant to stress and coping that have evolved from these disciplines. We will (a) give an overview of the principles of classical conditioning, operant conditioning, and cognitive-behavioral learning; (b) give examples of stress management intervention techniques that have been developed on the basis of these learning models; and (c) attempt to integrate these learning approaches with the concepts of emotion- and problem-focused coping in the cognitive appraisal model of stress.

CLASSICAL CONDITIONING

Imagine yourself lying relaxed on your favorite sofa. The TV is on. The popular movie *Jaws* has just begun, but you are immersed in a novel that has captured most of your attention. You are only minimally aware of the movie or of the music accompanying the opening scene during which a shark devours a young girl going for a swim. Suddenly, you realize that your heart rate has increased, your mouth has gone dry, and you have developed a sense of dread. Why? Where did it come from?

Without your even looking at the screen, the music accompanying the scene has elicited a stress reaction in you. As a result of the popularity of the film, and because the music *always* plays when the shark is on the attack, the music has come to be associated in most Americans' minds with the primeval fear of being devoured by a powerful predator. Consequently, the music has become a conditioned stimulus for fear. Thus, as noted in Chapter 1, fear is an *elicited* response or a *respondent*. We develop conditioned fear responses to certain situations or stimuli after they have been paired (or presented contiguously with) unconditioned stimuli that automatically or innately elicit a fear response.

Classical conditioning was first studied systematically by the Russian physiologist Ivan Pavlov, who was conducting experiments on salivation in dogs. Salivation is an adaptive reflexive or unconditioned response (UCR) that aids in digestion and that is normally elicited in a hungry animal in the presence of food. Pavlov noted that under certain circumstances the dogs salivated simply upon hearing him enter the laboratory and make other characteristic sounds that occurred whenever he fed the dogs. These sounds, which previously were neutral to the animals, had become a conditioned stimulus as a result of repeated association with an unconditioned stimulus (food) that automatically elicited salivation (an unconditioned response-UCS). After a while, the dogs salivated simply upon hearing the sounds. This learned (conditioned) salivation response (CR) was an example of classical conditioning. (See Figure 3–1.)

Conditioning of fear occurs in the same way. The most famous example of fear conditioning in the laboratory involved an eleven-month-old boy (Albert), who was conditioned to fear rats (Watson & Rayner, 1920). Previous to the conditioning process, Albert had been a "stolid and unemotional" boy who showed no fear of rats. During conditioning, he was presented a rat, and as he reached for it, a steel bar positioned behind his head was struck with a hammer, producing a loud sound. The clearly aversive sound (UCS) caused the infant to jump violently and whimper (UCR). After several pairings of the sound with the presentation of the rat, the presentation of the rat alone (CS) caused the child to whimper, cry, and crawl away. A conditioned anxiety response (CR) had been established to the rat. (See Figure 3–2.)

Further testing indicated that the response had generalized to similar stimuli (such as a rabbit, a fur coat, cotton wool, and a Santa Claus mask). The infant displayed similar reactions to these stimuli when tested two months later. Watson & Rayner concluded that such conditioned emotional reactions to previously neutral stimuli "persist and modify personality throughout life."

Figure 3–1

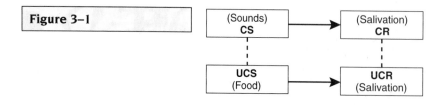

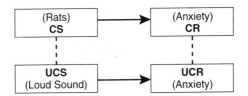

Figure 3–2

Subsequent findings have borne out Watson & Rayner's (1920) observations. For example, inability to function sexually is often the result of anxiety experienced in sexual situations resulting from a history of aversive associations. Some sexually inadequate persons have a history of being physically punished for engaging in exploratory sexual behavior. Others have had negative associations transmitted to them attitudinally and verbally by parents who themselves are sexually disturbed. Wolpe & Lazarus (1966) give an example of a male patient who was sexually adequate with prostitutes but not with "respectable" women, with this selective dysfunction resulting from parental teachings that respectable women are asexual and consent to sex only as an act of martyrdom. For another patient, nudity had become extremely aversive because his mother had insistently warned that gazing at nude persons of the opposite sex would result in blindness. Even though the attitudes transmitted may be illogical, repetitive presentation of negative information can produce strong aversive associations and can result in situation-specific anxiety. This situation is especially true when the disseminators are parents and the recipients are children for whom there is no other equally credible source of input.

Sometimes aversive associations are transmitted through observation alone without the individual's directly experiencing either physical punishment or negative attitudes. This outcome has been demonstrated in controlled laboratory studies as well as in clinical case studies (Bandura, 1986). For example, in a laboratory study, observers who heard a neutral tone and who then witnessed a model react with great pain (apparently in response to an electric shock) began to have negative physiological reactions to the tone alone, even though they never felt any pain themselves in conjunction with the tone (Berger, 1962). Clinical research has found that children who fear dogs differ little from nonfearful children in direct negative experiences with dogs; however, their parents are often very fearful and thus the children have had many opportunities to observe their parents' negative reactions to dogs (Bandura, Adams, Hardy, & Howells, 1980). Perhaps the most common type of conditioned fear that we experience is of the sort depicted in the example presented at the outset of the chapter. Playwrights and moviemakers know well that the success of a dramatic presentation depends in good part on the viewer's "suspending his or her disbelief" and vicariously experiencing all the emotions displayed by the protagonists.

Watson and Rayner's (1920) demonstration of how readily conditioned fears generalize to other similar stimuli has proven to be of importance in helping people deal with anxiety-related problems. For example, Grassick (1990) describes the case of a twenty-two-year-old unmarried art student who came to him for treatment of an extreme fear of receiving injections. In the course of questioning her with a standardized fear survey, Grassick found not only that she feared situations that bore an obvious relationship to her needle phobia (e.g., "seeing another person being injected," "dentists," "donating blood"), but also that she expressed fear of the display of interpersonal aggression (e.g., "angry people"), of items related to sexuality (e.g., "a nude man"), and of "dirt." In the course of treatment, it was revealed that her fears stemmed from repeated physical and emotional abuse by her parents during her childhood. The fear of being abused, which was quite rational given her past history, had broadened to include generalized irrational fears of the sight of the human body (including her own body) or of being touched in any way. Being injected with a needle represented the ultimate in intrusive physical contact and thus caused her extreme anxiety. Identifying these generalized fears was of crucial importance in treating her with a technique called systematic desensitization.

Systematic desensitization is one of three types of stress management techniques based on the classical conditioning model that we will describe in this chapter. The other two are exposure techniques and counterconditioning approaches using unconditioned stimuli. Desensitization and the exposure techniques are primarily used to diminish anxiety responses to feared situations, whereas counterconditioning techniques are used more broadly to change emotional reactions to problematic situations. The primary immediate goal of all of them is to directly change emotional responses to stressors, and thus they are classified as techniques designed to enhance emotion-focused coping.

Systematic Desensitization

Systematic desensitization involves three sets of procedures: (a) establishing a hierarchy of feared situations, (b) teaching relaxation, and (c) pairing relaxation with the feared situations in the hierarchy.

Table 3–1 lists some of the items in the hierarchy that was developed for the art student with a great fear of needles who was treated by Grassick (1990). The SUDS ratings in this table refer to "subjective units of discomfort," obtained both before and after the completion of treatment. These are the student's ratings of how much fear (from 0 to 100, where 100 represents extreme fear) is elicited by the thought of confronting each of these situations. It may be noted that these ratings are not always "logical" but rather are determined by the student's subjective responses based on her personal learning history. Thus, watching an injection in a movie is ini-

---

TABLE 3–1.   HIERARCHY OF SCENES FOR DESENSITIZATION OF A NEEDLE PHOBIA

Ratings of Scenes for Desensitization		
Scene	**SUDS Rating**	
	Pre	**Post**
1. The morning of the dentist's appointment	5	0
2. The dentist tells you that you need some work done	20	15
3. Picture of a syringe in a magazine	40	20
4. Watching an injection on TV	50	20
5. Lab technician preparing a syringe to give you an injection	60	40
6. A *grubby* lab technician holding your arm, about to give you an injection	70	50
7. Watching an injection in a movie	80	20
8. Needle entering your arm, subcutaneous injection	80	50
9. Watching serum being injected into your arm	90	50
10. Entering a blood donor clinic	90	70

Source: Reprinted from Grassick, *The fear behind the fear: A case study of apparent simple injection phobia,* 1990, with kind permission from Elsevier Science Ltd, The Boulevard, Langford Lane, Kidlington OX5 1GB, UK.

tially ranked as much more fearful than watching one on TV, and "entering a blood donor clinic" elicited as much fear as scenes depicting a needle actually entering her arm, with this scene maintaining the highest fear level after treatment.

Relaxation is taught typically by using the method of progressive muscular relaxation (see Chapter 7). Desensitization itself consists of having the client vividly imagine the scenes in the hierarchy, beginning with the least fear-arousing scenes, while at the same time experiencing relaxation. When possible, relaxation is paired with the client's actually experiencing the activities depicted in the hierarchy (in vivo desensitization). This method is preferred because sometimes people can learn to experience relaxation when imagining previously feared situations, but when they actually encounter the situations, the relaxation response may not generalize from imagery to the real world (degree of stimulus generalization is insufficient).

According to Wolpe (1990) the mechanism by which systematic desensitization works is *reciprocal inhibition*. According to this concept, by having the client experience a relaxation response in the presence of stimuli that previously elicited anxiety, the connection between the stimuli and the anxiety response is weakened. Concurrent with this inhibition, the relaxation response (which is the opposite of anxiety) is reciprocally strengthened. Thus in the case of the art student, prior to treatment, needles (and the other related stimuli), as a result of their association with aversive physical and interpersonal experiences, had become a conditioned stimulus for a strong anxiety response (as depicted in Figure 3–3).

After several months of treatment with desensitization the power of these stimuli to evoke an anxiety response in her had greatly diminished, and these stimuli had thus largely reverted to the status of neutral, nonthreatening stimuli. (See Figure 3–4.)

Exposure Techniques

Exposure techniques take a different approach to diminishing conditioned fears. One of the first of these to be developed, by Thomas Stampfl and Donald Lewis, was *implosive therapy* (Levis & Hare, 1977; Stampfl & Levis, 1967). Stampfl and Levis pointed out that when strong conditioned fear responses are learned, the stage is

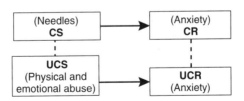

Figure 3–3

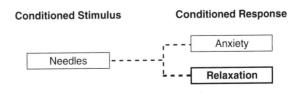

Figure 3–4

Reciprocal Inhibition: The strength of the relaxation response to the stimulus increases and surpasses that of the anxiety response, whose strength is simultaneously inhibited.

set for the development of second class of responses—*avoidance* responses. These responses are governed by the laws of operant learning (discussed later in this chapter). Thus, the art student in the previous example learned to avoid being in the presence of needles and other conditioned stimuli that evoked fear in her. To the extent to which these voluntary avoidance responses were successful in keeping her from being exposed to feared situations, they were reinforced and therefore more likely to occur. Thus, the conditioned fear stimulus (e.g., the sight or thought of needles) also became a cue (or *discriminative stimulus*, see p. 60) to initiate a well-learned operant (voluntary) avoidance response.

These avoidance responses are very persistent and difficult to extinguish because fear does not become conditioned to a single stimulus or event. Fear eventually becomes associated with a complex set of stimuli, and a given fear stimulus may elicit a *chain of memories* associated with it. These memories include nightmares, fantasies, and diffuse thoughts and impulses, all of which are part of the whole complex of what is feared and therefore avoided. Even though people often make attempts to confront some of the elements in the stimulus complex and may do so without experiencing excessive fear, they usually then have an experience with an infrequently experienced element in the stimulus chain (which could be an actual external event or a thought or fantasy symbolic of a feared event) that elicits a high level of anxiety. This experience serves to recondition fear to all of the elements of the stimulus complex and thus to reinforce the avoidance behavior.

Implosive therapy is based on the theory that in order to extinguish the fear response, this whole complex of stimuli must be experienced (that is, the client cannot be permitted to avoid the stimuli) *in the absence of any real punishment*. This method accomplishes two things. First, the conditioned fear stimulus is experienced, but without the unconditioned stimulus (punishment); eventually, therefore, the conditioned fear response will extinguish because there is no reinforcer to maintain it.[1] Second, as a by-product of this process, as fear diminishes the motivation to avoid the previously feared stimuli declines. This occurs because the reinforcer that was maintaining the avoidance was that it took the individual away from the painful experience of fear.

In contrast to the more gradual and deliberate approach used in systematic desensitization, implosive therapy emphasizes faster and more direct exposure to highly threatening material (presented in imagery). Another difference is that the scenes presented go beyond material that is explicitly presented by the client. Some of the scenes are based on the therapist's judgment regarding themes that likely underlie and have become part of the feared complex of stimuli. These themes often involve guilt, punishment, fears of castration, death wish impulses, etc. The goal is to re-create *every conceivable stimulus fragment* (both real and in fantasy) that has become an elicitor of fear, and to have the client experience these scenes in imagery as vividly as possible. An attempt is made to elicit *maximum* levels of anxiety, and to have the client hold the scene until it ceases to elicit anxiety. It is stressed that clients must not block out or pull away from the stressful images while their anxiety level is high. Doing this would reinforce the avoidance response and would not permit the anxiety response to extinguish.

---

[1] This is comparable to what would happen if Pavlov made the same sounds upon entering his laboratory, but no longer proceeded to feed the animals. The sounds had become conditioned stimuli for salivation because they were paired with the unconditioned stimulus of food. Once this reinforcer was no longer paired with the characteristic sounds, the conditioned salivation response to the sounds became progressively weaker until eventually it extinguished completely. In the case of the conditioned fear response, similarly, it is assumed that if the conditioned stimulus (feared situations) is repeatedly presented but without the unconditioned stimulus (punishment) that maintained the fear response, it too will extinguish.

The following excerpt from parts of some implosive therapy sessions with an individual with an intense fear of snakes illustrates the vividness of the imagery used with this technique:

> Okay, now put your finger out towards the snake and feel his head coming up. . . . Its head toward your finger and it's starting to bite at your finger. Put your finger out, let it bite—feel the fangs go right down into your finger. . . . Feel it gnawing, look at the blood dripping off your finger.—And the teeth of the snake are stuck right in your finger, right down to the bone. And it is crunching like on your finger there. Let it. Feel it biting, it is biting at your finger. . . .
>
> Okay, feel him coiling around your hand again, touching you, slimy, now he is going up on your shoulder and he crawls there and he is sitting on your chest and he is looking you right in the eye. . . . He is staring at you. He is evil looking, he is slimy, he is ready to strike at your face. . . . He strikes out at you, (Therapist slaps hands). Feel him bite at your face . . . let him bite. . . .
>
> Now he is going up by your eyes and he is starting to bite at your eyes, feel him bite at your eyes. Feel him bite, let him bite, feel his fangs go into your eyes and he is pulling at them and tearing at them and ripping at them. Picture what your face looks like. Get that sick feeling in your stomach. . . .
>
> (From Hogan, 1968, pp. 427–428)

Often, as scenes are presented, new memories associated with the fear are reactivated, and these memories provide material for new scenes. To exemplify how this process occurs, Levis (1980) describes the case of a female client with a tremendous fear of crowds. She attributed this fear to her body odor, which she was afraid others would detect. The first scene that she was asked to imagine involved variations of her having to attend a lecture with many people present where "she could feel the eyes of the audience" on her as she began to sweat. Imagining this resulted in diminished fear and less avoidance of people, but she still reported anxiety about her body odor. Scenes now focused on her imagining that she could smell the odor. When asked to list things that she associated with the odor, she reported that her main worry was about what people seated behind her were thinking. This led to memories of when she was six when a "girlfriend whispered to her friends that they shouldn't play with her because she was a bad girl and would let the boys touch her." From this memory, she went on to recollections about juvenile sex play, then to being molested by an adult male, and to further thoughts that people behind her knew what was happening and would tell her parents. This information led to new scenes involving the odor of sexual foreplay, which included her parents' finding out what was happening and rejecting her, then to scenes of her confessing her guilt to God, and finally being condemned to hell, where she smelled the sexual odor clearly as she was being burned with others staring at her and condemning her. Visualizing these scenes *in a safe environment* further alleviated her stress and decreased her avoidance of people.

Several variations of exposure therapy have been developed in recent years, some of which are less overtly frightening than implosive therapy. We describe these approaches in Chapter 9, and also give additional examples of the use of desensitization, focusing on how both exposure and desensitization can be used on a self-management basis.

Counterconditioning Techniques

Sometimes people experience stress that is the direct result of their own behavior, and though they are aware of this relationship they continue to engage in the behavior because they are unable to inhibit it. Prominent examples of these kinds of behaviors include alcohol and other substance abuse and behaviors involving sexual attraction to "inappropriate" stimuli including exhibitionism, violent sex, transvestism (cross-sex dressing), fetishism (sexual attraction to inanimate objects), and homosexuality.[2] Although these behaviors are operants (see next section) counterconditioning techniques are based on the assumption that these behaviors are engaged in because of prior classical conditioning. For example, it is assumed that for alcoholics, the sight and smell of alcohol have become attractive because they have been associated with an unconditioned stimulus that is innately reinforcing (alcohol is a central nervous system depressant that reduces anxiety). In *aversive counterconditioning* techniques, an attempt is made to reverse this conditioning by associating these stimuli with unconditioned stimuli that elicit a strong negative response. Among the unconditioned stimuli that have been used are electric shock, emetics (nausea-inducing drugs), and cognitively induced aversion (negative thoughts usually drawn from unpleasant experiences that have occurred while engaging in the "pleasurable" activity). It is assumed that once the reinforcement value of these stimuli has been reduced through classical counterconditioning, they will no longer be sought out and the problem behaviors will diminish.

An example of the use of aversive counterconditioning is presented in a case study by Lavin, Thorpe, Barker, Blakemore, & Conway (1961). The client was a truck driver who frequently dressed in women's clothing. This was a compulsive behavior that he had difficulty controlling (he was embarrassed because he occasionally appeared in public dressed as a woman) and that had become a source of stress in his marriage. As in systematic desensitization, a hierarchy was developed of the elements of the conditioned stimulus. In this situation, rather than using a fear hierarchy, the array consisted of the stimulus aspects of women's clothing that were most arousing for the client. For him, the most exciting element of cross-sex dressing was the sight of himself dressed in this way. A set of colored slides was made depicting the client in various stages of female dress from panties only to fully clothed. Furthermore, to make the stimuli as realistic as possible, a tape recording was made of the client describing himself in each scene (e.g., "I have now put on and am wearing a pair of ladies undies"), which was presented along with the slide.

The conditioning phase began with injecting the client with an emetic (apomorphine). As soon as he reported feeling sick (typically a headache followed by nausea), a slide was projected on the screen and the tape recorder was played. These stimuli were terminated after he had vomited . (See Figure 3–5.)

During Conditioning

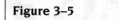

Figure 3–5

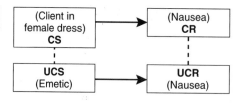

After sixty-six conditioning trials (about one every two hours for six days and nights), the client no longer was sexually aroused by cross-sex dressing, and on follow-up (six months after the completion of treatment) he reported continued lack of interest in the behavior. Both he and his wife expressed "relief at the removal of this obstacle to the happiness in their marriage."

Counterconditioning techniques have also been employed to help alleviate stress associated with sexual functioning by using sexual arousal as the main conditioning agent. In *orgasmic reconditioning*, the orgasm experienced during masturbation is used as a reinforcer to change sexual interest from fantasies and partners that are inappropriate and unattainable (and therefore a source of stress) to more appropriate and realistic fantasies. In this technique, the physical stimulation of masturbation is the unconditioned stimulus, and the sexual arousal and orgasm that is produced is the unconditioned response. During conditioning, the "appropriate" stimuli are paired in fantasy with the unconditioned stimulus, and if conditioning is successful, they become conditioned stimuli that now elicit a conditioned sexual arousal response.

Consider the case of a thirty-year-old-married man who could be sexually aroused only by sadomasochistic fantasies and activities (Marquis, 1977). As an adolescent, he had masturbated, arousing himself with fantasies that included whips, leather clothing, groveling, and picturing his (future) wife having intercourse with another man. These fantasies, which continued into adulthood, were a cause of negative feelings about himself and had also become a source of stress in his marriage when he pressured his wife to play roles in them. Treatment consisted of instructing the client to switch from his sadomasochistic fantasies to the image of his wife's face at the point when he sensed he was about to experience an orgasm during masturbation. Though switching fantasies was initially difficult, eventually (after about nine hours of treatment) he was able to control the fantasies and was able to have intercourse with his wife without inappropriate fantasies intruding. This "caused a marked increase in his self-esteem and greatly improved his relationship with his wife."

OPERANT CONDITIONING

In contrast to classical conditioning, operant conditioning deals with voluntarily *emitted* responses (operants). These are the kinds of behaviors that we ordinarily observe in others (e.g., social behaviors such as talking, gesturing, and laughing) as well as other behaviors that we use to control our environment. The emission of operants is determined by the consequences that they produce. That is, whereas respondents are influenced by stimuli that precede them, operants are controlled by stimuli that follow them. Operant behaviors that are followed by reward increase in frequency, whereas those that are followed by negative consequences tend to be emitted less frequently. Thus, the strength of operant behavior is dependent on its past effects in the environment.

Learning (or the failure to learn) appropriate operant behaviors is crucial to the stress and coping process. We are all motivated to secure certain primary reinforcers. These are reinforcers (e.g., food, sexual gratification) that satisfy physiologically based needs. Furthermore, we are all motivated to avoid and escape stimuli that produce physical pain or psychological distress. When we are infants and young children, much of our behavior is geared toward achieving these outcomes. In general, as we mature, internalized learned goals become more important as do the social consequences of our behaviors. We strive to meet performance expectations and goals that we have developed, and we try to learn how to elicit positive responses from people from whom we want approval (these are people such as parents, spouses, employers, and friends, who control reinforcers that we desire).

The importance of operant learning in stress and coping cannot be overemphasized. Operants are the behaviors that are visible to others, that others use to make crucial judgments about us—whether they like us, whether they think we are intelligent and competent, whether they want to be with us, whether we will be promoted on the job or graduate from school. Our success in emitting operants that meet our own internal criteria for approval, as well as the criteria of others who have at their disposal reinforcers that we value and punishers that we are motivated to avoid, are crucial in determining how we view ourselves. To the extent to which we do not learn what to say and how to act (or even how to dress) in social situations, and do not learn useful problem-focused skills in other highly valued areas (e.g., school, sports, on the job), these situations will produce aversive consequences (failure, taunting, rejection, exclusion from the group) and will therefore be appraised as stressful and will be avoided. Thus, we make efforts to learn how to act with peers, parents, lovers, employers, employees, at parties, at work, and in other situations where our behavior has important consequences. We find that different behaviors are "acceptable" to different people and in different situations. To the extent to which we either do not "learn the rules" (i.e., fail to learn what is expected of us and what behaviors will be met with approval by others in different contexts) or do not learn how to perform the required behaviors (or are unwilling or otherwise are inhibited from performing them), these situations become a source of stress. The notion that we need to learn which behaviors are appropriate in different situations or contexts is extremely important. We do not emit behaviors in a vacuum. We learn to *discriminate* as well as to *generalize* among stimulus situations. We learn to discriminate among certain cues very quickly because whether we discriminate accurately will determine whether our behavior will be reinforced. For example, a preadolescent boy will quickly learn to discriminate between nuances in his father's behavior, such as his father's facial expression, what he is wearing, his voice tone, where he is, and how he is holding himself. The boy learns, for example, that when his father is sitting in his favorite chair with his feet up, reading his favorite magazine and puffing on his pipe, it is likely that a request for an increase in spending money will be reinforced (Bijou & Baer, 1961). This set of stimuli has become a *discriminative stimulus* for the boy. It does not automatically elicit respondent behaviors as conditioned stimuli do, but rather marks a situation in which certain voluntary behaviors (operants) on the boy's part are likely to achieve desired consequences.[3]

This kind of discriminative learning can become increasingly refined with experience. Thus, the boy may learn that this set of stimuli is likely to mark a reinforcing situation only on Friday nights, and furthermore, that if his mother mentions an overdue bill to his father, almost any behavior that he initiates toward his father, regardless of where his father is or what he is doing, will be met with a rebuff (i.e., will produce an aversive stimulus) rather than a reward. On the other hand, the boy may learn that if his father is expansively discussing a success that he has achieved at

---

[3]In the example just given under classical conditioning, we noted that the sight or thought of needles had become, as a result of being paired with punishment (unconditioned stimulus), a conditioned stimulus that elicited fear. We noted that is had also become a *discriminative stimulus* in an operant sense. In this case, "needles" signified a situation in which an operant avoidance response was reinforcing because it enabled the student to minimize the aversive stress that she experienced when thinking about anything she associated with needles. Because the fear elicited by needles (an aversive stimulus) was reduced by an increase in operant behavior (avoidance), the fear reduction is considered a *negative reinforcer* in this situation.

work, regardless of where his father is or what else is happening, almost any request will be approved.

The latter is an example of operant stimulus *generalization*, which involves a failure to discriminate (Bijou & Baer, 1961). That is, some stimuli that are similar to an established discriminative stimulus (e.g., father relaxing in his easy chair) may be responded to as if they too signaled an occasion on which certain responses will be reinforced. Such generalization may or may not be appropriate. For example, after getting reinforced on several occasions when his father is relaxing in his easy chair, the boy may then make requests of his father at any time he seems to be relaxing and is also sitting down. Through trial and error, the boy may learn that he has inappropriately generalized and that his father must be sitting in that particular easy chair to assure a high probability of reinforcement. Over time, though, the boy finds that under certain circumstances stimulus generalization pays off. For example, because his parents and other adult relatives control so many desirable reinforcers (both positive and negative), he learns to attend carefully to their behavior, and he learns that certain cues suggesting relaxation or happiness on their part generally indicate a good time to make requests.

Just as stimuli are generalized and discriminated, so are responses. We learn that certain situations signify that a wide range of responses will be reinforced. When dad is relaxing in his easy chair, a boy may learn that almost any request involving money or extra privileges will be reinforced (response generalization); however, he also finds that this does not include use of his father's tools or his computer, so he quits asking for these privileges (response discrimination). Learning appropriate stimulus and response discrimination and generalization are crucial for adjustment. We need to learn when to do or to say the appropriate thing and *how* to do or say it. Appropriate generalization gives stability and consistency to our behavior; accurate discrimination gives it fluidity, flexibility, and specificity (Keller & Schoenfeld, 1950).

Failure to learn to discriminate and generalize appropriately can be a source of great stress, especially when there is "a lot on the line" (i.e., when an appropriate response will either produce highly desirable reinforcers or avoid or terminate a highly aversive outcome). This concept has been demonstrated in laboratory situations in which "experimental neuroses" have been induced in rats by forcing them to discriminate between similar visual stimuli in order to learn when a particular response will result in pain versus when it will result in a positive reinforcer (food) (Kimble, 1961).

Similar observations have been made of people when they have been put in extremely demanding situations that are very different from those that have been habitually experienced and in which it is unclear what needs to be done to avoid punishment. In such situations (e.g., captivity), some people, after a short period of trying to ascertain what they need to do to survive, simply give up. For example, Bettleheim (1960) describes some prisoners in the Nazi concentration camps during World War II who "came to feel that the environment was one over which they could exercise no influence whatsoever." These men who "stopped eating, sat mute and motionless in corners, and expired" (Seligman, 1975, p. 184) experienced what Seligman has termed "learned helplessness."

In some situations the individual knows what response to make but doesn't have the response in his or her repertoire. This is often the case with people who experience a great deal of stress in social situations. They know how they would like to behave with others—they are able to read cues accurately and know what they would like to say and do—but they do not have the skills (e.g., they are not verbally glib, they do not know how to dance) and thus they cannot obtain the outcomes that they desire. Other persons may have the needed social skills but are not adept at reading (discriminating among) cues. That is, they haven't learned when a particular response is likely to lead to reinforcement ("they say or do the wrong thing at the wrong time"). Still others have adequate social skills and have a good understanding of when to emit particular behaviors but are still uncomfortable in social situations. For such people, because they have had unpleasant experiences in social situations in the past, these situations elicit high-level anxiety and thus inhibit the emission of behaviors that likely would be rewarded. This kind of circumstance illustrates how an operant (e.g., asking a young lady for a date) that on one or more occasions meets with an aversive consequence (e.g., a negative response accompanied by a disparaging comment) can transform the situation in which the operant is emitted (social/dating settings) to a conditioned stimulus that elicits a respondent (anxiety) that inhibits the emission of future social behaviors in that situation.

Our discussion has centered on the crucial role that operant conditioning principles play in interpersonal adjustment and in moderating stress in social situations. A number of comprehensive programs have been developed, which in part use operant principles to help people deal with stress associated with dating, assertiveness, and other social stressors. These programs, which typically involve cognitive-behavioral as well as strictly operant components, are discussed in Chapter 7. Here, we will exemplify how operant conditioning can be used for stress management, emphasizing self-control procedures that (a) are easily applied to circumscribed problem areas like smoking and overeating, and (b) that involve application of strictly operant principles with a complex multistressor situation such as marriage counseling.

Operant Methods in Self-Control

Operant self-control techniques are useful in helping people deal with stress in two ways: (a) diminishing behaviors that they are engaging in to excess (e.g., smoking, overeating), and (b) teaching and shaping up behaviors that they wish to increase or perform more efficiently (e.g., studying, social interactive skills). In both cases we are typically dealing with behaviors that people are able to perform and are already enacting in certain situations. In the first case, they are causing stress, and by getting people to monitor when they are being emitted and the environmental contingencies (reinforcers) that are maintaining them, a plan is developed to reduce their frequency. In the second case, we are dealing with coping skills that need to be augmented or refined, and we use a similar analysis of situations and reinforcers to increase their probability of occurrence.

Diminishing Problematic Behavior: Overeating.   Because of its relationship to physical appearance and health, overweight and lack of control over diet are a source of stress for many of us. Many of the principles of self-control are exemplified in techniques used to moderate eating. These principles (adapted from Masters, Burish, Hollon & Rimm, 1987) include the following:

1. *Removing undesirable foods from the house.* Removing the foods will increase the time and effort involved in obtaining high caloric foods and thus decrease the probability of impulsive, unplanned eating.

2. *Modifying eating behavior.* After taking a mouthful of food, return the utensils to the table. Also, take short breaks during a meal. These changes allow attention to feelings of satiety and the realization that one does not *have to eat* in the presence of food.

3. *Stimulus narrowing.* Eat only in one place (for example at the dinner table), only at particular times of the day, and never when engaging in another activity (e.g., reading, watching television). This focusing brings eating under tighter stimulus

control, limiting the circumstances under which it is permissible, and removes secondary reinforcers that may have become associated with it.

4. *Changing the environment.* Include in the eating environment stimuli that are likely to elicit anxiety about overeating and thus to suppress eating (e.g., diet charts).

5. *Reinforcement.* Improved eating behavior (e.g., lower caloric intake, smaller portions) should be self-reinforced (e.g., treat oneself to a movie [no popcorn]) or reinforced by others who are knowledgeable of the treatment plan.

6. *Competing responses.* At times when impulsive eating is likely, other competing behaviors should be engaged in (e.g., going for a walk or drinking a large glass of water). The competing behavior should be initiated as early as possible in the response chain that otherwise leads to eating.

7. *Shaping.* These procedures should be gradually introduced in order of increasing difficulty (as perceived by the client) so that success is experienced at every stage.

Shaping Desired Coping Behavior: Studying. The following principles are adapted from Masters et al., 1987:

1. *Changing the environment.* Some students go to the school library as a logical place to study. For some, however, the actual reinforcers in the library are the social opportunities or a quiet place to doze off. An environment must be chosen where the probability of studying is high and where distractions and the opportunity for other reinforcers is low.

2. *Cue strengthening.* Select one area or desk that is to be used exclusively for studying. Only materials relevant to studying should be on that desk. The studying environment may be made more distinctive by adding a special element that is conducive to studying and to which you are not frequently exposed to (e.g., symphonic music by Beethoven). Over time these stimuli will become powerful discriminative stimuli for studying.

3. *Reinforcement.* Initially, set short-term goals for completion of periods of effective study that are realistic for you (e.g., ten to twenty minutes). Studying for extended durations may have aversive consequences (e.g., boredom) and inhibit future studying. Short study periods that are completed with a sense of accomplishment (rather than waiting until discomfort or boredom develops) followed by a reinforcer (e.g., the opportunity to socialize or sleep) are likely to be most effective.

Shaping Desired Coping Behavior: Marriage Counseling. Applications of operant self-control procedures are not limited to circumscribed problems such as eating and studying. They have also been used effectively with complex stressors such as marital distress, which involves interpersonal problems and usually several substressors. These approaches demonstrate that by isolating the stimulus conditions that are arousing stress, and by identifying procedures for modifying these conditions and motivating people to systematically apply them, a great deal of progress can be made in bringing seemingly overwhelming problems under control.

One illustration of successful implementation of operant self-control techniques to deal with marital stress is provided by Goldiamond (1965). The approach involved both lowering the rate of behaviors that were causing stress as well as promoting positive stress-reducing behaviors. Both partners wanted to maintain their marriage, but serious difficulties had arisen after the wife had committed the "ultimate betrayal" with her husband's best friend. Since that time, the husband screamed at his wife for hours on end or else spent hours sulking and brooding. Several procedures were introduced. Because the appearance of the house had become associated with their poor relationship, they were instructed to rearrange the use of the rooms and the furniture. The new environment would hopefully become a discriminative stimulus for their positive interactions. As another device, the word *farm* written on an index card was used as a cue to stimulate discussion during dinner about a topic that they readily conversed on (his mother-in-law's crazy ideas about farming). The husband's sulking was modified by requiring him to sit on a special "sulking stool" in the garage, where he "could mutter over the dignities of life for as long as he wished." His sulking, which had reached a high of seven hours in one day, disappeared entirely with the new contingency in place. Finally, to facilitate sexual relations, the stimulus value of the bedroom, which had come to be associated with discord, was changed. A yellow night light was installed, which was turned on when either felt "turned on" and kept switched off otherwise, thus further circumventing disharmony and promoting positive relations in this most sensitive arena.

A second approach involves use of *contingency contracting*. This procedure entails specification by each partner of situations or things that the mate does that produce stress and that need to be changed (target behaviors), along with the things they find sufficiently pleasurable (reinforcers) that would motivate them to change their behavior if these reinforcers were made contingent upon the emission of the target behaviors. Gullick (1973) compared the effectiveness of contingency contracting with conventional counseling and control procedures. Among the behaviors (stressors) targeted for change that were identified by couples using contracting were gum popping, sleeping on the couch, leaving hair in the sink, picking the nose, making jealous comments, making physical complaints, leaving makeup in the bathroom, and talking about events on "soap operas." Reinforcers that were chosen included ten minutes of extra sleep, the opportunity to watch a ball game on TV, being excused from ironing, a ten-minute back rub, thirty minutes of conversation with mate without TV, and the choice of the bathing suit worn by mate. Contracts that were subsequently drawn up consisted of agreements like the following: "If Jane spends less than one hour on the telephone on a given day, Richard agrees to fix her a martini before bedtime that evening." Gullick found contracting to be more effective in minimizing stressful behaviors and diminishing distress than traditional counseling or simply recording target behaviors without implementing contracts.

COGNITIVE PROCESSES IN LEARNING

Some critics have argued that the traditional operant and classical models provide overly simplistic explanations of how people learn. These critics maintain that learning is not an automatic process in which stimuli, responses, and reinforcers are mechanically associated; more complex cognitive processes, including awareness of contingencies, motivation, social influence, and personality differences are involved. Regarding operant conditioning, research consistent with this contention has shown that human operant conditioning is dependent upon awareness of the correct response-reinforcement contingency and that successful operant treatment produces not just the desired behavioral changes but also increases in feelings of mastery, self-confidence, and positive beliefs about the self (Murray & Jacobson, 1971).

Those who are critical of the traditional classical conditioning model emphasize research findings that indicate that there are other ways to develop fears and phobias than simply experiencing a previously neutral stimulus contiguously with an aversive unconditioned stimulus (Davey, 1992; Menzies & Clarke, 1995). Some of these findings were noted in Chapter 1 as well as earlier in this chapter, including the fact that we may develop fears without direct contact with aversive stimuli by observing others and through information that influences our beliefs and expectancies about the dangerousness of stimuli. It has also been argued that although the effects of systematic desensitization and the exposure therapies have been explained in terms of the traditional classical conditioning model, both techniques make extensive use of imagery (a cognitive activity), and it is likely that their effectiveness is due to changes produced in the "client's beliefs about internal reactions, self-concept, sense of mastery, or interpretation of the feared stimulus object" (Schwartz, 1982, p. 274) rather than simply to a mechanical relearning process.

Described next are three major treatment approaches that explicitly focus on teaching of cognitive strategies as a way of enhancing coping effectiveness.

COGNITIVE-BEHAVIORAL APPROACHES

Shawn Bradley was 6 feet, 8 inches tall as an eighth-grader, and as of this writing he is a 7-foot, 6-inch-tall 26-year-old and one of the tallest people on the planet. From a statistical standpoint, Bradley, a professional basketball player, is a freak. He is constantly reminded of this fact by others and could very well dwell on this aspect of his physical being and its disadvantages. But he chooses to view it in terms of its benefits: "I love my height. I've always loved being who I was. I wouldn't trade it for anything"; and this positive self-view is evident in his self-confident, friendly demeanor (Schuster, 1993, p. 1C). Others, in contrast, tend to view themselves and their circumstances in the most negative light. These people typically are ineffective copers and therefore are often anxious and depressed.

The cognitive therapies, in general, are based on the notion that anxiety (and our other emotions) are a product of our thinking—the personal meanings that we impose on reality (see Chapters 1 and 2). "Man is not disturbed by events, but by the view he takes of them" (Epictetus, a Roman philosopher often quoted by cognitive therapist Albert Ellis). For people who are chronically anxious—who tend to view events selectively in terms of potential threats and dangers ("what if this headache means that I have a brain tumor?"), the cognitive approaches stress alternative ways of thinking about their circumstances and themselves in relation to them. Cognitive therapists help clients "reframe stressful events" by using a variety of techniques including imagery, changing self-talk, and reconceptualizing the meaning of events and the coping resources at their disposal. These therapists help clients to assess the coping demands (emotion-focused and problem-focused) of particular stressors that they are dealing with and to formulate a plan of action to short-circuit the aversive emotional arousal engendered by those stressors. The term *cognitive-behavioral* is used to emphasize the fact that cognitions and behavior (and emotions) are interrelated. Though the centerpiece of these approaches is changing cognitions and information processing in order to alleviate emotional distress, behavioral performance-based procedures are used to produce changes in thinking, emotions, and behavior (Kendall, 1993).

Strictly emotion-focused techniques like progressive muscle relaxation, autogenics, and biofeedback focus on alleviating the muscle tenseness and physiological arousal components of stress (see Chapter 7). Problem-focused techniques like the skills-training techniques described in Chapter 7 focus on teaching coping skills that will render previously stressful situations neutral and nonthreatening because the situations can now be mastered. We classify the cognitive-behavioral therapies as "mixed" (both problem-focused and emotion-focused) because they usually have both components. They help us to change stress appraisals and to lower our anxiety (emotion-focused) by providing us with alternative ways of construing our environment. They may also be used to help us reconceptualize our environment and our relation to it so that we are better prepared and more motivated to try out problem-focused coping strategies.

Three major cognitive therapy systems have been developed: Meichenbaum's Stress Inoculation Training, Ellis's Rational-Emotive Therapy, and Beck's Cognitive Therapy. We describe each of these approaches and give examples of how they may be applied to stress and stress-related problems.

Meichenbaum's Stress Inoculation Training (SIT)

Meichenbaum's (1985, 1993) SIT is a comprehensive, loosely structured, yet flexible system that stresses teaching the particular mix of coping skills and strategies that are appropriate to the particular mix of stressors with which an individual is dealing. It thus teaches both emotion-focused and problem-focused coping strategies and differential application of strategies, depending upon the coping demands posed by particular stressors. Three broad phases of treatment are identified: Conceptualization, Skills Acquisition and Rehearsal, Application and Follow-Through.

The *Conceptualization* phase is based on the idea that people who are experiencing high levels of stress are preoccupied and sometimes overwhelmed by their discomfort. They have lost track and often have never had a good understanding of why they are experiencing stress. They often have incomplete knowledge of the stimuli that are eliciting stress, of the nature of a stress reaction (autonomic nervous system arousal, muscular tenseness, negative self-statements), and of what they need to do to regain control. The main goal of this phase is to help the client put the stress reaction in an understandable context. The nature, duration, and chronicity of the stressors that are eliciting discomfort are specified. Existing personal coping strengths and resources are identified, as are new skills or strategies (both emotion-focused and problem-focused) that might be useful in dealing with problematic stressors.

The *Skills Acquisition and Rehearsal Phase* involves teaching, shaping up, and practicing needed coping strategies. After the nature of the target situations has been assessed, the client is assisted in acquiring a particular mix of E-focused and P-focused coping strategies. Meichenbaum (1985, pp. 72–73) emphasizes that self-dialogue is a particularly useful technique both for diminishing stress level and for stimulating a problem-solving attitude. Consistent with the idea that different coping skills are necessary to deal with a stressor depending on our temporal relationship to it, he differentiates among the kinds of coping self-statements that are likely to be useful at different temporal stages. Here are some examples:

> *Planning for Stressor:* "I can develop a plan to deal with it," "Just think about what I can do about it" (P-Focused); "Stop worrying—worrying won't help anything" (E-Focused).
>
> *Confronting and Handling Stressor:* "One step at a time," "Look for positives, don't jump to conclusions" (P-focused); "Relax, I'm in control, take a slow deep breath" (E-Focused).
>
> *Evaluation of Coping Efforts and Self-Rewards:* "What can/did I learn from my try?" (P-Focused); "I made more out of stress than it was worth" (E-Focused).

Application and Follow-Through involves exposure to actual stressors through imagery and role-playing, and also practice in applying learned coping strategies. Using techniques such as booster and follow-up sessions, involving significant others in the training, and helping the client to learn how to bounce back from failures, efforts are made to ensure that learned coping strategies are used in actual situations and that they can be readily applied to new stressors as they are encountered.

One of the advantages of SIT is its flexibility and applicability to a wide range of stressors. For example, for patients facing major surgery under general anesthesia, there is no opportunity to change the situation instrumentally using problem-focused coping. Thus, an SIT intervention that was developed for surgical patients focused on enhancing emotion-focused coping strategies by teaching deep breathing, muscle relaxation, pleasant imagery, and positive self-statements. Patients who had been given SIT experienced less anxiety and pain after surgery, and they recovered more quickly than patients who had been given standard hospital instructions (Wells, Howard, Nowlin, & Vargas, 1986). In contrast, an SIT intervention for smoke divers (oil workers training to use smoke diving equipment in hot, dark smoke-filled surroundings) had to address both emotion-focused and problem-focused coping demands (Hytten, Jensen, & Skauli, 1990). Thus, trainee smoke divers were instructed in problem-focused skills (how to use the tactile sense and "cognitive pictures" to help orient themselves in total darkness) as well as emotion-focused anxiety management techniques (relaxed breathing, substitution of positive self-statements for negative self-talk) to help them function effectively under these highly stressful conditions. In summarizing the range of stressors to which SIT has been applied, Meichenbaum (1996) notes that empirical studies support its efficacy as a treatment for acute, time-limited stressors such as aversive medical examinations, ongoing intermittent stressors such as military combat, chronic stressors such as medical illness, and stressors involving multiple sequential components such as divorce and unemployment.

Ellis's Rational-Emotive Therapy (RET)

Albert Ellis traces the origin of his RET system to his own personal problems, which included fear of public speaking and anxiety about encountering women. After working with different therapy systems, including psychoanalysis, he concluded that the most important factor underlying disabling anxiety and other negative emotions is illogical thinking. In his many writings (e.g., Ellis, 1971; Ellis & Harper, 1975; Ellis & Whitely, 1979), he has identified a core group of beliefs that he thinks are widely endorsed and contribute to emotional distress in the majority of people. He calls these beliefs "*mus*turbatory" ideas because they are characterized by perfectionistic goals that can never be attained and therefore invariably lead to stress (e.g., the ideas that one must succeed every time and must be approved of and liked by everybody). Because these beliefs are so rigid and set up unattainable goals they lead to *awful*izing, another kind of self-defeating "absolutistic" thinking (e.g., "I didn't succeed, and it's awful—it's the end of the world").

The central technique in RET is the "curing of unreason by reason"—ridding people of the irrational ideas that are causing them emotional distress by disputing the ideas and substituting rational beliefs and attitudes. For example, the irrational belief that you must be totally competent and perform well in all areas in order to consider yourself a worthwhile person may be countered by the argument that this is an impossible requirement and therefore can only result in anxiety and feelings of inferiority. A more rational and realistic belief is that you should set your own performance criteria on the basis of your personal preferences and goals and then strive to achieve because doing so pleases you rather than trying to impress others. RET therapists are generally very active, directive, and confrontational. Techniques other than verbal persuasion, including role playing, modeling, and imagery, are used to convince clients of the irrationality and self-defeating nature of their belief system. Furthermore, clients are encouraged and challenged to engage in real-world activities that they have avoided or have been too anxious to perform because of their old belief system. For example, inhibited people are assigned to wear "loud" clothing in public or to refuse to tip a waitress who has given poor service, or even to go into a sex shop and conspicuously inquire about the different kinds of vibrators available. The purpose of these "homework" assignments is to demonstrate to people that though the homework may produce some discomfort, the catastrophic consequences that they have imagined do not eventuate, and that if these tasks are cognitively appraised in new ways (e.g., as adventures), they can be humorous and pleasurable.

Ellis's RET, which is the first contemporary therapy system that may be considered cognitive-behavioral, has undoubtedly been very influential (Kendall & Bemis, 1983). In addition, the self-help forms and self-instructional procedures that Ellis has developed (Ellis & Bernard, 1985), along with the self-monitoring and homework assignment components of his approach, make his system particularly amenable for use as a self-management technique. RET has generally fared well in research studies evaluating its effectiveness, though the methodological adequacy of many of these studies has been questioned (Engels, Garnefski, & Diekstra, 1993; Haaga & Davison, 1993). Also, like other cognitive-behavioral systems, it has come to subsume an increasingly broad array of techniques, thus making it more difficult to delineate its distinctive aspects and evaluate its efficacy.

Beck's Cognitive Therapy

Beck's Cognitive Therapy (Beck, Emery, & Greenberg, 1985) as applied to anxiety and anxiety disorders is a cognitive-behavioral system that shares many elements with Ellis's RET. Less emphasis is placed, however, on particular sets or types of beliefs (e.g., perfectionistic ones) that may be leading to elevated stress and behavioral problems. The focus is on identifying the stress-inducing faulty ideas or automatic thoughts associated with specific situations and on systematically questioning (using the Socratic method) the evidence for and against the logic of this thinking (e.g., "Are you confusing habit with fact?" "Are you taking selected examples out of context?"). On the basis of this interchange, efforts are then made to substitute alternative, more realistic interpretations of events (e.g., "He (the supervisor) is aloof from all the workers, not just me"), and to help the client learn to "decatastrophize" by helping him or her learn coping strategies (both problem- and emotion-focused) that can be used to deal with the situation. After "understanding" is achieved patients are encouraged, via homework assignments, to test out the new viewpoints and assumptions in the real world.

Beck's approach is most closely identified with the treatment of depression, though it is also widely used to treat anxiety disorders and stress-related problems. Commenting on the evidence for the effectiveness of CT, Kendall and Bemis (1983) conclude that its research credentials have largely been established with depressive disorders and that there is no solid evidence of its utility for other types of affective problems. More recent research, however, has validated Beck's approach and adaptations of it as an effective treatment for anxiety disorders (Chambless & Gillis, 1993).

$\mathscr{S}$UMMARY

1. Most fears are acquired through a classical conditioning process as a result of the occurrence of a previously neutral stimulus in conjunction with an aversive unconditioned stimulus. Sometimes aversive associations are transmitted through observation and information transmission alone without the direct experience of an aversive stimulus. As noted in Chapter 1, some fears are learned

more readily than others. Learned fears readily generalize to stimuli similar to the original conditioned stimulus.

2. Several important stress management techniques have been developed that are based on the classical conditioning model. These include systematic desensitization, exposure techniques (such as implosive therapy), and aversive counterconditioning techniques. Desensitization involves teaching relaxation, exposing the individual to increasingly fearful situations, and associating the relaxation response with those situations. Exposure techniques attempt to extinguish fear by having the individual experience highly feared situations in a safe environment. Aversive counterconditioning techniques use aversive unconditioned stimuli (such as electric shock) to reduce the reinforcement value of previously pleasurable but undesirable activities.

3. Operant conditioning is also involved in fear acquisition, because one way that situations can become aversive and associated with fear (via classical conditioning) is when they offer highly valued reinforcers (e.g., social situations) and people have been ineffective in learning how to acquire those reinforcers. Operant techniques (e.g., social skills training) can be used to teach acquisition and refinement of important problem-focused skills, as well as self-control of behaviors that are causing stress (e.g., smoking).

4. Cognitive-behavioral approaches emphasize the role of belief systems, self-appraisals, and information processing in determining stress responses. They focus on identifying the trains of thought underlying individuals' stress reactions, on getting them to examine and modify irrational ideas, and finally on getting them to engage in appropriate coping behaviors. Of the three major systems reviewed (Meichenbaum, Beck, Ellis), Meichenbaum's appears to be the most broadly applicable to stress management because it teaches a wide range of emotion-focused and problem-focused coping strategies that are tailored to an individual's coping needs, depending on the nature of the stressors being confronted.

$\mathscr{K}$EY TERMS

aversive counterconditioning   Classical conditioning-based procedure in which an aversive stimulus is paired with the performance of a problem behavior or the perception of an inappropriate stimulus in order to reduce the attractiveness of the behavior or stimulus.

cognitive-behavioral interventions   Techniques that help minimize stress-related problems by focusing on helping people reconceptualize or reframe their cognitive appraisals of events that they perceive as threatening.

conditioned response   In classical conditioning, the response that is elicited by the conditioned stimulus once learning has taken place. This response is almost identical to the unconditioned response. In phobias, the fear response becomes conditioned to a previously neutral stimulus as a result of the pairing of the stimulus with an unconditioned stimulus for fear (punishment).

conditioned stimulus   In classical conditioning, a stimulus that is neutral prior to learning. As a result of pairing with an unconditioned stimulus, it comes to elicit a conditioned response.

contingency contract   Based in operant conditioning principles; an agreement made between two parties (e.g., client and therapist, husband and wife) in which an exchange of rewards is made contingent upon the emission of certain behaviors on the part of each individual.

discriminative stimulus   In operant conditioning, an environmental cue that indicates to an individual that if a particular operant behavior is emitted at this time it is likely to be reinforced (positively or negatively).

exposure techniques   Based in classical conditioning theory; techniques used to diminish a stress response that has come to be associated with a particular stimulus by exposing the individual to this stimulus repeatedly, in the absence of any punishment or aversive experience. If treatment is effective, the stress response will extinguish and the conditioned stimulus will revert to the status of a neutral stimulus.

extinction   Gradual diminution of a learned response because the response is no longer associated with reinforcement. Operants extinguish when they are no longer followed by rewards. Conditioned responses extinguish when they are no longer paired with unconditioned stimuli.

generalization   Stimulus generalization: responses learned to particular stimuli also come to be made to similar stimuli (e.g., Little Albert learned to fear a white rat, and this response generalized to other white, furry stimuli); response generalization: a learned response to a particular stimulus may generalize to other similar responses (e.g., a boy finds that his father responds positively when he tells his father humorous stories from the *Reader's Digest* and the boy then attempts to elicit a similar positive reaction with off-color jokes that he has heard from friends).

implosive therapy   Exposure technique in which some of the imagery that is presented goes beyond the material presented by the client and is based on the therapist's judgment of the symbolic meaning of the feared stimuli to the client.

orgasmic reconditioning   Counterconditioning technique in which sexual arousal produced by masturbation is used as a reinforcing unconditioned response to alter sexual interests from stimuli that are inappropriate or unattainable to those that are appropriate and attainable.

reciprocal inhibition   Mechanism by which a fear response to a stimulus is replaced by a relaxation response in systematic desensitization (according to Joseph Wolpe).

reinforcer   In operant conditioning, any stimulus that when made contingent upon a response (i.e. follows the response), increases the rate of that response.

respondent   In classical conditioning, another name for an automatically elicited or unconditioned response.

stimulus narrowing   Technique in operant conditioning involving restricting the situations in which an individual may emit a particular problem behavior (e.g., smoking is restricted to the bathroom and eventually to the cellar).

systematic desensitization   Technique for treating extreme fear responses that involves developing a hierarchy of feared situations, teaching relaxation, and pairing the relaxation response with the stimuli in the fear hierarchy.

unconditioned response   In classical conditioning, an unlearned response (usually a reflex, such as the pupillary response to light) that is automatically elicited by an unconditioned stimulus.

unconditioned stimulus   In classical conditioning, any stimulus that (without prior learning) regularly elicits a particular response. Food is an unconditioned stimulus for the salivation response in a hungry person or animal.

CHAPTER **4**
Physiology of Stress

Janet slinks into her 10:00 a.m. Spanish class just as the instructor begins class. She avoids eye contact with the instructor and makes her way to the back of the room. She sits down behind several other students and shrinks into her seat. It is Friday, and that means that all the students are fair game to be called on to recite the dialogue from this week's lesson. Janet is a nervous wreck even when she is prepared to recite, and she is decidedly unprepared today. She would have cut class, but the instructor has a very strict attendance policy. Now that she is seated in the classroom, she would give anything to be anywhere else. There is no way to escape without making a scene, so she sits quietly praying that she will not be called on.

As she sits, Janet can feel the tension growing inside her. She is aware of her every heartbeat, her breathing is shallow, her hands are sweaty, and her mouth is dry. Someone is reciting in the front of the room, but she seems far away. Janet can only concentrate on controlling her growing tension. She is startled when a student just two seats away begins reciting. Her heart jumps to her throat, and a knot forms in her stomach, but the panic subsides somewhat when the instructor moves to someone seated near the opposite wall. Ten more minutes and she will be safe. Suddenly she hears her name called! All eyes in the room turn and look at her expectantly. Her throat is on fire, her face is beet red, and she feels nauseous. The instructor calls her name again, but she cannot speak. Janet sits dumbfounded as she sees the faces around her as if in slow motion. Her thoughts are drowned out by the sound of her heart pounding in her ears. The bell rings, and the other students leave, looking over their shoulders at her as they go.

Janet has experienced a stress response so strong that it borders on a panic attack. Her body responded as if she were in a life-

threatening situation. All of her physiological systems were involved in producing this response. The effects on her cardiovascular system (increased heart rate), gastrointestinal system (dry mouth, nausea), and somatic/muscle system (increased muscle tension) were particularly noticeable. However, other profound bodily changes were also occurring. Namely, the central nervous system, the endocrine system, and the immune system were all affected and in turn produced changes in other systems as part of the body's integrated response to stress. In this chapter, we will explore in more detail how the body responds to stressful situations.

For most people, stressors are associated with noticeable physiological and psychological changes. People report bodily symptoms such as sweaty palms, racing heart, churning stomach, and diarrhea. At the same time, they typically report a subjective sense of apprehension and dread. How are the subjective feelings of apprehension and dread related to changes in bodily functioning? How can simply appraising an event as threatening lead to such rapid bodily changes? Moreover, how are short-term physiological changes related to the stress-related disorders such as ulcers, coronary heart disease, headaches, and cancer?

Researchers have been grappling with these and related questions for some time. On some points we have a very clear idea of how stress exerts its effects on the body, but in other areas our knowledge is still in its infancy. For example, we have amassed a great deal of information and formed a fairly detailed picture of Cannon's fight-or-flight response, that is, the immediate physiological effects of stress. Questions concerning the nature of the relationship between exposure to stress and the development of disease have also received considerable attention. Researchers know a great deal about how stress hastens the development of illness and disease when laboratory animals are the objects of study. Answering questions regarding the relationship between stress and illness in humans has proved a much more complex undertaking.

This chapter will attempt to summarize our current understanding of the immediate physiological and psychological effects of stress. In order to do this, a review of the basic structure (anatomy) and function (physiology) of the nervous system is presented first. The review is divided into three parts representing the three most important body systems involved in the stress response. These three body systems are the **nervous system, immune system,** and **endocrine system.** A description of how each of these body systems responds to stress will be included in each section. This review of the anatomy and physiology of the key body systems that are involved in the stress response will provide the foundation for our discussion in the following chapter on specific stress-related disorders.

STRUCTURE AND FUNCTION OF THE NERVOUS SYSTEM

The stress response is both a psychological and a physiological phenomenon. Think about how you felt as the date for an important exam approached, for example, when you took your college board tests (e.g., SAT or ACT). Psychologically, you may have felt apprehensive or nervous. You may have felt as if you needed to review for the test but were too nervous to do so. At some point you may have concluded that further study or review was pointless, but yet that edge of apprehension and dread stayed with you. As you anticipated taking the exam (and perhaps during the exam itself), you may have noticed that your heart was beating faster, that your palms were sweaty, and that you experienced gastrointestinal distress. You may have had difficulty sleeping well the night before the exam, and you may have experienced a

Walter Cannon, who was one of the early pioneers in the stress-physiology area, first coined the term *fight-or-flight* response. The fight-or-flight (F/F) response describes the body's general activation that prepares it either to attack a stressor head-on or to retreat (quickly) in the face of a stressor. Both responses require an alert, activated organism to engage in some direct action. Cannon suggests that the F/F response is a vestige of our evolutionary past. The F/F response may have been adaptive when the typical stressors encountered in the environment were the dinosaur Tyrannosaurus rex and other reptilian contemporaries. However, the F/F response is maladaptive in modern society where most of the stressors encountered are of a *symbolic nature*. Specifically, most of the stressors faced by individuals in our society are not threats to physical safety (where preparation to fight or flee would be most appropriate), but rather, are threats to self-esteem (e.g., evaluation anxiety, social anxiety such as that induced in Janet by the Spanish class. Frequent, chronic activation of the F/F in response to symbolic stressors is thought to account for many of the deleterious effects frequently associated with stress (headaches, coronary heart disease, ulcers, etc.). Cannon's ideas have had great impact on the stress research field. The next several chapters are aimed at providing an overview of how stress affects bodily functioning and how it is related to illness and disease.

sense of euphoria after the exam was over. Not surprisingly, the psychological and physiological aspects of the stress response are intimately linked. These psychological and physiological responses to stress begin in the nervous system, which "sounds the alarm" when we appraise an event as stressful. Compared with the endocrine and immune systems, the nervous system reacts very quickly once the appraisal process has identified an event or a situation as threatening. The nervous system in turn influences the slower-responding endocrine and immune systems both directly and indirectly. These three body systems are interconnected and continually influence each other. However, our discussion of the nervous system will be more extensive because of its primary role in initiating the stress response.

Divisions of the Nervous System

The schematic in Figure 4–1 illustrates the relationships among the different divisions of the nervous system.

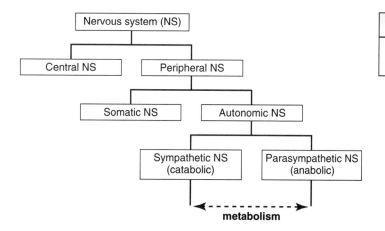

Figure 4–1

Divisions of the nervous system.

The nervous system is first divided into two primary divisions, the central nervous system (CNS) and peripheral nervous system (PNS). The CNS comprises the brain and spinal cord, and all other aspects of the NS are subsumed under the PNS. The PNS is divided into the somatic nervous system and autonomic nervous system. The somatic nervous system has also been termed the musculoskeletal NS or "voluntary" NS because of its involvement in the regulation of voluntary motor movements (e.g., running). The autonomic nervous system, on the other hand, regulates body functions over which we have little voluntary control. Functions regulated by the ANS include respiration, contraction of the smooth muscles (e.g., muscles that form the lining of blood vessels), and even "goose bumps" that appear on the skin when a person is cold, scared, tickled, etc. Finally, the autonomic nervous system is divided into the sympathetic and parasympathetic divisions. In general, these two divisions of the autonomic NS work together in a reciprocal fashion. The sympathetic NS is activated in the face of stress by the hypothalamus (a structure in the brain that is reviewed in the following section) and is responsible for preparing the body for "fight or flight." Activation of catabolic processes (energy consumption) is one consequence of sympathetic activity. In addition, blood flow increases to the brain but decreases to the stomach and intestinal organs during sympathetic activation. The parasympathetic division, on the other hand, works to conserve and store energy (anabolic processes) so that there is sufficient fuel ready when the sympathetic division is activated. Together, these two divisions of the ANS work to keep the metabolic process on an even keel, or in a state of equilibrium. One of the fundamental forces at work in nature, including our bodies, is constant pressure to maintain a state of equilibrium. When stress disrupts the equilibrium of the ANS or other body systems, adverse health consequences can occur.

Central Nervous System: Functions

In the previous discussion, our review of the divisions of the nervous system focused primarily on the divisions and functions of the peripheral nervous system. Because the PNS is very important in the stress response, we will return to elaborate on the functions of the PNS at later points in this book. For now, however, we will become familiar with the general outline of the structure and function of the NS and then will turn our attention to a more detailed discussion of the CNS.

As just noted, the CNS comprises the brain and spinal cord. The brain is the "command center" of the nervous system. Decisions made in the brain are communicated to the periphery by signals that pass down the brain through the spinal cord and then out to the appropriate peripheral target muscle or organ. At the same time, sensory information is constantly being transmitted from the periphery to the spinal cord and up to the brain, where the information is evaluated and further decisions are made. For example, using the vignette at the beginning of the chapter, imagine that you are in Janet's place and are called on to read a translation in Spanish class. The teacher's instructions represent auditory information that is collected in the periphery and sent, via the auditory pathway, to the areas in the brain that decode spoken language (even though your ears are on your head, they are still part of the peripheral nervous system). The brain, in turn, executes a number of split-second decisions. In this example, one CNS decision would probably be to make a spoken response, and therefore a message would be sent from the brain to the somatic nervous system to execute the necessary motor movements. If you are poorly prepared to read the translation and if you appraise the instructor's request as threatening, the brain may send messages that would activate the autonomic nervous system, specifically the sympathetic nervous system, to prepare the body for "fight or flight." Sympathetic nervous system arousal produces the immediate physiological symptoms of stress, such as sweaty palms, churning stomach, and pounding heart. These physiological symptoms in turn produce sensory information (you feel the sweat on your palms, the churning in your stomach, and the like), and this sensory information is sent from the peripheral sense organs to the brain, where it is evaluated and new decisions are made. Although this is a relatively simple example, it succinctly illustrates the interconnections between the CNS and PNS, as well as the primary role that the CNS plays in initiating the stress response.

Central Nervous System: Structure

The brain and spinal cord comprise an array of incredibly complex anatomical structures. In this review we seek merely to provide an overview of some of the most important brain structures involved in the stress response. In general, we can think of the brain as comprising three layers (MacLean, 1990). (See Figure 4–2.) If we could peel away the top two layers, we would find a core in the deepest part of the brain, much like the seed in the middle of a peach. The core of the brain, containing the deepest brain structures, is referred to as the hindbrain. The hindbrain regulates vital life functions such as general arousal and muscle tone. The brain layer that largely surrounds the hindbrain is called the midbrain. The reticular activating system (RAS) is the most important structure relevant to the stress response that passes through the midbrain. (We discuss the RAS in more detail in the next section.) Finally, the forebrain represents the top layer, the outside-most part being the cerebral cortex, which is often said to reflect that part of the brain that makes us uniquely human. The cerebral cortex controls language and largely accounts for what we experience as consciousness. It is here in the cerebral cortex that the appraisal process takes place. Events are evaluated as being threatening or nonthreatening, and the stress response is initiated. The fact that humans respond to symbolic stressors as if they were threats to physical safety is a consequence of our highly developed cerebral cortex and abilities in abstract reasoning. The ability of humans to use symbolic logic accounts for the reason that in humans, more so than in any other species, stress is in the past, the present, and the future. In fact, recent studies indicate that the body produces the strongest physiological response when a person is instructed to remember or imagine a stressful event, rather than when a person is actually exposed to the stressor.

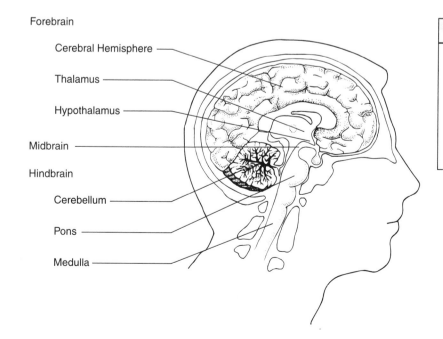

Forebrain
- Cerebral Hemisphere
- Thalamus
- Hypothalamus

Midbrain

Hindbrain
- Cerebellum
- Pons
- Medulla

Figure 4–2

Illustration of the three primary divisions of the brain; the hindbrain, midbrain, and forebrain. (From *Psychology: Principles and Applications*, 5/E by Worchel/Shebilske, © 1995. Adapted by permission of Prentice-Hall, Inc., Upper Saddle River, NJ.)

Generally these three layers of the brain are thought to reflect progressive advancements in evolutionary development. The forebrain, particularly the cerebral cortex, is the most advanced part of the brain. A number of important brain structures reside in the forebrain, in addition to the cerebral cortex. These structures include the basal ganglia (regulate motor movements), limbic system (regulates emotion), thalamus (routes incoming sensory information from the periphery to projection areas in the cerebral cortex), and hypothalamus (regulates the four F's of behavior: fighting, fleeing, feeding, mating). Each of these forebrain structures regulates their respective functions in concert with other brain structures (both higher and lower), and there is always information being transmitted among brain structures and between the CNS and the periphery. Midbrain and hindbrain structures serve in part as a communication conduit for the information coming from and going to the periphery.

One structure of particular importance in the stress response is the reticular activating system (RAS), which passes through both the hindbrain and midbrain and even projects up to the forebrain. The RAS is a diffuse, netlike web of nerve fibers that begins deep in the hindbrain, spreads upward through the midbrain, and interconnects with forebrain structures such as the thalamus. The pathways that bring sensory information from the periphery to the CNS have offshoots that interconnect with the RAS, while the main bundle of sensory fibers proceed to the thalamus and are then projected to higher brain centers. The offshoots of these sensory pathways that interconnect with the RAS serve to activate the RAS, In turn, the RAS through its diffuse network of fibers, produces arousal or activation in the many brain structures with which it interconnects. This activation by the RAS makes the brain more receptive or "alert" to incoming sensory information and facilitates the "decision making" functions of the cerebral cortex.

The arousal produced by the RAS facilitates our response to potential stressors by stimulating brain structures that are essential for activation of the stress reactivity pathways (peripheral nervous system, endocrine system) and by making the cerebral cortex ready to appraise the incoming stimuli as threatening or nonthreatening. Overactivation of the RAS, however, can have adverse effects on a person's health. The RAS adjusts to chronic activation by increasing the overall level of arousal so that rather than repeatedly responding to stimuli with increases in arousal, it simply keeps the level of arousal chronically high; that is, rather than "turning on and off" in response to transient stimuli, the RAS simply stays "on." This state leads to overactivity in all of the brain structures that the RAS interconnects with, including the brain structures associated with the stress-reactivity pathways. The RAS causes these structures to prepare for the "fight-or-flight response" before the cortex has appraised the stimuli as threatening or nonthreatening. Therefore, chronic activation of the RAS results in chronic activation of the stress reactivity pathways as well. Not surprisingly, your body systems are weakened and made more vulnerable to disease when they are constantly in "overdrive." One of the keys to stress management seems to be reducing chronically high levels of arousal, thereby returning the RAS to its normal pattern of functioning.

Central Nervous System: Neurons and Neurotransmitters

Each brain structure that was discussed previously comprises many hundreds of thousands of individual cells called neurons. Neurons share much of the same structure and function of cells in other parts of the body. However, neurons also have a number of specialized features that are unique to cells in the CNS.

Previously we have referred to communication among the different divisions of the nervous system and among the different structures of the brain in very general terms. Familiarity with some of the fundamental aspects of neurons described in the following section will provide a framework with which to understand some of the truly amazing features of neural communications, and ultimately of human consciousness. (See Figure 4–3.)

Neurons are simply specialized cells of the CNS. In order to send and receive information (we will use the terms *neural transmission* and *neural communication* interchangeably to refer to the process of neurons sending and receiving information), the neuron has two different types of projections that extend from its cell. These different projections are called the **dendrites** and the **axon.** Dendrites are relatively short, branchy projections, whereas the axon is a single long, slender projection with branches at the end known as terminal buttons. The terminal buttons of the axon contain small enclosures or pouches called vesicles. The chemicals inside the vesicles are called **neurotransmitters** and are very important for neural transmission. Although there are more neurons in your brain than stars in the galaxy, neurons do not communicate with each other via physical connections. Rather, there is a small space called the **synaptic cleft** that separates the axon of one neuron from the dendrite or cell body of another neuron. The terms **synapse** and **synaptic cleft** refer to the space between the axon of one neuron and the dendrite (or cell body) of another neuron. Sometimes we use the word *synapse* to refer to the relations and actions between two neurons. For example, we say that one neuron synapses on another to express the physical relation between two neurons; the term *synaptic activity* is a general term for events that occur in the synapse.

Neurons transmit information via an electrical-chemical process. If a neuron is sufficiently stimulated, it will send a wave of electrical energy down the axon to the terminal buttons. The wave of electrical energy that "fires" down the axon is called an **action potential.** When the action potential reaches the terminal button, the force of the energy pushes the vesicles against the membrane wall. The vesicle fuses

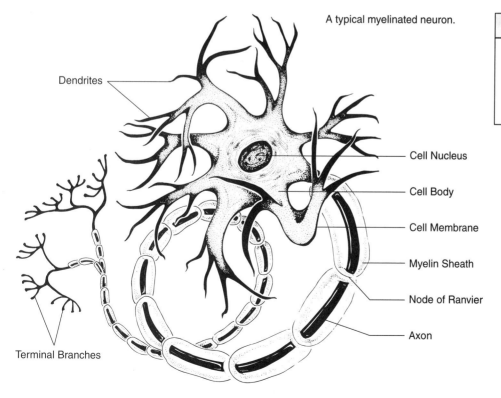

A typical myelinated neuron.

Dendrites

Cell Nucleus

Cell Body

Cell Membrane

Myelin Sheath

Node of Ranvier

Axon

Terminal Branches

Figure 4–3

Illustration of a neuron. (From *Psychology: Principles and Applications,* 5/E by Worchel/Shebilske, © 1995. Adapted by permission of Prentice-Hall, Inc., Upper Saddle River, NJ.)

with the membrane wall, and the pressure of the action potential causes the neurotransmitter substance to be released into the synaptic cleft. The neurotransmitters cross the synaptic cleft and interact with **receptors** imbedded on the surface of the dendrites (or cell body) of the adjacent neuron. The neurotransmitter molecule fits into its own receptor in a lock-and-key fashion. If the molecule released by the first neuron "fits" the receptor on the dendrites of the neighboring neuron, it causes relatively small waves of electrical activity to flow towards the cell body of that neuron. If a critical threshold of electrical stimulation is exceeded at the cell body, then the axon of the neuron "fires" a relatively strong wave of electrical activity (an action potential) down the axon to the terminal buttons, and the process of neural transmission proceeds from neuron to neuron.

In the previous section's discussion of the RAS, we noted that when the RAS is overactivated, it fails to "turn off" even after a stimulus, or stressor, has passed. At the level of the neuron, this failure means that neurons are firing more frequently than they normally should be. One of the changes that occurs in the brain as the result of this stress-induced increase in neuron firing is an increase in the growth of dendrites and in the number of receptors in the limbic system (the limbic system is one of the primary targets of the RAS). Remember, the body is always trying to maintain a state of equilibrium. When the RAS chronically activates the limbic system, there is an increase in neuron firing, causing an excessive amount of neurotransmitter substance to be released. The body tries to adapt to this state of affairs by producing more dendrites/receptors for the neurotransmitter substance to interact with. The net effect of this increase in dendrite/receptor growth is to make a person even more sensitive to limbic (emotional) stimulation. This helps explain why many people who are chronically stressed seem excessively emotional. Thus, the behavioral, emotional, and cognitive aspects of the stress response all have a biological basis.

Neurotransmitters

Some neurotransmitter substances are more intimately linked than others in producing the stress response. For example, one neurotransmitter substance in particular has been linked to the feelings of apprehension and dread that are often experienced when we are anticipating contact with a stressor. In the next section we will discuss specifically the relationship between neurotransmitters and anxiety. For now, we will lay the foundation for that discussion by reviewing the different neurotransmitter substances, receptors, and the main functions of each.

There are several different types of neurotransmitters, and each type of neurotransmitter substance has several different types of receptors with which to interact. (See Table 4–1.) Because the different receptors for each neurotransmitter substance have slight variations in shape, the receptors vary in how well the neurotrans-

TABLE 4–1. NEUROTRANSMITTERS IN THE BRAIN	
Neurotransmitters	**Action**
GABA	Inhibits anxiety; modulates anxiety
Dopamine	Modulates mood and reinforcement processes
Serotonin	Modulates mood, sleep, and pain
Norepinephrine	Excitatory neurotransmitter, modulates arousal processes (sleep/wakefulness)
Acytecholine	Involved in memory processes
Endogenous opiates	Modulates pain and feelings of euphoria

mitter chemical will "fit" into the receptor. There are many drugs that pass into the brain and interact with the different neurotransmitter receptors either to mimic the effects of the neurotransmitter or to block the neurotransmitter's effect. If a drug passes into the CNS and is about the same shape as one of the neurotransmitter substances, it will be able to mimic the effects of that neurotransmitter. On the other hand, drugs may get into the receptor but not really fit, like a broken key in a lock, and therefore the receptor is blocked. The actions of the neurotransmitter are reduced because many of the receptors are essentially filled with "broken keys." Drugs that block receptors in the brain are very useful tools in treating conditions caused by neurotransmitter substances that are "overactive." Schizophrenia, for example, is thought to be caused by excess dopamine in the brain (see Table 4–1); many people with this serious disorder are helped by drugs that block dopamine receptors. Drugs can affect neural transmission in a variety of other ways, such as facilitating or blocking the production of neurotransmitter substance in the axon. Not surprisingly, the drugs people take to relieve anxiety affect the chemicals in the brain. Of even more interest, however, is the developing literature indicating that the brain has receptors for chemicals that both relieve and perhaps cause anxiety.

Neurotransmitters and Anxiety

The neurotransmitter substance GABA (see Table 4–1) has been strongly implicated as an important mediator of the subjective feeling of anxiety that people experience during the stress response. That is, GABA seems to play a more important role in the experience of anxiety than do other neurotransmitters. Man-made drugs that are designed to reduce anxiety such as Valium and Librium (which belong to a class of drugs called benzodiazepines) seem to exert their anxiety-reducing effects by facilitating neural transmission in the GABA neurotransmitter system. The benzodiazepines bind to receptors adjacent to the GABA receptors and modulate the effects of GABA by slightly changing the shape of the GABA receptor, which in turn changes the GABA receptor's affinity (attraction) for the GABA molecule (Snyder, 1986). (See Figure 4–4.)

Because GABA exerts an inhibitory (calming) influence on other neurotransmitter systems, drugs such as Valium act to enhance the inhibitory effects of GABA. Although GABA receptors are found throughout the CNS and periphery, they are most concentrated in the limbic system, that part of the brain which regulates emotional behavior. Many scientists now agree that the binding of benzodiazepine drugs adjacent to the GABA receptors accounts for the antianxiety effects of these drugs (Sny-

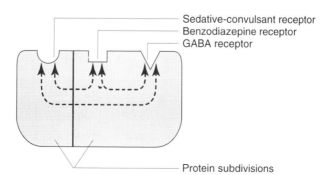

Sedative-convulsant receptor
Benzodiazepine receptor
GABA receptor

Protein subdivisions

A single protein molecule contains binding sites for GABA, benzodiazepines, and sedatives and convulsants.

Figure 4–4

Illustration of a GABA receptor. (From *Drugs and the Brain* by Snyder © 1986 by Scientific American Books. Used with permission of W. H. Freeman and Company.)

der, 1986). In fact, alcohol and other sedative drugs that people sometimes take to self-medicate the symptoms of stress and anxiety, interact with the benzodiazepine and GABA receptors to produce their sedative effects.

An important implication of this work relates to the fact that there are specific benzodiazepine receptors in the brain. The presence of a specific receptor that is receptive to benzodiazepine molecules suggests that there may well be an endogenous (naturally occurring in the body) antianxiety chemical/neurotransmitter in the brain. After all, Valium is a man-made substance; it is not likely that the brain would evolve in such a way as to produce receptors for substances there were just manufactured in the last three decades. Rather, the implication is that endogenous anxiety-reducing chemicals are naturally produced in the human brain. While this elusive anxiety-reducing chemical has not yet been isolated in the brain, the recent success of researchers in isolating endogenous opiates (another neurotransmitter substance discussed in more detail later in this chapter) increases our confidence that this substance will be isolated in the near future.

The search for naturally occurring Valium-like molecules has produced some fascinating discoveries. For example, there has been found a class of man-made drugs, the carbolines, that act as a benzodiazepine receptor blocker (they block the benzodiazepine receptor and therefore create effects opposite to those of the benzodiazepines). In an experiment with healthy volunteers, very small doses of the drug B-carboline produced intense anxiety in the participants. One subject became so anxious that he demanded a benzodiazepine be given to reverse the effects. The B-carboline also produced restlessness, and increased systolic blood pressure and pulse rate. However, from the subject's point of view, the most dramatic effect was the sense of extreme anxiety produced by the drug (see Braestrup & Nielsen, 1993). The fact that the apprehension and dread produced by B-carboline was reversed when the subject was given Valium is further evidence that the anxiety-inducing effects of B-carboline was the direct result of its ability to block the benzodiazepine receptor. More recently, intensive investigation of the morphology of the benzodiazepine receptor and the search for other benzodiazepine-like drugs has led to the development of new treatments for anxiety disorders and has greatly enhanced our understanding of the biochemical basis of anxiety (Chapter 10 discusses some of these treatments in more detail). As the mysteries surrounding the biological basis of anxiety are unraveled, it seems clear that the isolation of naturally occurring brain chemicals that relieve, and perhaps produce, anxiety is just around the corner.

STRUCTURE AND FUNCTION OF THE ENDOCRINE SYSTEM

The endocrine system is a complex system of glands that are located primarily in the periphery. The glands interact with each other and influence other body systems by releasing hormones into the bloodstream. When a person appraises an event as threatening, the glands of the endocrine system release a sequence of specific hormones. Many of the long-term illnesses associated with stress are thought to be caused in part by the overactivation of these glands and the release of these hormones.

Endocrine System Structure

Figure 4–5 illustrates the anatomical locations of the various glands that comprise the endocrine system. Several of these glands are of particular importance in mediating the stress response. Specifically, the pituitary and adrenal medulla are very active in regulating the stress response in the endocrine system. The various glands of the endocrine system communicate with each other by releasing hormones. Hormones are relatively large molecules that in many ways are analogous to neuro-

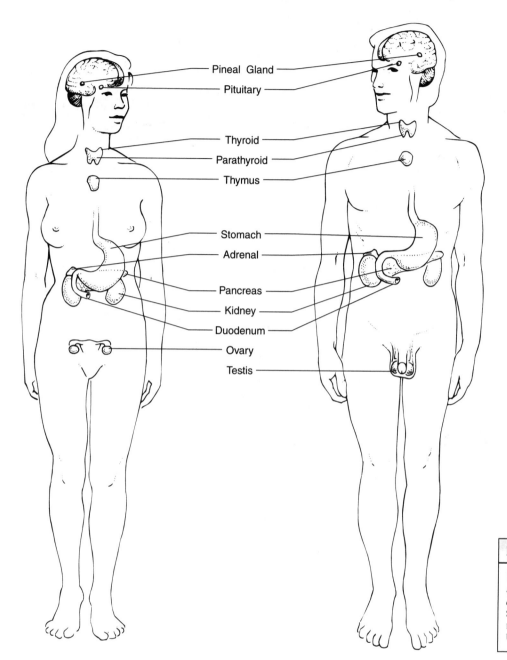

Pineal Gland
Pituitary

Thyroid
Parathyroid
Thymus

Stomach
Adrenal

Pancreas
Kidney
Duodenum

Ovary
Testis

Figure 4–5

Illustration of the endocrine glands in the body (From *Understanding Stress and Coping* by Smith, ©1992. Reprinted by permission of Prentice-Hall, Inc., Upper Saddle River, NJ.)

transmitter substances, only hormones are bigger and act more slowly. Hormones are released into the bloodstream, travel to their target organ, and exert their effects on the target organ/gland by locking into its respective receptor.

Endocrine System Function

The hypothalamus controls two stress reactivity pathways via its influence on the pituitary and adrenal glands. During stress, the hypothalamus secretes certain types of hormones (corticotroponin-releasing factor; CRF) into the bloodstream that activate the pituitary gland, which in turn secretes other hormones (adrenocorticotropic hormone; ACTH) that activate the adrenal gland. This pathway is referred to as the hypothalamic-pituitary-adrenal axis, or the HPA pathway. The adrenal gland secretes hormones, most notably the glucocorticoids. The glucocorticoids have widespread effects, including providing fuel for the fight-or-flight response, increasing blood sugar, mobilizing free fatty acids, decreasing the number of lymphocytes from other glands, and increasing blood pressure. It has been suggested that excessive activation of the HPA pathway has adverse effects on health. For example, the mobilization of free fatty acids has been associated with clogged arteries: decreasing the number of lymphocytes decreases the effectiveness of the immune system.

An additional stress reactivity pathway is more direct and involves activation of the adrenal gland by nerve fiber rather than by hormone release. Information is transmitted much more rapidly via nerve fibers than by hormones in the blood. This second stress reactivity pathway begins in the hypothalamus, which activates the adrenal gland directly. The adrenal gland secretes adrenaline and noradrenaline (also known as epinephrine and norepinephrine, respectively). When released by an endocrine gland (as opposed to the CNS or PNS), these substances are referred to as hormones. Adrenaline in particular serves to produce an effect virtually identical to that produced by direct nervous system stimulation (stimulation from the sympathetic nervous system, for example) with the exception that the response begins twenty to thirty seconds later and lasts considerably longer (ten times longer). Some of the most exciting and innovative research in the area of stress physiology is in the growing field of psychoneuroimmunology, which involves the study of the effects of psychological processes (i.e., stress) on the immune neuro-endocrine network.

STRUCTURE AND FUNCTION OF THE IMMUNE SYSTEM

The immune system protects the body from harmful substances that invade the body from outside (e.g., viruses, bacteria) or that are created internally by the body (e.g., mutant cells). The immune system is finely calibrated to produce a response of precise amplitude and duration to match the strength of the invading substance. Exposure to both short-term and chronic stressors disrupts the equilibrium of the immune system and ultimately can make the body more vulnerable to infection and disease. The brief review of the immune system presented in the following section is drawn largely from Boryensenko, (1987).

Immune System Structure

The body has many protective mechanisms, but the immune system is truly unique because its response can be very specific. The immune system is composed of two primary organs, the thymus and the bursa. These organs produce T-lymphocytes and B-lymphocytes, respectively, which are two of the important types of cells necessary to mount an attack on harmful substances in the body. Because they produce lymphocytes, the thymus and bursa are called lymphoid organs. Lymphocytes are the cells that permit the immune system to respond in a highly specific manner to particular substances that it recognizes as foreign to the body. Both types of lymphocytes require prior exposure to the antigen in order to make the highly specific and selective response against foreign invaders. This requirement accounts for the reason that children tend to get many colds and viruses, whereas adults are more resistant. During initial exposure to a virus, the lymphocytes become sensitized to the invading antigen. This process of sensitization allows the lymphocytes to recognize and resist the invader in future encounters, so that a person gradually develops "immunity" to a great many different strains of viruses.

Another important cell type produced by the immune system is the natural killer (NK) cell. As you might guess from the name, NK cells act to destroy cells that have been invaded by a foreign substance, including virally infected cells and certain tumor cells. NK cells work in a more general way than the T- and B-lymphocytes. Because the NK cells' response to invader cells is very general rather than specific, they do not need any prior exposure with the invading cell to be able to mount an attack against the invaders.

Immune System Function

The hallmarks of the immune system's ability to distinguish self from nonself are its diversity, specificity, and memory. Diversity is exemplified by the vast array of foreign substances to which the immune system responds. The response to subsequent encounters with the same foreign substance (antigen) is more rapid and potent than the first, demonstrating the specificity and memory of the immune system. The immune system is finely calibrated to continuously protect the body from foreign substances that invade the body from outside (exogenous antigens), as well as from foreign substances actually produced by the body itself (endogenous antigens). Table 4–2 illustrates the problems that might arise when the immune system is not functioning properly.

Since the immune system is precisely calibrated, disruption in its equilibrium (such as that caused by stress) can bring the organism closer towards disease. The table illustrates that a suppressed immune system makes the body not only more susceptible to infection from outside bacteria and viruses but also less able to destroy mutant cells, such as cancer, within the body. Similarly, an overactive immune system results in allergic responses and can lead to autoimmune disorders, whereby the immune system turns and attacks the body as if it were a foreign substance. In AIDS, for example, certain cells of the immune system itself are mistakenly targeted for destruction, thereby weakening the immune system in general and making a person much more susceptible to secondary diseases. Numerous studies suggest that stress can cause an imbalance in immune system activity in any of these four quadrants. Table 4–2 illustrates different types of health problems that may arise when the immune system is either overactive (makes too great a response to the antigen) or underactive (fails to make a strong enough response to the antigen). Antigens from the environment can invade our body (exogenous) or can be produced within the body itself (endogenous).

Immune System Measurement

Because stress can adversely affect immune system functioning and therefore make a person much more vulnerable to infection and disease, measurement of immune system integrity has become an important concern among stress researchers. Sev-

TABLE 4–2.   PATTERNS OF IMMUNE SYSTEM DYSFUNCTION

	Immune Activity	
	Overactivity	**Underactivity**
Exogenous antigen	Allergy	Infection
Endogenous antigen	Autoimmune	Cancer

Source: Boryensenko (1987), by permission of the Society of Behavioral Medicine.

eral key measurement procedures have been employed to assess the extent to which stress disrupts immune system functioning. *Skin-testing for delayed hypersensitivity* is a commonly used technique whereby a person is exposed to known antigens at a standard dose and then the extent of immune response is measured. The inability to react to a battery of antigens is termed **anergy.** Anergy reflects the fact that the immune system is in a hyporeactive state, meaning that the immune system is not being reactive enough; it is not attacking the antigens with normal strength. Anergy is associated with a variety of congenital deficiencies (those that exist at birth) and acquired (occur after birth) immunological deficiencies. AIDS patients, for example, frequently suffer from anergy.

Another common measure of immune system status is the *helper/suppressor cell ratio* of the T-lymphocytes. Ordinarily there are twice as many helper cells as suppressor cells; however, in many immunodeficiencies, the ratio is altered or even reversed. *Assays for lymphocyte activation* involve exposing a blood sample to a variety of antigens and quantifying the reaction of various lymphocytes. For example, natural killer (NK) cell activity is assayed by exposing the NK cells to chromium-labeled tumor cells (the chromium, which is radioactive, is bound to the tumor cells). The amount of radioactive chromium released after exposure to the NK is directly proportional to the number of tumor cells killed.

Immune System Functioning, Stress, and Health Outcomes

When measuring the effects of stress on immune system functioning, it is best to use several different measures of immune functioning. Kiecolt-Glaser and Glaser (1987), for example, reviewed data from several studies that used multiple measures of immune system function and concluded that commonplace stressful events are associated with transient impairments in immune functioning. Studies using medical students as subjects revealed significant declines in NK cell activity during final exams. Similarly, blood samples taken while medical students took an exam revealed a significantly lower percentage of helper T-lymphocytes related to a blood sample from these same students taken one month prior to the exam. The fact that the authors used two different measures of immune system functioning and the fact that the findings were replicated across several studies are strong evidence that "routine" stressors can have measurable effects on the immune system. However, the extent to which transient changes in immune functioning are related to health outcomes in humans is as yet unclear.

Animal studies, which examine the effects of more intense stressors than those we can use with humans, provide some of our best support for the link between stress, immune system changes, and changes in health status. Tobach & Bloch (1958) reported that the stress of overcrowding significantly reduced the survival time of mice that were exposed to acute tuberculosis infection. Since then, numerous studies have demonstrated a causal relationship between physical stressors and physical disease in animals. Shavit and Martin (1987) report that exposing rats to relatively long periods of intermittent footshock stress (shocking the feet of rats) both suppressed immune function and enhanced tumor growth. These and other studies suggest that under specified conditions, animals exposed to physical stressors exhibit both disturbed immune function and, in the long term, a higher incidence of disease (e.g., tumor growth). It is important to note that whether or not a stressor leads to physical disease depends on the type of stressor and the way that the stressor is presented. In the example of footshock stress and tumor growth, the parameters of the stressor, such as how frequently it was presented and how long the session lasted, influenced whether or not changes in tumor growth were observed.

Careful examination of some of the *short-term* effects of stress has allowed re-searchers to increase dramatically our understanding of how stress affects brain chemistry, systems of bodily functioning (e.g., endocrine and immune systems), and behavior. One well documented short-term effect of footshock stress is to produce a phenomenon known as **stress-induced analgesia (SIA).** Analgesia refers to a re-duced sensitivity to pain; thus, SIA is defined as an increase in pain tolerance that occurs in response to specific stressors. In the remainder of this section, we discuss neurotransmitters in the brain that produce the analgesia, and we give some exam-ples of the behavioral significance of SIA. A detailed description of the complex rela-tionship between SIA and immune functioning is provided in the box on page 86.

The analgesia produced by footshock occurs because **endogenous opiates** (natu-rally occurring opiatelike molecules) are released in the brain in response to this type of stressor. The general term for the endogenous opiates is *endorphins*, reflecting the fact that they are endogenous (endo) and morphinelike (orphin). The endor-phins are a recently discovered neurotransmitter system in the brain. Drugs such as codeine, morphine, and heroin, which are administered exogenously (enter the body from outside), are made from the opium poppy and interact with the endorphin re-ceptors to produce their effects. People generally take these drugs to relieve pain or to get "high." Thus, opiate molecules produce two major effects on the body, whether they are released endogenously (e.g., endorphins) or are administered ex-ogenously (e.g., morphine or heroin injection). These two effects are analgesia (re-duced pain sensitivity) and euphoria (strong pleasant emotions).

Given that we typically associate stress with feelings of anxiety and apprehen-sion, it may seem paradoxical that stress would produce analgesia and euphoria. One example of euphoria associated with stress is "runners' high," which refers to the experience of euphoria experienced by well-trained runners after a vigorous workout. The euphoria is due to the stress-induced release of endorphins in the brain (i.e., the physical stress produced by running triggers the release of endor-phins, resulting in a feeling of euphoria).

SIA may help explain a number of other behavioral and physiological effects of stress. The sensation-seeking behavior described in Chapter 1 may be maintained, in part, by the reinforcing effects of physiological arousal, particularly the reinforcing effects of endorphin-release in the brain. Acupuncture, a procedure that has been used for hundreds of years in China as an analgesic during surgery, exerts its effects by activating the endogenous opiate neurotransmitter system. During the acupunc-ture procedure, long, slender needles are inserted into specific spots on the body and then gently manipulated. For many years Westerners dismissed acupuncture as a hoax. Now, however, acupuncture is an increasingly accepted adjunct in the treat-ment of various pain problems and as an analgesic during surgery.

Researchers have gained a detailed understanding of the physiological processes that account for SIA and have begun to apply our knowledge of the endogenous opiate neurotransmitter in a variety of medical conditions in which pain is a primary symp-tom. With the biological basis of the phenomenon revealed, acupuncture, "runners' high," and the like are no longer associated with quackery. Yet for many people, the idea that stress could induce both analgesia and euphoria remains paradoxical.

Many people speculate regarding the functional significance of SIA (i.e., what is the adaptive function of an endogenous opiate system that is activated by stress?). From an evolutionary perspective, SIA may not be as paradoxical a phenomenon as it might appear at first glance. SIA may be an adaptive response by the body to make painful physical stressors easier to cope with. Similarly, perhaps the euphoric by-products of SIA also serve an adaptive function by positively reinforcing the escape behavior necessary in many situations in which there is a threat to one's physical well-being.

$\mathscr{W}$HAT TYPES OF STRESSFUL CONDITIONS
LEAD TO POOR HEALTH?

The main text alludes to two important points that warrant further discussion regarding the various effects of procedures used to produce stress-induced analgesia (SIA). First, it is important to remember that the short-term and long-term effects of stress on the body are often very different (e.g., short-term changes in immune function do not necessarily lead to long-term changes in health status). Second, subtle changes in the nature of the stressor can produce profound differences in the physiological response to the stressor. For example, a stressor such as footshock presented intermittently for a long period of time leads to an increase in tumor growth, whereas continuous shock for a shorter period of time has actually been associated with lower tumor growth.

In this sidebar section we elaborate on the complex effects of footshock stress to illustrate the intricacies involved in sorting out the relationship between stress and illness. The evidence is overwhelming at this point that there is a link between stress and disease. The question that researchers ask today is "Under what types of stressful conditions does stress lead to poorer health?"

There are a host of different stressful procedures that might be used in the laboratory to study the stress/illness relationship; footshock stress is used simply because it is a convenient (and fascinating) example. In the main text we learned that footshock stress is one of a number of procedures that cause SIA. We specifically discussed the role of the endorphins (endogenous opiates) as mediators of the SIA phenomenon. It turns out, however, that footshock stress can result in SIA without activating the endogenous opiate pathways. Whether stress produces analgesic effects via the endogenous opiate pathways or some other pathway (e.g., dopamine pathways) seems to be related to whether or not the stressor is linked to the long-term development of disease. In the main text we noted that long periods of intermittent shock were associated with increased tumor growth, whereas short periods of continuous shock actually made the organism more resistant to disease. Could it be that these differences in susceptibility to disease following stress are due to the differential activation of opiate versus nonopiate neurotransmitter systems? Shavit & Martin (1987) suggest this very explanation, and they provide interesting findings to back up their speculations. For example, rats in which morphine was directly administered exhibit significant decreases in their resistance to tumor challenge (morphine activates many of the same receptors activated by the release of the endogenous opiates). With both SIA procedures and direct morphine administration, the decrease in tumor resistance is in direct proportion to the NK cell suppressant effects of these procedures. This relationship is important because it demonstrates that the endogenous and exogenous opiate molecules both seem to be acting through similar mechanisms. Moreover, epidemiological studies reveal that morphine and heroin addicts develop cancers at a significantly higher rate than do the rest of the population (even when other risk factors such as smoking are controlled for).

In summary, a good deal of evidence now indicates that activation of the endogenous opiate neurotransmitter system (via opiate mediated SIA or direct administration of opiate substances) produces immunosuppressive effects that are linked to changes in health status.

STRESS AND ILLNESS RELATIONSHIPS

What is our experimental evidence that a causal relationship exists between stress and illness in *humans*? Remember, there are many ethical and practical constraints that make it difficult to directly assess the relationship between stress and illness in humans. Most of the early attempts to address this question were designed simply to test the hypothesis that a relationship exists between exposure to stressful life events and some indicator of health status (Dohrenwend & Dohrenwend, 1981). Much of the research was correlational in nature. Volunteers would fill out a questionnaire (e.g., Social Readjustment Rating Scale), asking them about life stressors that they had experienced, and these scores were then correlated with the subjects' reports of illness. In general, the correlation between major life events and *onset* of illness is relatively small. Recently, more complex models and methodologies have been employed to better assess the extent of the stress-illness relationship in humans. We will elaborate on these models in Chapter 5.

The correlational data in humans and the animal data converge to present a convincing picture that stress plays an important role in the development and exacerbation of illness in humans. Given that the stress and illness link is genuine and substantial, a reasonable follow-up question might be "Is stress-related illness an inevitable consequence of modern life?" One of the pioneers in the stress field, Hans Selye, seems to answer yes to this question. Selye proposed a three-stage model known as the *General Adaptation Syndrome* to describe the body's response to stress. He developed his model after observing that medical patients, in addition to the specific symptoms associated with their illness, exhibited a generalized pattern of symptoms that appeared consistently regardless of the diagnosis. This "syndrome of just being sick" was tested in the laboratory with animals. Different groups of mice were injected with various toxins that affected different organ systems, yet all the animals developed a stereotyped syndrome of symptoms. Moreover, this generalized response developed to a wide range of stressors, including heat, cold, and infection.

The three stages identified by Selye were alarm, resistance, and exhaustion. The alarm stage reflects the body's initial response to the stressor. A generalized state of arousal is produced, which is reflected in measurable changes in most body systems. In the resistance stage, the arousal is channeled more specifically into a limited number of body systems. These organ systems mobilize the body for more specific and precise response to the stressor. This response marks the body's attempt to adapt to the stressor via activation of the body system that is most efficient at responding to a particular stressor (e.g., immune system activation in the face of invading microbes). Chronic overactivation of body systems, however, leads to breakdowns and subsequent illness and disease. In the face of extreme unremitting stress, the body's resources may become depleted, and a stage of exhaustion sets in. Unable to resist any longer, the channeling of arousal to specific organ systems gives way to a nonspecific, generalized response that characterized the alarm stage. Major-organ breakdowns occur, and then death follows. This three-stage process involves adaptation of the body to the stressor but adaptation comes with a significant cost to one's health. Indeed, Selye referred to the stress-related illnesses as "diseases of adaptation."

Levine (1986) categorizes Selye's model as an "open-looped model of stress." Open-looped models view stress as a static system. The harmful effects of stress are thought to arise from gradual erosion of tissue and cellular integrity as stressors act cumulatively on a passive organism. Levine describes Selye's model as being analogous to a bank account ledger, where the consequences of stress have additive effects as the result of continually overdrawing one's energy resources.

"Closed-loop models of stress," however, view stress in the context of a systems model. A systems approach suggests that dynamic feedback patterns govern a wide spectrum of behavior and reflect the organism's capacity for order and stability. Stress in this model may be resolved or unresolved. These two types of stress are differentiated on the basis of their potentially progressive effects on the disorganization of the CNS. Unresolved stress occurs when equilibrium is not restored and therefore unstable, maladaptive states develop, much as Selye described in his GAS model. Far more common, however, is the experience of resolved stress in which activation is followed by a return to equilibrium. Feedback patterns among the various systems described (e.g., immune, endocrine) work together to promote order and stability in the organism in the face of a stressful stimulus. Activation of these feedback loops is not an "illness of adaptation" that progressively takes its toll on the body, but rather the activation reflects the natural resiliency of the human organism.

The development of stress-related physical disorders seems to be associated with stress levels that exceed the body's natural resiliency to "bounce back." In the following chapter, we will discuss a number of specific physical disorders, including ulcers, headaches, heart disease, and cancer, all of which are thought to be caused by or made worse by stress. We will build on the previous discussion of the nervous system, endocrine system, and immune system function to explain how stress may cause or exacerbate these disorders. We will also examine why some people seem to be more resilient/susceptible to these disorders than others.

*S*UMMARY

Walter Cannon first coined the term **fight-or-flight response** to describe the full-scale mobilization of bodily resources to respond to a threat to physical safety. This is an adaptive response from an evolutionary standpoint in that most stressors in our evolutionary past were threats to physical safety. In modern times, many threats that we face are symbolic in nature (e.g., threats to self-esteem), and circumstances often do not allow us to take problem-focused fight-or-flight action to short-circuit these stressors. Constant exposure to such conditions results in chronic maladaptive physiological arousal that likely contributes to stress-related illnesses such as headaches and coronary heart disease, and also affects the course of such illness as cancer and AIDS. This chapter covers basic anatomy and physiology relevant to understanding the relationship between stress and illness.

1. *Division of the Nervous System.* There are two major divisions of the nervous system: the central nervous system, comprising the brain and spinal cord; and the peripheral nervous system, which includes all other parts of the nervous system. The peripheral nervous system is divided into the somatic nervous system, which regulates voluntary motor movements (muscles); and the autonomic nervous system, which regulates functions that operate automatically without conscious control. There are two divisions of the autonomic nervous system: the sympathetic nervous system, which is activated by the hypothalamus and prepares the body for fight or flight; and the parasympathetic nervous system, which conserves and stores energy.

2. *Structure and Function of the Central Nervous System* (CNS). The brain is composed of three concentric layers. Beginning at the base of the brain, the layers are the hindbrain, midbrain, and forebrain. The forebrain contains many structures crucial to initiating the stress response, including the cerebral cortex (cognitive appraisal), basal ganglia (motor control), limbic system (emotional regulation), thalamus (directing incoming sensory information to higher brain centers), and the hypothalamus (initiating the two stress-reactivity pathways). The reticular activation system (RAS) is a weblike net of fibers that begins in the hindbrain, passes through the midbrain, and projects to the forebrain and activates the brain during stress. Chronic activation of the RAS is associated with brain damage and with potentially increased vulnerability to disease. The spinal cord is a conduit for information. The brain sends signals through

the spinal cord to the peripheral muscles and organs, and information from the peripheral muscles and organs pass through the spinal cord to the brain.

3. *Neurons and Neurotransmitters in the* CNS. Neurons are similar to all other cells in the nervous system but have a few additional specialized features. Neurons have short, branchy extensions called dendrites that extend from the cell body, and one long extension called an axon that allows the neurons to communicate with each other via an electrical-chemical process. The synapse is the space between the axon of one neuron and the dendrites (or cell body) of another neuron. Neurotransmitters are chemicals that are contained in vesicles at the end of the axon in the axon's terminal button. One neuron communicates with another when an action potential sends a wave of electrical energy down the axon and forces the neurotransmitter substance into the synapse. The neurotransmitter crosses the synapse and interacts with receptors on the dendrite of the adjacent neuron, causing small waves of electrical energy to pass up the dendrite towards the axon. With enough stimulation to its receptors, the adjacent neuron will "fire," sending a single large wave of electrical energy down its axon, and the process continues from one neuron (or from groups of neurons) to the next. Each neurotransmitter fits into its own receptor in a lock-and-key fashion. The neurotransmitter is the key that turns on the small waves of electrical energy when it interacts with its receptor. There are many different drugs that can either mimic or block the effect of a neurotransmitter. The neurotransmitter system most relevant to anxiety is GABA, which is concentrated in the limbic system and exerts an inhibitory (calming) influence. Valium and Librium are antianxiety drugs (benzodiazepines) that interact with the GABA receptor to facilitate the effects of GABA.

4. *Endocrine System: Structure and Function.* The endocrine system is a complex system of glands (e.g., hypothalamus, pituitary, adrenal) primarily located in the periphery. The glands interact with each other and influence other body systems by releasing hormones. The hypothalamus initiates two stress-reactivity pathways. The hypothalamic-pituitary-adrenal axis (HPA pathway) is the slow reactivity pathway. When an event is appraised as stressful, the hypothalamus secretes a hormone (CRF) that activates the pituitary, which in turn secretes a hormone (ACTH) that activates the adrenal gland. The adrenal gland secretes various hormones, including the corticoids, which fuel the fight-or-flight response. Excessive release of the corticoids is associated with decreased production of lymphocytes in the immune system, increased buildup of plaque on the lining of the arteries, and increased blood pressure.

5. *Immune System: Structure and Function.* The immune system is composed of two primary organs. The thymus produces T-lymphocytes, and the bursa produces B-lymphocytes. The immune system functions to protect the body from harmful exogenous and endogenous substances called antigens (viruses, bacteria, mutant cells). Lymphocytes permit the immune system to respond in a highly specific way to the antigens that it recognizes as foreign to the body. Natural killer cells (NK) work in a more general way to destroy cells that have been invaded by a foreign substance. The immune system, which is characterized by its diversity, specificity, and memory, responds to numerous foreign substances, and subsequent responses to foreign substances are more rapid and potent than the initial response. The immune system is generally a highly calibrated system that responds with precision, but factors such as stress can alter its response to make it overreactive or underreactive. Dysregulation of the immune system is associated with various types of illness and disease. Immune system functioning is measured with skin tests for delayed hypersensitivity, helper/suppressor cell ratio, and assays for lymphocyte activation. Numerous

studies have demonstrated a relationship between stress and changes in the various measures of immune system functioning. Recently, studies have been able to demonstrate a relationship between stress, changes in immune system functioning, and more long-term health outcomes.

6. *Stress and Illness Relationships.* Selye was one of the pioneers in the stress and illness research arena. He identified a three-stage (alarm, resistance, exhaustion) general adaptation syndrome (GAS) that all organisms go through when facing a severe physical stressor. The body mobilizes its resources in a fight-or-flight type of response during the alarm stage. If the stressor remains unresolved, the bodily mobilization plateaus in a resistance stage. Finally, if the stressor is not resolved, the body "gives up" in the exhaustion stage, leading to organ failure and death. Most stressors faced by humans are not severe, chronic physical stressors but rather are transient physical stressors or symbolic stressors. For these types of stressors, Selye's open-looped model of stress, which emphasizes stress taking an ever-increasing toll on the body over time, is probably not accurate. A closed-loop model in which the body's natural resiliency allows for adaptation to stress, and whereby the body generally returns to a state of equilibrium after exposure to a stressor, may better characterize the body's response to most everyday stressors.

$\mathcal{K}$EY TERMS

action potential   Wave of electrical activity that "fires" down an axon as a result of a rapid internal change from a negative (resting) potential to a positive (action) potential.

anergy   Inability of the immune system to react and attack antigens with normal strength.

antigens   Viruses, bacteria, mutant cells, and the like that act as "foreign invaders" of the body. Exogenous antigens are foreign substances that invade the body from outside, and endogenous antigens are foreign substances that the body itself produces.

autoimmune disorders   Disorders of the immune system in which the body does not recognize its own cells and mistakenly reacts to its own tissues as if they were antigens.

autonomic nervous system (ANS)   Division of the peripheral nervous system that deals with the regulation of the internal environment, over which we have little voluntary control (e.g., respiration). The ANS is divided into the sympathetic and the parasympathetic nervous systems.

axon   Long projection on a neuron that carries an action potential away from the body of the neuron.

benzodiazepines   Class of man-made drugs (e.g., valium) that are designed to reduce anxiety.

central nervous system   Primary division of the nervous system, which is composed of the brain and the spinal cord.

cerebral cortex   Outer layer of neural tissue that covers the cerebrum, where the majority of neural processing occurs.

closed-looped models of stress   Systems approaches that hold that feedback governs many behaviors and also reflects the capacity for equilibrium.

dendrites   Short, branchlike projection of the neuron that carries impulses inward from an adjacent cell.

endocrine system   Complex system of glands, located primarily in the periphery, that releases hormones that have an effect on another part of the body into the bloodstream.

endogenous   Naturally occurring within the body.

endogenous opiates   Naturally occurring opiatelike molecules called endorphins that produce two major effects: reduced pain sensitivity (analgesia) and strong pleasant emotions (euphoria).

"fight-or-flight" response   Body's general activation, due to physiological changes initiated by the sympathetic nervous system (e.g., increase in heart rate, blood glucose level), which prepares it either to attack a stressor head-on or to retreat quickly.

forebrain   Outermost layer of the brain; its key structures include the cerebral cortex, limbic system, basal ganglia, thalamus, and hypothalamus.

gamma-amniobutyric acid (GABA).   Most common inhibitory neurotransmitter, which is an important mediator of the subjective feeling of anxiety during the stress response; GABA receptors are most concentrated in the limbic system, the part of the brain that regulates emotional behavior.

hindbrain   Anatomical division of the brain located in the core of the brain.

hormones   Chemical substances that, like neurotransmitters, are produced by one part of the body and have an effect on another part; they are larger and act more slowly than neurotransmitters.

hypothalamic-pituitary-adrenal axis   Also known as the HPA pathway, it refers to the "slow" stress reactivity pathway of the endocrine system.

hypothalamus   Structure located in the forebrain that regulates fighting, fleeing, feeding, and mating, primarily through activation of the autonomic nervous system.

immune system   System that protects the body from infection through recognition and destruction of cells that are foreign to the body.

lymphocyte   Specialized white blood cell that has a significant role in the immune system because of its ability to recognize and destroy cells foreign to the body.

midbrain   Layer of the brain that largely surrounds the hindbrain.

natural killer cells   Cells that destroy cells that have been infected by a foreign substance; they do not require previous exposure to the antigen to initiate their immune response.

nervous system   Highly complex system of cells, tissues, and organs that control bodily actions and reactions via signals received from any part of the body; the signals are then relayed to the brain and spinal cord, where they are interpreted, and a signal is sent back out to the organs and muscles for appropriate action.

neuron   Specialized cell of the central nervous system that is capable of conducting, receiving, and transmitting electrochemical signals.

neurotransmitters   Molecules that are released from active neurons and that influence the activity of other cells by locking onto receptors on adjacent neurons.

open-looped models of stress   Models that view stress as a fixed system in which continual stress adds up and compounds existing problems.

parasympathetic nervous system   Division of the autonomic nervous system that works to conserve the body's energy stores (anabolic).

peripheral nervous system   Primary division of the nervous system that is located outside of the skull and spine; it is divided into the somatic nervous system and the autonomic nervous system.

receptors   Protein molecules that are located in or on a cell membrane; they cause changes in neurons when neurotransmitters bind to them (the neurotransmitter fits into the receptor in "lock-and-key" fashion).

somatic nervous system   Division of the peripheral nervous system involved with the regulation of voluntary movements (e.g., walking, dancing).

stress-induced analgesia (SIA)   Increase in pain tolerance that occurs in response to specific stressors.

sympathetic nervous system   Division of the autonomic nervous system that prepares the body for action ("fight or flight") when presented with a stressor; it consumes energy (catabolic).

synaptic cleft   Space that separates the dendrite of one neuron from the axon or cell body of another neuron.

CHAPTER 5
Stress and Illness

Walt Kersey works as an air traffic controller (ATC) at one of the busiest airports in the world. It is a high-pressure, high-stakes assignment that requires supreme concentration and skill. Initially, Walt found the job demanding, even exhilarating. He was quite competent at his job, but after just three years, he developed an ulcer and high blood pressure. One morning he drove to the airport through a heavy fog and knew that making visual contact with the planes on the ground would be difficult that morning. This was nothing new for Walt; he had been working the tower for twelve years and had come to accept changing weather conditions as part of his job. Usually the early morning fog burned off well before the flow of air traffic picked up in mid-morning. On this day, however, the humidity in the air was heavy, and the fog clung thickly to the ground. Walt's level of concentration went up several notches (as did his heart rate and other autonomic functions) as the air traffic picked up throughout the morning and the fog refused to budge. He made frequent contact with the pilots on the ground, constantly noting their position on the tarmac and runways. He could not see the planes on the ground, so he knew that the incoming pilots would not be able to see them either. The ground fog made it increasingly difficult to track the ground positions of outgoing flights and to track the "blips" in the air at the same time. He alone was responsible for the air traffic on runways 5 and 6, and right now he concentrated on preventing one plane from landing while another was crossing the runway to prepare for takeoff.

Walt stayed completely focused on the positions of his planes, smoothly guiding their takeoffs and landings and acting as a traffic cop at the busy intersections on the tarmac. But the smooth rhythm of his routine was broken when one of the planes coming *in for a landing reported trouble with its landing gear. The sequencing of the landings had to be disrupted as Walt instructed the pilot to circle the airport again and follow standard procedures for tracing and fixing the source of the problem. He stayed completely focused on his task, but he could feel the tension ripple through the tower as other ATCs became aware that he had a problem situation. Walt's supervisor came over to help realign the landing sequence and monitor the progress of the malfunctioning plane's repair efforts. So far this was a fairly routine incident that plane crews correct in time to land in the next pass of the airport. However, if the plane had to attempt a belly landing, air traffic would have to be diverted and emergency crews sent to the runway, and there was a high probability that there would be injury or loss of life. Walt knew all this, but he was smooth and experienced. His heart was beating quickly, but he appeared cool as a cucumber. Suddenly, the bright light of a fireball caught his peripheral vision, and a cold panic gripped him as he heard from behind a terrific crash.*

In that instant Walt's heart was in his throat, and he was soaked in his own sweat. The tight knot he always had in his stomach became a stranglehold. He quickly checked the position of his planes as frantic calls from airborne pilots came in, confirming what he knew without looking; an incoming plane had crashed and burned on the runway parallel to his own on the other side of the tower. In the first seconds after the realization that a crash had occurred, Walt wanted only to make sure none of his planes were involved. In moments he verified that his planes were safe, and he was overwhelmed by feelings of both relief and guilt. Jim Keaton, an ATC for almost as long as Walt, was the controller in charge of Flights 603 and 239, which were now burning uncontrollably on runway 2. Having stabilized the positions in his own airspace, Walt glanced over his shoulder and came face to face with the gruesome realities of the cost of a simple lapse in concentration: two planes were in flames, shrouded in an eerie fog, the nose of one plane embedded under the wing of the second plane. A man engulfed in flames was beating himself wildly as he writhed on the ground. Walt knew that debris, including bodies and body parts, were strewn across the runway and infield. For the first time that morning, he was grateful that the fog obscured his view. As Walt turned back to his own station, he could feel pangs of pain in his abdomen and a tightening in his chest as he fought to suppress the nausea swelling up inside him.

In Chapter 1, we noted that for humans, a stressful event does not merely exist in the present. Remembering past events and anticipating future events give stressful events an opportunity to impact us long after the event itself has subsided. No one embodied that paradox more fully than Walt. The events that transpired this day haunted him in his dreams. Moreover, he did not work a day without worrying that these events might be repeated. In the months and years that followed, Walt would develop a variety of physical disorders, and many people who heard Walt's story were drawn to the conclusion that his stressful job was largely to blame.

The reader who assumes that Walt's health problems are more or less the result of the stressful work environment is probably correct. The quandary lies in calculating "more or less." Is stress the primary contributor or only a minor contributor to Walt's health problems? Many people believe that ATC work is associated with such high levels of stress that in the long run, anyone in that job would suffer ill effects from stress both in terms of performance and of health. This notion is reflected in federal law (Public Law 92-297) that requires ATCs to retire at an earlier age and with fewer years of service than other federal employees in order to protect the ATCs from the negative effects of stress. On the other hand, is it possible that Walt's stressful job would have little effect on his health if it were not for some genetic predisposition or dispositional coping style that made him especially vulnerable to the effects of stress? This idea has some merit, since several studies suggest that, as a group, ATCs do not experience their jobs as any more stressful or exhibit substantially more health problems that do people in other jobs (e.g., Melton, McKenzie, Wicks, Saldivar, 1978).

In general, it has been quite common for different studies to reach different conclusions regarding the extent to which stress influences the development of various health problems, and studies examining ATCs have been no exception. The relationship between stress and illness has proved to be a difficult and sometimes controversial area of study. However, some points of general agreement have emerged over the course of literally thousands of studies by researchers from many different scientific disciplines. Namely, most researchers agree that stress is an influential variable in the development and maintenance of many physical problems. The "more or less" problem remains controversial and should be examined carefully because of its ramifications for personal lifestyle decisions (e.g., job choices, treatment choices, etc.). For example, we could not in good conscience recommend that Walt quit his job because of its stressfulness because we do not know enough yet to make predictions about how important stress is, or will become, to a *single individual's* health outcomes.

In this chapter we will sift through some of the complexities involved in assessing the stress-illness relationship and provide a broad understanding of the difficulties involved in this type of research. The experimental evidence establishing the stress-illness relationship and some of the methodological problems in this area of research will provide a point of departure for reviewing specific health problems. A review of the evidence linking stress to several different types of health problems will illustrate how evidence converges to support the stress-illness connection and will reveal how much farther we need to go to answer the "more or less" question regarding the extent to which stress is associated with the development of specific disorders.

EXPERIMENTAL EVIDENCE ESTABLISHING A STRESS-ILLNESS RELATIONSHIP

We noted earlier that Walter Cannon was one of the first people to highlight the importance of symbolic stressors (threats to one's self-esteem) in triggering the fight-or-flight response. He inferred that changes in sympathetic nervous system activity triggered in the fight-or-flight response resulted in illness or disease, but he did not empirically test his idea. In the previous chapter we also mentioned that the best evidence available for establishing the link between stress and illness comes from studies evaluating the effects of physical stressors on animals. You may recall that Hans Selye exposed animals to severe physical stressors and observed a general adaptation syndrome (GAS) characterized by gradual deterioration in bodily function that eventually resulted in death. To move forward in our understanding of the stress-illness relationship, a procedure to assess for the purely *psychological* effects of stress needed to be developed.

Jay Weiss and his colleagues conducted some of the most systematic experimental research in this area (Weiss, 1971, a,b,c). He refined a test procedure that separated the effects of the physical stressor per se from the psychological aspects of the stressor. For example, in the foot shock procedure mentioned in the previous chapter, we did not discuss whether it was the shock itself that was related to tumor growth or whether it was the fear of being shocked. Weiss's procedure allows us to evaluate the physical effects of the shock independently of the psychological effects of the shocks.

The general procedure that Weiss developed involved testing rat triplets in one of three different conditions. Using triplets ensured that any differences that might be observed in the rats later were not the result of differences in the genetic makeup of the rats. Each rat was placed in its own experimental chamber, and separate electrodes were attached to each rat's tail. The electrodes were capable of delivering an electric shock that the rats would find painful but was not strong enough to cause tissue damage. An illustration of the testing apparatus is presented in Figure 5–1.

Thus far we have described three genetically identical rats being exposed to identical experimental procedures. What follows is a description of the different experimental conditions for the three rats. For Rat Number 1, a tone is sounded that serves as a signal to press the lever or else be shocked. If Rat 1 presses the lever, it avoids the shock, but if it does not respond before a predetermined amount of time has elapsed, a shock is delivered to the tail. Rat 1 is in an **escape/avoidance** condition. The animal can respond during the tone to prevent the shock from being administered (avoid the shock). If the rat fails to respond during the tone, it is shocked and must respond to terminate the shock (escape the shock). The procedure is set up in such a way that occasionally Rat 1 makes a mistake and fails to respond in time to avoid the shock but is able quickly to escape the shock by pressing the lever once the shock begins.

Meanwhile, Rat Number 2 is in an identical chamber with an identical lever. However, its lever is inactive. Pressing the lever has no effect on the shocks. Rat 2 has no prior experience with the lever ever being active. In this procedure, Rat 2 is experimentally "yoked" to Rat 1. Whenever Rat 1 is shocked, Rat 2 is also shocked, a procedure that is referred to as a "yoked-control" condition. This procedure insures that

Figure 5–1

Typical experimental apparatus in Weiss's studies. The rat on the left (Rat 1) can avoid the shock by pressing the lever. The rat in the center (Rat 2) cannot avoid the shock and gets shocked whenever the rat on the left gets shocked. The rat on the right (Rat 3) never receives a shock. The rat in the middle develops the most ulcers. (Weiss, 1977). From *Psychopathology: Experimental Models* © 1977 by Martin E. P. Seligman and Jack Maser. Used with permission of W. H. Freeman and Company.

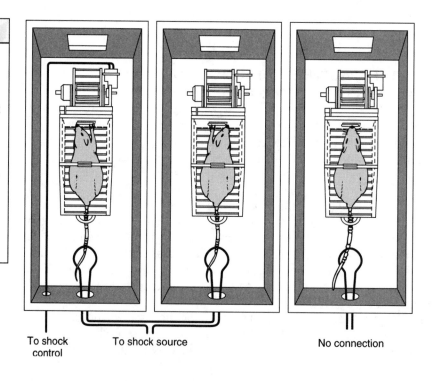

To shock control   To shock source   No connection

both Rat 1 and Rat 2 are exposed to identical physical stressors (they both receive the shocks with the same frequency, intensity, and duration); only the psychological context varies between the two conditions.

Rat 3 is in a "no-shock control" condition. It is treated exactly the same as the other two rats, but it never receives a shock.

Which rat is more likely to develop a physical illness from these procedures, and why? Rat 1 has to pay attention and work hard to avoid the shocks, but at least it has some control over the situation. Rat 2, on the other hand, does not have "work," but occasionally it receives shocks in an unpredictable and uncontrollable manner. It turns out that the extent of physical pathology that results from these three conditions can be summarized as 2 . 1 . 3. The yoked-control condition of Rat 2 produces the most severe physiological symptoms (e.g., ulcers); the escape/avoidance condition of Rat 1 results in moderate levels of ulceration; and the no-shock control condition of Rat 3 provides a baseline to compare the effects of the other two conditions.

The implications of these findings are far-reaching. Although Rats 2 and 1 received identical exposure to the *physical* stressor, they *did not* exhibit the same amount of physical pathology. This result tells us that although the shock itself had adverse effects (since both Rats 1 and 2 developed more ulcers than Rat 3, who received no shocks), the psychological effects of being in the yoked-control condition somehow led to more profound physical pathology. The crucial psychological variable that differed in these two conditions was **controllability** of the stressor. Rat 1 had control over the stressor, whereas Rat 2 had no control. This same type of experiment has been replicated hundreds of times, with many different species, with similar results. In general, the less control that the organism has over a stressor, the more severe the health outcomes; and, conversely, the more control an organism has over a stressor, the better the health outcomes. Interestingly, the researcher who first pioneered this test procedure, Joseph Brady, predicted the opposite relationship. His story is described in the box on page 98.

Weiss was able to demonstrate conclusively that psychological factors affect health outcomes by separating the physical dimensions of the stressor from the psychological dimensions. Note, however, the limitations in our ability to generalize from these findings. We can conclude from Weiss's work that physical stress alone (shock) can cause ulcers (Rat 1) and that physical stress (shock) plus psychological stress (uncontrollability) causes even more ulcers (Rat 2), but we *cannot* conclude that psychological stress alone causes ulcers or other physical impairment. This inability to generalize is problematic because most of the stressors that people face day in and day out are not physical stressors; rather, they are threats to our self-esteem (**symbolic** stressors in Cannon's terminology). For example, on a typical day, we may feel stressed because we want to perform well on a test, make a good impression on a date, or deal with criticism from a boss. But it is difficult to determine conclusively that these types of psychological stressors *cause* illness in humans. When conducting stress research with humans, we cannot control for all relevant confounding variables or employ true experimental designs; therefore, establishing causal relationships between stress and illness in humans has proved difficult.

METHODOLOGICAL ISSUES IN STRESS-ILLNESS RESEARCH

True experimental designs allow us to make inferences about causal relationships between two variables. For example, we might take one thousand people and randomly assign them to one of two groups. If one group was exposed to a known psychological stressor and the other group was not *and* if we were able to hold all other relevant variables constant across groups, we could infer that any differences in health status that

JOSEPH BRADY'S EXECUTIVE MONKEY EXPERIMENT

Joseph Brady preceded Jay Weiss in attempting to separate the effects of physical stressors from psychological stressors on the development of physical illness. Brady believed that psychological stress was a significant factor in illness onset. In particular, he thought that high-powered executives who were constantly pressured by deadlines and decision-making responsibilities were probably very vulnerable to stress-related disorders. For the many reasons cited in the text, however, Brady was unable to test his idea on human subjects. Therefore, he devised an animal model to test his ideas. Brady (1958) tested monkeys in an escape/avoidance procedure that presumably mimicked the essential features of the stress experienced by human executives.

Brady used pairs of monkeys as his subjects. One monkey in each pair was designated the "executive" monkey, and the other monkey was termed the "yoked-control" monkey. Both monkeys were placed in restraining chairs (i.e., they sat in chairs that restricted their movements), and each monkey had access to a lever. The executive monkey could press his lever to prevent the delivery of a painful shock. The other monkey was yoked to the executive monkey in that whenever the executive monkey received a shock, the yoked-control monkey also received a shock. Lever-pressing by the yoked-control monkey had no effect. The escape/avoidance task was arranged so that the shocks were delivered relatively frequently (every twenty seconds) unless the lever was depressed, thereby postponing the delivery of the shock (for one minute). Under these conditions, the executive monkey pressed the lever at very high rates, and both monkeys received relatively few shocks. The yoked-control monkey rarely pressed the lever because doing so had no effect on shock delivery (or anything else). The yoked-control monkey simply was shocked every time the executive monkey failed to press its lever in time to prevent a shock.

During the typical experiment, a six-hour "danger" period during which the escape/avoidance task was in effect alternated with a six-hour break for eating, drinking, and sleeping. This sequence continued around the clock, twenty-four hours a day, for the duration of the experiment. During the six-hour breaks, the two monkeys were treated exactly the same. Thus, both monkeys shared the same shock frequency, shock intensity, and shock duration. They were restrained to the same degree and were treated similarly during the break periods. The two monkeys differed only in that the executive monkey repeatedly had to make decisions and take action to forestall unpleasant events, but the yoked-control monkey did not.

Brady thought that this experimental procedure was a reasonable analogue to real-life executives. The executive monkey was responsible for the welfare of both partners, just as the decisions of an executive at a major corporation affect the welfare of many of his or her coworkers. Of course, with the monkey pairs, it is less likely that the executive monkey "knew" that it was responsible for the yoked-control monkey or that the yoked-control monkey "knew" that the executive monkey's failures to lever-press caused the shocks received by both monkeys. Nevertheless, just as Brady had predicted, within a short time the executive monkeys died of perforated ulcers, whereas the yoked-control monkeys remained healthy. (See Figure 5–2.) This finding is surprising, since, as noted in the text, Weiss and others have conclusively demonstrated that animals in a yoked-control condition—animals that have no control over the stressor (e.g., shocks)—experience the greatest amount of physical pathology.

How can we reconcile the discrepancy between Brady's and Weiss's findings? It turns out that there was a methodological flaw in Brady's experiment. Rather than randomly assigning his monkeys to the two test conditions, he assigned monkeys that were known to respond at higher rates to the executive-monkey condition. Unfortunately, later research revealed that higher rates of responding predispose animals to ulcers (Weiss, 1971). Also, though a red light served as a cue in Brady's experiment to indicate to the executive monkey that it was in a shock-avoidance period, there was nothing to indicate during that period exactly when the shock was coming. Therefore, the executive monkeys had no signal to indicate that their responses would be effective, and they worked much harder than they actually had to in order to avoid the shocks. Uncertainty about whether a coping response is effective seems to increase the risk of ulcer development. We conclude from this finding that control reduces stress to the extent that an individual is sure his or her responses will be effective.

Figure 5–2

The "executive" monkey (left) has learned to press the lever in its left hand, thereby preventing shocks to both animals. The yoked-control monkey (right) has lost interest in its lever, which is a dummy. Only the executive monkeys developed ulcers. (Photograph from Brady, 1958, Walter Reed Army Institute of Research)

developed over time were due to the psychological stressor. It is easy to do this with physical stressors and rats, but it is very hard with people. With people, relevant variables that would have to be held constant would include factors like what the subjects ate and drank, how much sleep they got, how much TV they watched, how much exercise they got, what their work and home environments were like, what their prior health status was, and countless other variables (including genetic makeup) that are related to health. Because it is impossible to control all these variables with human subjects, we must use correlational and quasi-experimental designs. Correlational research assesses the relationship between two variables but does not permit inferences regarding whether one variable causes a change in the other variable. Quasi-experimental designs, such as **retrospective** and **prospective** studies, fall somewhere in between correlational research and true experiments in terms of the inferences that are permitted. In general, quasi-experimental designs are more powerful than correlational designs but are less powerful than true experiments.

In a retrospective study, the experimenter might study a group of people who already have the disorder of interest and might compare them with another group of subjects ("controls") who do not have the disorder to see how the stress levels of the two groups differ. Typically, subjects are asked to report on the frequency and intensity of stressors that they experienced during a period of time prior to being diagnosed with their illness. The Social Readjustment Rating Scale (SRRS) (Holmes & Rahe, 1967) was the first of these types of assessment instruments. Some sample items from the SRRS are presented in Table 5–1.

A problem with the retrospective approach is that people's memories of past stressors may be influenced by the fact that they are sick at the time of questioning. A more rigorous design is the prospective study, in which the experimenter might assess the stress levels and coping styles of a group of healthy subjects and then might track the subjects over time to see whether the assessment instruments can predict who develops a particular disorder and who does not. This type of design also is limiting, since no single study can establish a causal relationship. However, if the results of multiple studies using correlational and quasi-experimental designs converge, reporting similar results, then we can be increasingly confident that stress plays a major role in the development and maintenance of the physical disorders being studied.

Another method for handling the ethical and practical constraints of doing certain types of research with humans is to develop an animal model for the human disorder. Weiss's work with the yoked-control procedure is an example of the use of an animal model to test the stress-illness connection. If we could develop a good animal model to test the effects of purely psychological stressors on animals, we would be able to overcome some of the main obstacles in this area of research. Un-

---

TABLE 5–1.   SAMPLE ITEMS FROM THE SOCIAL READJUSTMENT RATING SCALE

Each life event is given a weighted point value (Life Change Unit) that reflects how much disruption or stress that event caused the person. The original scale consisted of forty-three items. Respondents indicate how many of these events occurred in the last twelve months and then sum up the LIfe Change Units. Higher scores indicate greater vulnerability to the negative physical effects of stress. More recent life-change inventories ask the respondents to appraise the life event as negative or positive.

Life Event	Life Change Units
Death of a spouse	100
Divorce	73
Death of a close family member	63
Marital reconciliation	45
Addition to family	39
Son or daughter leaving home	29
Change in social activities	18
Christmas season	12
Minor violations of the law	11

Source: (Holmes & Rahe, 1967).

Reprinted with permission from *Journal of Psychosomatic Research* 11(2), 1967:213–218, Elsevier Science Inc.

fortunately, we do not have good psychological stressors for rats. Your average laboratory rat does not seem to be concerned about whether or not the other rats like it or how well it's going to do on the next exam. Therefore, whereas it seems logical simply to extend Weiss's work with animals, the absence of relevant psychological stressors for animals precludes this approach.

Another methodological problem in establishing a causal link between stress and illness is distinguishing between illness and illness behavior. That is, we must be able to differentiate between an *objective* clearly defined physical illness and the *subjective* report of that illness. Any time that a person reports that he or she is sick, there are both physiological and psychological forces at work. Physiological processes produce bodily symptoms. For example, activation of the sympathetic nervous system increases heart rate and perspiration. These are both physical processes that we can measure. However, psychological processes such as attention, attribution of meaning, and appraisal are also at work, and they influence whether a person says or does anything about the symptoms. Figure 5–3 illustrates a simplified model of how stress influences both psychological processes and physiological processes to influence both the illness behavior and the illness.

Keeping in mind the model presented in Figure 5–3, we can delineate four categories of stress-related illnesses. The four categories are the **somatoform disorders, psychophysiological disorders, somatogenic disorders,** and **accidental injuries.** Each category differs in the extent and the manner in which stress influences the physiological processes that lead to illness and the psychological and behavioral processes that lead to illness behavior. For each of the four major categories, one exemplar disorder will be highlighted, and the evidence linking stress to the development of that disorder will be reviewed in detail. The stress-illness relationship for other disorders in each category will be summarized more briefly.

Throughout this review, remember that stress is only one of many possible causal variables that lead to illness and illness behavior. Being stressed does not mean that you will necessarily become ill, and saying that you are sick does not necessarily mean that you are stressed. Disease progression is a multiply determined process in which stress is only one of many contributors. On the other hand, establishing stress as an independent risk factor is not to be trivialized. Since we have potent interventions to manage stress, it is important to determine the extent to which stress and coping contribute to various disease processes, so that we may develop appropriate interventions.

In the review that follows, we take a fairly conservative look at the evidence linking stress to illness. There is no doubt that psychological stress per se has demonstrable effects on physiological processes. In general, however, the data are very convincing that the body is resilient to stress and usually adjusts to stressful conditions in an adaptive manner. For example, numerous studies assessing the effects of

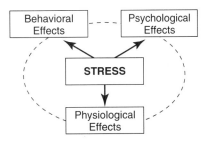

Figure 5–3

Multi-modal effects of stress. This diagram illustrates the influence of stress on physiological, psychological, and behavioral processes. Stress influences all three domains of functioning, and the three domains can influence each other.

stress on immunity reveal that the immune response of stressed persons generally falls within normal limits (Rabin, Cohen, Ganguli, Lysle, & Cunnick, 1989). The body seems to have a "bend but don't break" defense system against stress. It is possible for the body to "break" if stress is excessive or if our coping strategies are very rigid, but the normal outcome is for the body to bounce back from stress.

SOMATOFORM DISORDERS

Somatoform disorders are not typically included in a discussion of stress-related disorders, because they reflect psychological rather than physical problems. The term *somatoform* literally refers to a disorder that is physical (somatic) in form only. Disorders such as somatization and hypochondriasis are examples of somatoform disorders. The hallmark of all somatoform disorders is the complaint of physical symptoms that have no clear physical (organic) basis. Furthermore, there is strong evidence that the symptoms are linked to psychological factors or conflicts (American Psychiatric Association [APA], 1994). Many people confuse somatoform disorders with psychosomatic disorders. The definition of a psychosomatic disorder is actually very different from that of a somatoform disorder. Psychosomatic disorders are disorders where clear organic pathology (e.g., ulcers, tumors) is present, and these physical changes are caused or exacerbated by psychological factors such as stress.

Somatoform and psychosomatic disorders do, however, share two essential features. First, they are both characterized by physical complaints. However, in the somatoform disorders, a physician cannot find a physical basis for the complaint, or if a physical problem is diagnosed it is insufficient to explain the magnitude of the complaint. In the psychosomatic disorders, the magnitude of the complaint is congruent with the magnitude of the underlying organic pathology. Second, they are both stress-related disorders. In the somatoform disorders, stress primarily activates psychological processes. Arousal of physiological and behavioral pathways may occur, but these are secondary to the psychological processes that lead to the physical complaint. For example, consider a person who thinks that he is about to have a heart attack at any time that he feels stressed and notices that his heart rate has increased. In the psychosomatic disorders, stress results in a physical complaint primarily because the stressor activates physiological pathways that in the long run leads to physical disorders. Activation of the psychological and behavioral pathways occurs after the activation of the physiological pathways. Differentiating between the somatoform and psychosomatic disorders is often very difficult.

Hypochondriasis

Hypochondriasis is a somatoform disorder characterized by an unrealistic interpretation of physical signs or sensations as abnormal, which leads to a preoccupation with the fear of having a serious disease (APA, 1994). Most us have overblown some physical symptom at some time in our lives. Perhaps we have felt fatigued and then worried that this fatigue might be the first sign of AIDS, or have thought that mild abdominal pain was appendicitis. For most people, these types of worries come and go. Either the symptoms resolve themselves and we quit worrying, or we have the symptoms checked out by a physician and then follow the physician's recommendation. A formal diagnosis of hypochondriasis is not given unless the unrealistic fear or belief persists despite medical reassurance, or unless it causes impairment in social or occupational functioning. Informally, many patients are labeled hypochondriacs, somatizers, or worse (e.g., malingerers) when the physician cannot find a diagnosis that matches the symptoms that the patients present.

Stress and Hypochondriasis.   Though anxious people tend to have more somatic complaints (Barsky, Goodson, Lane, & Cleary, 1988), there is little evidence that persons diagnosed as being hypochondriacal experience more stressful life events than do others (Warwick & Salkovskis, 1990). Many authors suggest that hypochondriacal complaints and the constant searching for sympathetic medical care represent a maladaptive way of coping with stressful life events (e.g., Ford, 1986; 1995). This view suggests that rather than experiencing more life stress or more organic pathology than others experience, hypochondriacal or somatizing patients simply lack the skills needed to cope adaptively with the normal stressors of life. These people are typically described as having failed in ordinary pursuits and lacking in basic social competencies (e.g., Wooley, Blackwell, and Winget, 1978). While there are virtually no empirical data testing this assumption, the "poor coping" model of hypochondriasis and somatization is extremely prevalent in the medical community.

Biological Mechanisms Linking Stress to Hypochondriasis.   Some authors disagree with this "poor coping" view of hypochondriasis and instead emphasize biological mechanisms in the development and maintenance of hypochondriacal behavior. One prominent model of hypochondriasis suggests that perceptual and/or cognitive abnormalities cause hypochondriacal patients to overreport somatic symptoms (Barsky, 1979; Barsky & Klerman, 1983; Feuerstein, Labbe, & Kuczmierczyk, 1986). Specifically, this model predicts that hypochondriacs amplify normal bodily sensations. That is, they experience normal bodily sensations as more intense and more noxious (i.e., more stressful) than do others (Barsky & Klerman, 1983; Feuerstein et al., 1986). Perhaps hypochondriacs are physiologically "hard-wired" to experience sensory stimuli as more intense and more unpleasant and therefore are more likely to report and act on their symptoms. Data that support this model indicate that hypochondriacs have lower sensory and pain thresholds relative to controls (Bianchi, 1971; Hanback & Revelle, 1978). Consistent with this is a recent study that revealed that hypochondriacal subjects exhibited greater elevations in heart rate when exposed to a painful stressor and that they rated the stressor as significantly more unpleasant relative to nonhypochondriacal control subjects (Gramling, Clawson, & McDonald, 1996). Some have theorized that hypochondriacs have higher baseline (resting) levels of autonomic nervous system arousal, but this study (Gramling et al., 1996) and others (Tyrer, Lee, & Alexander, 1980) have found that hypochondriacs actually exhibit significantly lower baseline heart rates relative to controls.

Several authors note that physiological sensitivity is probably neither necessary nor sufficient to account for the full clinical picture of hypochondriasis (Warwick & Salkovskis, 1990). However, it may turn out that additional psychophysiological studies with hypochondriacs will prove that there are physiological underpinnings that predispose certain individuals to develop the emotional and cognitive dysfunction characteristic of hypochondriasis.

Related Somatoform Disorders

Conversion disorder is historically one of the most fascinating of the somatoform disorders. This disorder is characterized by loss of, or alteration in, physical functioning due to psychological needs or conflicts. Typically, the symptom presentation defies current understanding of anatomy and physiology. "Glove anesthesia," for example, is a conversion disorder in which the physical complaint is that there is a total lack of feeling in the hands but that the arms are unaffected—an anatomical impossibility. Yet true conversion disorder patients are unaware of any conscious effort on their part to cause the symptoms. They are unresponsive to stimuli such as a pin prick or a hot match. Frequently, the symptoms appear when the person is experiencing psychological conflict, and some thus have speculated that the patient "converts" the psychological conflict into somatic symptoms that will force resolution of the conflict. For example, a study examining students in a naval aviator-training program revealed that a surprising number of students developed conversion symptoms (e.g., blurred vision, double vision) that forced them to quit the training program. The authors of the study suggest that these patients developed conversion symptoms because the psychological conflict produced by their admitting that they were failing because of lack of ability or fear, was an unacceptable alternative (Mucha & Reinhardt, 1970).

A problem with conversion disorders and other somatoform disorders is that patients with symptoms that are particularly difficult to diagnose may be given this label by physicians, even though their symptoms are actually the result of real physical problems. One study that looked at the long-term outcomes for patients diagnosed with conversion disorder found that a startling 30 percent of the patients were dead five years later, and that the causes of their deaths were disease processes that could have explained the symptoms presented at the time the patients were diagnosed with conversion disorder (Watson & Tilleskjor, 1983).

Because patients with somatoform disorders and those with psychosomatic disorders make similar physical complaints, it is often difficult for a physician to determine whether the causes of the complaints are primarily physical or psychological (Kellner, 1990). In general, the diagnosis of somatoform disorder is a "diagnosis of exclusion," which means that once a physician has ruled out known physical explanations for a symptom complaint, the physician assumes that the patient has a somatoform disorder. Unfortunately, history is full of examples of persons who had been labeled with a somatoform disorder by a physician but who were later diagnosed as having a real physical problem. Typically, correct diagnosis depends on technological improvements that make the physical problem easier to diagnose, or on the worsening of symptoms that makes the physical dysfunction more apparent.

PSYCHOPHYSIOLOGICAL DISORDERS

The psychophysiological disorders are one type of the psychosomatic disorders (the somatogenic disorders are another). Traditionally, they are defined as physical disorders with clear organic pathology that are caused or exacerbated by stress. The disorders that are associated with stress-induced elevations in muscle tension such as tension headache, temporomandibular joint disorder (pain in the jaw and muscles of the face), and some types of low back pain are classified as psychophysiological disorders. Other examples include ulcers (which we learned from Weiss's work are clearly stress-related), coronary artery disease, asthma, and irritable bowel syndrome. Pain disorders associated with elevated levels of muscle tension are by far the most frequently reported of the psychophysiological disorders and are the most difficult to distinguish from the somatoform disorders.

We will use temporomandibular disorder as the exemplar psychophysiological disorder and will review in detail the evidence establishing it as a stress-related disorder. The stress-illness relationship for several other disorders will be summarized together later in this section.

Temporomandibular Joint Disorder

The temporomandibular joint (TMJ) is the "hinge" that connects your upper and lower jaw. If you bite down gently on your molars and place your fingers towards the back part of your jaw (towards your ear), you can feel the TM joint and surrounding muscles tense. Temporomandibular joint disorder (TMD) is actually a cluster of related facial pain disorders involving the muscles of mastication (chewing muscles) and/or the temporomandibular joint (McNeill, Moh, Rugh, & Tanaka, 1990). TMD prevalence rates in the general population have been estimated to range from 26 to 75 percent (Solberg, Woo, & Houston, 1979). The pervasiveness of these disorders and the negative impact that orofacial pain has on chewing, talking, and drinking, indicate that TMDs represent a serious health problem.

Stress and TMD.   Daniel Laskin's work in this area first gave rise to the idea that stress plays an important role in initiating the behavioral/physiological sequence that leads to TMD pain (Laskin, 1969; Greene, Olson, & Laskin, 1982; Laskin & Block, 1986). Laskin's general model, which has been refined by others (Haber et al., 1983; Parker, 1990) suggests that *stress* triggers *muscle hyperactivity* in the muscles of mastication, possibly via various oral habits (such as teeth clenching or lip biting). This process in turn leads to elevated tension in the muscles and subsequent *pain*. This model has a great deal of intuitive appeal. However, a review of the empirical literature linking stress to the development of TMD is still somewhat controversial (e.g., Haber, Moss, Kuczmierczyk, & Garrett, 1983; Kapel, Glaros, & McGlynn, 1989; Lundeen, Sturdevant, & George, 1987). Although it is too soon to say that stress *causes* TMD, we can say at this point that stress is strongly associated with TMD. Three lines of evidence demonstrating the relationship between stress and TMD are presented in the following sections.

Retrospective Self-Report Evidence.   Much of this research has simply assessed the relationship between TMD symptoms among patients already diagnosed with TMD and has looked for differences in self-reported life stress. Studies using this approach found that TMD pain patients have higher stress levels (Lundeen et al., 1987), have experienced more physical injury–illness events and social support losses (Marbach, Lennon, & Dohrenwend, 1988), report more anxiety, and have lower pain tolerances than pain-free "normal control" subjects (Katz & Rugh, 1986). The problem with these studies, however, is that they fail to establish a temporal relationship between stressful events and pain onset. That is, it is not clear from these types of studies whether stress causes TMD or whether having TMD simply makes life more stressful.

Muscle Reactivity Evidence.   Since stress is thought to cause increased muscle tension, which in turn causes muscle pain, evidence pertaining to the level of muscle tension (technically referred to as electromyogram or EMG) among TMD sufferers is relevant to understanding the role of stress in the development of TMD. Many studies have found heightened masseter muscle (one of the larger muscles involved in chewing) EMG when TMD subjects were exposed to experimental stressors. For example, one study compared masseter EMG in TMD and control subjects after exposure to two experimentally induced stressors (painful electric shock and a difficult puzzle). TMD subjects showed significantly more masseter EMG activity during a prestressor baseline condition and during the stressor itself relative to a nonsymptomatic control group (Thomas, Tiber, & Schireson, 1973). Several other researchers report similar findings (e.g., Mercuri, Olson, and Laskin, 1979). However, other studies (Gale, & Carlsson, 1978; Moss & Adams, 1984) have failed to demonstrate elevated levels of masseter muscle EMG in TMD patients under experimental stress or no-stress conditions. Flor and Turk (1989) have reviewed and critiqued the TMD literature relevant to the hyperactivity model and found the methodology of many of these studies to be inadequate. We believe that when naturalistic stressors are employed and measurement techniques are improved, heightened EMG levels among TMD patients will be consistently observed.

Evidence from Treatment Outcome Studies.   If TMD pain is caused by stress-induced elevations in masseter EMG, then treatments that reduce the level of tension in these muscles should have beneficial effects. Behavioral treatments such as relaxation training and biofeedback, in which muscle tension-control is a central feature, have been successfully applied to TMD pain (e.g., Clarke & Kardachi, 1977; Salter, Brooke, & Merskey, 1986). These findings have led most researchers to conclude that relaxation training techniques are efficacious (Gale, 1986; Scott, 1981). However, because many of these studies did not actually measure masseter EMG levels, the improvements reported in TMD patients may be a **"placebo"** response rather than the result of any actual change in EMG levels. In summary, it is clear that interventions which emphasize tension control of the musculature are effective treatments for TMD; however, it is not clear whether these interventions work by lowering tension in the masseter muscles per se.

Behavioral Processes Linking Stress to TMD Pain.   Oral habits such as teeth clenching and grinding, lip biting, and nail biting have been implicated as the behavioral response to stress that triggers elevated EMG and subsequent TMD pain (Moss et al., 1982). We suggest that these oral habits are a form of schedule-induced or **adjunctive behavior** (Gramling, Grayson, Sullivan, & Schwartz, 1996; Sturgis & Gramling, in press). A dictionary definition of *adjunct*, "something joined or added to another but not essentially a part of it," provides a general sense of the nature of adjunctive behaviors. Generally speaking, adjunctive behaviors occur in conjunction with other behavior but seem to serve no useful purpose. Pacing, finger tapping, and knuckle cracking are other examples of behaviors that may be adjunctive. Some researchers suggest that these behavioral adjuncts are an adaptive outlet for the surplus arousal that is triggered by stress or frustration (Tinbergen, 1951). We think that oral habits like teeth grinding and clenching, lip and nail biting, are behavioral responses that initially develop in response to negative emotion and become ingrained ("unconscious") habits over time. A habit reversal intervention, whereby facial-pain patients are taught to identify, interrupt, and reverse their pain-producing oral habits, is an effective treatment for many patients with TMD symptomatology (Gramling, Neblett, Grayson & Townsend, 1996).

Biological Mechanisms Linking Stress to TMD.   The most frequently cited and researched biological mechanism in the Stress>>>>TMD model has been stress-induced hyperactivity in the muscles of mastication. Much of that research was described earlier in the review of evidence supporting the Stress>>>TMD model. Currently there are about as many studies reporting negative findings as there are studies reporting positive findings. The methodological problems cited by Flor and Turk (1989) probably account for the failure to observe consistently positive results. The use of naturalistic stressors and improved measurement and methodology will likely lead to more consistently positive findings in the future.

If oral habits are an important link in the stress>>>muscle hyperactivity>>>TMD pain sequence, then there must be a biological mechanism to account for the persistence of these behaviors in light of the painful consequences that they produce. To the extent that oral habits are in fact a form of adjunctive behavior, then the literature pertaining to the neurophysiology of adjunctive behavior might shed some light on this question. Dantzer (1989) cites a wide array of neurophysiological data and concludes that adjunctive behaviors represent a general behavioral and neurophysiological response to aversive stimuli. We believe that oral habits such as teeth clenching may have adaptive value in reducing the immediate arousal of sympathetic nervous system activation associated with stress, as well as reducing the harmful impact of hormonal responses to stress.

Other Psychophysiological Disorders

Coronary Heart Disease.   Stress takes its toll on the cardiovascular system in a number of different ways. The expression "scared to death" provides a literal explanation for some instances of sudden cardiac death. For example, during natural disasters, a percentage of people die from heart attacks without sustaining any other injuries. In skydiving accidents in which a parachutist dies because the chute fails to open, it is often the case that "they were dead from a heart attack before they ever hit the ground." These are just a few examples of the clinical lore suggesting that sudden cardiac death can be stress-induced. The biological mechanism for stress-induced sudden cardiac death involves excessive release of epinephrine and norepinephrine during stress. These catecholamines in turn can cause cardiac arrhythmia (irregular heart beat), which can be fatal in severe cases.

Stress-induced sudden cardiac death can happen to anyone but occurs most frequently in persons who have ongoing cardiovascular problems such as hypertension (high blood pressure) and coronary artery disease (hardening of the arteries). Stress is an important risk factor for both of these chronic cardiovascular problems. The release of catecholamines by the autonomic nervous system and the release of various stress-related hormones (glucocorticoids and mineralcorticoids) via the hypothalamic-pituitary-adrenal axis, have a cumulative negative effect on the heart and blood vessels by means of a number of different mechanisms. The damage from these chemicals is largely due to the fact that they remain in the bloodstream for extended periods of time rather than being "burned off" through fight or flight. Both the catecholamines and stress hormones cause an increase in blood pressure, which can damage the inside wall of the blood vessels. The glucocorticoid called cortisol, which is released by the adrenal gland during stress, is associated with an increase in free fatty acids in the bloodstream, which in turn leads to plaque buildup on the lining of the blood vessels. The catecholamines also act to enhance blood coagulation as well as "bad" cholesterol, which when combined, thicken the inside wall of the blood vessels. As the blood vessels narrow over time, it becomes increasingly difficult for the heart to pump sufficient blood through the increasingly narrow passage in the blood vessels. These are just a few of the stress-induced biological mechanisms that lead to high blood pressure and coronary heart disease.

Coronary Prone Behavior: The Type-A Personality.   The physiological sequence just described happens to everyone at any time when the fight-or-flight response is engaged. However, for people with a **Type-A** personality, the cardiovascular system seems to be overresponsive to stressors. For these people, elevations in blood pressure and in heart rate during stress are noticeably greater, and the time that it takes for the heart rate and blood pressure to return to resting values is noticeably longer than for non–Type-A-personality people. During the 1950s, Friedman and Rosenman (1974) set out to study systematically the relationship between personality and coronary heart disease. They had noticed in their cardiology practice that the front edge of the upholstery on the chairs used by patients always wore out first, but that this pattern of wear and tear was not evident in other medical practices. They took this as evidence that their cardiac patients were literally "on edge" and came to believe that there was a pattern of specific behaviors that characterized the coronary-prone person. The cluster of behaviors that they identified are listed in Table 5–2.

People without these characteristics are classified as Type-B and can be thought of as more "laid back" literally and figuratively relative to the Type-As. The global Type-A behavior pattern listed in Table 5–2 has been investigated in numerous studies and has (with a few exceptions) supported the idea that Type-A is a risk factor for coronary heart disease (CHD) (e.g., Booth-Kewley & Friedman, 1987). As further research has been conducted, the most "toxic" element of the Type-A behavior pattern

TABLE 5–2.	**CHARACTERISTICS OF THE GLOBAL TYPE-A BEHAVIOR PATTERN***

1. An overriding drive to achieve goals and a strong need for recognition and advancement.
2. Intense competitiveness (e.g., seeks to win games played against small children) so extreme that it alienates family and coworkers.
3. Time urgency and impatience characterized by a chronic sense that there is not enough time to accomplish objectives. Constant involvement in varied tasks involving deadlines and time pressure.
4. A tendency to speed up mental and physical tasks, and high levels of mental and physical alertness.
5. Hostility and aggressiveness.

*General Characteristics originally identified as part of the Type-A Coronary Prone Personality.

that has emerged is hostility or anger, particularly hostile cynicism. Matthews (1988) and Smith (1992), who have reviewed the literature in this area, conclude that hostility is a significant risk factor for CHD. Table 5–3 presents items from two of the most commonly administered questionnaires used to assess Type-A behavior in general and hostility in particular. Although the Type-A behavior pattern remains an area of intense research in the psychological literature pertaining to CHD, recently other psychological constructs, particularly depression, have received renewed attention as well.

Ulcers.   The early research on the effects of stress on physical functioning focused on ulcer development largely because an ulcer is a clear-cut, easily quantified physical disorder. An ulcer is a lesion in the lining of the stomach or intestines. Selye and Weiss provide compelling evidence that physical and psychological stressors, respectively, are important contributors to the development of ulcers. Stress presumably hastens the development of ulcers because activation of the sympathetic nervous system during the fight-or-flight response leads to a reduction in activity all along the gastrointestinal (GI) tract (i.e., mouth, esophagus, stomach, small intestine, large intestine, anal opening). This reduction occurs because the stomach and the rest of the GI tract are not essential for preparation for fight or flight. During periods of sympathetic nervous system activation, the relative amount of hydrochloric acid in the stomach increases. At the same time, the relative inactivity of the GI tract leads to a reduction in mucous production in the GI tract (which is why the mouth goes dry when one is stressed), and therefore the lining of the stomach is not as well protected from the hydrochloric acid. Together these changes result in a state of high vulnerability for the stomach.

You may never have an ulcer, but you probably have had some first-hand experience with other stress-*related* dysfunction of the GI tract. For example, stress results in the release of epinephrine in the periphery, and epinephrine causes increased contractility of the large and small intestines, leading to transient bouts of diarrhea when stressed. A dry mouth and "butterflies" in the stomach are other stress-related GI symptoms.

Ulcers provide a good example of a common phenomenon observed among the psychophysiological disorders: namely, that the most severe consequences of stress to the body often occur *after* the stressor has terminated. For example, in examining

---

TABLE 5–3. ITEMS FROM TWO COMMONLY ADMINISTERED QUESTIONNAIRES ASSESSING TYPE-A BEHAVIOR

Sample Items from the Jenkins Activity Survey*

1. Is your everyday life filled mostly by
   a. problems needing a solution?
   b. challenges needing to be met?
   c. a rather predictable routine of events?
   d. not enough things to keep me interested or busy?
2. When you listen to someone talking, and this person takes **too long** to come to the point, how often do you **feel** like hurrying the person along?
   a. Frequently
   b. Occasionally
   c. Almost Never
3. How often do you find yourself hurrying to get places even when there is plenty of time?
   a. Frequently
   b. Occasionally
   c. Almost never
4. When you play games with young children about 10 years old (or when you did in past years), how often do you purposely let them win?
   a. Most of the time
   b. Half of the time
   c. Only occasionally
   d. Never
5. Would people who know you well agree that you take your work too seriously?
   a. Definitely yes
   b. Probably yes
   c. Probably no
   d. Definitely no
6. How is your temper nowadays?
   a. Fiery and hard to control
   b. Strong but controllable
   c. No problem
   d. I almost never get angry
7. How often do you go to your place of work when you are not expected to be there (such as nights or weekends)?
   a. It is not possible on my job
   b. Rarely or never
   c. Occasionally (less than once a week)
   d. Once a week or more

Respondents are instructed that the Jenkins Activity Survey asks questions about aspects of behavior that have been found helpful in medical diagnosis. Each person is different. There are no right or wrong answers. For each question choose the answer that is true of you. The sample items reflect the global Type-A Behavior Pattern characteristics listed in Table 5–2.

Sample Items from the Cook-Medley Hostility (Ho) Scale†

1. When someone does me wrong, I feel I should pay him back if I can, just for the principle of the thing.

(continued)

TABLE 5–3. *(continued)*

2. I think most people would lie to get ahead.
3. Someone has it in for me.
4. I don't blame anyone for trying to grab everything he can get in this world.
5. It is safer to trust nobody.
6. I have often felt that strangers were looking at me critically.
7. Most people make friends because friends are likely to be useful to them.
8. It makes me feel like a failure when I hear of the success of someone I know.
9. People generally demand more respect for their own rights than they are willing to allow for others.
10. There are certain people whom I dislike so much that I am inwardly pleased when they are catching it for something they have done.

Respondents are instructed to answer the items above as either true or false. In general, most of the time, does the item describe you? For each of the items, a response of "true" would be scored as indicating higher levels of hostility. Hostility is thought by many to be the most "toxic" component of the global Type-A personality.

Source: Jenkins, C. D., Rosenman, R. H., and Friedman, M., 1968. By permission of Mosby Publishing Co.
†*Source*: Minnesota Multiphasic Personality Inventory (MMPI). Copyright © 1942, 1943 (renewed 1970) by the University of Minnesota. Reproduced by permission of the University of Minnesota Press.

the relationship between stress and the Type-A personality, it is the prolonged elevation of blood pressure after the stressor has terminated that is most damaging. Presumably, Type-A individuals' tendency towards hostility and aggression keeps them agitated and aroused as they ruminate about the stressor long after the stressor (e.g., an unpleasant encounter with the boss) has subsided.

Similarly, the stomach may be most vulnerable to ulcers *after* a *long* period of stress is over (Sapolsky, 1994). During a protracted period of stress, your body "cuts corners." Acid secretion is inhibited, and as a result, the protective thickening of the stomach walls and mucous secretion diminishes. When the stressful period ends, you begin to eat again (often in large amounts), and normal amounts of acid are secreted to aid in digestion, but your stomach with its thinned walls cannot defend against the acid and so is easily damaged. Thus, argues Sapolsky, ulcers are formed, but less so during exposure to a stressor than during the recovery period; and from the standpoint of getting ulcers, you are better off being under constant stress than repeatedly going through long periods of stress followed by periods of low stress.

Migraine headachers show a similar pattern. Namely, though they may have a migraine at other times, they are most vulnerable to migraine after a long period of intense stress. During intense stress, vasoconstriction seems to dampen the dysregulation of the cerebral vasculature that characterizes this patient population, preventing the onset of headache pain. However, once the stressor is removed, "the flood gates open." The blood vessels relax and dilate, and the underlying dysregulation is exaggerated—fluctuating between extreme vasoconstriction and extreme vasodilation and subsequent headache pain.

Ulcers also serve as a good example of how the distinctions between the different categories of stress-related disorders are becoming increasingly blurred. Remember that earlier in this chapter we mentioned that it is often difficult to differentiate complaints of physical symptoms that are somatoform in nature from those that are psychophysiological. Similarly, the distinction between a psychophysiological disorder and a somatogenic disorder is not always clear-cut. It is with good reason that ulcers have been the prototypical psychophysiological disorder for many years. Numerous researchers have demonstrated strong evidence that physical and psychological stress cause ulcers (e.g., Selye, 1956; Weiss, 1977). However, there is new evidence that the primary culprit may be a corkscrew-shaped bacterium called Heliobacter pylori and therefore that the effects of stress on the development of ulcers must be more indirect (e.g., weakening the immune system). Stress exposure and the resulting sequence of physiological processes initiated in the digestive tract may serve to increase vulnerability to this bacterium, which is the proximal cause of the disease. Ulcers may therefore be more accurately classified as a somatogenic disorder (see the following section) than as a psychophysiological disorder. Our understanding of the immune system is growing geometrically, and it would not be surprising if other disorders thought to be psychophysiological in nature turn out to be better classified as somatogenic.

SOMATOGENIC DISORDERS

In the somatogenic disorders, stress makes the body more vulnerable to disease-causing viruses or bacteria. Unlike the psychophysiological disorders, however, stress per se does not cause the disorder. As we learned in the previous chapter, stress has profound effects on the immune system and can lead to a reduction in immune system integrity. However, a virus or some other pathogen must be present in the body for you to become ill. For example, Walt (the highly stressed ATC), would not contract the flu or any other viral or infectious disease if the pathogens were not in his body.

Cancer

There are at least two hundred different types of cancer. What these different types of cancer share in common is an abnormal reproduction of cells. By the time that we reach adulthood, the rate at which new cells develop is equal to the rate at which old cells die. With cancerous cells, the rate of growth is about the same, but because these cells do not know when to "turn off" or stop dividing, their rate of increase grows unchecked and can turn into massive tumors. A normal cell can become cancerous by being exposed to a carcinogen, which is simply any substance that is capable of causing cancer. Tobacco products are the most well-known carcinogenic substances. A carcinogen can cause a normal cell to become abnormal by entering into the cell nucleus and binding to the genetic material (the DNA) that resides inside every cell nucleus. This abnormal cell is called a mutation; if the cell divides, the mutation will be spread to the new cells. Typically, these mutant cells do not divide any more rapidly than normal cells; they simply do not quit dividing at the point where a normal cell stops. This constant division can transform a single mutant cell into a cancerous tumor.

There are other ways that a cell might mutate, including exposure to certain types of energy, such as ultraviolet light and X-rays and by other endogenous processes that we do not yet fully understand. It is probably the case that potentially cancerous cell mutations occur in all of us with some regularity, but the natural killer cells in our immune system destroy them before they cause any damage. The immune system may fail to protect us from cancer if it becomes "overloaded" with carcinogens, that is, if there are so many mutations occurring that even a strong immune system is overwhelmed. Similarly, if the integrity of the immune system has been compromised by some other process, such as another serious illness or chronic stress, it might not be able to mount an effective defense against the mutant cells, even when there are relatively few mutant cells to combat.

Stress and Cancer.   Most of the studies linking stress to the development of cancer in humans are retrospective studies. A study by Jacob and Charles (1980), for example, studied the parents of twenty-five children who had cancer and compared them with the parents of twenty-five children without cancer. They found that families with children diagnosed with cancer reported significantly more stress in the year prior to the child's diagnosis than did the families of children not diagnosed with cancer. This finding suggests that increased stress levels in these families may have contributed to the development of cancer.

One of the problems with these types of retrospective studies, however, is that the cancer experience itself can influence one's memory of stressful life-events. A clever study that overcame this confound was reported by Cooper & Faragher (1993). Women admitted to a hospital for breast lump biopsies (which would determine whether or not the lump was cancerous) were administered a stressful-life-events scale prior to the biopsy (i.e., before they knew whether they had cancer), as were a group of women without breast lumps. Women who turned out to have cancer more frequently experienced a major stressful life-event in the two years prior to diagnoses than *either* the benign-breast-lump group or the healthy women "controls." Furthermore, in a five-year prospective study, it was found that individuals who developed cancer were significantly more likely to report the loss of a significant relationship and poorer job stability in the five years prior to diagnosis compared with individuals who developed benign lung tumors (Horne & Picard, 1979). Taken together, these and many studies like them suggest a moderately positive correlation between life stressors and the development of cancer.

Cancer-Prone Personality.   For the most part, the studies just described link the frequency of life stressors, or the person's appraisal of the severity of life stressors, to the development of cancer. There is another body of literature that links a person's dispositional way of coping with stress to the development of cancer. This research focuses on the so-called "Type-C" or cancer-prone personality. A number of retrospective studies (e.g., Temoshok & Dreher, 1992) suggest that trait depression, hopelessness, and lack of emotional expression are correlated with the development and progression of cancer. Prospective studies also converge on the finding that lack of emotional expression (suppression of negative emotion, unassertiveness, docility) is correlated with cancer (Grossarth-Maticek, Bastiaans, & Kanazir 1985; Shaffer, Graves, Swank, & Pearson, 1987).

One of the most striking findings among the prospective studies was reported by Grossarth-Maticek et al. (1985). In this study over 1,350 residents of a small industrial town in Yugoslavia completed a psychosocial questionnaire and an assessment of smoking behavior. Ten years later the researchers found that scores on an eleven-item Rationality/Anti-Emotionality scale included in the preassessment battery predicted the incidence of cancer with 93 percent accuracy. Of the 166 people who had died of cancer in the preceding ten years, 158 had answered yes to ten or eleven of the items shown in Table 5–4.

To follow up on these startling findings, Grossarth-Maticek and colleagues conducted a prospective treatment study. One hundred healthy subjects thought to be at high risk for cancer on the basis of their high scores on the Rationality–Anti-Emotionality scale, were randomly assigned to one of two groups. One group was taught a variety of behavioral techniques to facilitate the expression of emotions, and the other group received no treatment. Ten years later none of the subjects in the treatment group had been diagnosed with cancer, whereas sixteen of the

TABLE 5–4.   RATIONALITY–ANTI-EMOTIONALITY SCALE

People who answered yes to ten or eleven of these items were reported to have an incidence rate of cancer forty times greater than people who answered yes to three or fewer of these items.

1. Do you always try to do what is reasonable and logical?
2. Do you always try to understand people and their behavior, so that you seldom respond emotionally?
3. Do you try to act rationally in all interpersonal situations?
4. Do you try to overcome all interpersonal conflicts by intelligence and reason, trying hard not to show any emotional response?
5. If someone deeply hurts your feelings, do you try to treat him rationally and to understand his way of behaving (so that you hardly ever attack and deprecate him or treat him purely emotionally)?
6. Do you succeed in avoiding most interpersonal conflicts by relying on your reason and logic (often contrary to your feelings)?
7. If someone acts against your needs and desires, do you nevertheless try to understand him?
8. Do you behave in almost all life situations so rationally that only rarely is your behavior influenced by emotions only?
9. Is your behavior frequently influenced by emotions to such a degree that from a purely rational point of view, it would have to be regarded as nonsensical and detrimental?
10. Do you try to understand others even if you do not like them?
11. Does your rationality prevent you from attacking others, even if there are sufficient reasons for doing so?

Source: Reprinted by permission of the publisher from Grossarth-Maticek, Bastiaans, & Kanizer, *Journal of Psychosomatic Research, 29*, 167–176. Copyright 1985 by Elsevier Science Inc., 655 Ave. of the Americas, New York, NY 10010.

no-treatment control subjects had died of cancer. The results are somewhat controversial, given that we rarely see such strong predictive power from brief self-report measures (Eysenck, 1990). However, populations in two German communities have participated in a similar study that has yielded similar results (Eysenck, 1991). Both of these studies are quite provocative, and several of the other prospective and retrospective studies converge to a general point of agreement, namely, that characteristic patterns of emotional expression (i.e., general style of coping with unpleasant events with an unemotional, detached, or docile demeanor) are important correlates in the development and progression of cancer.

Biological Mechanisms Linking Stress and Coping to Cancer.   It is generally assumed that to the extent that stress and coping styles contribute to the onset and promotion of cancer, they do so by weakening the immune system. Numerous animal studies have demonstrated that exposure to extreme uncontrollable physical stress has profound effects on the immune system, and often these changes are related to the development of cancer. As described in the previous section, human studies provide evidence that stress and certain coping styles are risk factors for cancer. Numerous studies of human participants indicate that psychological stress is associated with changes in immune system functioning, such as the helper/suppressor cell ratio and assays for lymphocyte activation. However, for the most part, studies of stress effects on immunity have shown that the immune responses of stressed persons fall within normal ranges (Rabin et al., 1989). Scientists across many different scientific disciplines are at work trying to find a way to test the full model of the stress-immunosuppression-cancer link in humans. These scientists are trying to demonstrate empirically that increased stress causes changes in immune system functioning and that these changes are related to cancer initiation and promotion.

One of the lessons from the previous chapter was that the body is very resilient and adaptive. Most of the time, stress-related changes in immune-system functioning are transitory adaptive responses to stress-related changes in the autonomic and endocrine systems. The fact that stress is sometimes associated with changes in the immune system that actually retard tumor growth (as discussed in Chapter 4) tells us that when the full story is known, it will be more complicated than simply that stress causes cancer or that a certain coping style causes cancer.

Acquired Immunodeficiency Disorder (AIDS)

AIDS is one of the most well-known and deadly of the immune system disorders. The disease is marked by a progressive loss of immune system competence with resulting vulnerability to infections and malignancies. The disease progression begins when a person becomes infected with the human immunodeficiency virus (HIV-1). Over time an HIV-1 infected person develops AIDS-related conditions (ARC), which may include symptoms such as fatigue and increased incidence of viruses and infections. When the immune system becomes extremely weak, the disease progresses into full-blown AIDS. At this point, the individual is vulnerable to very serious diseases, including rare forms of cancer. The primary target of HIV-1 is the T-helper/inducer cell, a major regulatory cell of the immune system, the loss of which is associated with many different immunological defects. Initially the HIV-1 virus results in a large drop in the number of T-helper/inducer cells, but the numbers tend to plateau for several years following this initial decrease. The efficacy of antiretroviral therapy for HIV infection has fostered new hope that medical interventions will lead to the eventual control of the HIV disease process (Berger, 1996). The time interval between initial infection and endpoint diagnosis of AIDS can vary from five to fifteen years, and as new treatments continue to emerge, we can expect the average time interval to become even longer. Increasingly, AIDS researchers have come to view this disease as a chronic illness, and interest in the relationship between stress and longevity among AIDS patients has increased.

Stress and AIDS.   Our understanding of whether and how stress influences the progression of AIDS is still in its infancy. One of the unique stumbling blocks in researching the effects of stress on illness progression in AIDS patients is the fact that AIDS is often associated with neurological impairment. AIDS patients often develop memory problems and sometimes lose awareness of their impaired condition. Self-report measures of stress level and coping strategies are difficult to interpret under these conditions (Klusman, Moulton, Hornbostel, & Picano, 1991). Those studies that have correlated stress level, coping style (e.g., hardiness), and immune system status variables have produced widely varying results depending on the exact measures that are used and the disease stage in which the patients were tested (Antoni, Schneiderman, Fletcher, Goldstein, Ironson, & LaPerriere, 1990; Gorman, Kertzner, Cooper, Goetz, Lagomasino, Novacenko, Williams, Stern, Mayeux & Ehrhardt, 1991; Kertzner, Goetz, Todak, Cooper, Lin, Reddy, Novacenko, Williams, Ehrhardt, & Gorman, 1993; Lutgendorf, Antoni, Ironson, Klimas, Kumar, Starr, McCabe, Cleven, & Fletcher, 1997). For example, prolactin levels, which are typically increased during stress, are elevated in asymptomatic HIV-1 positive homosexual men in some studies but not in others (Gorman, Warne, Begg, Cooper, Novacenko, Williams, Rabkin, Stern, & Ehrnhardt, 1992).

Nevertheless, the increasing interest in the relation between behavioral factors and immune functioning and disease progression among HIV-1 positive individuals has led to the development of several stress-management interventions for HIV-1 positive individuals (Antoni et al., 1990). In one recent study, researchers demonstrated that a stress-management program composed of moderate aerobic exercise elevated the T-helper/inducer count of asymptomatic men infected with HIV-1 (LaPerriere, Fletcher, Antoni, Klimas, Ironson, & Schneiderman, 1991). These results are promising but should be interpreted cautiously (LaPerriere, Ironson, Antoni, Schneiderman, Klimas, & Fletcher, 1994). It is not known whether the same effect would be observed if an exercise program were implemented at a later stage in disease progression, and we are not yet sure that an increase in T-helper/inducer cells of this magnitude is actually related to longevity. In another study, asymptomatic healthy homosexual men who were tested for the HIV-1 virus but did not know the results received stress management training five weeks prior to notification of their HIV-1 status. A similar group of men was assessed but did not receive the stress management intervention. After the HIV-1 test results were revealed comparisons were made between the HIV-1 positive men in the two groups. In general, the authors concluded that participants who had received the stress management intervention, particularly the relaxation training, experienced a positive change in immune system functioning including an increase in T-helper/inducer cells (LaPerriere, Antoni, Schneiderman, Ironson, Klimas, Caralis, & Fletcher, 1990).

The use of stress management techniques to enhance the quality and length of life among HIV-1 persons will likely proliferate long before these interventions meet accepted standards of demonstrable effectiveness. This phenomenon is similar to that already observed with anti-viral drug interventions for AIDS. The need is so great, and the alternatives so few, that an unproven intervention is considered a far better choice than no intervention.

ACCIDENTAL INJURIES

During the immediate aftermath of the accident described in the beginning of this chapter, Walt was busy diverting air traffic to alternate airports and sequencing those planes that had to land on alternate runways. The plane with the landing gear problem landed without incident. Following four months of intensive investigation, the FAA released its report on the accident and cited several contributing factors. The main cause listed for the accident was not the fog but rather was human error on the part of the ATC responsible for runway 2. Jim Keaton had given clearance for a small commuter plane to take off on runway 2 just before landing gear problems had been radioed in to Walt. Jim watched as the supervisor walked over to assist Walt. Jim listened to the pilot-to-tower communication, hoping to get a sense of how serious the problem was. Jim's attention was brought back to his own position when a request for confirmation on runway 2 came over his radio set. He acknowledged, not realizing that the request for runway 2 was actually made by an incoming pilot who was unclear about for whom the previous transmission had been intended. Ordinarily a mistake like this would not have fatal consequences. Inexplicably, however, the mistake was not caught. The FAA transcript was clear—Jim had okayed two planes on the same runway at the same time! Subsequent to the accident, Jim was relieved of his duties. Although Jim had grimly "held it together" during the investigation, he fell apart emotionally and physically after his dismissal. He became despondent and was unable to secure comparable employment. Later he developed severe ulcers and migraine headaches even though he ended up working in a seemingly "low stress" clerical position.

We have all had personal experience with the old adage "haste makes waste." Often when we feel stressed, such as when we are in a hurry, we make mistakes.

Sometimes the mistakes are "simple" ones and cause no real harm. But on other occasions, feeling stressed can contribute to a serious accident. In the vignettes that began this chapter and this section, we saw that a stress-related lapse in concentration led to a collision between two airplanes, resulting in the death of over two hundred people. It has been estimated that over 88 percent of all accidents are attributable to human error (Heinrich, 1931; Petersen, 1984) and one of the important factors that precipitate human error is stress. Murphy (1987) proposed a stress-accident model wherein stress-related symptoms (e.g., anxiety) result in decrements in worker capabilities (e.g., slower reaction time), which in turn increase accident risk. This model assumes that a number of all accidents are the result of temporary, unsafe behaviors brought about by stressor-induced disorganization of workers' capacities (Murphy, 1987).

Murphy's model of stress-related accidents fits well with the model illustrated in Figure 5–3. Stress-related accidents seem to occur when stress affects psychological processes such as attention, which in turn have behavioral (unsafe behavior) consequences. The "stressor-induced disorganization of workers' capacities" can be used to help explain the human error exhibited by Jim Keaton, the air traffic controller in charge when flights 603 and 239 crashed and burned on runway 2. Jim's attention and concentration were already stretched to capacity that morning. The extra demands on his concentration imposed by the ground fog made him feel anxious, and the crisis situation developing on the other side of the tower distracted him, making him vulnerable to human error. We should note that all the other air traffic controllers were exposed to the same working conditions, and none of their flights crashed. This fact suggests that, as in the other stress-related disorders that we have discussed, stress is an important contributor to, but almost never the sole cause of, stress-related illness behavior, illness, and accidents.

Stress and Accidents.   In addition to anecdotal accounts implicating stress as a causal variable in accidents, there are a variety of research studies that support this conclusion. Petersen (1984), for example, summarizes the effects of stress (acute and chronic) on work-related accidents and concludes that high stress levels are an important risk-factor in work-related accidents. Moreover, stress-management programs have been shown to reduce employee accidents (Steffy, Jones, Murphy, & Kunz, 1986).

Motor vehicle accidents are another class of accidents in which the role of stress has become increasingly apparent (e.g., Redlemier & Tibshirani, 1997). Lourens (1990) proposed a model suggesting that while perceptual and cognitive factors are important determinants of traffic accidents, motivation, emotion (i.e., anger & anxiety) and intention are equally important. He concludes that stress can distort these cognitive processes and can contribute to motor vehicle accidents. Consistent with this model is evidence that the use of cellular phones, particularly when combined with other sources of inattention on the road, is a significant risk factor for motor vehicle accidents (Violanti & Marshal, 1996). Moreover, higher levels of stress (both on and off the road) are associated with an increased number of traffic offenses in both men and women (Simon & Corbett, 1996). A recent study that examined both occupational stress and motor vehicle accidents suggests that occupational stress is associated with a higher incidence of road accidents among company car drivers (Cartwright, Cooper, & Barron, 1996).

Coming full circle from our opening vignette, it is interesting to note that emotional stress has been identified as a risk factor for aviation accidents associated with "pilot error" (Raymond & Moser, 1995). Like the literature examining the effects of stress on errors made by air traffic controllers, however, the empirical data needed to make strong causal inferences are not yet well developed in this area. Nevertheless, the bulk of the evidence emerging from this area of research suggests that stress is likely an important contributor to accidental injuries. This area of study warrants more rigorous research designs to delineate more clearly the role of stress and accidents.

CONCLUSIONS

The evidence that we have reviewed suggests that stress is a precipitant of many different types of health-related problems. It is clear that our understanding of the psychological and physiological processes that account for the stress-illness link is just now beginning to take definitive form. One of the difficult questions that we have only hinted at so far concerns the reason why the stress-illness relationship manifests itself in such different forms in different people. That is, why are some people vulnerable to stress and others not, and why does stress seem to be associated with ulcers in one person but cancer in someone else?

Several models have been developed that seek to account for the discrepant effects of stress across different individuals (e.g., Dohrenwend & Dohrenwend, 1981). The three models depicted in Figure 5–4 illustrate the main components of these models.

The victimization model reflects the closed loop model suggested by Selye. This approach posits that severe stressful conditions (e.g., concentration camp imprisonment) are likely to lead to adverse health outcomes (even death via the general adaptation syndrome) in all but the hardiest individuals. The stress-strain model is somewhat more complex. Sometimes this model is referred to as the "weak-link" hypothesis, suggesting that constant activation of psychophysiological process leads to a breakdown in the weakest of the organ systems. Presumably people differ in terms of which organ systems are most susceptible to the effects of stress, and this variation accounts for the reason why stress is associated with GI disorders in some people and immune system disorders in others. Finally, the vulnerability model includes personal dispositions and the social context as important mediators of the stress-illness relationship. Personal dispositions are both physiological as in the weak-link model, and psychological as in dispositional ways of coping such as we described in the cancer-prone personality. An important social context variable is a person's social support network. A good deal of research has addressed how social support "buffers" the negative effects of stress as well as how the social context interacts with personal dispositions to affect health outcomes (see Chapter 2). The fact that people can vary in many ways in terms of their physiological and psycho-

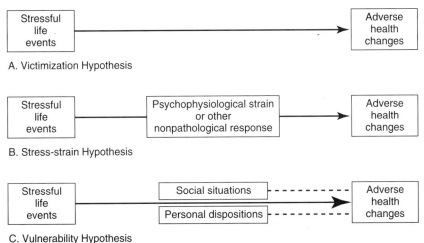

A. Victimization Hypothesis

B. Stress-strain Hypothesis

C. Vulnerability Hypothesis

Figure 5–4

Three models of stress and illness illustrating potential moderating variables in the stress-illness relationship. (From Dohrenwend & Dohrenwend, 1981.)

logical dispositions, as well as can the social context in which they experience stressful life events, helps account for the diversity that we see in the development of stress-related health problems.

SUMMARY

1. There is experimental evidence establishing a stress-illness link. Studies evaluating the effects of prolonged physical stressors on animals, such as the animal studies performed by Hans Selye, established a causal link between physical stress and the development of illness. Jay Weiss conducted systematic studies evaluating the effects of psychological stress independent of physical stressors on the development of illness. He found that animals that could not predict or control the stressor developed the most serious physical problems compared with animals exposed to identical physical stressors that could predict and/or control the stressor. Controllability and predictability of stressors are key variables in understanding how much physical harm may be incurred by exposure to a stressor.

2. Regarding methodological issues in stress-illness research, it is difficult to establish definitive causal relationships between exposure to stressors and the development of illness in humans, because it is usually impossible to use true experimental designs. Most studies are correlational or quasi-experimental, making causal inferences tenuous. Retrospective studies are frequently used in this area of research, but this design is very limited. Prospective studies, on the other hand, are a much more powerful research methodology. Even though studies are generally not true experiments, when many studies produce similar results, there is more confidence that a causal link exists between stress and the development of illness.

3. Stress has behavioral, physiological, and psychological effects, and therefore the types of disorders that can be considered stress-related are more than simply physical disorders. Four classes of disorders are identified as stress-related: somatoform disorders, psychophysiological disorders, somatogenic disorders, and accidents. In each case, stress is thought to be one important factor, though not the only factor, in the expression of the disorder.

4. Somatoform disorders are a collection of psychological disorders in which there are physical complaints for which no organic basis can be found. The report of physical symptoms is theorized to reflect psychological processes (e.g., poor coping, need for attention, "unconscious" avoidance of unpleasant or feared situations). The different somatoform disorders include hypochondriasis, conversion disorder, and somatization disorder. Stress and anxiety are thought to increase symptom-reporting among the somatoform disorders by increasing physiological arousal, thereby making an already sensitized person more likely to attribute changes in physical status (e.g., increased heart rate) to some disease process. Others theorize that the somatoform disorders simply reflect a poor coping strategy used by individuals unable to cope with the normal stress and strain of daily living.

5. Psychophysiological disorders involve physical problems where there is demonstrable organic pathology that is caused or exacerbated by stress. Temporomandibular joint disorder (TMD) is a stress-related disorder in which stress is thought to trigger maladaptive oral habits such as teeth clenching, which in turn cause elevated levels of muscle tension in the masseter muscles,

leading to facial pain. Retrospective self-report data indicate that persons with TMD report higher levels of stress in the preceding year relative to pain-free individuals. Treatment outcome studies suggest that interventions that teach people to lower the levels of tension in these muscles are effective, providing strong support for the stress-muscle hyperactivity model. Oral habits may be a form of adjunctive behavior.

6. Ulcers have been one of the most extensively studied psychophysiological disorders. Selye demonstrated the link between physical stressors and the development of ulcers, and Weiss conducted numerous studies linking psychological stress to ulcers. Recent evidence suggests that ulcers are linked to a particular bacterium, indicating that stress effects on ulcer development may be more somatogenic rather than psychophysiological as previously thought. Coronary heart disease (CHD) is considered a psychophysiological disorder in that a specific behavioral style, the Type-A behavior pattern (TABP), has been shown to be an independent risk factor for CHD. Hostility, measured by the Cook-Medley Hostility Inventory, seems to be the most "toxic" component of the global Type-A behavior pattern. The TABP is often assessed with the Jenkins Activity Survey.

7. In the somatogenic disorders, stress per se does not cause a physical problem. Stress acts to make the body more vulnerable to bacteria, viruses, and so on, generally by disrupting the function of the immune system. Moderate positive correlations have been reported between exposure to life stress and the development of cancer. The search for the cancer-prone personality, (Type-C personality) reveals that trait depression, hopelessness, and lack of emotional expression are the strongest personality variables associated with cancer. The eleven-item rationality anti-emotionality scale has been used in retrospective and prospective studies, and high scores have consistently been associated with the development of cancer. AIDS is an autoimmune system disorder caused by the HIV virus. Stress presumably reduces the ability of the immune system, making the body more vulnerable to the opportunistic infections that characterize AIDS. Stress management programs have been shown to increase measures of immune system competence as well as psychological adjustment. It is too early to tell whether stress management will have a measurable effect on longevity.

8. The observation that stress can lead to accidents is summed up in the phrase "haste makes waste." Most accidents are the result of human error and are often associated with fatigue and stress. Stress seems to influence accidents by diverting a person's attention from the task at hand. Murphy proposed a stress-accident model whereby stress or anxiety results in decrements in workers' capabilities, which in turn increase accident risk.

9. Numerous models have been proposed attempting to account for the discrepant effects of stress across different individuals (i.e., why do different people develop different stress-related illnesses?). Three main models include the victimization model, the stress-strain model, and the vulnerability model.

 **EY TERMS**

adjunctive behavior Behavior such as teeth clenching, finger tapping or pacing that occurs in conjunction with other behaviors but that seems to serve no useful purpose; such behaviors may become habitual.

biofeedback Method that teaches how to gain more control over biological functions (e.g., elevated muscle tension) through monitoring physiological processes, making the individual aware of his or her bodily responses, and consciously trying to control the measured response (see Chapter 7 for further detail).

carcinogen Cancer-causing agent.

conversion disorder Somatoform disorder characterized by loss of or alteration in physical functioning due to psychological needs or conflicts.

correlational research Type of research that assesses the relationship between two variables but does not permit inferences regarding whether one variable caused a change in the other.

electromyogram (EMG) Graphic representation of the electrical activity associated with muscle tension.

epinephrine Hormone (a catecholamine, also called adrenaline) that is secreted by the adrenal medulla in situations that are appraised as stressful; the physiological changes that it brings about help prepare the body for action.

escape/avoidance condition Condition in an experiment that places a subject in a situation requiring a specific response (e.g., pressing a lever) in order to terminate an aversive stimulus (escape) or avoid it (avoidance).

hydrochloric acid Major component of gastric juices whose job it is to break down food during digestion.

hypochondriasis Somatoform disorder characterized by an unrealistic appraisal of physical signs or sensations as abnormal, leading to a preoccupation with the fear of having a serious disease.

norephinephrine Stress hormone (also called noradrenaline) that is released via the endocrine system as part of a stress reaction and that possesses some of the excitatory action of epinephrine.

placebo Inert substance that is identical in appearance to an experimental substance being tested in an experiment; it is used to control for the nonspecific, suggestive effects of the substance or treatment being evaluated.

prospective study Study that initially assesses the condition of a group and that then tracks the group under investigation over a period of time to see whether the assessment procedures can predict who will develop a disorder and who will not.

psychophysiological disorder Type of psychosomatic disorder in which there is clear organic pathology (e.g., heart disease) and in which psychological stress is a likely causative factor or has contributed to the exacerbation of the patient's condition.

quasi-experimental design Type of research design that does not provide the experimental controls of a true experimental design but that generally allows stronger causal inferences to be made than simple correlational designs.

retrospective study Research design in which inferences about current or past functioning are made on the basis of data collected after an event or behavior has actually occurred.

somatoform disorder Disorder in which persons present physical complaints or symptoms but in which there is no clear medical, organic basis for the disorder.

somatogenic disorder Disorder in which chronic stress makes the body more vulnerable to disease-causing viruses and bacteria and thereby influences the onset and course of the disease.

stress-strain model   Sometimes referred to as the "weak-link" hypothesis, suggesting that constant physiological activation leads to a breakdown in the weakest organ systems.

temporomandibular joint disorder (TMD)   Group of related facial pain disorders involving the chewing muscles and/or the temporomandibular joint.

Type-C personality   Also called the cancer-prone personality; it is based on findings that trait depression, hopelessness, and lack of emotional expression are correlated with the development and progression of cancer.

Type-A behavior pattern   Also called the coronary prone behavior pattern; it describes a cluster of behaviors (e.g., time urgency, intense competitiveness, an overriding need to achieve) that has been linked to increased risk of coronary heart disease. One aspect of the Type-A Behavior Pattern, hostility, may be the most "toxic" component.

variable   Any part of an experiment that can fluctuate and be measured (dependent variable) or can be manipulated by the experimenter (independent variable).

victimization model   Closed-loop model suggesting that severe stressful conditions are likely to lead to adverse health outcomes in all but the hardiest of individuals.

vulnerability model   This model states that personal dispositions (physiological and psychological) and the social context (i.e., social networks) are important mediators of the stress-illness relationship.

CHAPTER **6**
Stress Management: Introduction

Managing stress is on everybody's mind these days. Some "experts" claim that as a problem area for American society stress has reached "pandemic" dimensions (Robinson, 1990). As a result, we are constantly being bombarded with information about how we can improve our chances of living healthier and longer lives (forestalling our inevitable progressive deterioration and demise), avoid death-dealing diseases (e.g., AIDS, cancer), be successful (i.e., avoid failure), and minimize contact with a wide range of other undesirable happenings that seem to be on the increase (e.g, air and water pollution, marital strife, plane accidents, terrorism, cyanide in your grapes, alar in your apples, computer viruses, corporate downsizing)—all of this in the context of the progressive thinning of the ozone layer and the "nuclear age" (which offers the continuous possibility that it could all end at any time).

Thus, it is not surprising that much energy is being devoted to developing techniques that promise to enable us to lower our stress levels, and that "stress management" in its many guises has become a growth industry in this country. But despite the claims of entrepreneurs who market audiotapes and videotapes, self-help books, and other products that "guarantee" instant stress reduction there continues to be confusion regarding what techniques are in fact useful and how to apply them (Matheny, Aycock, Pugh, Curlette, & Cannella, 1986; Nicholson, Duncan, Hawkins, Belcastro, & Gold, 1988). Given this state of affairs, our intent in this section of the book is to provide an organizational framework for classifying the major stress management techniques, and information on how they were developed, how they can be used, and on their effectiveness. In our companion workbook (Gramling & Auerbach, 1998) we give detailed instruction on how to select the techniques that are likely to be most effective for particular problems, how specific coping skills can be acquired and applied to those problems, and how to monitor and track progress in skill acquisition and application.

In this brief introductory chapter, we will outline the general features that distinguish stress management techniques from other psychological interventions, review developments in the mental health fields and in American society that have influenced the growth and tremendous popularity of the stress management movement, and finally present an overview of the organization of the following three chapters in Part III.

WHAT IS STRESS MANAGEMENT?

From the most general standpoint, stress management interventions are defined as any procedures designed to enhance the ability of people to cope with stressors or with the negative emotions elicited by them. However, such a broad definition would include traditional psychotherapy, electroconvulsive therapy (ECT), and even prefrontal lobotomies—all of which are designed to help people adjust better to life stressors and dysphoric emotions. Therefore, in addition to the major requirement of enhancing coping ability, there are other distinctive features that set stress management techniques apart from other psychological interventions designed to make people feel better.

First, stress management techniques are designed for the generally adequately adjusted person confronted with difficult circumstances. In contrast to traditional psychotherapy these techniques are oriented toward teaching coping skills rather than producing basic changes in personality traits, and for the most part they are not designed to deal with long-standing behavioral problems that are serious enough to merit a psychiatric diagnosis.[1] *Second*, most are behaviorally oriented. That is, they involve using techniques derived from classical conditioning, operant conditioning, or the more recently developed cognitive-behavioral approaches. *Third*, they are generally short-term, limited in scope, and oriented toward producing change as quickly and efficiently as possible. *Fourth*, emphasis is on self-administration, self-monitoring, and learning to establish one's own goals and develop one's own treatment program with minimal ongoing guidance from professionals. Although most of the approaches that we will review in this book require initial guidance and instruction from professionals to be used most efficiently, all have important elements that can be continued to be used by people on their own. Thus, from this standpoint, traditional psychotherapy, which requires continued interaction with a professional in a formal mental health setting, is excluded, as are somatically based medical techniques such as electroconvulsive therapy.

DEVELOPMENT AND POPULARITY OF STRESS MANAGEMENT

Several related developments in the mental health fields and in society as a whole have influenced the development and tremendous popularity of stress management. These include (a) the growth of the community mental health and crisis inter-

---

[1]The dividing line between serious maladjustment and moderately distressing emotional problems is not precise. Some of the stress management procedures that we will describe were developed to treat stress-related problems which are circumscribed (e.g., phobias), but which can nonetheless produce significant distress (see Chapter 1 for a more detailed discussion). Also, as noted in Chapter 5, stress is a causative factor in serious physical disorders, and stress management techniques are useful in alleviating these disorders or in helping people cope with the stress associated with them.

vention movements, (b) the diminishing influence of the "mental disease" model of psychopathology, (c) disenchantment with traditional psychotherapy along with the development of the behavior therapies, and (d) changes in the popular attitude toward mental health and self-help (Auerbach, 1986).

The community mental health movement gained its initial burst of momentum during the 1960s when it became embedded in the spirit of social action and progressive legislation of the Kennedy and later the Johnson administrations. The movement is oriented toward identifying and changing stress-producing aspects of the community rather than focusing on how psychopathology originates within the person, and it emphasizes early detection and prevention of psychological problems in order to avert development of severe mental disorders that would require long-term treatment by professionals (Bloom, 1984).

The 1960s were also a period of social upheaval characterized by widespread mistrust of traditional institutions. As a result community-based "rap" centers, drop-in clinics, crisis intervention telephone hotlines, and other nonestablishment agencies became popular vehicles for dealing with stress-related problems (Butcher & Koss, 1978). The underlying philosophy of these services was that "normal" people can be *expected* to experience periods of distress brought about by transitory circumstances. Furthermore, these people could be given guidance and taught how to help themselves by ordinary people who were specially trained but did not have formal training in a mental health specialty (paraprofessional volunteers). Sometimes the most effective help could be provided by "peers," who had already experienced and worked through the stressor that the person in crisis was now confronting (e.g., widows counseling the newly widowed; Silverman, 1974).

The main principle was that if helped early enough and taught to use their own resources and existing social support systems, people could deal effectively with even major stressors and avoid becoming mental health "patients." Formal entry into the mental health system, formal labeling with a psychiatric diagnosis, treatment by a professional and/or hospitalization increasingly became something to be resorted to only if all else failed. This emphasis continues today and applies even to hospitalized psychiatric patients who are returned and reintegrated into the community as quickly as possible.

Thus, the emergence of the community mental health movement was an expression of broad dissatisfaction with the established mental health system and of doubts that many came to have regarding the necessity and effectiveness of long-term psychotherapy. It was becoming increasingly recognized that many problems that people have are primarily situational and that crisis intervention or other brief interventions that are focused on helping them cope with those stressors would be sufficient to get them back on track. Expensive, long-term therapy that usually has the much broader goals of changing personality dispositions, values, self-views, attitudes, and so on may not be necessary.

These ideas were growing not only among professionals. Beginning in the 1970s, there clearly came to be increasing public acceptance of the idea that it is "okay" to have psychological problems and to try to learn and grow from dealing with those problems. The idea that having psychological problems is a sign of personal weakness (or worse, a "mental disease") and therefore not to be talked about has become minimized. There is widespread acceptance of the notion that situational problems that can cause a great deal of distress are normal, even to be expected. Losing your job, getting divorced, having to deal with your children growing up and leaving home (the "empty nest"), having a child with a substance abuse problem, or having one yourself are seen as aspects of everyday living that can be handled without necessarily seeing a psychiatrist or a psychologist for long-term psychotherapy.

Much of this acceptance has been fostered by the media, especially television talk shows such as "Donahue" and "Oprah" that reinforce the notion that stress-related problems are a part of everyday experience (rather than something shameful to be hidden) and that it is admirable to face such problems head-on. Even the idea that "you can be your own shrink" has been promoted recently by one psychiatrist who urges people to solve their own problems with brief therapy techniques and without the help of a professional (Zois, 1992). Recent research reviews indicate that self-administered psychological treatments achieve outcomes comparable to those obtained from treatments administered by therapists (Christensen & Jacobson, 1994).

Another response to disenchantment with traditional psychotherapy was the development, beginning in the 1950s, of intervention techniques based on learning theory. These "behavioral" techniques, though coming from a much different tradition than crisis intervention and other community-based approaches, share with them a situational orientation, a reluctance to use traditional psychiatric labeling, and an emphasis on demystifying the whole process of helping people change. In the behavioral techniques, the goals of intervention and the way that they will be achieved are made explicit from the outset. There is no presumption of an underlying illness that will manifest itself in another problem once the original problem has been removed ("symptom substitution"). Many of today's widely used stress management interventions are identical to or are directly derived from behavioral techniques.

OUTLINE OF PART III

All stress-management procedures are behaviorally oriented, and many are clearly grounded in learning theory. But no single conceptual model satisfactorily integrates all of the techniques that meet the criteria for "stress management" procedures as just noted. Furthermore, the techniques themselves are extremely diverse. They include procedures that teach general stress management skills, as well as those that are specific to particular kinds of stressors, those that are geared toward preventing stress as well as those designed to help adjustment to past stressors, techniques designed for individuals as well as those delivered to groups or even entire communities, and techniques that are designed to teach direct control of stress levels (emotion-focused interventions) as well as those designed to teach mastery of problematic situations that are eliciting stress (problem-focused interventions). This diversity, along with the lack of an encompassing conceptual model, makes it difficult to classify stress management interventions and present them in a systematic manner.

The overall framework that we will present emphasizes the importance of taking an objective, analytic approach toward the use of stress management interventions. Consistent with the concepts presented in Chapters 1 and 2, stressors need to be evaluated in terms of the nature of the coping demands (problem-focused, emotion-focused) that they are imposing at a given time. Stress management interventions should be selected for use on the basis of their potential effectiveness for helping people address those demands, not because they are currently popular. Thus, in describing interventions, we specify as best we can, considering the current state of knowledge, how interventions can be used to elicit coping strategies that are most appropriate given the demands of the stressors that are being confronted. In our companion volume (Gramling & Auerbach, 1998), we present specific techniques for conducting an ongoing evaluation of the effectiveness of interventions in producing desired changes.

In Chapter 3 we reviewed the relationship of the principles of classical conditioning, operant conditioning, and cognitive-behavior modification to stress management. These learning models have served as the basis for the development of many important techniques, and we gave examples of these techniques and how they may be applied to enhance coping to specific stressors. In Chapter 7 we present an overview of *basic* stress management approaches. These include emotion-focused (progressive muscle relaxation, autogenics biofeedback, meditation) as well as problem-focused (general problem-solving approaches) techniques.

The final two chapters in Part III focus most directly on the application of stress management techniques to particular kinds of stressors. The chapters are oriented around the idea, mentioned in Chapter 1, that stress occurs in the "past, the present, and the future," that temporal orientation is a significant motivator of human behavior in general (see Karniol & Ross, 1996), and that it is one of the most important characteristics of stressors that determine how we cope with them (Auerbach, 1986; 1992). We start, in Chapter 8, with "the future." In this chapter we concentrate on techniques that are designed to prevent stressors, to minimize the likelihood that we will be confronted with them if they do occur, or at least strengthen our ability to manage them should we have to deal with them. As already noted, because prevention is strongly associated with community psychology, many of the prevention procedures that we discuss are directed toward groups or entire communities. Some of them involve influencing people to change their *beliefs* and *attitudes* in order to get them to engage in preventive behaviors; they therefore have a strong *cognitive* component. In the last chapter in Part III (Chapter 9), we address the question of *postvention*, or what can be done to aid people in adjusting to the negative effects of stressors *already encountered*. Many postventive techniques are based on the classical conditioning model and the cognitive-behavioral models presented in Chapter 3. In Chapter 9 we elaborate on these techniques, with emphasis on how they may be applied in self-management.

CHAPTER 7
Basic Techniques

In this chapter we describe the "basic" techniques that are used to teach emotion-focused and problem-focused coping skills. In general, we use the term *basic* to denote fundamental procedures or strategies. However, for emotion-focused techniques, we use the term *basic* to denote procedures that are widely used on an ongoing basis to moderate emotional arousal but that may also be adapted to dealing with specific stressors. Of the four emotion-focused techniques that we discuss (progressive muscle relaxation, meditation, autogenics, biofeedback), progressive muscle relaxation has been used most widely as a component of techniques designed to enhance coping with specific stressors (see Chapters 3 and 9). In the problem-focused area, we describe one general problem-solving model (D'Zurilla & Goldfried, 1971). We also describe programs that have been developed for teaching social skills, which is a stress-relevant problem area for most people at one time or another.

EMOTION-FOCUSED INTERVENTIONS

In this section we outline the most widely used psychological approaches designed to moderate emotional arousal produced by stressor exposure. In doing so, we focus on what have been classified as the "relaxation" approaches. These include four widely recognized techniques that have been shown to reliably produce decrements in stress-related emotional arousal: progressive muscular relaxation, meditation, autogenics training, and biofeedback.

We use the term *emotion-focused* interventions with some caution. The *intent* of these techniques is to dampen stress-related arousal, and available research generally supports their effectiveness in doing so using both physiological and self-report outcome measures. However, it has not been established exactly how these techniques influence particular coping behaviors. It has been argued that the impact of these approaches is largely cognitive, that by lowering aversive arousal these approaches let people believe that they can cope with what was previously thought to be uncontrollable and that they thus lead to the execution of problem-focused coping behaviors (e.g., Goldfried, 1971). It should also be noted that the approaches we describe are the more "formalized" approaches. Many others are widely used (see Rosenthal, 1993, for an overview). Some of these approaches, such as martial arts movement disciplines or acupuncture, are highly structured but are used for a variety of purposes. Others, such as distraction, exercise therapy, massage therapy, and prayer are widely used informally but not in formal ways and so have not been extensively researched. Still other modalities, such as music and breathing, appear to have strong relaxation effects, but because they are often used in combination with the basic techniques their impact is difficult to isolate.

Progressive Muscle Relaxation

Progressive muscular relaxation (PMR) involves systematically tensing and then relaxing different groups of skeletal (voluntary) muscles, with the subject's attention directed toward discriminating between the contrasting sensations produced by the two procedures. The technique was originated by Edmund Jacobson (1924; 1938). His research led him to conclude that tension involved the effort manifested in the shortening of skeletal muscle fibers. Therefore, relaxation (the lengthening of those fibers) was viewed as a logical treatment for the tension that occurred when a person reported anxiety. From a physiological standpoint, PMR lowers emotional stress levels because it reduces proprioceptive input to the hypothalamus, thereby reducing sympathetic nervous system arousal (McGuigan, 1993).

Jacobson's (1924) original PMR procedure, which consisted of relaxing up to fifty muscle groups, took several months to master. As currently practiced, PMR involves a far smaller number of muscles. This practice commonly involves the following sixteen muscle groups in the following order (Bernstein & Borkovec, 1973, p. 25):

Dominant hand and forearm

Dominant biceps

Nondominant hand and forearm

Nondominant biceps

Forehead

Upper cheeks and nose

Lower cheeks and jaws

Neck and throat

Chest, shoulders, and upper back

Abdominal, or stomach, region

Dominant thigh

Dominant calf

Dominant foot

Nondominant thigh

Nondominant calf

Nondominant foot

Cycles consist of a 7-second tension phase followed by a 45-second relaxation phase. Each of the muscle groups is tensed and relaxed twice. About six sessions are generally necessary to obtain proficiency (Bernstein & Borkovec, 1973; Lichstein, 1988). McGuigan (1993) notes that it is important to work with tensions of increasingly lower intensity so that eventually these subtle tensions may eventually be readily identified in areas such as the minute muscles of the tongue and eyes. Also, he states that suggestion (e.g., "your hands are heavy, you are getting more and more relaxed") should be avoided because it inhibits the learning of relaxation as a response to tension cues and increases dependence on the therapist (making self-management more difficult). Bernstein & Borkovec, however, recommend that when progressing to the muscles of the chest, shoulder, and upper back, breathing cues should be added, and that following the relaxation of a muscle group, suggestions (e.g., "notice the slow and regular breathing") should be made that are paced to coincide with the client's breathing rhythm. They also emphasize that home practice is an important component of the learning procedure. Two daily practice sessions of 15 to 20 minutes separated by at least 3 hours are advised.

A number of variations in PMR have been developed to facilitate its use as a self-management procedure. They are designed to enable rapid relaxation in everyday situations without its being evident to others that effort is being made to relax. These *self-control* techniques (abstracted from Bernstein & Borkovec [1973] and Lichstein [1988]) include the following:

1. Condensation of training from the sixteen muscle groups noted above to seven muscle groups, and then finally to four groups, by combining sets of muscles (e.g., eventually the muscles of the left and right arms, hands, and biceps are combined into a single group and tensed and relaxed at the same time).

2. Training the client to achieve relaxation in response to a self-produced cue (cue-controlled relaxation) by having him or her relax, breathe deeply, and verbalize a word such as "calm" or "control" or "relax" during exhalations. Eventually the word is subvocalized (changed to a self-statement). Hopefully, this training will result in relaxation with the cue word becoming associated with relaxation. The client may then chant the word nonvocally to relax when faced with a stressful situation. Subsequently, the five deep breaths are changed to moderately deep breaths. In addition, clients are asked to relax with their eyes open. These changes are also designed to facilitate unobtrusive relaxation without alerting others in everyday situations.

3. A *recall* procedure is introduced. After relaxation is a well-learned response, the client learns to focus on and remember the feelings associated with tension release. This procedure is designed to eliminate the need to produce actual muscle tension in order to experience relaxation. The client may be instructed to associate a cue word (e.g., "calm") or counting with these feelings (e.g., "As you remain very deeply and completely relaxed, I'm going to count from one to ten, and as I count . . . allow all of the muscles to become even more deeply relaxed . . . ;" Bernstein & Borkovec, 1973, p. 36).

4. Lichstein (1988) emphasizes the importance of clients' acquiring the philosophy that relaxation is an *active* coping skill that can be applied systematically to actual situations. An essential component is learning to recognize signs of stress arousal in its earliest stages. This involves self-monitoring and detecting changes in thoughts, physical sensations, and overt behaviors that signify increases in arousal. Figure 7–1 illustrates the changes in these three areas that might accompany the stressor "secretary made an error." Again, the emphasis is on detecting mild to moderate levels of stress arousal so that self-control relaxation can be practically ap-

		THOUGHTS	SENSATIONS	BEHAVIORS
100% **Extreme**	Out of control	My business is going down the drain and my life is ruined.	headache; heart throbbing; stomach cramps	shouting insults
75% **Excessive**	Inappropriate conduct	She is constantly wasting my time with her errors.	heart beating faster	criticizing secretary in loud voice; hands on hips
50% **Moderate**	Public events	I can't believe how many times she makes this mistake.	mild chest and shoulder tension	sigh; annoyed expression
25% **Mild**	Private events	She misspelled customer's name.	stomach discomfort	none
0% **Normal Calm**				

Briefly describe situation ____ Secretary made error. _____

Example of completed homework assignment in self-monitoring of arousal.

Figure 7–1

Emergence of emotional distress. (From Lichstein, K., 1988. By permission of John Wiley & Sons, Inc.)

---

plied before arousal reaches "out of control" levels. Clients prepare for applying relaxation skills to everyday situations by practicing self-relaxation (taking moderately deep breaths, counting or chanting cue words subvocally) while tying shoes, dialing the telephone, and so on. (See Chapter 9 for further discussion of anxiety self-management techniques.)

Adverse effects of relaxation training have been reported but appear to be infrequent. These effects have generally been grouped under the label "relaxation-induced anxiety" (Heide & Borkovec, 1984) and include increased anxiety due to fears of losing control, intrusive worrisome thoughts, and changing bodily sensations. McGuigan (1993) maintains that these effects occur largely in the commonly used "briefer" derivations of Jacobson's original PMR technique, which rely heavily on suggestion. In discussing abbreviated methods, Bernstein & Carlson (1993) suggest that these anxiety phenomena may consist of minute episodes of hyperventilation in susceptible individuals, and that teaching diaphragmatic breathing skills may avert these difficulties. In general, it is important to prepare clients beforehand for the sensations and subjective experiences that they will face during relaxation and to provide them with skills (e.g., use of pleasant imagery) to manage any adverse effects that they might encounter.

Lichstein (1988) has summarized the research findings on the efficacy of PMR. He notes that Jacobson's early laboratory experiments beginning in 1927 showed that PMR reliably reduced muscle tension in both normal and highly anxious individuals, and that this effect was accompanied both by changes in cognitive activity and by decreases in blood pressure and in changes in measures of heart function. However, although Jacobson's experiments were carefully conducted, shortcomings in experimental design and lack of formal statistical analysis of data diminish confidence in his findings. More recent controlled clinical studies with various kinds of patients indicate that PMR reliably reduces state anxiety and has been used successfully to treat a range of psychophysiological disorders, including hypertension, migraines, muscle contraction headaches, and chronic pain. Abbreviated PMR has been found to be effective in treating psychophysiological and other stress-related disorders, and is particularly effective when training is presented individually rather than in a group format and when patients are provided with audiotapes for home practice (Carlson & Hoyle, 1993). Lichstein concludes that although there has been no basic research on self-control relaxation, clinical studies indicate that it is a particularly effective intervention for phobias and that it often produces general anxiety decrements beyond the boundaries of the targeted stressor.

Meditation

Although classified (along with progressive muscular relaxation, autogenics, and biofeedback) as one of the major "relaxation" procedures, meditation is also used to achieve other, more subjective goals, including "contemplation and wisdom" and "altered states of consciousness" (Lichstein, 1988). In contrast to these other techniques, meditation has a strong cultural and Eastern religious/spiritual heritage (in Zen Buddhism and yoga) and some varieties of it demand a particular lifestyle of its practitioners.

Meditation has come to denote a wide range of approaches rather than a particular well-delineated set of procedures. Although meditation is difficult to describe succinctly, two broad categories of procedures have been identified: focal or "concentrative" approaches that involve focusing attention on a single stimulus such as a word, a phrase, or an image, and diffuse or "nonconcentrative" approaches that encourage openness and expansion of the meditator's field of attention (Carrington, 1993; Lichstein, 1988). Focal forms of meditation are the more common of these two approaches and usually involve concentration on and repetition of a *mantra*, which is a word, a sound, or a phrase thought to have particularly calming properties. In one very popular form of meditation, transcendental meditation (TM), a special mantra is selected that is said to be particularly appropriate for each meditator. TM has been criticized because of the secrecy of the mantra (Girdano, Everly, & Dusek, 1990).

Although there are different types of meditation, there are several basic elements that are common to most approaches and that seem to be best suited to stress reduction (Benson, 1975; Girdano et al., 1990; Lichstein, 1988). These elements include the following:

1. A *"quiet" environment*. There should be as few distractors as possible. These distractors include external impingements (e.g., noise sources such as the phone; dimming the lights and closing the eyes "quiet" the visual environment) as well as internal stimuli. Regarding the internal environment, Girdano et al. (1990) suggest muscular relaxation as a good way to minimize physiological tension prior to meditating.

2. A *"mental device."* Attention should be consumed by a benign stimulus, e.g., a mantra (as in TM), repetition of another calming word or phrase, or focus on a tactile sensation, on one's own breathing, or on an external object. In his "secularized" meditative technique, Benson (1975) recommends the use of the word *one* because

of its neutrality and lack of cultic association. The basic strategy is to "quiet the mind" by occupying it with an emotionally neutral stimulus.

3. A *"passive" attitude.* A major goal is attainment of an attitude of "unconcerned acceptance" (Lichstein, 1988). As noted by Girdano et al. (1990, p. 292), in most meditative techniques consciousness is directed "away from the logical, cause-and-effect, goal-directed" thinking that characterizes us much of the time. Achievement of the meditative state cannot be forced.

4. A *comfortable position.* This may include sitting in a chair, lying on the floor or a mat, etc. An uncomfortable position is a source of distraction.

Some practitioners put less emphasis on the specific meditative techniques that are used than on the "state of mind" achieved through consistent application of a given set of procedures. Carrington (1993) emphasizes the need to communicate the "meditative mood," which she defines as "a subtle atmosphere of tranquility best transferred through nuances of voice and tonal quality" (p. 154).

Carrington (1993) has recently reviewed the research literature on the effects and effectiveness of meditation. She concludes that "all of the simplified meditation techniques . . . rapidly bring about a deeply restful state" (p. 141) without loss of alertness and decreased physiological arousal, as indicated by findings of lowered oxygen consumption, decreased heart and respiration rates, increased electrical resistance of the skin, and decreased concentration of blood lactate. She further notes that "when practiced regularly," meditation produces other concrete beneficial behavioral changes such as diminution of stress-related physical symptoms, diminished use of addictive nonprescription drugs, and increased physical stamina and productivity. In one study (Alexander, Langer, Newman, Chandler, & Davies, 1989), elderly volunteers who practiced transcendental meditation not only showed more improvement on measures of mental and physical health and cognitive flexibility, but also had significantly better survival rates over a three-year period than did no-treatment control subjects or those taught a "mental relaxation" technique.

Formal research has not detected any particular individual difference variables that indicate the types of people more prone to be attracted to or benefit from meditation (Carrington, 1993). However, clinical experience suggests that persons with a more spiritual bent seem to be drawn to the technique, especially the "cultic" forms of it. For some people, meditation becomes a virtual way of life, and there are reports of negative side effects experienced by people who meditate for several hours a day rather than for the recommended period of 15 to 20 minutes no more than twice a day. These side effects include psychotic episodes. Carrington also cautions that abbreviated versions or "analogues" of authentic meditation training are unlikely to be useful because they eliminate the subtle contextual aspects that are an essential component of all meditative approaches.

Autogenics

Autogenic training (AT) is a technique that has been widely practiced outside this country but that has been less popular here. It is based on the work of German neurologist, Johannes Schultz, who described it as a self-hypnotic procedure; the term *autogenics* is derived from the Greek words *autos* and *genos* and literally means "self-exercise" or "self-induction therapy" (Linden, 1993).

The major characteristics of AT include maintenance of an attitude of passive concentration, minimization of extraneous stimulation (i.e., noise, light, physical discomfort) and focus on internal sensations, and repetition of a series of verbal formulas designed to induce relaxation. Passive concentration implies a casual, unconcerned attitude about any specific goals or outcomes and a general lack of apprehensiveness while maintaining awareness and alertness (Luthe, 1983). Passive concentration and reduction of external stimulation are characteristic of meditation as well as of AT. Also, as in mantra meditation (and cue-controlled muscular relaxation), an attempt is made to get the user to focus on certain phrases or images that can then serve as cues for particular relaxation responses.

Like biofeedback, AT focuses directly on moderating autonomic nervous system arousal. AT is differentiated from other relaxation approaches by the use of six exercises, or "formulas," each of which targets a particular bodily function and is designed to produce specific sensations. These exercises emphasize feelings of warmth and heaviness, smooth and even breathing, and slow, regular beating of the heart. Their major features are as follows (adapted from Linden, 1993, pp. 214–219):

Exercise 1 involves producing muscular relaxation, beginning with the dominant arm, through suggestions of heaviness ("The right arm is very heavy") and quiet ("I am very quiet").

Exercise 2 focuses on producing the experience of warmth, and through suggestions of warmth (adding "the right arm is very warm" to suggestions of heaviness and quiet), it aims at increasing blood flow throughout the circulatory system. It is felt that sensations of heaviness and warmth and associated blood vessel dilation will generalize to the entire body and produce a tranquilizing effect.

Exercise 3 teaches people to be sensitive to the regular and steady activity of their own heart. The suggestion that is repeated is "The heart is beating quietly and strongly" or "quietly and regularly."

In *Exercise* 4, through repetition of the phrase "it breathes me," smooth and regular breathing is integrated in with muscular, vascular, and heart relaxation.

Exercise 5 focuses concentration on feelings of warmth in the solar plexus, which is seen as "the most important nerve center for the inner organs." The suggestion "sun rays are streaming quiet and warm" is repeated during this phase.

Exercise 6 capitalizes on the "well-known relaxing effect of a cool cloth on the forehead." The phrase "the forehead is cool" is repeated.

Linden emphasizes that it is important to engage in a "taking-back" procedure after each session, which consists of activities designed to bring the individual from a relaxed state back to alertness. The procedure involves bending the arms and stretching them, breathing deeply in and out, and opening the eyes.

AT users are encouraged to supplement standard formulas with images that are personally meaningful and especially useful, given the nature of the stress-related problems they have. For example, Charlesworth and Nathan (1982, p. 153) describe creative imagery used by hypertensive individuals in conjunction with autogenic training to regulate their blood pressure: "A person who worked in gas transmission saw a pipeline system and was able to open up valves and decrease pressure or redirect flow. Others saw the heart connected to a system of flexible hoses." Another person with an irregular heartbeat "discovered she could increase her heart rate control by imagining a small girl, swinging rhythmically under a tree, while the wind gently blew through her blond hair (p. 152)."

A side effect reported by most AT practitioners is "autogenic discharges." These are paradoxical anxiety symptoms (e.g., jerks, spasms) that indicate "facilitation of neuronal discharge activity from various areas of the brain that appear to be overloaded" (Luthe, 1983, p. 173). They are viewed as comparable to "relaxation-induced anxiety" symptoms occasionally observed in connection with progressive muscular relaxation, and although usually considered unwanted by trainees they are viewed by some as signs of progress in "reducing physiological and psychological inhibition" (Linden, 1993). Autogenic discharges aside, Luthe (1983) lists a wide range of physical conditions (e.g., cardiovascular problems, hypoglycemia) as well as various psychological states (e.g., psychotic states, chronic anxiety) that contraindicate the use of AT.

Favorable findings have been reported for AT when applied to a wide range of clinical problems, as well as for enhancing ability to perform under stressful conditions (e.g., sports, interpersonal functioning) (Luthe, 1983). However, many studies are poorly designed and lack appropriate controls (Pikoff, 1984). Considering appropriately controlled research, findings evaluating the effectiveness of AT indicate that it is about as effective as the other major relaxation interventions (biofeedback, meditation, PMR) in alleviating stress-related symptoms but that there is considerable variability depending on the specific disorder (Linden, 1993).

Biofeedback

The major objective of biofeedback is to teach control of stress-related physiological responses that have been operating in a maladaptive fashion. The technique teaches control of these responses (e.g., blood pressure, muscle tension) by using two devices: (a) an instrument that measures the physiological response and feeds that measurement back to the individual in an understandable way (e.g., by giving a digital representation of the heart rate in beats per minute), and (b) teaching the individual to be sensitive to subtle internal stimuli that affect the response system in question and thereby to produce changes in that response system. Individuals use different techniques and typically proceed by trial and error to find the way that most efficiently produces the desired changes for them. It is crucial that feedback is immediate so that the individual can associate what he or she is doing mentally to relax (e.g., imagery, calming self-talk) with the physiological change that is taking place.

One form of biofeedback focuses on learning to regulate the electrical activity in the brain (see Girdano et al., 1990). The biofeedback device in this case is an electroencephalograph (EEG), which measures brain-wave activity. The intent of this form of biofeedback is for the individual to learn to control the dominant brain-wave frequency in a particular area of the brain. The goal is to maintain dominance of alpha waves, which have been associated with the state of calm and relaxation combined with alertness that practitioners of meditation and autogenics also strive to achieve. Alpha waves are contrasted to very slow delta waves that are dominant only during sleep, with theta waves that are slightly faster than delta waves and seem to be dominant during internally oriented states such as daydreaming, and especially with beta waves which are faster than alpha waves and are associated with states of intense concentration and orientation to external events. Although beta wave activity does not necessarily indicate a stress response, it is almost always dominant when the stress level is elevated.

Blanchard and Epstein (1978) have outlined the history of the development of biofeedback to its current status as a major relaxation technique. The term *biofeedback* did not come into widespread use until 1969. Prior to about 1960, it was generally thought that responses like heart rate and stomach acid secretion that were under the control of the autonomic nervous system were strictly respondents. That is, it was assumed that they were involuntary and could not be brought under voluntary control. A group of experiments conducted in the 1960s challenged this assumption (see Katkin, 1971). For example, in an early study Shearn (1962) found that human subjects could change their heart rate if doing so enabled them to delay the occurrence of an electric shock. Later studies by Neal Miller and associates at Yale University provided even more dramatic findings. In one investigation, DiCara and Miller (1968) showed that with proper reinforcement (electrical stimulation of the "pleasure centers" of the hypothalamus), rats could be trained to constrict and dilate the tiny blood vessels in one ear relative to the other and thus regulate blood flow to the ears. Findings such as these, which seemed to show that under the proper conditions we can voluntarily control a wide range of our innermost functions, generated tremendous excitement. Katkin (1971, p. 23) proclaimed, "Between now and 1984 you may well discover that you can voluntarily reduce your blood pressure, set your heart to beat at any rate you desire, and tell your kidneys just how fast to produce urine for your maximum convenience."

But the results of these studies have never been consistently replicated. As noted by Roberts (1985, p. 939), "We still have no convincing evidence that the autonomic nervous system can be taught by operant methods independently of mediation by striate muscles" (muscles that mediate voluntary activity). Though the mechanisms accounting for its effects are not clear, biofeedback nonetheless has become a widely used and generally accepted technique for producing relaxation (lowered levels of physiological arousal), and some specific effects have been documented.

Conclusions

Relaxation techniques in general are widely used by people in informal ways to moderate anxiety and to deal with stress-related somatic problems (Eisenberg, Kessler, et al., 1993). PMR is easily learned and widely accepted by most clients, and using the self-control relaxation techniques just described may be readily transferred to use in everyday situations. Many practitioners (e.g., Smith, 1986) feel that PMR is particularly appropriate for beginners and should be learned before techniques like meditation or autogenics are attempted. PMR is also widely used in conjunction with systematic desensitization. Overall, it is generally viewed as the most basic and reliable of the techniques and seems to have, to a lesser degree than the others, adherents who have a vested interest in its effectiveness.

Meditation in its various forms (especially transcendental meditation) has a dedicated core of adherents and is widely used to treat stress-related somatic disorders that are thought to stem from chronic overactivation of the autonomic nervous system. However, Holmes (1984) found that there was no methodologically sound research evidence that meditation was any more effective than simple resting in lowering physiological arousal, or evidence that it facilitates control of stress arousal in threatening situations. He concluded that "the claims made for meditation have far exceeded the existing data" (Holmes, 1985, p. 730). As already noted, the efficacy of biofeedback has also been called into question (Roberts, 1985), and it has been concluded that AT has not generated sufficient methodologically sound research. But in the most recent authoritative review, Lehrer & Woolfolk (1993) conclude that on balance all of the major techniques are generally effective and "produce significant decreases (in stress arousal) on a broad array of measures." This also appears to be the consensus of opinion among those who work with these techniques on a day-to-day basis.

Lehrer and Woolfolk (1993) also address the question of whether the different techniques have specific effects or whether they all elicit a global undifferentiated relaxation response, as Benson (1975) has proposed. They conclude that a number of specific effects are evident. For example, they note (p. 510) that both AT and biofeedback have specific effects on the particular autonomic response systems being trained, that PMR appears to have specific effects on the musculoskeletal system, and that meditation "may have stronger cognitive effects" (p. 510). Lehrer and Woolfolk also point out that people may be differentially receptive to different techniques. Even though most relaxation methods work best with people who are internal in their locus of control orientation, biofeedback tends to work better with externals. This difference is attributed to the fact that internals feel that they can control their stress levels through practice and thus work on and apply their techniques on their own. Biofeedback is more congruent with an external orientation because it relies on an external machine, and success is less contingent on persistent practice outside of the office setting.

DEVELOPING PROBLEM-FOCUSED COPING SKILLS

Despite the crucial role that problem-solving plays in stress management, for the public and for many psychologists it is not viewed as a stress management tool to nearly the same degree as are the emotion-focused strategies. As we have emphasized previously, effective emotion-focused coping is usefully deployed on a short-term basis to manage overwhelming stress and to deal with situations that we cannot control instrumentally. But the essence of effective stress management is acquiring a repertoire of skills that enable one to manage problematic situations, building on and refining those skills, learning when and where they will be effective, and actually implementing them when they are called for.

What motivates us to initiate action rather than avoid or deny or use other emotion-focused coping mechanisms in the face of challenging and stressful situations? The primary factor is our conviction that we ourselves are capable of doing what is necessary to achieve the outcomes we desire. Bandura (1977, 1986) has termed this sense of potential mastery an "expectation of self-efficacy." Without this conviction that we can execute the behaviors needed to defuse problematic stressors, we will not attempt to do so and will not persist in the face of obstacles. The most powerful influence on judgments of self-efficacy is exposure to stressors accompanied by direct experiences of personal mastery—mastery that is cognitively appraised and recognized as such by the individual. Expectations of personal efficacy are also influenced by vicarious experience (viewing or visualizing others coping successfully with threatening events), by verbal persuasion (encouraging people to believe that they can master situations), and by reducing or relabeling the source of their emotional arousal (because people tend to view somatic arousal or fatigue in challenging situations as a sign of vulnerability, which in turn debilitates performance). Mastery of particular kinds of situations produce expectations of efficacy specific to those situations. People over time develop a more general sense of their effectiveness as problem-solvers across situations.

Recent research findings confirm that the perception of having good, general problem-solving ability enhances stress-coping effectiveness and overall psychological adjustment. People who view problems as challenges and who actively approach problems and deal with them with dispatch report fewer dysfunctional thoughts and irrational beliefs (Heppner, Reeder, & Larson, 1983), are less trait anxious and depressed (Heppner, Baumgardner, & Jackson, 1982; Neal & Heppner, 1982), and report experiencing less stress (D'Zurilla & Sheedy, 1991) than those who view problems as threats to well-being, respond to them with negative emotions, and put off dealing with them. Self-appraised effective problem-solvers have been found to see less threat in stressful situations, perceive more options for coping, and use more problem-focused coping and less emotion-focused coping than ineffective problem-solvers (MacNair & Elliott, 1992). Among college students, effective problem-solving is more predictive of effective study habits than is academic ability (Elliott, Godshall, Shrout, & Witty, 1990) and is associated with less premenstrual pain (Elliott, 1992), and among spinal-cord injured patients it is associated with less depression and psychosocial impairment (Elliott, Godshall, Herrick, & Witty, 1991).

In the next section we outline a well-known model that articulates general principles that may be used to enhance problem-focused coping and self-perceptions of mastery: D'Zurilla and Goldfried's Problem-Solving Model. The remainder of this chapter is then devoted to a discussion of ways of teaching and developing social skills.

D'Zurilla and Goldfried's Problem-Solving Model

D'Zurilla and Goldfried's (1971) model is a cognitive-behavioral approach that involves specifying problematic situations, generating problem-focused response options, trying out solutions, and evaluating their effectiveness (see D'Zurilla & Nezu, 1989; Nezu & D'Zurilla, 1989, for specific application of this model to stress management).

Four major stages or sets of processes are posited as necessary for effective problem-solving. The first stage, *Problem Definition and Formulation*, involves taking on a "can-do" problem-solving orientation, specifying the primary problem areas in clear, operational terms, and differentiating them from more peripheral and less crucial areas. This procedure is necessary because when people are depressed and anxious, they tend to dwell on their negative emotions, globalize, and adopt an external "out of control" orientation. *Generation of Alternatives* involves brainstorming possible solutions (again stated in concrete, operational terms) in a "freewheeling" fashion without concern for their utility or appropriateness, and formulating these solutions in terms of specific actions. A freewheeling and noncritical set towards potential solutions opens up creativity and originality, and likely produces a greater quantity of viable options. *Decision Making* entails estimating the consequences of following particular courses of action. The final stage, *Verification*, involves implementing the selected solutions and evaluating the desirability of the consequences that they produce.

D'Zurilla (1986) describes an application of this problem-solving approach with a client (Mr. C) who had become anxious and depressed after his wife of twenty-six years had left him. Several interrelated stress-inducing problem areas were identified. Among them was his intolerance of seeing his wife with her new boyfriend (Dave), whom he saw as a threat to his reestablishing a relationship with his wife. Mr. C initially stated the problem as "How can I make Dave get out of my wife's life?" Further exploration revealed that the primary problem was actually "How can I get my wife back?" Mr. C's review of his past attempts to deal with this problem and remaining alternative actions at his disposal led to the conclusion that he had no viable options in this area, and that he needed to accept the problem as insoluble and beyond his control.[1] This conclusion led to a reformulation of the problem with Dave (whom he had previously threatened with violence) as "How can I control my anger and aggressive behavior toward Dave?" Two alternatives were generated which seemed to be potentially useful. First, he cognitively reappraised the meaning (to him) of his wife's relationship with Dave, moving from self-deprecating self-views (e.g., "It shows that I am inadequate") to equally plausible nondemeaning conceptualizations (e.g., "We had different interests and values and were bound to drift

---

[1] One form of problem-focused coping that may be effective is to decide that realistically, we cannot instrumentally control a situation in the way we would like (e.g., direct confrontation) and that we should develop alternative problem-focused strategies. In some situations we may decide correctly that it is in our interest to cede control to others who are more capable of making decisions about our welfare (see Burger, 1989). This is often the case in health care situations in which we relinquish much control to the "experts" (the medical staff). Even in these situations, persons with a good sense of self-efficacy remain alert to relevant information, constantly assess the validity of decisions being made about them, and readily ask questions or even make suggestions regarding their own care (see Auerbach, 1989; Miller, Brody, & Summerton, 1988).

apart"). Second, from a more strictly problem-focused standpoint, he decided to avoid situations where he was likely to see Dave and his wife together and to act "friendly" should he encounter them together.

Mr. C learned to apply this systematic problem-solving approach to other areas. He realized that his unrealistic hope of winning his wife back had also deterred him from dealing in a systematic problem-solving fashion with other stressors, such as anxiety over meeting women and establishing new relationships. This area was boiled down into specific subproblems such as "Where can I go to meet women?" "How can I let women know that I am available?" and "How can I make myself as attractive as possible to women?" Alternative solutions to each subproblem that had a reasonable probability of success were considered (e.g., Parents Without Partners functions, church or work-related activities, and singles bars are places to meet women, or he could place ads in the newspaper or respond to ads by lonely women); the solutions that Mr. C felt most comfortable with were implemented. These generally met with success. Over time Mr. C became increasingly adept at systematically applying this analytic problem-solving approach to diverse problems as they emerged, and consequently his anxiety level declined and his overall mood and level of self-esteem was enhanced.

Problem-solving models vary in sophistication and in the complexity of the decision-making rules that are their essential components. When there are few alternatives available, sometimes the most efficient way to decide on a course of action is to follow a set of simple rules, as illustrated in Figure 7–2.

Social Skills

We all face the challenge of learning appropriate problem-focused social skills, and failure to do so can produce high levels of stress (see Chapter 3). Particularly among high-school-age and college-age men and women, social situations, having to interact with strangers, and dating situations are significant sources of anxiety (Kolko & Milan, 1985). For example, one survey found that 64 percent of college students rated dating concerns as their major problem (McEwan, 1983). Another survey found that almost a third of a sample of undergraduates described themselves as somewhat or very anxious in dating situations (Arkowitz, Hinton, Perl, & Hamadi, 1978).

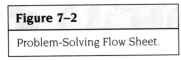

Figure 7–2

Problem-Solving Flow Sheet.

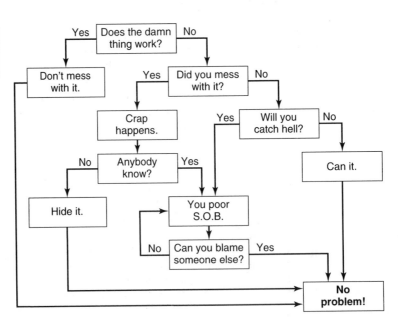

Further, Kolko and Milan note that these concerns about initiating and maintaining opposite-sex relationships are frequently associated with other adjustment problems (e.g., academic difficulties, depression) and may presage broader psychosocial difficulties in adult life.

Given the prevalence of social situations as a stressor, we further illustrate generic problem-focused interventions by discussing social skills training programs. A number of different variations of these programs have been developed. These variations have been largely oriented around tailoring the teaching of these skills to specific populations with specific needs, such as divorced individuals, the elderly, parents who need to train children, and the mentally retarded (L'Abate & Milan, 1985). Because meeting and initiating contact with others, especially those of the opposite sex, is the most common stress-related social problem we will focus on heterosocial and dating skills in exemplifying the content of social skills training programs.

Examples of Heterosexual Social Skills Training Programs

Social skills programs are *situation*-oriented. It is assumed that insufficient skills in social situations lead to performance failures, so that these situations thus elicit anxiety when they are encountered. Therefore, the focus is on identifying problematic situations and on the teaching, rehearsal, and reinforcement of responses that will enable the individual to deal skillfully with those situations. The description in the next sections, following the outline provided by Curran, Wallander, & Farrell (1985), highlights the main elements of the training programs developed by Curran (1977), Curran, Monti, & Corriveau (1977), Lindquist, Framer, McGrath, MacDonald, & Rhyne (1975), Twentyman & McFall (1975), and West, Goethe, & Kallman (1980). All of these training programs use a *group* therapy setting. This format allows clients to practice skills with each other, to receive feedback from peers, and to respond to new situations as they arise in the group, thus promoting generalization of skills to a wider range of situations (West et al., 1980).

1. *Identifying Frequently Encountered Stressful Social Situations.* Either situations are predetermined or particularly stressful situations are identified by using a standardized questionnaire. Here are some examples:

Asking for a date

Dealing with the first physical contact (kiss, holding hands)

Uncomfortable silences

Turning down a date

How and when to end a first date

Dealing with a goodnight kiss

2. *Providing Information.* Initial information is provided regarding what is meant by good heterosocial skills and how they can be used effectively. Participants are told why a social skill is important and how it can be used productively, and they are also given examples of inappropriate uses of a skill. For example, Curran (1977) starts by presenting the idea that people have misconceptions that contribute to the anxiety that people experience when trying to start a conversation and to keep it going. Many people think that they shouldn't talk about trivial things, that if they are not talking about something "meaningful" then they are not accomplishing anything and are coming across poorly. In fact, participants are told, casual conversation serves important purposes. It informs people of a person's attitudes and values, and the

extent to which people are congruent in these areas is an important determinant of how much they like each other. Furthermore, relationships need to start somewhere before they can move to a more intimate level.

Specific information can then be given (or demonstrated visually by using a model) regarding how and when to initiate a social contact and how to use specific conversational skills during a social interaction. For example, men are taught to attend to cues that indicate whether a woman is likely to be receptive to an approach (e.g., making eye contact, smiling) versus those that indicate probable lack of receptiveness (e.g., wearing a wedding ring). They are given examples of possible "opening lines" to use (e.g., "Is anyone sitting here?" "Have you decided what you're doing this summer yet?") (Lindquist et al., 1975). During a conversation, useful skills include nonverbal behaviors such as using eye contact and head nods to show interest and attention, decreasing one's interpersonal distance and using posture to indicate comfort with the other person, or using gestures and alterations in voice tone or volume to emphasize a particular point, as well as verbal behaviors such as the use of open-ended questions and reflective statements to indicate interest and to encourage the other person to continue talking (West et al., 1980). Further information is provided on how to continue a conversation (e.g., comment on a friend or an interest that you may have in common), how to extend a conversation (e.g., changing topics at least once), and establishing future contacts (e.g., "Can I call you sometime?" "Will you be taking a break later?").

3. *Rehearsal.* An essential part of training is continued repetition of newly learned responses to enhance the probability that they will be used in actual situations. The most widely used practice format is role-playing.

The following are examples of role-play situations used by West et al. (1980, p. 50) in their skills-training program. *Initiating a conversation:* "You are on a break at your job. You see a guy who is about your age. He works in another part of the store, and consequently you don't know him very well. You would like to start talking to him. What would you do?" *Maintaining a conversation:* "You are talking to a guy at work, and he is explaining how he missed the bus, thus getting to work late. He pauses. You want to continue the conversation. What would you say?"

After skills are practiced in role-play situations, clients may be assigned to try out and rehearse their skills in practice dating situations. In some programs, therapists arrange dates for clients, either with other clients or with confederates (e.g., Christensen, Arkowitz, & Anderson, 1975). In others, clients are given assignments to engage in social contacts outside of the therapy session without assistance from the therapist (e.g., invite a woman for coffee). In these instances, clients are prepared for such encounters by having them review the skills that they have learned and express anticipated difficulties so that alternatives and suggestions can be offered by group members and by the therapist.

4. *Performance Feedback and Generalization.* Learned skills are shaped through feedback provided by peers or group leaders and through self-reinforcement. One powerful format is playing back and commenting on videotape recordings of role-plays. Another involves having clients report back to the group on attempts to carry out assignments outside of the group. Clients are encouraged to review and evaluate their own performance (what she or he did, how others reacted, how he or she felt). The group is encouraged to adopt a problem-solving strategy and generate alternative approaches in giving feedback for unsuccessful ventures. Successfully completed assignments and attempts to persevere in the face of anxiety are reinforced by the group leader and members (Lindquist et al., 1975).

Hopefully, as skills are shaped in therapy sessions they will be increasingly applied and will meet with success in the natural environment. Generalization of skills that are learned in a controlled setting such as a therapy group to the real world is never assured. Therapy groups offer continuous modeling, appropriate feedback and reinforcement, and encouragement to emit appropriate behaviors in fearful situations. None of these are consistently available in everyday life.

As noted by Milan and Kolko (1985), *self-control* techniques can be taught to clients in order to enhance generalizability of learned skills. These techniques emphasize various combinations of systematic application of problem-solving strategies to decide on solutions and of teaching self-talk to encourage, guide, and reinforce performance of appropriate behaviors. The goal is to teach broad, general coping strategies that can be applied to a variety of conditions. These techniques all have a strong *cognitive* component and we will provide more detail on them later when we discuss cognitive interventions.

Evaluation of Effectiveness.   Curran et al. (1985) reviewed studies evaluating the effectiveness of heterosocial skills-training programs. They concluded that participants in training programs showed significantly more improvement over the course of treatment than did people in control groups that controlled for the passage of time (pretreatment and posttreatment evaluations only), or over those that gave subjects the same amount of attention by a therapist but not the crucial ingredients of skills training. The evidence for maintenance of treatment-gains at followup is more tentative and therefore requires more research before definitive conclusions can be made.

Assertiveness Training

Assertiveness is an important aspect of social competence, and assertiveness training is an essential component of social skills training. Some feel that assertiveness should be incorporated under social skills training rather than treated as a separate topic; however, we examine it separately because of its great popularity and strong association with the special needs of women (Galassi, Galassi, & Fulkerson, 1984).

Assertiveness refers to a group of operant behaviors that fall under the category of social skills. In general, assertiveness refers to direct and clear expression of one's thoughts and feelings and desires in a socially appropriate way. The "socially appropriate" caveat excludes behaviors that are threatening or punishing or that in any way violate the legitimate rights of others.

Three general groups of assertive behaviors have been identified. These include *expressing positive feelings* (e.g., affection, giving and receiving praise), *self-affirmation* (e.g., refusing unreasonable requests, expressing personal opinions), and *expressing negative opinions* (e.g., expressing justified anger).

Assertive behavior is differentiated not only from passive behavior but also from aggressive behavior. Charlesworth and Nathan (1982, pp. 335–340) outline the multiple ways in which these three kinds of behaviors can be contrasted. *Passive* behavior is characterized by withholding forthright expression of thoughts and feelings and by allowing others to take advantage. There is frequent use of apologetic words (e.g., "I guess," "I'm sorry") and also of nonverbal indicants of acquiescence and deferral to the wishes of others (e.g., voice is soft and hesitant, frequent head-nods when others are speaking). Passive behavior allows avoidance of conflict with others in the short term but usually produces feelings of frustration, anxiety, and anger in the long term, and others come to depreciate and lose respect for the person. *Aggressive* behavior is characterized by direct expression of thoughts and feelings but in ways that blame and imply threats. "Your voice is loud—your eyes are narrow, cold, and staring—your hands are in fists or your fingers are pointed at the other person." Whereas aggressive behavior often gets the person what he or she wants in the short term, it is at the expense of others who feel humiliated and angry and in the long term it produces alienation from others. In contrast to these less adaptive styles *assertive* behavior is characterized by clear, tactful statements that are communicated in a calm, assured manner. Because the assertive person is direct and aboveboard, others are likely to feel respected and are likely to trust that person and to feel free to express themselves forthrightly. Furthermore, the assertive person often achieves goals without feeling compromised or producing dysphoric emotions in others.

Galassi et al. (1984) reviewed studies that evaluated the effectiveness of assertive behaviors in contrast to aggressive and passive behaviors in achieving desired goals, and the impact that these behaviors have on others. They found that, in general, assertive responses result in more compliance, and elicit greater respect and sympathy and less dislike from others than aggressive behavior. Passive behavior tends to be rated as pleasant and friendly by others but is generally less effective than assertive behavior. One study (Linehan, Brown, Nielsen, Olney, & McFall, 1980) examined the effects of different kinds of assertive responses. In terms of general effectiveness, direct assertiveness (e.g., "No thanks, I need to have some alone time") and empathic assertiveness (e.g., "I know you feel bad, but I just can't help you") were rated highest, followed by flattery, apology, stretching the truth, helplessness, and indirectness.

Origins of Nonassertiveness.   Assertiveness involves emitting certain classes of verbal and nonverbal operants (those that involve expressing emotions, standing up for one's rights, and expressing displeasure) with others. Why are some persons less comfortable emitting these behaviors, and why have some never learned how to emit some of these behaviors? It is not easy to provide precise answers to these questions. There is evidence that some people are born with a propensity to be shy. Their temperament is such that they tend to be inhibited with people and to avoid unfamiliar nonsocial situations as well (Kagan, Snidman, & Arcus, 1993), and they are thus predisposed to be less assertive. However, even among those with a predisposition toward social inhibition, learning history plays a significant role in molding nonassertive behavior. As a result of a variety of experiences, many of us have come to accept the idea that we shouldn't assert ourselves, that it is socially inappropriate, that one shouldn't "rock the boat" or "stick out your neck," that it is best to conform, because those who express their feelings and attitudes are flaunting authority and looked on with disfavor by others. Parents often play a strong role in developing this type of attitude. They may model passive behavior by rarely expressing their feelings and thus implicitly teaching that this is the way to behave; or more explicitly, parents may selectively reinforce passivity and behavior oriented toward social obligations and punish assertive behavior. Wolpe (1990) notes that this behavioral style is often encountered in devoutly religious persons who have been taught that it is a moral imperative to turn the other cheek. It should be noted that inappropriately aggressive behavior may be learned and reinforced in the same manner, and that it is also sometimes underwritten by moral teachings of a different sort ("It's a dog-eat-dog world out there"; "If you don't get them first, they'll get you").

Learning histories of this kind can have two types of consequences that are detrimental to the learning of appropriate assertive behaviors. First, social situations that call for assertive behavior may come to have aversive properties and thus elicit anxiety in a classical conditioning sense. The aversiveness may stem from several sources: (a) a history of punishment received from parents or other adults when the individual attempted to behave assertively in such situations; (b) negative consequences delivered by peers (e.g., lack of popularity or, at the extreme, social ostracism) for overly passive or overly aggressive behavior, (c) negative self-statements in response to the lack of positive feedback from others in social situations (e.g., "Nobody seems to like me, I don't know what's wrong with me"). Second, as a result of these negative experiences that would lead to an avoidance of social situations, as well as parental restrictions (e.g., parents who restrict normal social interactions such as dating or sports), there may be limited opportunities to learn appropriate assertive behaviors.

Thus, two broad types of problem areas may develop: (a) a classically conditioned fear and resulting avoidance of social situations calling for assertive behavior, and (b) a deficiency in (operant) assertiveness skills and a resulting lack of knowledge of when and how to apply them.

Learning Assertiveness Skills.   Assertiveness difficulties tend to be situation-specific. Most of us are able to be comfortable behaving assertively in some ways with some people (e.g., refuse requests made by friends), but may experience anxiety and are "reduced to jelly" when the need arises to be assertive in particular ways with others (e.g., expressing justified annoyance to parents). Before a program of change can be initiated, specific areas of discomfort must be identified. In our companion workbook (Gramling & Auerbach, 1998) we present a situation (person) by behavior format for assessing assertion difficulties.

Assertiveness training programs generally involve the same major components outlined earlier under social skills training programs. These include doing a situation by person assessment in order to identify specific assertive behaviors in conjunction with particular target persons, rehearsal of assertive behaviors using a role playing format, and then trying out newly learned skills in actual situations. Sometimes a range of problematic situations is identified, and, as in systematic desensitization, a hierarchy of situations in order of increasing difficulty (as perceived by the client) is developed and dealt with progressively. The following are items from a hierarchy developed for "a 25-year-old woman having an affair with an older married man who appears to be indifferent to her feelings" (reprinted from Masters et al., 1987, p. 105).

1. He phones to tell you he may not be able to see you the following weekend, offering no reason.
2. You complain about his mistreatment, and he calls you a "bitch" and won't respond further.
3. You want to tell him off, but you fear losing him as a result.
4. You want to tell him you no longer wish to see him.

Role playing often includes role reversal in which the therapist takes the part of the client, and the client plays the role of the target person. This enables the therapist to model appropriately assertive behavior for the client and also provides an opportunity for the client to experience the actual impact that assertive behavior has on others.

A variation on role playing that is useful for self-management assertiveness training involves a cognitive technique called *covert modeling* (Kazdin, 1976). The main component of this approach involves having an individual imagine scenes in which a model acts assertively, and thus the technique may be used to handle stressful situations as they come up in everyday life. The following is an example of a scene used for covert assertive modeling (reprinted from Kazdin, 1976, p. 479):

> Picture yourself at a concert with a friend. A few people in the row behind you are making a lot of noise and disturbing everyone. It seems they have a comment to make every few minutes which everyone can hear. A person sitting next to you (the model) turns around and says, "Will you please be quiet."

Logically, it might be expected that visualizing oneself as the model would be most effective. However, Kazdin has obtained data indicating that clients who imagine several different models show greater behavior change, suggesting that this approach produces greater generalization.

Passive-Aggressive Behavior.   Wolpe & Lazarus (1966) point out that sometimes in situations in which one's rights are being violated, a direct expression of feelings is not an effective way of dealing with the situation. In such situations one may have to resort to *passive-aggressive* behavior. Passive-aggressive behavior has been called "sugarcoated hostility, aggression with an escape clause" (Wetzler, 1992). It involves indirect and covert ways of expressing resistance and achieving one's ends that are designed to preclude retaliation by the target of the behavior. It is the type of behavior that over the long haul elicits distrust and hostility in others, but in particular instances may be a reasonable strategy for dealing with a stressful situation.

Wolpe & Lazarus (1966, pp. 52–53) give an example of such a situation. They describe the case of a young lawyer with a very desirable job who was being unduly harassed by a senior partner who continually found fault with his work and lectured him on petty details. Explanations that he offered to the partner were ignored, as were complaints to the other partners, and he concluded that an honest discussion with the partner at a time when the partner was not lecturing him would be to no avail.

> Therapeutic attention was then devoted to the implementation of subtle tactics which might serve to discourage the employer's prolonged and denigrating lectures. Mr. G. F. was instructed to make casual inquiries from the secretaries and other office personnel regarding the senior partner's idiosyncrasies and possible vulnerabilities. At the next session the patient informed the therapist that the senior partner was reputed to be a hypochondriac. He added, "I don't know whether this is relevant but the typists are also very amused by Mr. J's great pride in his tailor-made suits."
>
> The therapist asked Mr. G. F. if he was able to feign a worried expression when his principal next engaged in one of his tirades and to interject with some assumed statement of concern regarding the state of his employer's health. He was exceedingly amused at the idea of this proposed gambit and said he would certainly attempt to apply it. A second tactic was also proposed. In the midst of one of his employer's declamatory speeches Mr. G. F. was required to dust real or imaginary specks of dandruff from his employer's clothes. For this purpose behavior rehearsal procedures were employed in which the patient enacted this behavior with the therapist.
>
> At the following interview, 3 weeks later, Mr. G. F. was jubilant. He described an occasion when his employer lit his pipe and settled back in his customary manner to deliver one of his harangues. Mr. G. F. recounted how he had riveted his gaze on his employer's left cheek and (approximately 10 min. later) his employer had demanded to know what he was staring at. "I put on a worried frown as though my discovery was too dreadful to repeat and said 'Nothing Sir. Excuse me for asking Sir, but are you feeling quite well?'" The senior partner was reported to have replied, "Why what's wrong?" whereupon Mr. G. F. said "Nothing Sir, nothing at all." The interview was terminated less than 2 min. later. Mr. G. F. subsequently used a variation on the ploys he had rehearsed. He had learned that his principal was extremely self-conscious about his balding head. "The next time he started with me I just kept staring at his head. The lecture ended after about 5 min. instead of the usual hour or longer . . . I repeated the same performance 3 days later. Since then the boss has given me a very wide berth."

Evaluation of Effectiveness.   Galassi et al. (1984, p. 367) concluded that "Based on self-report and laboratory performance measures, it appears that effective assertion training treatments can be constructed based either on behavior rehearsal or a modeling foundation. However, evidence for generalization of treatment effects to in vivo behavior continues to be meager as are data about the reactions of significant others to the new behavior patterns of individuals who have received assertion training."

$\mathcal{S}$UMMARY

1. Basic techniques are classified into two categories: (a) those that are primarily designed to moderate stress-related emotional arousal (emotion-focused techniques) and those that are designed to teach problem-solving skills (problem-focused techniques).

2. Of the four emotion-focused techniques, PMR is probably the most versatile. It can be used by itself to help moderate the overall level of emotional arousal or as part of systematic desensitization to moderate stress responses to specific stressors. It may also be readily adapted for use as a self-control technique and be applied in specific situations.

3. Meditation may involve a wide range of techniques; many meditative approaches have a spiritual component and have an Eastern religious heritage. Research findings indicate that meditation can be an effective means of lowering stress-related arousal and minimizing other negative stress effects.

4. Autogenic training, like meditation, emphasizes inducing passive concentration and a focus on phrases or images that serve as cues for relaxation. Like biofeedback, it attempts to directly reduce autonomic nervous system arousal; it also has elements of suggestibility similar to hypnosis.

5. Biofeedback is designed to teach voluntary control of stress-related, autonomically mediated physiological responses, such as muscle tension and heart rate. It is widely used clinically and well accepted by clinicians and the public, although the mechanisms accounting for its effects have not been definitively established.

6. Emotion-focused coping skills are useful on a short-term basis and in low-control situations. Effective stress management, however, ultimately involves acquiring and appropriately applying instrumental skills to manage problematic situations. General problem-solving models, such as Goldfried and D'Zurilla's, have been applied effectively to a wide range of stress-related problems. Other models have been applied specifically to persons with social skills deficits and assertiveness problems, with good success.

$\mathcal{K}$EY TERMS

assertiveness Direct and honest expression of thoughts and feelings in ways that are considerate of and that do not violate the rights of others.

assertiveness training Form of social skills training that generally involves identification of situation (person)–specific behavioral deficits, rehearsal of appropriate assertive behaviors in role playing, and trying out newly learned behaviors in actual situations.

autogenics Emotion-focused coping technique that induces relaxation through the use of six exercises that target different bodily functions.

biofeedback Emotion-focused technique in which an individual learns to influence stress-related physiological responses not ordinarily under voluntary control (e.g., blood pressure); it involves providing immediate, understandable feedback (e.g., a digital presentation) of the response level so that the individual can learn to associate a relaxation procedure with appropriate response changes.

covert modeling   Using imagined scenes in which a model behaves effectively to help motivate appropriate behavior in actual situations.

D'Zurilla & Goldfried's Problem-Solving Model   Cognitively based approach that involves specifying stressors, generating response options, trying out different solutions, and testing their effectiveness.

passive-aggressive behavior   Indirect ways of expressing negative feelings toward others that are designed to minimize retaliation by the target persons.

progressive muscle relaxation   Emotion-focused technique in which relaxation is produced by systematically and progressively tensing and then relaxing different muscle groups; an essential component of systematic desensitization.

mantra   In meditation, a calming word or sound that is repeated verbally or mentally.

meditation   Term used to denote a wide range of emotion-focused techniques that usually involve relaxation procedures ("quieting the mind") as well as various rituals and postures ("quieting the body"); the mental aspect emphasizes concentration on a particular subject or image.

social skills training   Behaviorally and situationally oriented programs designed to teach social skills and minimize anxiety in social situations (often involving dating and heterosexual relations).

CHAPTER 8
Prevention

Prevention is a compelling concept. If the factors that cause negative events can be identified and somehow modified or eliminated, these events will occur less often or not at all. When prevention procedures are not implemented or are not effective, the alternative is treatment, which is typically more expensive and exacts an added cost in human suffering. In medicine, preventive activities have had a significant impact in reducing the prevalence of most diseases and have generally been more effective than treatment services (Bloom, 1984).

As used in medicine and public health, the concepts of prevention and treatment refer to decreasing vulnerability to (prevention) or limiting damage resulting from (treatment) disease. A disease entity (e.g., schizophrenia) is identified, evidence is accumulated about its etiology and course, and preventive and treatment procedures are implemented on the basis of these data. These concepts may also be usefully applied to stress management. But stress management, in contrast to the disease-centered model of medicine and public health, is oriented around sources of stress. It focuses on how to use behavioral techniques to prevent stressors (which may or may not be diseases) from occurring, on how to help people avoid coming in contact with them if they do occur, and on minimizing the chances of experiencing negative effects if they do come in contact with them (Auerbach, 1986, 1992).

Two broad types of programs have been developed to provide people with ways of averting stressors in their lives or with skills to cope with stressors should they be exposed to them. One type is *global* in its approach. Rather than being oriented around particular kinds of stressors or problem areas, these programs are designed to help people address a broad range of problems or to provide them with general skills that are applicable in dealing with a range of stressors. The second group of approaches target *specific* stressors. They have as their goal motivating people to take preventive action to avoid exposure to dangerous stressors (e.g., diseases such as AIDS or cancer) or to prepare them to deal effectively with specific stressors that they are likely to encounter. The bulk of this chapter will consider approaches targeting specific stressors. First, however, we give an overview of more global programs.

GLOBAL STRESS MANAGEMENT PREVENTION PROGRAMS

One kind of global preventively oriented stress management program is designed to teach broad-based coping skills. Many such programs are now available through commercial organizations providing workshops as well as self-help books and audiotapes and videotapes that promise to teach you how to "control the stress and tension in your life." They often focus on a single favored technique and are rarely evaluated in terms of the extent to which people follow through with recommended activities or of how useful they are. One program ("Success Over Stress") developed by Jason, Curran, Goodman, & Smith (1989) is notable because of its scope and its innovative use of the media, along with supplemental written materials, in an attempt to reach a significant segment of a large community, and because of efforts made to evaluate its effectiveness.

Teaching Coping Skills: A Media-Based Program

The Success Over Stress program was based in Chicago and aired by a television station twice a day for two weeks during regularly scheduled news programs. Local celebrities appeared on commercials to promote the series, and the program was presented by a popular local anchorman. Local volunteers, representing different population segments, were filmed and their progress was monitored as they tried the ten-day program. The program thus made use of positive role models and trusted public figures as well as easy-to-identify-with average community residents to facilitate acceptance and promote participation.

The program contained an educational component as well as information on coping techniques. The positive and negative aspects of stress were presented, as was information on how we respond physiologically, behaviorally, and cognitively to stress exposure. Viewers were taught how to evaluate the impact that specific stressors have on them and the coping strategies that they were currently using, and then directed them to consider alternative coping strategies both for these stressors and for other stressors should they encounter them. Information on using self-management coping techniques ranging from challenging unrealistic beliefs to marshaling social support in dealing with specific stressors was then presented, along with instruction on how to evaluate their effectiveness and on ways to reward oneself for effective coping. An example of how one of the coping techniques (challenging unrealistic beliefs) was presented is illustrated in Figure 8–1.

Though it presented some information on the negative effects of stress and stress-related habits such as smoking and substance abuse, limited use was made of fear arousal as a motivational tool. The emphasis was more on positive growth and on the beneficial effects of learning how to identify stressors and apply coping techniques in a positive way. Data collected on a subsample of 84 viewers (of an estimated 300,000 or more who viewed the programs daily) indicated that more than half tried the techniques that were portrayed (such as deep breathing, challenging beliefs, progressive relaxation, exercise, and humor), used them on numerous occa-

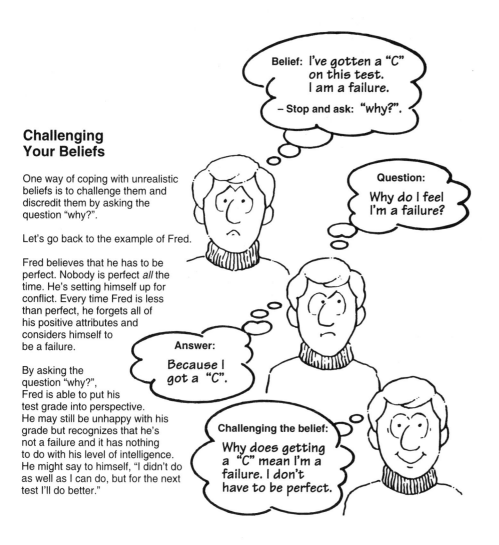

Challenging Your Beliefs

One way of coping with unrealistic beliefs is to challenge them and discredit them by asking the question "why?".

Let's go back to the example of Fred.

Fred believes that he has to be perfect. Nobody is perfect *all* the time. He's setting himself up for conflict. Every time Fred is less than perfect, he forgets all of his positive attributes and considers himself to be a failure.

By asking the question "why?", Fred is able to put his test grade into perspective. He may still be unhappy with his grade but recognizes that he's not a failure and it has nothing to do with his level of intelligence. He might say to himself, "I didn't do as well as I can do, but for the next test I'll do better."

Figure 8–1

Challenging your beliefs. (Reprinted by permission of the American Lung Association of Metropolitan Chicago.)

sions (deep breathing and humor were used most frequently), and rated them as helpful. Though there wasn't a "no-treatment" control group to provide comparative data, people who tried the program showed significant pre-post improvement on measures of psychological adjustment.

Crisis Intervention Hotlines

In contrast to programs like Success Over Stress that teach broad coping strategies, crisis intervention hotlines provide specific resources and information to help people deal with stress-related problems. In this sense, hotlines are more *reactive* than proactive. We present them here under the category of prevention programs because their development was grounded in the idea that people under stress should have a resource that they could feel comfortable turning to at a moment's notice, without having to disclose their identity and without having to deal with the stigma of being identified as someone with a "mental problem." It is the hope that in this way, people would feel more comfortable seeking help and would receive it at the earliest stages of dealing with a stressful problem, so that serious psychopathology would be prevented. Rather than having people deal with a psychologist, psychiatrist, or other mental health professional, help would be provided by nonprofessional volunteers specially trained in telephone counseling techniques.

Crisis intervention, in general, overlaps a great deal with stress management. Both approaches emphasize using one's own resources as much as possible, achieving eventual self-sufficiency, and avoiding, if possible, the traditional mental health setting and treatment by professionals. A major difference is that crisis intervention has much more of an "emergency" connotation. Crises refer to highly stressful events, usually of sudden onset, that strain coping capability to the limits. We thus rarely use the adjective *chronic* to describe crises, as is sometimes done to characterize stressors. Also, in contrast to the behavioral (learning) heritage of most of the recognized stress management interventions, the most important influences on the growth of crisis intervention hotlines were the community mental health movement (described in Chapter 6) and particularly the increased attention paid to suicide prevention in the late 1950s and 1960s by clinical and community psychologists.

When crisis intervention hotlines were first developed, they were organized around the main goal of suicide prevention. Farberow (1974, p. 18) characterized suicide as the "epitome of crisis, the best example of an emotion-laden psychiatric emergency heightened by the fact that a life is at stake." The basic techniques for telephone crisis intervention were developed at the Los Angeles Suicide Prevention Center, which was established in 1958 (McGee, 1974). The following major intervention principles were established for nonprofessional volunteers serving as crisis intervention workers (Farberow, Heilig, & Litman, n.d.):

1. *Establish a relationship and maintain contact.* For callers to hotlines who are under stress and often confused and hesitant, it is important that the voice on the other end of the line represents a "real" person. Thus the crisis worker must quickly project empathy and "communicate by his attitude that the person has done the right thing in calling" (Farberow et al, n.d., p. 4). One simple mechanism at the outset is for the volunteer to identify herself or himself by first name, to request the name of the caller, and to use it in addressing the caller. In tone of voice and manner of speech the worker should project an air of calm, reassurance, and confidence. Hesitant callers should be gently encouraged to talk (e.g., "I know it must be hard for you to put your feelings into words"). The objective is for the caller to feel understood and supported (Slaikeu, 1990).

2. *Identify and clarify the nature of the problem that has prompted the call.* Callers are sometimes very emotional and therefore disorganized in their presentation. It is important to clarify with them the central conflicts that they are dealing with so that action plans can be developed. Initially, open-ended questions such as "What has been happening recently to make things so difficult for you right now?" are useful (Slaikeu, 1990).

3. *Evaluate suicidal potential.* Certain factors have been identified as indicating a higher risk of suicide. These include being of the male sex, being advanced in age, having a mental disorder, having a difficult or unhappy marital status (persons who are divorced, widowed, separated, and never married—particularly men—are at higher risk) (Buda & Tsuang, 1990; Tuckman & Youngman, 1968), and having made a previous nonimpulsive attempt at suicide (Suokas & Lonnqvist, 1991). Regarding the latter, it is estimated that nearly three-fourths of suicide committers have previously attempted the act (Resnik, 1980), and it is believed that the greater the lethality of the last attempt the higher the present risk (Sommers-Flanagan & Sommers-Flanagan, 1995). Although females call crisis hotlines more often than males, females are lower suicidal risks (Diekstra, 1989). The suicide rate for adolescents in general has been increasing in recent years (Kaplan & Sadock, 1996), with substance abuse often a complicating factor with this group. There is consistent evidence that a history of physical or sexual abuse is a risk factor for suicide or suicidal symptoms in children and adolescents (Wagner, 1997).

Aspects of emotional functioning should also be attended to. Suicide is associated with severe depressive states that are most commonly reflected in such complaints as difficulty in sleeping, poor appetite, lack of energy, social withdrawal, feelings of failure and worthlessness (Miles, 1977), and, in particular, the expressed belief that the future is hopeless (Beck, Brown, & Steer, 1989). Depressed persons may also exhibit agitation, restlessness, and overt anxiety and tenseness. It is believed that when these symptoms are evident, suicide risk is increased because they are indicative of energy and motivation for committing the act (Resnik, 1980). Possibility of suicide is further enhanced when a specific stressful incident has recently occurred, particularly one involving loss (e.g., of a job, of health, of a marital partner) (Hatton, Valente, & Rink, 1977). HIV infection increases suicide risk substantially. The risk of suicide in men between the ages of twenty and fifty-nine who know they have been infected is thirty-six times that of men in the general population who are in this age category and who do not have such knowledge; this risk factor is likely due to stress possibly interacting with the dementia that accompanies AIDS symptoms (Marzuk, 1991; VandeCreek & Knapp, 1993).

Crisis workers should not avoid asking questions regarding suicidal inclinations on the part of the caller if the caller appears to be at risk. Suicide risk is higher to the extent that the individual has invested time and energy in making preparations (e.g., changed a will, left notes) and committed himself or herself to a detailed and realistically lethal plan (e.g., bought a gun, set a time and place).

4. *Assess the caller's internal strengths and resources.* Prior to formulating an action plan, an estimate should be made of the caller's ability and willingness to cope actively with his or her situation. Positive indications include an accepting response to the crisis worker's initial suggestions and improvement in mood and cognitive focus as the interview progresses.

5. *Formulate an action plan and mobilize the caller's resources.* Crisis intervention workers are not trained to be therapists. Their primary goal is to understand the caller's problem in order to get them assistance in the easiest way possible. A first priority is to get the caller to consider readily available resources (friends, family, clergy, family physician, employer) that he or she may not be considering because of current stress level; for example: "Who do you usually talk to when you're down?" "Where is he?" "How can you contact him now?" Rather than the crisis intervention worker's trying to solve the caller's problem on the phone, the main objective is to refer the caller to resources that can provide help. In some cases (e.g., where there appears to be potential for suicide), this referral is to a mental health or social service agency. Workers typically have extensive resource materials at their disposal to help them make the appropriate referrals.

A number of research investigations have been conducted assessing the effectiveness of crisis intervention hotlines and suicide prevention programs (Auerbach, 1983; Auerbach & Kilmann, 1977). Some programs have tried to show that their presence has resulted in a decrease in the suicide rate in the communities that they are serving; however, this is not a practical enterprise because adequate control groups cannot be established and determination of death by suicide often cannot be reliably established. Also, though many crisis centers have been organized around the primary objective of suicide prevention, suicide is a relatively atypical event, and the majority of calls involve stress-related problems or sometimes simply requests for information unrelated to suicide. Even using non-suicide-related outcome measures (e.g., changes in caller stress level during the course of a call, follow-up contacts with callers to evaluate their reaction to the phone contact, determining whether callers actually showed up for referrals that were made by the crisis worker), it is very difficult to determine definitively the effectiveness of crisis centers or how they affect their communities. It is clear, however, that most callers view crisis center contacts as positive experiences. In addition, even though problems spanning the temporal spectrum are addressed by hotlines, they serve an important preventive function by providing easy access to social support and friendly advice for people who might be unwilling to turn elsewhere for help.

STRESSOR-SPECIFIC PREVENTION PROGRAMS

Two broad types of preventive stress management interventions can be distinguished: (a) those that are aimed at stressors that we are not likely to confront in the near future and that we do not consider to be *imminently* dangerous, and (b) those that we know we are about to confront or are likely to confront in the near future. We have used the terms "distal anticipatory stress" and "proximal anticipatory stress" respectively (Auerbach, 1986; 1992) to distinguish between these two types of stressors, and therefore we classify preventive interventions according to this categorization.

Distal Anticipatory Stress

Engaging in long-term preventive behavior *makes sense*. We should all wear seat belts, install dead bolt locks on our doors, watch our diets and exercise, engage in "safe sex," perform self-examinations for potentially cancerous tumors, and so on. However, as noted in Chapter 1, unlike the Vulcan Mr. Spock in *Star Trek*, we humans are not always logical. We usually attend most closely to matters of immediate concern to us and are inconsistent in our efforts at problem-focused preventive coping with stressors not on our immediate horizon. This neglect occurs because energy invested in dealing with potential misfortunes exacts a cost in diminished flexibility and spontaneity, delay of gratification, and limitation of our range of potentially reinforcing activities. In other words, it is just no fun spending your time looking out for potential dangers, and most of us are unwilling to invest significant time or energy in doing so.[1]

Thus, much of our anticipatory coping with events that we do not consider to be imminently dangerous or to have a high probability of ever affecting us is of the emotion-focused variety. We rationalize ("I've been driving for twenty years and have never been in an accident"), intellectualize ("The chances of getting cancer are very small no matter what you do") or use other mechanisms to temporarily block out our fears. With breast cancer, for example, information has been widely disseminated that early detection of lumps via self-examination and mammograms greatly enhances the probability that a patient will survive and lowers the possibility that disfiguring treatment will be necessary. But the fear that as a result of detecting a tumor there will be immediate confrontation with the fact that a breast or even one's life will be lost causes women to avoid preventive examinations (Crook & Jones, 1989).

What kinds of long-term preventive stress management programs are possible or have been attempted? We classify them into three groups: those in which we try to minimize (a) the likelihood that a negative event will occur, (b) the likelihood that

---

[1]At the other end of the continuum are people who are preoccupied with warding off danger. People who become engrossed in this activity to the point where it clearly interferes with their overall adjustment are classified as suffering from an obsessive-compulsive anxiety disorder (see Chapter 1).

we will be exposed to the event if it does occur, and (c) the possibility that we will be damaged by the event if we are exposed to it.

Lowering the Incidence of Potential Stressors.   Efforts at eliminating or at least lowering the frequency of occurrence of stressful events is prevention at the most basic level. If these endeavors are successful, no other preventive activities will be necessary. Medicine has had some notable successes in this regard when specific causes of diseases have been identified (e.g., the virus that causes polio) and when vaccines have been developed that have effectively eradicated the diseases.

In stress management, rather than isolating a microorganism or a genetic defect, we need to identify the attitudes and behaviors that promote the occurrence of stressors and change those attitudes and behaviors. This approach is obviously not possible for stressors such as natural hazards (e.g., earthquakes, tornadoes) and is viable only for stressors whose occurrence is influenced by attitudes or behaviors. For example, there is considerable evidence that sexual assault is fostered by unfounded beliefs about rape (e.g., "In the majority of rapes, the victim is promiscuous or has a bad reputation," "Women who get raped while hitchhiking get what they deserve," "A woman who is stuck-up and thinks she is too good to talk to guys on the street deserves to be taught a lesson") that encourage or justify it (Burt, 1980). Men who are identified as unusually likely to rape tend to endorse such beliefs and furthermore believe that rape is not aversive to women—that, in fact, women desire and enjoy it. In contrast, among college men, a greater knowledge about rape trauma and the perception of rape as more aversive is associated with fewer pro-rape attitudes and lower self-reported likelihood of raping (Hamilton & Yee, 1990). Therefore, educational interventions targeted at potential offenders that are designed to alter such mythical beliefs, or programs aimed at children designed to promote egalitarian sex-role attitudes, should be effective in decreasing the incidence of rape. Although attitude change and educational programs that have been conducted have met with some success in modifying attitudes, they have not demonstrated that attitude change results in decrease in actual incidence of rape (Schewe & O'Donohue, 1993).

Another approach used with persons who are chronic offenders and who are therefore likely to continue their behavior, is direct behavioral interventions. Some programs use aversive counterconditioning techniques (see Chapter 3) in which aversive unconditioned stimuli such as nausea-inducing drugs are associated with rape-related stimuli in an effort to diminish the rapists' sexual arousal to these stimuli. These approaches are sometimes supplemented by procedures in which sexual arousal to normal heterosexual stimuli is enhanced, along with the teaching of social skills and normal "dating" behaviors (Abel, Blanchard, & Becker, 1976). It is assumed that having a deficiency in heterosocial skills is one reason why some chronic offenders turn to rape and continue to rape, and that if such skills are taught, these offenders will be less likely to engage in the behavior in the future.

Preventing Exposure to Stressors/Minimizing Negative Consequences If Exposed to Stressors: Persuasion and Attitude Change.   If we cannot eliminate or greatly reduce the occurrence of stressors, what can be done either to minimize the number of people who will be victimized or to diminish harm done to them if they are exposed? Again, the problem facing psychologists is that, in many ways, we are not rational in our decision making about potential threats. We tend to overestimate the threat in risks that are short-term compared with the risks associated with events that are far in the future, we are unduly optimistic when assessing our own risks compared with those of others (Jeffrey, 1989), and we overestimate the risks involved in highly publicized events or activities and underestimate the risks in more common, unspectacular ones (see Chapter 1). For example, though cigarette smoking is indisputably a cause of death and disease (and second-hand smoke likely threatens family members and others in the immediate vicinity) and though these facts have been widely publicized, more than one-third of Americans continue to smoke (Koop, 1986). Many women do not examine their breasts for early detection of tumors, people continue to engage in unsafe sex and drug-use practices despite the AIDs epidemic, and so on. Furthermore, as just noted, though the most *logical* way to minimize likelihood of exposure to a noxious event like cancer is to take problem-focused action, we often reduce our anxiety with rationalizations of the "it can't happen to me" variety or with other defensive emotion-focused mechanisms.

Since the 1950s behavioral scientists have been conducting laboratory experiments and field studies in an attempt to determine how to persuade people to take problem-focused action to lower the likelihood that they will ever encounter stressful, life-threatening diseases such as cancer (e.g., stop smoking, eat a low-fat diet, exercise regularly) or at least to minimize their damaging effects by detecting their presence at an early treatable stage (e.g., have regular mammograms, perform breast or testicular self-examinations). Initially, disease prevention and health promotion campaigns conducted through the media were based on the assumption of rationality. It was supposed that if people were educated as to the risks of certain behaviors and the benefits of preventive and detection behaviors, they would change their behavior (i.e., they would act rationally). But, simply providing factual information does not result in people's taking protective or preventive action. Messages must be attended to, and people must be convinced that the preventive behavior is possible and that the benefits of engaging in the behavior outweigh the costs (i.e., that it is a worthwhile activity for them).

Two general factors have been found to be important in persuading people to change their behavior. These involve characteristics of the communicator and the communication.

1. *The communicator*. Communicators must be believable. Factors that contribute to believability are their attractiveness, their apparent level of expertise, and their degree of trustworthiness or sincerity (Baron, Byrne, & Kantowitz, 1978). In information transmitted via the media (as in the Success Over Stress program), this might involve using well-known athletes, actors, or public figures as communicators. In some cases, believability has been enhanced by using well-known spokespersons who have also been victims (e.g., a popular actor who is dying of cancer).

In instances in which particular groups are targeted, more specifically appropriate communicators can be used. For example, in discussing ways to control cancer in African Americans (in whom cancer rates are particularly high) prevention and early detection programs should make use of the tradition of oral communication in the black community and should use local residents who are cancer survivors, as well as family, friends, and existing leaders in the black community who have already earned people's confidence, to spread the message that cancer can be prevented by taking appropriate action (Bloom, Hayes, Saunders, & Flatt, 1987). In one AIDS prevention program in New York City, this principle was used by having former addicts provide street outreach in drug "shooting galleries" where they gave on-the-spot information on AIDS risk and instruction in needle disinfection methods (St. Lawrence & Kelly, 1989).

2. *The communication*. Much of the early research on how to frame persuasive communications centered on the role of motivating behavior change by arousing fear. "Fear appeals" have been used in antismoking campaigns, in messages designed to promote safe driving and good dental hygiene, and in other health-promotion crusades. An example of a fear-arousing antismoking presentation that threatens dire consequences for smokers is presented in Figure 8–2.

The pictures say it all.

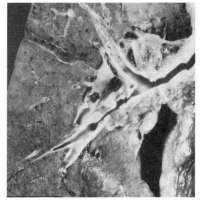

Healthy lung

Smoker's lung
(Emphysema)

AMERICAN
CANCER
SOCIETY

Figure 8–2

Example of a fear-arousing
communication. (From the
American Cancer Society.)

In general, fear arousal has been found to have positive effects. Fear-arousing messages produce more strongly stated intentions on the part of people to engage in the recommended preventive behavior (e.g., smokers to moderate or stop smoking, high school students to adopt safe driving practices, people to floss their teeth) and also tend to produce actual behavioral changes (Sutton, 1982). Why does fear-arousal work? One approach suggests that it moderates defensive (emotion-focused) avoidance or denial and brings attention to the need to actively do something (problem-focused coping) to prevent exposure to the stressor (Janis, 1982). For example, a commentator recently noted that "most young people feel invulnerable to AIDS." AIDS is prototypic of the type of stressful event that is universally dreaded yet which produces a tremendous approach-avoidance conflict. Sex is a powerful drive, and especially among youth there is a strong tendency to block out the potential negative consequences and seek out the strong positive reinforcers associated with sexual activity. Furthermore, health authorities sometimes inadvertently reinforce this false sense of invulnerability by communicating misleading information about health threats. In the case of AIDS, emphasizing IV drug use or homosexual anal intercourse as risk factors can have negative effects. It may foster the incorrect conclusion among people such as sexually active heterosexuals or homosexuals who refrain from anal intercourse that they are not at risk, even when other aspects of their behavior are risky (St. Lawrence & Kelly, 1989). This feeling of invulnerability is not exclusive to youth, as exemplified by the case of basketball star Magic Johnson who engaged in unprotected sex with numerous women and finally contracted the HIV virus.

From the standpoint of stress management, the question is, how can information about health threats and ways to minimize these threats be transmitted in order to maximize the probability that people will act on this information and engage in preventive or early detection behavior? Fear arousal is one factor, but there is evidence that undiluted fear alone may not be an effective motivator. Illustrative of this point is the situation regarding testing for the HIV virus, which causes AIDS. Given the wide dissemination of information regarding high-risk behaviors and the deadly consequences of AIDS, fear levels are apt to be very high among those in high-risk groups, such as gay men. Yet, significant proportions of gay men decline to be tested for HIV infection, and of those who volunteer for testing, almost 40 percent do not want knowledge of their results (Coates, Stall, et al., 1988).

If heightened fear increases the sense of vulnerability to a threat without providing a clear way of short-circuiting it, it may further increase defensive avoidance and disrupt effective problem-focused coping. But fear can be an effective motivator of early detection and preventive behaviors if people believe that there is a way for them to respond to the danger effectively and with few costs to them. Therefore, to be most effective, fear-arousing information needs to be accompanied by *specific action plans* presented in a way that allows people to feel that they are capable of executing the plans without having to experience pain or further stress (Cleary, 1987; Leventhal, Meyer, & Nerenz, 1980). For example, in motivating women to conduct breast self-examinations, not only should they be given reassurances about their ability to properly and easily perform the examination, but also they should be provided with clear information about what they can do if a lump is detected. For other detection examinations (e.g., a mammogram), having anxieties associated with attending a medical clinic, interacting with possibly insensitive personnel, and encountering any hazards associated with the tests themselves need to be addressed in a reassuring manner.

Several other factors have been found to influence the effectiveness of messages designed to elicit preventive and early detection behavior. These include strengthening long-term (versus momentary) beliefs in the severity of the danger (Sutton, 1982), using case histories to illustrate points (Taylor, 1995), and frequently repeating messages and presenting them in a variety of formats. Regarding the latter, one successful AIDS prevention campaign included putting "slogans and logos on bar napkins, cups, and matchbooks to reinforce risk reduction," having "posters placed in bars and businesses," as well as holding "in-the-home parties that presented risk-reduction information through informational games, demonstrations, and question and answer sessions" (St. Lawrence & Kelley, 1989, p. 24).

There is also evidence that prevention and early detection recommendations are most persuasive when they emphasize that *the recipient* is *personally responsible* for engaging in the behavior rather than leaving it up to others. Rothman, Salovey, Turvey, & Fishkin (1993) showed women who had less than 50 percent of the number of recommended screening mammograms one of three types of videotaped messages about getting a mammogram and detecting cancer. One of these tapes communicated an "internal" message emphasizing a *woman's own responsibility* for getting a mammogram and detecting breast cancer (e.g., "Eight out of 10 lumps that you might find will not be breast cancer," and "While it is not known yet how to prevent breast cancer, the value and benefits of *your* finding it early are well-known"). The "external" tape emphasized *a doctor's responsibility* (e.g., "Eight out of 10 lumps that *are* found will not be breast cancer," and "—the value and benefits of finding it early are well-known"). The subtle wording differences in the presentations had an effect on whether the woman adopted the recommendations. Women who viewed the presentation that emphasized one's own responsibility for maintaining health obtained significantly more mammograms during the year following the presentation.

Thus far in our discussion of ways of motivating people to take action to ward off a potential stressor, we have used examples of *prevention* behaviors as well as *early detection* behaviors. Prevention behavior (e.g., stopping smoking, changing one's diet) is designed to preclude or to forestall exposure to a stressor (cancer). That is, if smoking and a high-fat diet are, in fact, significant causative factors in cancer and if they are avoided, an individual will hopefully never confront the disease. Early detection behaviors (e.g., mammography, testicular examination) detect a problem (cancer) at its earliest stages, so that any negative consequences are minimized. Promoting detection behaviors thus falls under the category of "minimizing negative consequences if exposed to a stressor." Recent research suggests that information that promotes detection behaviors may need to be formulated differently from information that promotes prevention behaviors, at least in terms of one particular variable, to be most effective. Detection messages tend to be more persuasive when they are framed in terms of *potential loss* (e.g., "We will show that failing to detect breast cancer early can cost you your life") rather than potential gain (e.g., "We will show that detecting breast cancer early can save your life") (Banks, Salovey, et al., 1995, p. 180), whereas messages framed in terms of *potential gains* are more effective in inducing preventive behaviors such as the use of sun screen to prevent skin cancer (Rothman, Salovey, Antone, & Keough, 1993).

Minimizing Negative Consequences If Exposed to a Stressor: Skill-Based Approaches. We noted earlier that one approach to trying to prevent a stressor like sexual assault from happening, or at least minimizing its incidence, is to try to change widespread attitudes that condone it as a legitimate behavior. But culturally based attitudes are neither easily nor quickly changed on a large scale. Given that the incidence of sexual assault continues to rise and that most women want the freedom to live an active existence without being constantly on the alert for an assault, a reasonable alternative is to acquire the skills to defuse a situation should it become threatening. A number of intervention programs have been developed to achieve this aim by teaching women how to defend themselves against sexual assailants in the event that they are attacked. These programs are based on findings that active resistance on the part of women, especially in the early phases of an assault, is often effective in deterring the assailant (Ozer & Bandura, 1990; Thomas, 1977). Many women feel, however, that when faced with a usually much larger individual with hostile intent, they are powerless to do anything about it.

Ozer and Bandura (1990) developed and carefully evaluated a program designed to empower women in such situations. More than a third of the women had been physically assaulted at one time or another, and almost a third had experienced forced sexual intercourse in one or more relationships. Using simulated assaults, an instructor modeled the delivery of disabling blows to vital areas of the body, safe ways of falling and striking an assailant, use of firm verbal warnings and yelling, and other relevant skills designed to deter or disable an attacker (see Figure 8–3). These skills were practiced until mastered. The women also received information and encouragement designed to enhance their beliefs that they could in fact use their skills effectively if necessary. This program was effective, compared with a control condition, not only in that it enhanced feelings of personal control, lowered perceived vulnerability to assault, and reduced the amount of negative thinking and anxiety about a possible sexual assault, but also in that it resulted in greater participation in and less avoidance of recreational activities, evening social events, and travel to different community settings.

Similarly, a number of programs have been developed to teach children how to be alert to and to deal with potential sexual abuse situations, though these programs have proved more difficult to evaluate than the programs for adults. For example, Wurtele, Saslawsky, Miller, Mars, & Britcher (1986) taught children when it was okay to have their "private parts" touched and how to deter a potential molester verbally (e.g., saying **no** in a big voice) and motorically (e.g., getting away, telling someone about the threat). Harvey, Forehand, Brown, & Holmes (1988) showed that such programs can be used effectively with children as young as kindergarten age. Among the things that they taught the children was to "identify *who* can sexually abuse children (e.g., a stranger, a familiar adult, a teenager),"—"recognize when 'something wrong' is happening to me," "learning to tell someone what happened,"

Figure 8–3

Action photographs of some of the types of disabling blows perfected in the simulated assaults.
(From Albert Bandura)

and that "it is acceptable to break a promise and disobey an adult if the adult is trying to sexually abuse them" (p. 432).

Proximal Anticipatory Stress

Sometimes we know that we are about to be exposed to a stressor or we are presented with warning signs that imminent confrontation is likely. In these circumstances, stress levels often equal or exceed those experienced during actual stressor exposure (Nomikos, Opton, Averill, & Lazarus, 1968; Spacapan & Cohen, 1983). Thus, in contrast to "distal" situations, where stressors are far in the future and raising fear level is a strategy used to motivate preventive behavior, in "proximal" situations fear level suddenly escalates and often interferes with adaptive problem-focused coping.

Some stressors, like sexual assault or child sexual abuse, can be avoided totally if early warning signs (e.g., suggestive remarks, inappropriate touching) are attended to and appropriate withdrawal behaviors are initiated. But there is a common human tendency to manage stress by engaging in maladaptive emotion-focused coping in the face of warning signals. We are prone to deny cues indicating impending dangers and overinterpret them as "normal." For example, Janis & Mann (1977) pointed out that many people, when experiencing acute chest pains and other symptoms indicating possible onset of a heart attack, respond with some form of denial. Some take active steps to demonstrate to themselves that their symptoms *could not* indicate a heart attack by engaging in vigorous activity that actually could increase heart damage. Others simply repress the signs and delay seeking treatment. Similarly, "emotional and personal blocks" have been found to impede the detection and reporting by professionals of potential or ongoing sexual child abuse (Finkelhor & Hotaling, 1983, p. 3; cited in Swift, 1986). This tendency to distort warnings of impending danger in active avoidance situations has also been observed during the prelude to natural disasters. For example, Fritz and Marks (1954) found that of those people who were exposed to an Arkansas tornado and who noted a roaring sound prior to the actual impact, less than one-third appraised the sound as implying a seriously threatening event and that many interpreted it as indicating a passing train.

For some stressors (such as many natural hazards), even if warning signs are interpreted correctly, there is insufficient time to escape. In such cases people are taught beforehand what they can do to increase their probability of survival and to minimize losses (see Table 8–1).

For some stressors that require problem-focused coping, avoidance or escape is not even an option because of physical impossibility or because of your designated role, or commitments that you have made you are obligated to deal with a stressor should it present itself. Consider the situation that airline pilot David Cronin found himself in (see Chapter 2). Like Captain Cronin, we all like to think of ourselves as being able to "think on our feet"—capable of reacting quickly, rationally, and decisively in a sudden emergency. Yet people often lose their composure and make poor decisions in these circumstances. One recent, highly publicized example involved the crew members of the USS *Vincennes*, who in 1988 accidentally shot down an Iranian civilian airliner that they had mistaken for a fighter plane. All 290 passengers were killed. As a result, congressional hearings were held, and the Office of Naval Research expanded its programs on decision making under stressful conditions (Adler, 1993).

What contributes to cognitive inefficiency and poor choices during states of panic or near panic? The worst errors are made when stress level gets so high that an individual becomes hypervigilant (Janis, 1982). The individual becomes so attuned to any potential threat that attention either becomes diffused and shifts continually

	TABLE 8-1. EXAMPLES OF ADAPTIVE AND NONADAPTIVE BEHAVIOR IN NATURAL DISASTERS		
Hazard	**To Increase Survival and Minimize Loss**	**To Decrease Survival and Maximize Loss**
Earthquake	Stand in door frame.	Run out of building.
Hurricane	Evacuate low-lying areas before storm.	Have hurricane party.
Flash flood	Climb up and out of canyon.	Say in house or climb onto roof.
Tornado	Seek shelter in basement or protected structure.	Attempt to drive to safer place.
Avalanche	Evacuate perpendicular to flow.	Attempt to outrun avalanche.
Tsunami	Move to high ground.	Go to the beach after first wave.
Lightning storm	Seek low-lying area.	Stand under tree.

Source: Sorenson & Mileti, 1987, by permission of Cambridge University Press

without any focus or becomes overly rigid and narrowly focuses on petty details. This condition is most likely to happen when it is not clear what needs to be done and when it appears that there is insufficient time to arrive at a solution. A high work load and (in group situations) poor communication among team members and the failure of a leader to clarify the meaning of threat cues and to issue authoritative directives (as in the case of the crew of the *Vincennes*) enhance the probability that inappropriate action will be taken (Adler, 1993; Janis, 1982).

What can be done to maximize the probability that people will use good judgment and act effectively when suddenly confronted with an emergency situation? Clearly, knowledge of the specific problem-focused skills needed to deal with the situation and prior training and experience in applying those skills are of paramount importance. For example, communities that cope most effectively with natural hazards such as earthquakes are those that have had a lot of prior experience with a particular hazard and have trained community organizations (e.g., hospitals, schools, mental health agencies, law enforcement agencies) and leaders to instantaneously adopt specific functions and roles geared toward minimizing the effects of the stressor. In addition to basic physical needs, these functions include dealing with psychological distress in uninjured survivors, witnesses, and disrupted families (Columbia Area Mental Health Center, 1974).

On a more individual level, it is not the all-around superhero or superheroine (as portrayed in contemporary films) who always "keeps his or her cool" and seems destined to take charge in all situations who typically surfaces as the leader and problem-solver in emergencies; more often it is the people who have the specific problem-focused coping skills needed to deal with the situation at hand (Barton, 1969; Chapman, 1962). For example, in a disaster in which houses began to blow up as a result of a rush of illuminating gas, it was the normally low-status delivery-truck drivers who could turn off house valves who directed procedure and defused the situation (Wenger, 1978). Sometimes, these skills are obtained via specific training given as part of a designated role or job function because of the likelihood of encountering a particular stressor. For example, medical personnel who are likely to encounter violent patients in emergency rooms or psychiatric settings are trained to identify occasions when patients are likely to become agitated, as well as behavioral cues indicating agitation; also, they are taught listening skills for calming patients, self-defense techniques, and ways to apply restraints if necessary (Jacobs, 1983; Rice, Helzel, Varney, & Quinsey, 1985). In situations in which no one has special skills or knowledge relevant to the situation, the best alternative is to apply general problem-solving strategies (see Chapter 7) to the situation at hand.

Emotion-focused coping can play both a positive and a negative role in dealing with emergencies. From the negative standpoint, the extended use of avoidance, wishful thinking, and other emotion-focused coping strategies that might result in distortion or disregard of important warning cues in a situation that calls for rational problem-solving and immediate action, is damaging. In stressful *group* decision-making situations (as in the *Vincennes* situation or in policy-making situations like the Cuban missile crisis in President Kennedy's administration), it is important to avoid "groupthink." This is a kind of maladaptive emotion-focused coping in which in-group pressures and the desire to come to a consensus about what to do produce selective inattention, forgetting, and rationalizing that result in poor decision-making (Aldag & Fuller, 1993; Janis, 1972).

From a positive standpoint, if people are being trained to cope with a situation in which initial stress levels are likely to be very high, they should be instructed in how and when to use emotion-focused, as well as problem-focused, coping strategies. The use of emotion-focused coping (induced by techniques such as muscular relaxation, deep breathing, calming self-talk, and appropriate cuing; see Chapter 7) helps moderate initially disabling stress levels so that the individual is better able to assess cues and make rational decisions regarding appropriate actions to take. For example, former Nazi concentration camp inmates pointed out that one of the most important things that enabled them to survive after suddenly being plunged into a living nightmare was the ability to use emotion-focused mechanisms (denial, detachment, passive submission) to deal with the nearly overwhelming panic that they experienced initially. This technique, however, had to be *very quickly* followed by the development of the relevant problem-focused coping skills that matched the demands of the situation. These skills included developing "an exquisite sensitivity to the mood of the guards and constant alertness to opportunities for gaining extra food or better work assignments" and finding other prisoners who spoke the same language and then cultivating mutually supportive relationships with them (Schmolling, 1984, p. 114). Those who remained detached and didn't follow through with appropriate problem-focused coping quickly died (see Chapter 2).

In other situations, brief use of emotion-focused coping early in a stress situation is important because it provides opportunities to use problem-focused coping that may not be available later on. In hostage situations, for example, opportunities to escape are greatest during the highly stressful early phases of the abduction (when hostages are often left unguarded with easy access to escape routes and there is still general confusion). However, these opportunities are rarely acted upon by hostages because they are literally "frozen with fear" (Strentz, 1996). In sum, when suddenly confronted with a high-stress situation, judicious, *short-term* use of emotion-focused coping facilitates rational decision-making and execution of the problem-focused behaviors needed to resolve that situation.

A last category of proximal prestress situations to consider are those whose onset is less sudden and thus do not require quick decision-making regarding a course of action, yet which require preparation in order to maximize coping outcome. For many of these situations, we have some control or forewarning over time of onset, but we know that we will have to confront the situation sometime in the near future. Some such events are associated with the passage of time itself (e.g., retirement, the prospect of widowhood after a spouse's long illness). Others are fairly common events in which we choose to submit to short-term unpleasantness in order to receive longer-term anticipated benefits.

Among the latter type, perhaps the most prevalent are invasive and dangerous medical and surgical procedures that we undergo in order to increase longevity and enhance health status. Considerable research has been undertaken evaluating the efficacy of stress management interventions, which are administered just prior to stressor exposure and are designed to enhance patient adjustment and possibly speed recovery. On the surface there would seem to be little opportunity for a patient about to have surgery to use problem-focused coping (other than refusing to have the operation), and thus interventions designed to promote problem-focused coping would be unlikely to be effective. But it has been found that there are individual differences in how people facing medical stressors respond to different interventions. People who are generally information seekers (monitors, internals) respond better when they get detailed information regarding the impending stressor (which likely promotes a sense of active involvement and control) than do those people (blunters, externals) who are more likely to deal with stress by distracting themselves or avoiding the situation (see Chapter 2; Auerbach, 1989).

It has been pointed out, however, that in developing interventions, we need to take a closer look at the coping demands of the situations that people are facing, as well as at individual differences in coping dispositions (Auerbach, 1989). Some surgeries and medical examinations (e.g., those in which the patient is conscious and must follow instructions) are more likely to be perceived as having controllable elements, and thus problem-focused interventions (e.g., specific information about the procedures to be followed, sensations that will be experienced, and ways in which the patient can facilitate things by cooperating with the physician) are more likely to have a positive effect. In contrast, in procedures that involve loss of consciousness and those that portend an uncertain future (e.g., surgery involving tangible threat of death or severe debilitation or disfigurement), interventions geared toward inducing emotion-focused coping (e.g., reinforcing perceptions of support and caring from others, teaching techniques such as relaxation and attention redirection to pleasant fantasies) would likely produce a more positive response.

In summary, in proximal prestress situations in which time of onset of the stressor is known, it is important to take the coping demands of the stressor as well as individual differences in coping style into account in developing stress management interventions. Because findings in this area are still far from definitive, more research is needed (see Auerbach, 1989).

$\mathscr{S}$UMMARY

1. Prevention, in stress management, involves using behavioral techniques to preclude stressors from occurring, to help people avoid coming in contact with them if they do occur, and to lower the chances that damage will be done if they are confronted.

2. Prevention programs may be divided into those that teach broad-based, widely applicable skills (e.g., "Success Over Stress" media series, crisis intervention hotlines) and those that are oriented around specific stressors.

3. Stressor-specific programs include those that are designed to stimulate behaviors that will minimize the occurrence and damaging effects of stressors or to

avoid stressors that are not imminently threatening ("distal" stressors), as well as those that are likely to be confronted in the near future ("proximal" stressors).

4. Techniques to lower the incidence of distal stressors include changing unfounded beliefs that foster a stress-inducing behavior such as rape, or working with persons who have a high probability of emitting the behavior (e.g., chronic rapists) to minimize their likelihood of repeating the behavior.

5. Techniques to minimize exposure to distal stressors and to minimize negative consequences if stressors are encountered include changing attitudes in order to motivate change in prevention and early detection behaviors, respectively. This area, which is particularly applicable to maintaining physical health, includes prevention behaviors such as sunscreen use, dieting, exercising, and avoiding smoking and unsafe sex, and early detection behaviors such as mammography, and breast and testicular self-examination. Messages delivered by believable communicators that have an element of fear-arousal but that also contain specific action plans, elements of reassurance, and emphasis on personal responsibility on the part of the recipient for engaging in the behavior have been most effective in stimulating behavior change. Detection messages tend to be more persuasive when framed in terms of potential loss whereas preventive messages are more effective when framed in terms of potential gains.

6. Effective skill-based programs have also been developed to teach individuals how to cope with potential stressors (e.g., training women to use self-defense skills to deal with potential sexual assault situations, teaching children to use verbal and motoric skills to deter potential molesters).

7. A common reaction when fear level elevates in the face of an imminent (proximal) stressor is to deny warning cues or overinterpret them as "normal."

8. Effective management of imminent, highly stressful situations (emergencies) usually requires brief use of emotion-focused coping to moderate stress level, quickly followed by judicious decision-making and emission of the appropriate problem-focused behaviors to modify or avoid the situation to the extent possible. Prior knowledge of necessary skills and training in applying them are of paramount importance in mastering such situations.

9. In other proximal prestress situations (e.g., impending surgical operation), onset is less sudden, and there is more time to prepare. The extent to which problem-focused versus emotion-focused interventions are useful in preparing people for such situations depends on individual differences in coping styles and the perceived controllability of the situation.

KEY TERMS

crisis intervention   Treatment procedures designed to help people adjust to highly stressful events, usually of sudden onset, that strain coping capability.

crisis intervention hotlines   Telephone services, usually staffed by paraprofessional volunteers and usually available on a twenty-four-hour basis, designed to provide advice and guidance to persons in crisis.

distal anticipatory stress   Stress induced by consideration of events that are not of immediate concern to us but that we may confront at a future time; these events require long-term anticipatory coping behavior (e.g., minimizing smoking, exercising, and eating healthy foods to deter future illness).

early detection behavior   Anticipatory coping behavior designed to detect early signs of a potentially stressful event in order to minimize its negative impact (e.g., performing self-examinations to detect potentially cancerous tumors at an early, treatable stage).

global stress management prevention programs   Broad-based programs that teach general coping skills or programs that are applicable to a wide range of stressors rather than being oriented around teaching ways of coping with particular stressors.

prevention   Behavior designed to forestall the occurrence of stressful events, which often involves long-term anticipatory coping behavior (see earlier).

proximal anticipatory stress   Stress induced by contemplation of stressors that we think we are about to confront in the near future; coping effectively with such stressors as well as with ongoing stressors often involves judicious use of both emotion-focused coping (quickly moderating very high stress levels) and problem-focused coping (making good decisions and taking appropriate action).

CHAPTER 9
Postvention

In postvention, rather than planning for potential threats, we are dealing with stress engendered by harm or losses that have already been sustained. In this sense, postvention is *reactive* whereas prevention is *proactive*. In discussing prevention, we distinguished between "distal" and "proximal" stressors. We similarly distinguish between distal and proximal aspects of the poststress period. However, we want to emphasize that in contrast to the prestress period, where the line of demarcation between these two phases is explicitly defined by the presence of a distinct warning that an aversive event is about to occur, clear poststress stages have not been established with empirical research. This is a somewhat controversial area because many practitioners erroneously base their interventions on the assumption that the same emotions are experienced by victims of particular stressful events (e.g., that depression is inevitable following a loss such as the death of a loved one) and that the process of coping must follow a uniform path (e.g., that feelings of grief must be actively confronted rather than denied) for stress victims to recover (Silver & Wortman, 1980; Wortman & Silver, 1989).

Although there is little evidence for uniform poststress stages of response, it is clear that exposure to stress (especially traumatic stress) produces both short-term and often long-term adjustment problems. Furthermore, there are important differences between the coping strategies that are associated with good coping outcome immediately after a traumatic event versus those that are most often effective many years later (Schulz & Decker, 1985). Rape victims are a traumatic stress group that has been particularly well studied. Research with rape victims indicates that although the trauma persists for months or years for many victims (Frank, Anderson, Stewart, and Dancu, 1988), substantial improvement in social adjustment typically occurs over the first four to six months following the attack (Atkeson, Calhoun, Resick, & Ellis, 1982; Resick, Calhoun, Atkeson, & Ellis, 1981). In a recent review, Resick (1993) concludes that most rape victims experience an acute emotional reaction that lasts about three months, although some continue to experience anxiety and depression-related problems that interfere with social and sexual adjustment for much longer periods. In general, the findings support the notion that different treatments are likely to be most useful for those who seek help immediately after the assault versus treatment seekers who delay (Kilpatrick & Calhoun, 1988).

In this chapter we will first consider the types of intervention procedures most appropriate for helping people deal with the short-term effects of stress exposure (proximal poststress period). This section will be relatively brief because there has been comparatively little methodologically sound research that allows us to conclude what particular procedures are most effective. Psychologists and other practitioners are more likely to be sought out after some passage of time following stressor exposure when it has become apparent to the victim that there are residual problems that continue to interfere with adjustment. Techniques used for proximal poststress intervention usually are classified as "emergency psychiatric care," as "psychological first aid," or as forms of crisis intervention. In the more extensive section that follows on distal poststress intervention, we will focus on the stress management techniques based on the classical conditioning model that we introduced in Chapters 1 and 3, with emphasis on self-management applications of these procedures.

PROXIMAL POSTSTRESS INTERVENTION

The lack of a solid body of information on how to help people in the immediate aftermath of exposure to a stressor is due to the inherent ad hoc nature of the situation. Because stressors are often sudden and unexpected there is little time to plan interventions or to systematically examine the effects of different treatments. Observations of people exposed to a range of traumatic stressors, including rape, natural disaster, and widowhood, indicate that for many the initial reaction is one of shock and relative psychological immobility, leaving them minimally receptive to attempts to foster problem-focused coping strategies (Auerbach, 1986, 1992). Procedures designed to foster short-term emotion-focused coping, including encouragement to reconcile oneself temporarily to the fact that one has little control, are likely to be most productive in this situation (Strentz & Auerbach, 1988; Suls & Fletcher, 1985). It has been conjectured that such interventions will likely be delivered most effectively in a manner projecting empathic understanding by kin, or at least by persons of similar social background and life experiences as the victim (Bailey, 1988; Thoits, 1986).

It is clear that aggressive, problem-oriented coping interventions centered on the victim are unlikely to be productive during this early period, and that efforts are often most usefully directed toward those who have a close relationship with the victim and others on the periphery. Such indirect interventions take different forms, depending on the nature of the stressor. For example, the initial reaction of husbands, boyfriends, or fathers to a woman's rape is often to blame the woman or to become enraged at the assailant. Thus, an important intervention task at this early stage is to counsel these persons whom the victim looks to for support that they should invest their energy in being supportive, rather than in being vengeful toward the assailant or reproachful or overprotective toward the victim (Thomas, 1977). In bereavement situations, there is a tendency among family members to avoid discus-

sion of the death to protect each other, whereas it would be more helpful to promote intrafamily support and sharing of grief in order to minimize the burden of the
widowed individual (Kleiman, 1977). A different set of dynamics is involved in the
immediate aftermath of a natural disaster. In this situation, resources are used most
effectively to reinforce the emergence of leaders who model altruism and cooperation. This step is important because it is the most effective way of drawing community consensus away from counterproductive tendencies toward looking for
someone or some group to blame or scapegoat. Such indirect community-based
interventions have proved more useful than aggressive outreach programs by mental health workers geared directly toward disaster victims (Barton, 1969; Taylor,
Ross, & Quarantelli, 1976).

Relatively few stress management programs have been designed expressly to aid
victims of specific stressors in the immediate postimpact period. An exception is
Kilpatrick & Veronen's (1983, pp. 178–182) Brief Behavioral Intervention Procedure
(BBIP), which is designed to treat recent rape victims (one day to two days post-
rape). Aspects of the procedure are similar to some of the approaches with long-
term victims, a main difference being recognition that recent victims have limited
capacity for sustained participation and that any intervention needs to be brief. The
BBIP is a four- to six-hour treatment package designed as a "prophylactic treatment
which may short-circuit the development of phobias and other (long term) rape-
related problems." The main procedures in this program include (a) after first having
the victim relax (using deep-muscle and deep-breathing relaxation techniques),
gently encouraging the victim to recall details of the assault and to express feelings
that she had blocked out or forgotten; (b) educating the victim regarding how fears
are developed and maintained via classical and operant conditioning—fear is presented as a normal reaction that is expressed physiologically, behaviorally, and cognitively and is something that can be controlled; (c) attempting to reduce feelings of
guilt and responsibility for the rape by discussing with the victim societal forces and
myths that are perpetuated that encourage rape; and (d) teaching both emotion-
focused coping (deep breathing, relaxation) and problem-focused coping strategies
(encouraging assertiveness in calling the police, deciding whom the victim will in-
form, and resuming activities that they have avoided because of fear).

Foa, Rothbaum, & Steketee (1993) concluded that this promising intervention
program has not been sufficiently evaluated to definitively establish its utility. However, Foa, Hearst-Ikeda, & Perry (1995) developed an eight-hour program for recent
(of less than two weeks) female sexual or nonsexual assault victims that included
the educational and relaxation components of the BBIP, and added elements that
are part of Foa and colleagues' exposure-based approach with long-term rape victims (reliving the assault in imagery, confronting feared but safe situations, identification of distorted cognitive assumptions about coping ability; see later). This program was found to be more effective than a control condition in reducing PTSD
symptoms in the assault victims two months after the assault and in alleviating depression and "reexperiencing symptoms" five-and-a-half months postassault.

Mental health personnel in medical emergency rooms or psychiatry services are
faced with a somewhat different challenge than interveners who are dealing with victims of a known stressor. Emergency medical personnel are often confronted with
persons in intense emotional distress whose situational circumstances are not clear
and when there is minimal time available to obtain basic information. An additional
complication is that in contrast to victims of natural disasters and other circumscribed events—who do not usually manifest psychotic behavior, extreme aggression, or suicidal tendencies—these are problems not infrequently encountered in
the emergency medical setting.

Current emphasis in this setting is on trying to anticipate major problem areas
and to develop treatment guidelines for frequently encountered crisis populations

with special needs, such as the elderly, suicidal adolescents, rape and domestic violence victims, recently diagnosed AIDS patients, and substance abusers (Ellison, Hughes, & White, 1989). Because psychotropic drugs are widely used to control anxiety as well as psychotic and acting-out behavior, an important task for psychiatric personnel is to learn to distinguish between anxiety states and agitated psychotic behavior and then to make quick decisions regarding appropriate dosages of medications needed for rapid tranquilization. An additional complication is that the most widely prescribed antianxiety drugs, the benzodiazepines, may precipitate uncharacteristically aggressive behavior in highly anxious patients (Ellison et al., 1989). (See Chapter 10 for further discussion of the use and abuse of drugs for stress management).

Exactly when the initial acute reaction period ends so that trauma victims can begin to resume constructive problem-solving activity has been a matter of some controversy. As already noted, approximately three months has been identified as the critical interval for many rape victims. Among crisis intervention specialists, a widely held assumption is that most victims reestablish "a stable emotional equilibrium" within six to eight weeks after stressor exposure (Bloom, 1984; Caplan, 1964). But an examination of studies of victims of different types of major stressors, including rape and natural disaster victims, prisoners of war, and concentration camp survivors, as well as people exposed to relatively milder stressors such as a surgical operation, indicates that there is no single uniform time course. Rather, the degree and duration of emotional dysfunction resulting from stress exposure seems to be determined largely by the severity of the stressor, modified by individual differences that might soften the impact of the stressor or that might result in its being appraised as relatively less disruptive by some people versus others (Auerbach, 1986). Among these individual differences are personality traits such as hardiness and optimism that are associated with greater stress resilience, past mastery of coping skills that could be applied to the present situation, and the availability of socially supportive relationships that serve as a protective buffer (see Chapter 1).

Victims of aversive life experiences are usually expected by others to "weather the storm" and eventually return to their previous level of emotional stability (Silver & Wortman, 1980), and some people have in fact endured the most profound traumas (such as concentration camp internment) and have managed ultimately to resume "normal" lives (Leon, Butcher, Kleinman, Goldberg, & Almagor, 1981). However, many persons, even after initial behavioral problems and emotional distress have seemingly stabilized, experienced long-term adjustment problems that are clearly traceable to exposure to the stressor. Some victims seem to "continually reexperience the crisis for the rest of their lives" (Silver & Wortman, 1980, p. 308). This fact is evident in many Holocaust victims who experience chronic emotional and interpersonal problems and are never able to resolve guilt feelings over having survived (Eitinger, 1980), in people grieving over the loss of a spouse or child in a car accident, who four to seven years after the event "continue to ruminate about the accident or what might have been done to prevent it and "[who] appear to be unable to accept, resolve, or find any meaning in the loss" (Lehman, Wortman, & Williams, 1987, p. 218), and in some rape victims who seem to maintain a "core of distress" that persists for years (Ellis, 1983).

In the next section on distal poststress intervention, we will describe intervention approaches that have been used with persons who are dealing with long-term stress-related problems. These interventions will include those used for people who can clearly identify a focal event (e.g., rape) or a series of events (e.g., Vietnam war experiences) that are undoubtedly the source of their continuing maladjustment, as well as for those who have less debilitating specific fears (e.g., a snake phobia) that are assumed to be the result of past classical conditioning, even though a particular past experience may not be readily identified as the source of the stress reaction.

DISTAL POSTSTRESS INTERVENTION

Previously, in Chapter 3, we outlined both the theoretical rationale behind systematic desensitization and the exposure techniques, and gave examples of how they may be used to help people cope with acquired fears. In this chapter we give examples of some variations and extensions of their use, emphasizing self-management applications. We also discuss use of cognitive-behavioral approaches and other more specialized techniques that have been developed to help people cope with long-term stress-related problems.

Because we are emphasizing self-management, it might be useful at this point to review considerations involved in determining whether to embark on a self-management program versus consulting a professional (Flanders, 1976; Marks, 1978). First, Marks, a strong proponent of self-management treatment for stress-related problems, emphasizes that the presence of certain conditions indicates the need to consult a professional before proceeding further. These conditions include emotional states involving extreme depression, especially where there is serious suicidal ideation, and when substance abuse is involved (especially with alcohol or sedative drugs). Another contraindication, specifically when using exposure techniques that initially induce elevated anxiety levels, is the presence of diseases such as heart trouble, asthma, peptic ulcer, or colitis that might be exacerbated by increased short-term anxiety. Second, specific fears that can be linked to particular stressors are far more amenable to self-help than are vague complaints such as "I want to feel better about myself." Self-evaluation and behavioral self-monitoring procedures that are an essential part of any good self-management plan help you zero in on specific problems, identify causative factors, and clearly spell out goals so that well-defined self-treatment plans can be developed (see Gramling & Auerbach, 1998; Watson & Tharpe, 1993). Third, motivation and persistence are especially important if there is no professional to provide prodding and continual encouragement. Friends and family can be an important source of emotional support and also can become active partners in the self-change project.

Systematic Desensitization

The theoretical rationale for systematic desensitization and the elements of the procedure are described in Chapter 6. In this section we focus on self-management applications of desensitization (self-directed desensitization). In this approach, the client typically first consults briefly with a therapist in order to build a hierarchy of feared situations and to learn the basics of deep-muscle relaxation (clients are often provided with a cassette recording of muscle relaxation exercises to use at home). Hereafter, clients self-administer the desensitization procedure.

Krop and Krause (1976) used this approach with a twenty-six-year-old graduate student. She had developed an intense fear of sharks and an avoidance reaction to the beach as an adult, after witnessing several large sharks from a beach at which she frequently swam. Her fear was heightened after she had read about sharks and assisted shark fishermen in catching and cutting the jaws from a shark as part of a course requirement. (This experience exemplifies how conditioned fears may develop as a result of observation and indirect contact, without any direct punishment.) Subsequently, she reported experiencing "out of control panic" when at the beach. This panic was particularly debilitating for her because as a Florida resident many of her social activities were centered there.

Items in her hierarchy ranged from "walking on the beach on a clear, calm day" (relatively low stress) to walking "knee deep in the water and seeing a fin 50 feet away" and "swimming in the ocean in water 10 feet deep" (high stress). She worked

her way through the hierarchy (at home) by using the deep-muscle relaxation techniques she had learned, while simultaneously imagining the scenes in the hierarchy.
Imagery was combined with in vivo exposure as she was instructed to go gradually
into the ocean and engage in the behaviors described in the hierarchy, combining
these experiences with relaxation. At a ten-month follow-up, the student was reported to be "enjoying swimming and other ocean-related activities with no anxiety"
even after seeing the movie *Jaws*.

Another case study illustrates how desensitization can be implemented with minimal professional involvement by enlisting the help of family members and using
creative ways of simulating the feared situation at home (Kvale & Bruce, 1992). The
client was a nineteen-year-old man who was diagnosed with advanced cancer. In addition to all the other stressors associated with this disease, he had developed a severe phobia of undergoing an important diagnostic examination, magnetic resonance imaging (MRI; described in Chapter 1). He stated that he would "rather
undergo a (very painful) bone marrow aspiration than have another MRI." On the
basis of reading material that he was given and on two visits with psychologists, the
patient, with help from his parents, formulated a hierarchy of feared situations (see
Table 9–1), practiced relaxation skills, and implemented the desensitization procedure at home.

TABLE 9–1.   DESENSITIZATION HIERARCHY FOR MRI EXAMINATION

SUD'S (Subjective Units of Discomfort) Level (0–100)	Anxiety-producing Situations* Related to the MRI Procedure
5	I am going to have an MRI exam in two days.
7	We are driving to the Mayo Clinic for treatment.
10	We are walking into the waiting room at the clinic.
20	The nurse calls my name.
25	We walk up to the nurse.
30	She takes me back to the exam room.
35	They lay me on the table and strap me in.
45	They put a cover over my head and slide me into the machine.
55	The first course of tests starts and lasts ten minutes.
65	I hear a pounding.
70	The frequency of the pounding increases.
70	The pounding stops suddenly.
75	The pounding cycle repeats two more times.
80	They pull me out of the machine and give me an injection.
85	They push me back in.
90	The pounding begins more frequently.
95	The pounding is shaking my head.
100	The pounding cycle repeats two more times but for longer periods.

*Situations generated as described in the patient's own words.

The most unique aspect of the procedure was that rather than using imagery or in vivo exposure to the elements in the fear hierarchy, the parents constructed a simulated MRI machine out of a board and a 50-gallon barrel and used it during home desensitization trials. Among other things, they also put a pail over the patient's head to simulate the confining helmetlike device that is used during MRI, and then they pounded on the roof of the barrel to simulate the distressing noise that occurs during the MRI procedure. After the desensitization procedure was completed, the patient underwent the next MRI with no expression of anxiety and no evidence of avoidance behavior.

In general, controlled studies have found self-directed desensitization to be as effective as standard therapist-directed desensitization (Rosenbaum & Merbaum, 1984).

Variants of Desensitization.   Anxiety management training (AMT; Suinn & Deffenbacher, 1988; Suinn & Richardson, 1971), like desensitization, uses exposure to anxiety-arousing scenes and relaxation training. In contrast to desensitization, hierarchies of feared stimuli are not developed. This step is viewed as unnecessary and overly time-consuming, especially when several hierarchies need to be developed and modified to deal with multiple fears. In line with the position espoused by Goldfried (1971), it is argued that the focus must shift from teaching clients to associate relaxation with specific external situations that are fear-arousing to teaching them to recognize the bodily feelings and cognitions that signal the presence of anxiety and to associate relaxation with these internal stimuli.

In AMT, clients are initially trained in progressive muscle relaxation and to visualize a past event that is anxiety-arousing. Subsequently, imagery of a scene associated with relaxation or with personal success is used to enhance relaxation. The purpose of visualizing a fearful scene is to get clients to focus on *how* they experience anxiety and to recognize bodily sensations and self-talk that signify mild to moderate levels of stress. Clients are taught to associate feelings of relaxation with feelings and thoughts associated with anxiety arousal. Because (in contrast to traditional desensitization) little attention is paid to the stimuli that are eliciting anxiety in real life, AMT should be particularly useful for clients who have difficulty identifying these stimuli (such as those suffering from panic disorder or generalized anxiety disorder; see Chapter 1).

By focusing on exactly how anxiety is experienced (physiologically, behaviorally, cognitively) and by teaching self-monitoring, AMT allows clients to prevent higher levels of arousal by identifying feelings of stress in the early stages and instituting relaxation imagery as soon as these feelings are identified. Suinn and colleagues maintain that this allows clients to more readily generalize their learning to new situations, whereas relaxation learned in desensitization is more specifically tied to particular stimulus hierarchies. AMT is similar to the self-control relaxation techniques described in Chapter 7 and to other procedures such as applied relaxation (Ost, 1987) that stress the use of relaxation as an active self-management technique. Suinn & Deffenbacher (1988) list a number of published studies demonstrating the effectiveness of AMT as a stress management intervention, including several in which it was as effective as standard desensitization and self-control desensitization.

Exposure Therapy

We have described the basic elements of exposure therapy (implosive therapy and flooding) and its theoretical grounding in the classical conditioning model of learning in Chapter 6.

One important current application of the Stampfl & Levis (1967) implosive therapy model is with Vietnam veterans experiencing combat-related post-traumatic stress disorder (PTSD) (Lyons & Keane, 1989). As in the original model, the therapist is active and directive. The therapist begins by developing imagery that brings the client into the setting, engaging the senses as fully as possible: "You are now going on a journey back in time, back to Vietnam. You will be able to hear, smell, taste, and feel everything as if you are really there." (Lyons & Keane, 1989, p. 144). Subsequent imagery gets increasingly specific, stressing both stimulus and response cues ("You feel the chopper lifting off—NOW—you feel it deep in your stomach") (p. 146).

It is not critical that situations be created as they precisely occurred. The crucial element is that the imagery elicits fear related to the trauma that was experienced. The client should not be allowed to reduce his or her fear level by changing or otherwise escaping from the scene. Each element of the trauma must be concentrated on until it no longer elicits high fear levels. In contrast to the Stampfl-Levis implosive model, a "flooding" approach is taken in developing imagery, with focus on sensations, cognitions, and feelings associated with the actual trauma that was experienced. No attempt is made to evoke imagery that is associated with hypothetical childhood conflicts or other speculative psychodynamically based events. Progressive muscle relaxation and relaxation-based imagery are used to enhance imagery skills and build patient-therapist rapport at the outset, and also to provide the patient with another technique to cope with intrusive memories and deal with stressful situations.

Several other variations on and expansions of the exposure approach have been developed in recent years. We first describe these variations before briefly discussing self-management applications of exposure techniques.

Foa & Kozak's Exposure Model.   Foa & Kozak (1986) developed an exposure therapy model based on Lang's (1979) bioinformational model that conceives of fear as a complex informational structure consisting of stimuli, responses, and the meanings associated with them. According to this approach, in order for fear to be reduced and for avoidance behaviors to be diminished in people who have experienced trauma-inducing stressors, they must be exposed to stimuli that both (a) reactivate the fear memory and (b) provide new information that "includes elements that are incompatible with some of those that exist in the fear structure, so that a new memory can be formed" (Foa & Kozak, 1986, p. 22). When, for example, dog phobics are confronted with dogs during exposure therapy *but are not bitten*, the "dog-fear" information structure is changed to incorporate this new incompatible information that dogs are unlikely to injure them. This accounts for the reduction in fear that they experience when they next encounter dogs.

There is much similarity between the rationale and procedural aspects of this approach and the implosive therapy model developed by Stampfl & Levis. In both approaches, clients are encouraged to remember and relive *all* aspects of their traumatic experience, as illustrated by the following excerpts from the remembrances of a rape victim. "I see this person in the doorway of the stairwell and he seems to be rushing at me" (external stimuli)—"and my heart is pounding" (physiological reactions)—"he says, 'Get on the bed,' which again surprises me—I didn't expect that— it's the first time I suspect rape" (cognitive appraisals)—"I think this man is really dangerous, he can really hurt me and I have to be careful" (feared consequences) (Rothbaum & Foa, 1992, pp. 220–221).

In both methods, emphasis is on imagery, but with the client rather than the therapist generating the script. In vivo exposure is used occasionally. For example, for rape victims, in vivo exposure is assigned as homework with the hierarchy consisting of major situations that are avoided but that are realistically safe (e.g., going to parties, going out alone, talking to men). Both techniques use a gradual approach at the outset of therapy and emphasize not terminating imagery if the client continues to show distress. Foa, Riggs, Massie, & Yarczower (1995, p. 490) tell clients, "If you start to feel too uncomfortable and want to run away or avoid it by leaving the image, I will help you stay with it." It is essential that clients remain with the feared image until their anxiety level decreases so as not to reinforce avoidance of the feared situation.

An important difference is that Foa & Rothbaum, in contrast to Stampfl & Levis, have focused on treating persons who have been exposed to the original trauma relatively recently, as adults. Thus many of the PTSD victims whom they treat "not only suffer from conditioned fear to stimuli that remind them of the original trauma, but also display fear and avoidance of the memory of the trauma itself," and in exposure treatment they have concentrated on getting clients to "re-experience the feared trauma itself" (Rothbaum & Foa, 1992, p. 219). As with Lyons & Keane (1989) their approach thus emphasizes "flooding" and does not include the implosive therapist's technique of introducing symbolic images based on psychodynamic theorizing. Finally, in this model there is some attempt to introduce "corrective" information into the imagery (e.g., "But you are going to survive") if the patient gets extremely distressed.

Rothbaum & Foa (1992) note that critics have argued that with rape victims, it is inappropriate to decrease their fear to a situation that they should be fearful of and should avoid. Rothbaum & Foa reply that the fears of rape victims (or other trauma victims) never completely extinguish and thus that there will always be an avoidance tendency, maintaining that exposure therapy helps reduce the intense psychological pain associated with the experience. This aspect is poignantly represented in a quote from one of their clients, who described each session of exposure therapy as "peeling a layer off of an onion, and after a few sessions, you get to the stinky part in the middle, and then it doesn't stink anymore" (1992, p. 222).

In a study with rape victims Foa, Rothbaum, Riggs, & Murdock (1991) empirically demonstrated the effectiveness of their approach. Rape victims who met the criteria for PTSD (see Chapter 1) were given either supportive counseling, a cognitive-behavioral stress management intervention that included muscular relaxation and elements of Meichenbaum's, Beck's, and Ellis's cognitive-behavioral approaches (see Chapter 7), exposure therapy, or they were assigned to a control group in which treatment was delayed. Exposure therapy involved having the patients imagine the rape scene as vividly as possible and then describe it aloud in the present tense. Patients were prompted to include *all* memories, including what they saw, smelled, heard, and felt. Patients' descriptions were tape-recorded, and they were told to listen to the description at least once daily. Additional homework included actually exposing themselves to situations that they had come to fear and avoid as a result of the rape experience. All of the treatments produced improvement in emotional functioning immediately after treatment. The cognitive-behavioral treatment produced the most improvement on PTSD-related symptoms (such as reliving experiences, nightmares, flashbacks, avoidance of thoughts of the assault) immediately after treatment, but exposure therapy was most effective in reducing these symptoms at a longer-term follow-up period (three-and-a-half months after treatment).

Levis's Memory Reactivation Approach.   In Levis's (1991, 1995) recent adaptation of the original Stampfl-Levis implosive model, he describes an approach in which the therapist plays a much less active role than in the original implosive approach (in this respect it is similar to the Foa/Kozak/Rothbaum technique). Levis reports that in many of his clinical cases, after being presented imagery pertaining to their presenting problem, patients often began to report "strange and puzzling associations" that appeared unrelated to the material in the imagery. When these associations were re-presented to the patient, they elicited other "puzzling" associations. Eventually "these disjointed associations came together in what appeared to be a stored memory of a traumatic conditioning event." Typically, the activation of one memory led to another until memory of a coherent traumatic event was evoked.

For example, Levis (1991) describes a patient who reported seeing a white field in imagery whenever she closed her eyes. Instructions to focus on the white field led to a white table, seeing a bottle on the table, hearing background noise, the smell of alcohol, and through successive associations to a summer cottage with a white hallway. Eventually, after repeatedly encouraging the patient to confront these stimuli, a complete memory was recovered. She was four or five years old. The noise that she heard was from a party that her parents were having. Her parents had been alcoholics and would force her to drink beer until she gagged. They and her uncle had also repeatedly brutally abused her both sexually and physically on these occasions. According to Levis, when memories of traumatic events are retrieved in this way, there is remarkable improvement in emotional functioning as well as in the physical symptoms that often accompany unresolved trauma (see box pages 183–184).

Levis (1991) argues that the key to symptom removal is "complete extinction of the affect associated with the memories driving the symptom." Furthermore, he notes that once the memory retrieval process begins, it cannot be altered by the therapist. "Patients regularly correct you if the cues suggested were not part of their memory. It appears the process of recovery has a life of its own" (Levis, 1991, p. 419).

Eye Movement Desensitization and Reprocessing (EMDR).   EMDR, a treatment technique recently developed by Shapiro (1989, 1995), is based on the assumption that the disturbing emotions associated with the memory of a traumatic event can be diminished if rhythmic side-to-side eye movements are generated while the client is visualizing the traumatic event. Clients are first required to create a visual image of the disturbing event. Then, while they are holding the image, they are asked to follow with their eyes the therapist's finger as it rapidly moves laterally across their field of vision. Shapiro (1994) claims that in contrast to traditional desensitization and exposure techniques, EMDR produces a fundamental change in clients' memories of the traumatic event, rather than simply modifying their stressful reaction to the event. She claims that EMDR is superior to systematic desensitization because it does not require establishing hierarchies or prolonged relaxation training and that it is superior to other exposure techniques because high levels of anxiety are not elicited.

Tallis & Smith (1994) note that although EMDR has "been enthusiastically and favorably received by the academic community" and that initial clinical reports (e.g., Marquis, 1991; Wolpe & Abrams, 1991) indicate that it is an effective treatment for posttraumatic stress, in their own research they found no evidence that induced rapid eye movement facilitates emotional processing. In one recent study (Jensen, 1994), it was found to be minimally effective in reducing symptoms of PTSD in Vietnam combat veterans; but in another study (Wilson, Becker, & Tinker, 1995) it was effective in reducing self-reported anxiety and in presenting complaints and increasing positive cognitions in individuals who had been exposed to a range of traumatic events. EMDR has undergone explosive growth in recent years and has a dedicated group of adherents. However, concerns have been expressed regarding the aggressive way in which it has been marketed to professionals, its claims of applicability to a wide range of clinical disorders (Rosen, 1996), and the lack of scientific foundation for the physiological model and concepts underlying the technique (Lohr, 1996). As of this writing, it continues to be a controversial procedure in need of further validation with controlled treatment outcome research.

Disclosure.   Pennebaker (1990) has recently been investigating the "healing" effects of simply opening up and confiding to others the details of traumatic events that have been experienced. In a series of studies, he found that Holocaust survivors who disclosed more about their personal experiences during World War II had better long-term physical health, as did college students who expressed their thoughts and feelings about coming to college or their emotions surrounding a traumatic event. Studies with college students showed that disclosing resulted in fewer health-center visits and improved immune system functioning. Pennebaker has found that although talking or writing about emotional trauma is painful in the short run and can be risky because we can never be sure about how others will react, most people when given the opportunity readily do so. He (Pennebaker, 1989) found that most people disclose topics pertaining to interpersonal conflict, intimacy, and loss through death or divorce. Esterling, Antoni, Fletcher, Margulies, & Schneiderman (1994) studied the effects of disclosing on a measure of immunological functioning in college students and found that talking about stressful events was more effective than writing about them. Both were more effective than a control condition in which students wrote about trivial topics. The following is an excerpt from a twenty-year old college student given the opportunity to talk about her stressful experiences:

> I love my parents. We have a perfect family life. My parents always support me in whatever I do. . . . My father has been such a bastard. I know that he has something going with his secretary. My mother takes it out on me. I have to wear the clothes she wants, date the boys she wants. I'm even at SMU because she went here, even though I wanted to go to UT.
>
> (Reprinted from Pennebaker, 1989, p. 211)

What accounts for the beneficial effects of confiding? Agger & Jensen (1990) suggest that it provides a means of reframing a painful experience and the shame and guilt associated with it in a way that makes it meaningful for the victim. Former concentration camp inmate Bruno Bettleheim saw it as "a way of convincing myself that my life was still of some value, that I had not lost all the interests that once gave me self-respect" (Bettleheim, 1960, p. 105). Pennebaker (1989) views confiding as providing some of the same benefits obtained by people undergoing Freudian psychoanalysis. It gets people to reconfront experiences that they have blocked out and to achieve some insight into why they are feeling distressed, and it also provides an opportunity to release pent-up emotions.

Cognitive Processing Therapy. Cognitive Processing Therapy (CPT; Calhoun & Resick, 1993) is an approach developed specifically for sexual assault victims experiencing symptoms of posttraumatic stress disorder. It is of interest because it adds a cognitive component to the exposure model and also contains elements of Pennebaker's disclosure approach. Calhoun & Resick argue that although exposure to traumatic memories in a safe environment alters the fear structure and enables habituation to the feared stimulus, there may be no changes in other emotional reactions that continue to cause the victim distress. "Victims may still blame themselves and feel shame, disgust, anger, or confusion, all of which could be sufficiently intense to facilitate intrusive memories, arousal, and avoidance reactions" (p.59). Thus, in addition to reliving the event without experiencing punishment, the victim is also exposed to *information* that corrects misattributions and maladaptive beliefs regarding the event itself and expectations for the future. The focus is on "stuck points" or conflicts between prior beliefs (e.g., "My decision not to tell my parents about being raped was cowardly") and new corrective information or beliefs (e.g., "My decision was not cowardly but was motivated by my desire to protect my parents and therefore was courageous"). In the exposure component, rather than using imagery, clients are instructed to write about the event in detail, including sensory experiences, feelings, and thoughts at a time and in a place when they are comfortable and feel free to express their emotions. They are then instructed to read the account to themselves daily and subsequently aloud to the therapist. Initial findings on the effectiveness of CPT are promising (Resick & Schnicke, 1992).

Short-Term Dynamic Psychotherapy.   Sometimes posttraumatic stress is treated by using short-term dynamic psychotherapy (which is related to psychoanalysis). In this approach (Horowitz, 1984), treatment is based on the observation that PTSD is characterized by attempts to deny and "numb" the memories of past traumas as well as by the intrusive flashbacks that reinstate those memories in consciousness. As described by Fairbank, Schlenger, Caddell, & Woods (1993), the therapist, at times when avoidant symptoms predominate, tries to remove the blocks to processing and encourages encountering the event—but only to the point where this is tolerable. When that limit is reached, the patient is encouraged to turn away from the traumatic memories until they become more manageable. This process continues until ultimately the full meaning of the event to the victim can be "explored and worked through." Conventional psychoanalytic therapy for dealing with trauma is far more complex and cumbersome. It is described as a process of altering unconscious intrapsychic conflicts pertaining to aggressive drives that have been brought about by exposure to traumatic stress (Emery, Emery, & Berry, 1993).

Self-Management Applications of Exposure.   Proponents of exposure treatment have been particularly interested in developing self-exposure approaches that minimize the amount of time a client needs to spend with a professional therapist. In general, the results of studies comparing self-exposure to therapist-directed treatment (reviewed by Marks, 1987, and Ost, Salskovskis, & Hellstrom, 1991) have been promising. These studies evaluate self-exposure approaches in which the client is given a written treatment manual with diaries to record homework and then proceeds without the aid of a therapist, as well as those approaches in which there is ongoing contact with a therapist (or sometimes a spouse who serves as cotherapist) who helps guide homework assignments and evaluate progress. Marks (1987; Al-Kubaisy, Marks, et al., 1992), an ardent proponent of self-management exposure treatment, argues that in those reported instances in which phobics did not benefit from self-management exposure they were not properly instructed or did not practice the technique sufficiently.

Recently there has been increased use of in vivo exposure as the means of contact with feared stimuli because it is the most cost-effective (Marx, 1987). Live self-exposure reduces therapist contact time because imagery material does not need to be developed, and the problem of generalizing from imagery to actual situations is obviated. However, it has been pointed out that some patients are too fearful to begin live exposure immediately and that for some phobias (e.g., earthquakes), live exposure is impractical (Wanderer & Ingram, 1991). Live exposure, whether self-managed or therapist-guided, can also be more unpredictable than imaginal exposure conducted in a controlled home or office environment. This fact is exemplified in the humorous recollection of a veteran therapist (see box on page 179).

Wanderer & Ingram (1991) report successful use of a flooding self-management technique in which clients visualize their most frightening scenarios and fantasies and then describe their feelings. These descriptions are tape-recorded, and a three-minute tape is made of the period when arousal is at its highest. For their homework assignment, clients are instructed to replay this tape repeatedly until the stress level diminishes and the stimulus can be confronted without discomfort. In addition to recommending live self-exposure, Marx (1987) has concluded that when possible, long exposure periods are more effective in reducing fear than shorter ones and that rapid exposure produces habituation to fears faster than slow exposure.

"Be Prepared"

At the culmination of a long and arduously graded exposure treatment with an agoraphobic patient who, among other things, could not ride the elevator at her apartment, the fateful day for an in vivo exposure in the elevator arrived. Living on the sixth floor of an inner-city apartment required her, when grocery shopping, to place the bundles inside the elevator, press her floor number, then run up the stairs as quickly as possible, hoping that no one else would call for the elevator before it got to her floor.

As I drove to her apartment to meet her in the lobby, the sky darkened and it began to rain, with the thunderstorm approaching the intensity of Disney's "A Night on Witch Mountain." I must say that my own cognitions while driving included traces of uncertainty as to the wisdom of this exposure on this particular day.

When greeting her in the lobby, she more eloquently summarized my unspoken concerns, and I quite adeptly used paradox and said, "how fortunate it is to have such a wonderful thunderstorm available for the exposure today." I believe this to have been my undoing, for, in addition to her anxiety, I aroused the wrath of the gods.

The exposure proceeded; first one floor, then two, then me going up three floors and her following alone, and up and up. Finally, the acid test: up six floors alone. I waited in the lobby as she entered the elevator. The lights flickered. I watched the dial: 1, then 2, and finally the 6th floor light came on and . . . all the lights went out in the building. I quickly turned in panic to find the superintendent of the building coming out of a doorway with the emergency lights on, saying, in broken English, Mrs. X was stuck in the elevator and didn't I know that she was deathly afraid of it.

Images raced through my mind: I saw her lying dead in the elevator; then my name plastered on the front page of the *Times*. Mustering as much control as possible, I asked the super how we could get power back on, and only then noticed that the entire neighborhood was pitch black. My fate was sealed (so was my patient's). I tried, however feebly, to engage step one of the problem solving model (problem orientation; or stop and think). It didn't work; I had a problem of gargantuan proportions.

Then, the emergency door next to the elevator opened and out came my patient with flashlight in hand. I was drenched in sweat; she was desert dry.

What I had failed to observe in the exposure session was her purse in which she religiously carried a virtual cornucopia of emergency equipment ranging from food and water to medical supplies. She was, in fact, prepared for anything and had just gotten off at the 6th floor when the lights went out. She hastened to remind me that whereas I had forced her to gradually reduce the size of the purse (originally a knapsack) as well as its contents in previous road exposures, she proved the adage about always being prepared for any emergency.

Post script: Soon after, the lights came on, and I said, "Back on the elevator, without your bag."

CONCLUSIONS AND CURRENT ISSUES

If there is one factor common to all of the major approaches used to help people adjust to posttraumatic stress, it is confrontation. All of the techniques that we have discussed involve getting people to face memories, thoughts, or images of past traumatic occurrences that they have suppressed. In this sense, even systematic desensitization can be considered an "exposure" approach, though contact with feared stimuli is more gradual than in the flooding techniques, and elicitation of high levels of anxiety in desensitization is avoided. It should be noted that some exposure approaches involve the use of "graded" or gradual exposure to feared stimuli, and even in techniques such as implosive therapy and flooding, which quickly phase in exposure to highly aversive imagery or events, there is some initial exposure to less aversive stimuli.

An implicit assumption of all the exposure techniques is that we need to deal actively with and somehow reprocess or recondition memories of past aversive events if we are to get past them and diminish their influence on our lives. From this standpoint, perhaps the flashbacks (spontaneous reexperiencing of traumatic events in memories and dreams) that are commonly endured by PTSD victims represent a natural tendency to engage in this reconfrontation process. The techniques that we have discussed are effective because they accelerate and concentrate this process through extended and repeated presentation of the material under conditions that minimize distractions and opportunities to avoid it (Rachman, 1980). Disclosure (and systematic desensitization) do this in the most gradual fashion, whereas the flooding approaches are the most directly confrontational.

Of the approaches discussed, disclosure is the most amenable to direct self-use. For most people, both systematic desensitization and the exposure techniques usually require some initial professional guidance, after which both may be used effectively on a self-management basis. Innovative in vivo techniques have been developed to facilitate self-management applications, such as telephone-guided self-exposure for housebound agoraphobics (McNamee, O'Sullivan, Lelliott, & Marks, 1989), and citizen's band radio-guided desensitization and mobile-phone-guided exposure for individuals with severe driving phobias (Flynn, Taylor, & Pollard, 1992; Levine & Wolpe, 1980).

A recently developed alternative to in vivo exposure is the use of virtual reality as the means of exposure to feared stimuli. This approach integrates a range of high technology sensory input devices to immerse the individual in highly realistic computer-generated environments that change in a natural way with head and body movements. Experienced inside a helmet, environments developed for acrophobics (persons with a pronounced fear of heights) include "a virtual hotel with an open elevator that took (acrophobic) students up 49 stories, as well as a series of ever scarier balconies and bridges—the precipices were frightening enough to induce vomiting, sweaty palms and rubbery knees in most of the students, who stood on a 4-foot by 4-foot platform as they guided themselves ever higher with a hand-held mouse ('The latest head trip,' 1996)." Initial reports indicate that exposure via virtual reality is an effective treatment for acrophobia (Rothbaum, Hodges, et al., 1995), and it seems to be potentially useful as a self-management technique. EMDR and psychodynamic psychotherapy appear to have no potential for use as self-management techniques.

In the 1960s and 1970s, desensitization came to be viewed by many professionals as the standard treatment for phobias and other anxiety disorders. Though the question of how it works has not been resolved, its efficacy as a clinical technique is supported by research findings, and it is widely accepted by professionals (Deffenbacher & Suinn, 1988). Recently, exposure techniques have gained more prominence, especially in the treatment of agoraphobia, panic disorder, social phobia (Rapee & Barlow, 1993), posttraumatic stress-related conditions (Fairbank et al., 1993), and obsessive-compulsive disorders (Sturgis, 1993). Swinson & Kuch (1989) note that for agoraphobia and panic disorder, the treatment of choice has gradually evolved from desensitization to exposure-based treatments, and that for approximately 80 percent of patients self-directed exposure is "rapidly effective and improvements are maintained over years." Marks (1987) argues that exposure to feared stimuli is *the* critical variable in producing change (in desensitization as well as flooding and implosive therapy), and omitting exposure or simply using relaxation or cognitive approaches does not produce fear reduction.

In studies comparing exposure and desensitization, some have found desensitization to be superior (e.g., Weinberger & Englehart, 1976, for speech anxiety; Smith & Nye, 1973, for test anxiety), and others have favored exposure (e.g., Marshall, 1977, for snake phobia; Jacobson, 1991, for needle phobia). It has been argued that exposure treatments are inappropriate for some anxiety-related problems (e.g., sexual dysfunction) that have been effectively treated with systematic desensitization (Deffenbacher & Suinn, 1988). Also, some studies have shown flooding to be superior or comparable to desensitization in effectiveness but rated lower by clients and therapists on satisfaction and preference (Crowe, Marks, Agras, & Leitenberg, 1972; Rudestam & Bedrosian, 1977; Suarez, Adams, & McCutcheon, 1976).

Exposure has been used to effectively treat children with PTSD (Lipovsky, 1991; Saigh, 1989) and in one case to treat a child with a simple phobia (of dogs) after desensitization had failed (Sreenivasan, Manocha, & Jain, 1979), but the intense levels of anxiety elicited in clients have caused some to question the acceptability of exposure treatments, especially with children (King & Gullone, 1990; King, Hamilton, & Ollendick, 1988). Exposure treatments clearly produce more subjective discomfort in clients and some therapists. However, recent research (reviewed previously) indicates that they are the most effective behavioral treatments for clinical level anxiety disorders and PTSD.

We have had little to add in this chapter on cognitive-behavioral techniques. This is not because they are not powerful and well-accepted interventions, but rather because outside of the well-delineated systems described in Chapter 7, cognitive-behavioral applications are often based on general guidelines (sometimes associated with one of these systems) rather than on set procedures. For example, De Jongh, Muris, et al. (1995), in successfully treating dental phobics, used a cognitive intervention "largely based" on Aaron Beck's model. Patients' generalized beliefs about dentists (e.g., "dentists are clumsy and sadists, and everything goes wrong when they treat a problem") were disputed and shown to be irrational when dentists' actions were objectively examined and discussed (e.g., "an injection of a local anesthetic might initially cause pain in an inflamed area, but this was necessary in order to remove an infected tooth while minimizing overall discomfort—and if the patient had not waited so long to come for treatment, the whole procedure might have been done painlessly"). Of the more structured interventions discussed in this chapter, Foa & Kozak's and Calhoun & Resick's (cognitive processing therapy)—both of which include "corrective information" in their procedure—have the most explicit cognitive elements.

A current trend is the development of combination treatment packages, which sometimes include both exposure and relaxation or desensitization (as in Lyons & Keane's, 1989, adaptation of flooding therapy for PTSD—described previously) and also cognitive-behavioral procedures as components (e.g., Barlow, Craske, Cerny, & Klosko, 1989; Roberts, 1989). In general, multicomponent treatments that include cognitive-behavioral techniques (such as cognitive restructuring using Beck's or Ellis's model or Meichenbaum's multimodal stress inoculation training) as a major element have been shown to be effective treatments for panic attacks (Rapee & Barlow, 1993) and PTSD (Fairbank et al., 1993).

It should be noted that many cognitively oriented therapists (cf. Goldfried, 1971) hold that the effectiveness of *all* anxiety management techniques is due to changed cognitions that are produced about oneself. This view is, of course, consistent with the cognitive appraisal model of stress and coping espoused in this volume. From this standpoint, positive changes produced by desensitization and exposure are not regarded as being due to a mechanical relearning process (reciprocal inhibition, extinction of a feared response respectively) but rather to the learning of a new set of cognitions (e.g., "I am not afraid when I see a snake," "I can handle this situation"), and it is these new self-views that are thought to be the critical factor enabling individuals to cope more effectively with future stress. Thus, it is argued, *all* change is cognitively mediated, and all of the relearning techniques are cognitive-behavioral even if they do not label themselves as such or explicitly attempt to change cognitions. In this vein, a common observation of experienced clinicians using exposure techniques with PTSD patients (rape victims, Vietnam War veterans) is that initially, patients' memories of the traumatic event are extremely constricted and difficult to access. As the visceral fear response is extinguished by using exposure techniques, these memories are far more easily verbalized. This opening of access to previously suppressed cognitive schemas in nonpunishing circumstances seems to enhance the fear extinction process and thus plays a crucial role in "curing" the patient.

We have similarly not mentioned applications of problem-focused coping, such as social skills and assertiveness training, in dealing with distal poststress reactions. As noted in Chapter 7, these are extremely important techniques in dealing with interpersonal stress when anxiety has developed through a prolonged conditioning processes and resulted in major skill deficits. Situations in which a stress experience has radically changed life demands also require skill-building and problem-solving, in addition to learning fear reduction through emotion-focused techniques. For example, some widows who had depended on their husbands to manage financial affairs, make repairs, and do the driving often have these tasks cared for by a male relative in the weeks following the spouse's death. But this support is usually withdrawn rather suddenly, and the widow must now take on these responsibilities as well as learn to relate socially as a single woman without a husband, and deal with any residual emotional distress that she is experiencing (Glick, Weiss, & Parkes, 1974).

When the original aversive conditioning events have engendered traumatic stress, or in other situations in which the level of stress currently experienced is debilitating (as in panic attacks or some phobias), the primary goal is to minimize the stress elicited through the teaching of emotion-focused coping techniques. Teaching problem-focused coping, then, becomes a possible adjunct depending on the needs of the individual. Some investigators are producing interventions tailored to specific problems that address both emotion-focused and problem-focused coping needs in a single comprehensive package. For example, Turner, Beidel, Cooley, Woody, & Messer (1994) developed a treatment program for severe social phobics that included exposure as well as social skills and problem-solving training, in order to address their emotional distress as well as their social inhibitions and impaired academic and occupational functioning. Similarly, Frueh, Turner, Beidel, Mirabella, & Jones (1996) reasoned that although exposure treatments effectively deal with the emotional distress components of PTSD (e.g., nightmares, intrusive memories, flashbacks, physiological arousal, and subjective emotional distress), they do not alter deficits involving problem-focused coping skills that accompany this condition (e.g., problems in interpersonal relations, social withdrawal, employment difficulties). Therefore, they developed a multicomponent treatment that included social skills training, as well as intensive exposure therapy, in order to address both the problem-focused and emotion-focused coping deficiency components of PTSD.

Finally, no discussion of long-term stress would be complete without addressing the current controversy regarding the authenticity of memories of victims of traumatic events (especially those pertaining to sexual abuse). The traumatic memories of Vietnam veterans, adult sexual assault victims, and Holocaust survivors are unquestionably authentic. But what about adults who claim to have experienced sexual abuse during childhood? In recent years, stories of adults who have "recovered memories" of past sexual abuse by parents, teachers, priests, and babysitters have surfaced—some by well-known entertainers, some involving Satanic rituals, and even sexual assaults by extraterrestrials (see Remembering "Repressed" Abuse, 1992; Sagan, 1993). Why has there been a sudden upsurge of such stories? Are the alleged victims' memories accurate—did these events actually occur? Does it matter if they are real? These issues have become highly controversial and the subject of much debate. See the box on pages 183–184 for a discussion of these issues.

$\mathcal{T}$HE RETURN OF THE REPRESSED—OR FALSE MEMORIES?

One of the cardinal concepts in Sigmund Freud's psychoanalytic theory is that the psychological problems we experience as adults stem from sexual traumas during childhood that were unresolved and repressed—forgotten and rendered unconscious because they were too stressful and overwhelming to deal with at the time. Freud later concluded that most of these memories of early trauma—which were revealed (or "uncovered") during psychoanalytic treatment of adult patients—were fantasies rather than memories of actual events. But he thought that they were highly significant nonetheless, because they represented wishful thinking (e.g., they were symbolic of an unconscious desire to have sex with one's mother or father) and needed to be explored and resolved if a patient was to be "cured."

Freud's ideas were highly controversial when he first proposed them around the turn of the century. However, though they have continued to be influential with some practicing psychotherapists, they have been rejected by many others who orient their treatment of psychological trauma around learning-based models (as described in this chapter) rather Freudian-based psychodynamic techniques. But the specter of Freud has recently reappeared as stories of adult children accusing their parents of having abused them sexually during childhood and infancy surface almost daily in the popular media. In most of these cases, the adult "survivors" claim that they have become newly aware of their repressed memories of being abused as a result of psychotherapy or some other social support process. In some cases, parents have been convicted or successfully sued in civil cases by their children solely on the basis of the childrens' report of newly unearthed repressed memories. In the wake of these actions, a heated controversy has developed between the supporters and the opponents of the "recovered memory" movement.

Loftus (1992, 1993) has recently addressed this issue. She notes that the high incidence of confirmed sexual child abuse makes it clear that this is an enormous problem that demands immediate attention. Furthermore, she points out that patients who recover such memories are generally supported by practicing psychotherapists who "are impressed with the emotional pain (and physical symptoms) that accompanies the expression of memories" (Loftus, 1992, p. 16) and who believe that they represent actual events. For example, Levis (1991) a researcher and clinician who uses exposure therapy with his patients, describes various physical symptoms that he has observed in patients which coincide with the nature of the abuse that they say they have experienced, and that usually precedes the visual image of the recovered event. In one case,

"A patient reported the appearance of bumps or sores on the outside and inside of her genital area. Medical examination could not determine what these marks were. . . . A scene was developed in which the patient was asked to visualize these sores and focus on the pain. A number of associations were produced and incorporated into the scene as the memory was fully decoded. The elicited memory revealed that the mother discovered her daughter (the patient) had sex with her husband, stripped her naked, and forced her to sit in the chair for a very long period. The mother periodically came into the room where the patient was being punished and grabbed and pulled her skin both around and inside the vaginal area. . . . Photographs of the patient's bumps on her body were consistent with the type of marks reportedly produced by the mother's sadistic activities. Once the full memory was recovered and the accompanying emotional affect extinguished by repeating the memory, the physical symptoms disappeared as quickly as they materialized" (Levis, 1991, p. 416).

But Loftus (1992, 1993) and others point out that there are reasons to be cautious about uncritically accepting reports of such memories. Consistent with Freud's conclusions, Dawes (1991) notes that there is experimental evidence that we often reconstruct the past on the basis of how we would like it to have been or how we think it should have been. Loftus notes that though some claim to remember being abused during early infancy, most studies indicate an inability to recall events prior to the age of three or four. Memories could be honestly believed, she notes, but could still be false. These beliefs could be influenced by contemporary popular writing, especially the best-selling book *The Courage to Heal* (Bass & Davis, 1988) which tells the reader, "If you are unable to remember any instances (of child sexual abuse) like the ones mentioned above but still have a feeling that something abusive happened to you, it probably did," (p. 21) or by therapists themselves who sometimes, on the basis of only a "suggestive history," tell patients that they definitely have been traumatized.

(continued)

Another factor that contributes to the recent proliferation of claims of recovered memories of child sexual abuse and their broad acceptance is the increasing readiness of people to identify themselves as victims. In American society, membership in a victimized group is no longer a stigma. Rather, it is more often met with understanding, sympathy, and special privileges, and can be a source of positive identification and self-esteem. But, as illustrated by a cartoon that recently appeared in newspapers throughout the country, much of the public is beginning to view the current upsurge of suddenly recovered memories with increasing skepticism.

Why does it matter whether or not reports of sexual child abuse are authentic? Loftus (1992, 1993) argues that (a) the lives of parents and others who may be falsely accused are unfairly damaged and (b) if we uncritically accept uncorroborated allegations, true cases of abuse will be disbelieved and will not get the serious attention that they merit. Furthermore, she asks rhetorically, if actual childhood sexual abuse has serious negative consequences, what are the effects on people of suggested or "implanted" memories of abuse that did not actually occur?

"WAIT A MINUTE!....I FEEL A LONG-REPRESSED MEMORY BUBBLING UP!....HOLD IT! NO, WAIT, NEVER MIND... IT WAS THAT TUNA CASSEROLE FROM LAST WEEK."

Reprinted with special permission of King Features Syndicate.

Summary

1. Postvention involves helping people deal with stress produced by an event that they have already encountered.

2. Proximal poststress procedures help people deal with the short-term effects of stress exposure. The initial reaction to a traumatic stressor is often shock, and therefore victims are usually not receptive to aggressive, problem-oriented interventions at this time. Provision of social support is crucial during this period. Psychotropic drugs can be used to provide rapid sedation if necessary but must be very carefully prescribed.

3. The length and severity of the acute reaction period is variable, and depends on the severity of the stressor and individual differences that affect appraisal of stressfulness and coping ability. Some people continue to have adjustment problems stemming from exposure to stressful events for the rest of their lives.

4. Interventions for long-term stress-related problems include systematic desensitization, anxiety management training (a variant of desensitization), and various forms of exposure therapy. The latter includes Stampfl & Levis's groundbreaking implosive therapy, in which clients are in part presented symbolic imagery based on psychodynamic speculations, and several more recently developed variations of exposure therapy that take a pure flooding approach, using only imagery associated with traumatic events that were actually experienced.

5. Other variations of exposure therapy include (a) Lyon & Keane's approach, which incorporates relaxation skills and was developed for use with Vietnam veterans; (b) Foa & Kozak's approach, which focuses on treating individuals who have been exposed to the original trauma relatively recently and which has been applied largely to rape victims; (c) Levis's memory reactivation approach, in which the therapist is relatively inactive and functions primarily as a stimulator of the "memory retrieval process," and which has been mainly applied to female victims of childhood sexual and physical abuse; (d) EMDR, which uses induced eye movements to enhance the visual image and "reprocessing" of the disturbing event; (e) disclosure, in which details of the traumatic event are reviewed and disclosed either in writing or orally; (f) Calhoun & Resick's cognitive reprocessing therapy, which was designed specifically for sexual assault victims and which includes an informational component designed to alter maladaptive beliefs that the victim may hold about her role in the event; and (g) short-term dynamic psychotherapy, which focuses on resolving unconscious conflicts brought about by exposure to trauma.

6. There is little evidence to support the adage that "time heals all wounds." Treatment outcome data indicate that previously experienced traumatic events must somehow be reencountered and reprocessed in a safe environment. All of the effective posttraumatic stress adjustment techniques in some way foster active confrontation with memories or images of these events that have been avoided or suppressed.

7. Many clients, after having received brief professional guidance, have effectively used exposure as well as systematic desensitization (in vivo and/or imaginal) on a self-management basis.

$\mathcal{K}$EY TERMS

anxiety management training   Variant of systematic desensitization that focuses on teaching clients to identify stress responses at low levels and associate them with relaxation in order to prevent high levels of arousal from developing.

brief behavioral intervention procedure   Procedure developed to help recent rape victims problem-solve and deal with their emotional distress; designed to avert long-term problems.

cognitive reprocessing therapy   Exposure-based treatment approach, in which the client writes about the traumatic event, that also includes an explicit information component designed to correct maladaptive beliefs and meanings attributed to the event.

disclosure   Technique in which people confide to others, orally or in writing, the details of traumatic events that they have experienced. This approach is particularly amenable to use on a self-management basis.

distal poststress interventions   Procedures designed to help people cope effectively with the long-term aftereffects of exposure to a stressor.

eye movement desensitization and reprocessing (EMDR)   Relatively recently developed exposure technique in which side-to-side eye movements are induced by a therapist in order to enhance the image of a traumatic event.

Foa & Kozak's exposure model   Exposure approach, theoretically based on Lang's bioinformational model, in which clients are encouraged to relive their traumatic experiences; it has been applied most often to relatively recently assaulted rape victims.

flooding   Exposure approaches in which emphasis is on presenting to the client sensory material representative of the actual trauma that was experienced; no attempt is made to present stimuli that are thought to be symbolically relevant but which were not actually experienced.

Levis's memory reactivation approach   Exposure treatment in which the therapist plays a relatively nondirective role, encouraging patients to associate trauma-based images until memory of a coherent traumatic event is elicited.

postvention   Interventions designed to help people cope effectively with the stress resulting from past aversive experiences.

proximal poststress interventions   Procedures designed to help people cope effectively with the short-term aftereffects of exposure to a stressor.

recovered memories   Memories of past sexual/physical abuse "recovered" from adult "survivors" who state that (usually as a result of psychotherapy) they have become aware of previously forgotten childhood abuse after many years.

self-directed desensitization   Systematic desensitization in which the client and sometimes his or her family or friends take primary responsibility for implementing the procedure, usually after first consulting briefly with a professional therapist.

short-term dynamic psychotherapy   Application of traditional psychodynamic psychotherapy to deal with posttraumatic stress.

CHAPTER **10**

Drugs of Use and Abuse in Stress Management

John is a twenty-seven-year-old Gulf War combat veteran. He grew up in a small town where just about everyone knew everyone else. His circle of friends in high school were a close-knit group who had known each other all their lives. John was a "B" student in school. He played several sports but truly excelled at wrestling. An active member of the youth group at church, he did not drink or smoke and had no disciplinary problems, but then that was true of most the kids he grew up with. John left for college after high school graduation and made new friends but never forgot his old ones. Like many members of his unit, John joined the Marine Reserves while in college as a way to help pay tuition. He had never considered the Marines as a career, but he enjoyed working with his unit and became an excellent marks-man while in the reserves. During his college days, John described himself as a "typical" student, going to classes, taking tests, play-ing in the intramural sports leagues, and partying on the week-end on occasion.

After graduation, John married his high school sweetheart and began working as an intern at a large corporation. John's wife was three months pregnant with their first child when the Gulf War began. Incredibly, he went from being on the fast track in corporate America to the front lines in Iraq in less than forty-eight hours. He was a part of the frontal assault on Iraqi troops when the U. S. forces literally overran, and ran over, Iraqi troops in southern Iraq. Tanks and assault carriers pushed over and through the Iraqi lines. Trenches full of Iraqi troops were over-run, and those that did not surrender were buried as wave after wave of U. S. armed personnel carriers propelled over and through the trenches. John remembers vividly looking back at the trenches just crossed and seeing only the caved-in trenches with *an occasional pair of hands sticking up out of the sand, sometimes with the fingers still wiggling. When John looked up, he was particularly distressed at the sight of a soldier, now not more than a skeleton in uniform, still holding his gun upright in the burned-out remains of a truck. Out of nowhere machine gun fire rang out, hitting John in the shoulder and back and fatally wounding two of his close buddies. There were very few U. S. casualties during the Desert Storm operation. Unbelievably, two of them, buddies he had been to college with, lay sprawled next to John, and nothing he could do could bring them back to life. John's heart raced, and his mind swirled, "What will I tell their families?" he thought. As blood oozed out over his uniform, John could feel himself losing consciousness, and he prayed that this was all a bad dream, and if not, he prayed that he would die.*

As fate would have it, John lived, but his bad dream was just beginning. From the moment he regained consciousness, John couldn't help thinking that if he had paid more attention to his surroundings that day, his friends would not be dead. John returned home to his still-pregnant wife and with continued physical therapy was able to return part-time to his position as an intern at the company. Although he was very relieved to be home again with his family, John could not shake the thoughts of guilt surrounding the deaths of his friends. He frequently found himself thinking, "Why did I survive?" and "I should have been able to prevent their deaths." He felt guilty, angry, and depressed. In the midst of his emotional turmoil, his wife and friends saw the same good guy John on the outside and seemed to treat him as if the war never really happened. He tried to act like the same old John, but he did not feel like the same person any more. He was troubled by his heightened sensitivity to noises or sudden movement. He began to scan the environment whenever he and his wife went out, and he often found himself anxious in crowded places, and eventually refused to go out in crowded public situations at all. He was especially bothered by feelings of guilt and bad memories before going to bed at night. His heart would race, and his mind would swirl when the distractions of the day faded to the quiet solitude of the evening. He began sleeping less and waking more often with nightmares of past events.

John tried to push these symptoms aside, and he hoped that with time he would return to his normal self. To help him get to sleep one night, John drank several shots of rum, and though he did not really care for the taste, he found the drink surprisingly soothing. It seemed to relax his body and let his mind rest. He was able to go to sleep almost immediately. Soon afterward, John began drinking regularly to help "unwind" before going to bed. He started drinking during the day, and he found this allowed him to block out the persistent feelings of anxiety and guilt. But as John's drinking became more regular, his wife complained that he was becoming emotionally distant and was not taking enough care of his home and family. John responded to her complaints by isolating himself as much as possible and drinking even more.

At his wife's insistence, John scheduled an appointment with their family physician, Doc Johnson, someone John had known all his life and someone John's wife thought he would be able to talk to. He told the doctor of his difficulties with his marriage and new baby, and he described his trouble getting to sleep and his feelings of anxiety in public places. John's doctor listened patiently, and when John was through talking, Doc Johnson explained that he was just experiencing the normal stress and strain of fatherhood. John's doctor never asked about the use of alcohol, and John did not offer this information. John would never volunteer that he was depressed and anxious all the time, or that he had troubling nightmares and

daytime flashbacks, and persistent feelings of guilt surrounding his wartime expe-
rience. He would never offer this information, but he sure wished the doctor would
ask. Instead, John was sent home with a prescription for Valium and was in-
structed to take it easy and be grateful for the good life, friends, and family that he
enjoyed. John filled the prescription and was amazed at how the drug seemed to
drain the tension out of his body and mind, and left him feeling more peaceful than
he could ever remember. "Maybe the doctor knows what's best after all," thought
John. However, John began increasing the dose of the Valium, and when that
didn't work as well as it had before, he drank more. After almost a year, John de-
cided that the drug wasn't working very well any more and he was tired of having
to practically beg old Doc Johnson into giving him another prescription, so he
stopped taking the drug when he ran out of pills. John experienced a tremendous
increase in his anxiety and sleep problems; it seemed to be far worse than any time
in the past. To compensate, John increased his alcohol consumption and began
experimenting with other drugs, including marijuana, morphine, and even heroin.
He retreated into his own world, and watched as his marriage, friendships, and
livelihood crumbled in the wake of his addiction to sedative drugs.

You have probably guessed that John is suffering from posttraumatic stress disorder (PTSD). PTSD is an anxiety disorder in which drugs are frequently misused and abused. For example, as many as 80 percent of Vietnam veterans with PTSD have alcohol-related problems (Jelinek & Williams, 1984). The tendency to use drugs and alcohol to manage or "self-medicate" anxiety is commonly reported by substance abusers diagnosed with PTSD as well as those diagnosed with other types of anxiety problems. As you have learned in this text, there are effective nonpharmacological treatments available for people with PTSD and other anxiety disorders. For some anxiety problems that we will review in this chapter, there is evidence that specific types of antianxiety medication can be helpful, but PTSD is not one of these disorders. Almost all drugs used to manage anxiety in PTSD are misused or abused whether by prescription or "self-medication." Interestingly, people like John, who develop substance abuse problems in trying to cope with their trauma and who had no prior alcohol or drug problems, tend to reduce or eliminate drug use as their PTSD symptoms decrease in intensity and frequency during psychological treatment (Jelinek, 1984).

Throughout this book and in our workbook (Gramling & Auerbach, 1998), we have emphasized a self-management approach to stress and anxiety problems. Learning anxiety-management skills, either through self-management techniques or with the assistance of a cognitive-behavioral therapist, is an extremely effective way of reducing anxiety and increasing one's confidence in the ability to manage stressors to be encountered. Yet, we must acknowledge that many people seek medication for their anxiety problems. For some of the most serious forms of anxiety disorders, there are medications that are very useful, especially when used in combination with cognitive-behavioral interventions. We want the reader to be aware of what types of drugs are effective and what types are ineffective in treating different types of anxiety and stress-related problems.

It is important to note that a prescription (or nonprescription) medication is not a magic bullet for the treatment of stress-related problems. There are many reasons to be cautious about the use of medication in the treatment of anxiety. Some antianxiety drugs are overprescribed, some have adverse side effects, and some have substantial potential to be overused and abused by the person suffering from anxiety. Sometimes the use of an antianxiety medication, whether prescribed or not, can actually hinder the effectiveness of anxiety-management procedures used in cognitive-behavioral interventions.

Although it is commonly believed that many people who abuse drugs with sedative properties initiate drug use as a means of self-medicating their anxiety (e.g., O'Connell, 1989; Julien 1995), the empirical research in this area is not well developed (Gregorious & Smith, 1991). Presumably, people suffering from anxiety often discover that specific types of drugs are negatively reinforcing (drug-taking reduces the aversive state of anxiety) (Weiss, 1991), and thus self-medication with alcohol or other drugs represents an attempt to reduce or eliminate persistent symptoms of anxiety (Khantzian, 1985).

The types of drugs that people use to manage their anxiety range from legal substances such as alcohol and over-the-counter medication to prescription medications and even illegal drugs. Misuse and abuse of antianxiety drugs can occur with prescription drugs as easily as with illegal drugs. For example, prescription drug abuse can occur when physicians overprescribe because of patient pressure (patients come in demanding certain drugs for their condition, and it is easier to prescribe the drugs than to argue with the patients); or lack of knowledge on the part of the physician (the physician might prescribe the same antianxiety drug for all anxiety symptoms without trying to uncover the type of anxiety disorder that the patient is suffering from) (Ziedonis, 1995). People use drugs in the treatment of all forms of anxiety, from transient anxiety states like test anxiety to the chronic anxiety problems that merit formal diagnoses, and there is always the potential for abuse when drugs are involved in the treatment of anxiety. It is not that drugs are all bad, and if you are currently taking a prescription medication, do not discontinue the drug without discussing it with your physician. There can be serious side effects with abrupt withdrawal of some of the antianxiety medications. (See box on page 191). One of the problems with the use of medication in stress management is that it is very easy to slide into a pattern of excessive use and abuse. Hopefully, this chapter will provide information that will make you more knowledgeable and informed when talking to your physician or when considering "self-medicating" your anxiety.

A MODEL FOR DRUG USE AND ABUSE

As many have noted, drug abuse is difficult to define (Kleber, 1990). With respect to drugs used to control anxiety, we find that differentiating between appropriate and inappropriate use (including alcohol, over-the-counter, prescription, and illegal drugs) is often not clear-cut. A continuum approach for the use and abuse of psychoactive drugs has been described (Julien, 1995) that is adapted in the following section to apply specifically to antianxiety agents. The stages of use and abuse include the following:

1. *Accepted medical or recreational use.* Medical use would include the use of medication for the treatment or prevention of diagnosed disease or alleviation of physical or mental discomfort. The use of medication prescribed by a knowledgeable physician who is able to diagnose accurately the various types of anxiety disorders would clearly be included in this category. What constitutes accepted recreational use is mostly a function of your reference group. If your grandmother ran a bar well into her 70's (as did the second author's—and she's 90 now and still drinking the occasional "ice tea"), you might have a more liberal view of what constitutes accepted recreational use of antianxiety drugs than a person who was raised a Mormon in Salt Lake City, Utah. At least with respect to legal substances, the authors suggest that the dividing line between accepted drug use versus misuse (described later) is best determined by each individual. A person of legal age who goes out with friends and

DRUGS ASSOCIATED WITH INCREASED ANXIETY

There is a good chance that there are foods that you eat, over-the-counter medications that you take, and even commonly prescribed drugs that can cause or exacerbate feelings of anxiety, tension, and restlessness. Any persons trying to manage their anxiety level should consider taking an inventory of the foods and drugs that they ingest to determine whether they include ingredients that may be contributing to feelings of anxiety. We list and describe here some of the most common dietary/medication contributors to anxiety.

Caffeine.   Caffeine is the most widely used central nervous stimulant in the United States and the world at large. Probably everyone knows that caffeine can keep you awake, make you restless, and increase anxiety, but you might not realize how pervasive this drug is and how much it contributes to feelings of anxiety, especially among people who are already anxious. The pharmacological effects of caffeine can occur at doses as low as 50–200 mg. Chances are that you are aware that caffeine is found in coffee, tea, and cola drinks. If you are trying to manage your anxiety, one of the first things to consider is the reduction or elimination of caffeine use. The typical caffeine content of these beverages is 29–176 mg for coffee, 150 mg for tea, and 30–65 mg for a 12-ounce cola drink. Caffeine also can be found in chocolate (about 25 mg for a small bar), and many chocolate lovers are unaware of this association. Another often overlooked source of caffeine is aspirin. Many manufacturers of aspirin tablets also add a substantial dose of caffeine (15–150 mg). You can avoid these products by checking the ingredients on the label. If the aspirin product contains caffeine, it will be listed as an ingredient along with the dosage. A surprising number of prescription analgesic medications also contain caffeine including Darvon, Fiorinal, and Norgesic.

Over-the-counter medications that contain caffeine include cold remedies, diuretics, and various stimulants advertised to keep a person awake (e.g., No Doz) or as an aid in weight reduction (caffeine has a mild appetite-suppressant effect). Moreover, a variety of prescription drugs contain caffeine or theophylline or theobromine, both of which belong to the same class of drugs as caffeine and which also have similar central nervous system effects. Bronchodilators, for example, which are used in the treatment of asthma, may contain theophylline, which is associated with nervousness, anxiety, and insomnia.

Sympathomimetics.   The sympathomimetics stimulate the sympathetic nervous system and thereby create physiological symptoms similar to the stress response when the sympathetic nervous system is stimulated "naturally." These drugs are found in a range of products including some cough and cold preparations, nasal sprays, some eye-drop preparations, and some respiratory drugs. Ephedrine is one example that until recently could be found in the form of pseudoephedrine in dozens of over-the-counter cold medications.

Beta-Adrenergic Stimulants.   As you might guess from the name of this class of drugs, these drugs have the reverse effect on the body as the beta-blocker drugs discussed in the main text. These types of drugs are often used in the treatment of respiratory disorders and may be associated with nervousness, tremor, increased heart rate, and palpitations. Literally dozens of bronchodilators, largely used in the treatment of asthma, are beta-adrenergic stimulants.

has a few beers in order to "unwind" after completing a nerve-wracking test would likely be included in the accepted recreational-use category by the vast majority of people.

2. *Drug misuse.* Drug misuse is the use of any drug (legal or illegal) for a medical or recreational purpose when other alternatives are available, practical, or war-

ranted, or when drug use endangers either the users or others around them. For example, a person who drinks a few beers after taking a big exam and then drives home intoxicated would fall into the category of drug misuse. Similarly, the person who is very anxious prior to a big exam, drinks a few beers to "self-medicate" anxiety, and falls asleep without studying, resulting in very poor performance, would fall into the category of drug misuse. In general, a recreational drug is misused when it impedes the user's social, occupational, or family functioning, when it results in a preoccupation with drug use, or when it endangers the physical or mental health of the user or others. With respect to prescription drugs, a physician who prescribes an antianxiety drug such as Valium for a patient without making a thorough assessment or simply because the patient requested it is promoting and allowing drug misuse.

3. *Compulsive abuse.* When a person uses a drug despite adverse social or medical consequences and has developed an intense reliance on self-administered drugs, the pattern of behavior is considered compulsive abuse. John, from our opening vignette, slipped into compulsive abuse when he began to rely on alcohol to help him get to sleep every night and "had to have" his Valium every day in order to be able to function. Another sign of compulsive abuse was shown when John began begging and demanding more of the drug from Doc Johnson, and Doc Johnson's going along with it contributed to John's problem.

4. *Addiction.* Addiction, which is the most extreme result of drug misuse, is characterized by overwhelming involvement in drug use and in securing its supply. Drug use pervades the person's life and controls his or her behavior. This is the state that John eventually fell into. The signs of addiction were present in the later stages of his compulsive drug abuse and became full-blown as John's life began to revolve around obtaining and using drugs. Like many others who become addicted to drugs, John lost his job, his family, and his friends as drugs became more and more the center of his life.

DRUGS OF USE AND ABUSE IN STRESS MANAGEMENT

There are a variety of drugs, legal and illegal, prescription and nonprescription, that are frequently used and abused by persons trying to manage their anxiety. In the section that follows, several of the most frequently used antianxiety drugs are presented. Some of these drugs, such as alcohol, will be familiar to you. Others, such as some of the tricyclics, may be unfamiliar, or you may not have realized that they could be used as antianxiety medications. Each of these drugs or class of drugs has an accepted medical or recreational use (in terms of the model of drug use and abuse described earlier). All of these drugs can be misused, and some have a very high abuse potential. Interestingly, the drugs for which we have the best data as effective antianxiety medications have the lowest potential for abuse and addiction.

Benzodiazepines

Because the benzodiazepines have been the most frequently prescribed drugs in the treatment of anxiety, we will carefully examine these drugs and the risks associated with their use. The first benzodiazepine (Librium) was introduced in 1960, and its powerful antianxiety effects forever changed the landscape of anxiety management. The benzodiazepines are associated with rapid relief from subjective feelings of anxiety. Slight variations in the benzodiazepine molecule led to the development of over a dozen benzodiazepine compounds. Table 10–1 presents the generic name and the more familiar brand name of some of the most frequently prescribed benzodi-

TABLE 10–1.	TRADE NAME AND GENERIC NAME FOR COMMONLY USED BENZODIAZEPINES

Trade Name	Generic Name
Long-Acting Agents	
Valium	Diazepam
Librium	Chlordiazepoxide
Dalmane	Flurazepem
Paxipam	Halazepam
Centrax	Prazepam
Tranxene	Chlorazepate
Intermediate-Acting Agents	
Ativan	Lorazepam
Klonopin	Clonazepam
Dormalin	Quazepam
ProSom	Estazolam
Short-Acting Agents	
Versed	Midazolam
Serax	Oxazepam
Restoril	Temazepam
Halcion	Triazolam
Xanax	Alprazolam

azepines. Because most people are more familiar with the trade names and they are generally easier to remember, we will henceforth use the trade name when referring to a specific drug. However, if you were to research these drugs in the library, you would want to look them up by the generic name, since that is how most scholarly publications refer to these drugs. Each of the various benzodiazepines listed in Table 10–1 has antianxiety properties, and each has a slightly different profile (shorter versus longer acting, more or less selective, and so on). In addition to their antianxiety properties, these drugs also have sedative effects, muscle relaxant effects, and anti-convulsant properties.

Through the mid-1970s, there was an exponential increase in the use and misuse of the benzodiazepine drugs, with over 100 million prescriptions written in a single year when the use of these drugs was at its zenith (Smith, 1991). This era of benzodiazepine-prescribing has been roundly criticized on many grounds. Most frequently, the criticism has been that these prescribing practices "medicalized" what in many cases were simply problems of daily living. Rather than encouraging moderately distressed anxiety sufferers to learn new coping skills, physicians gave them a pill that was thought to be a "magic bullet" and sent them on their way. Derisive terms, such as "mother's little helper" came into use to describe the tendency to use medications to solve problems of daily living. The tendency to overprescribe these drugs was termed "legitimized drug abuse" and likened to sweeping one's problems into a "pharmacological closet." On the other side of the debate, the critics were accused of "pharmacological Calvinism" (if a drug makes you feel good, it must be bad), and some questioned whether physicians have the right to exercise value judgments in denying a patient a legal medication (Smith, 1991). The same pattern of debate appears again in this decade in the battle over Prozac, "the Librium of the '90s." Although the rate of prescribing benzodiazepines has slowed (88 million prescriptions in 1990), they remain one of the most frequently prescribed medications in the United States.

A less philosophical and far more pragmatic concern regarding overprescription of the benzodiazepines has been the increasing awareness of the adverse side effects associated with their use. In classic pharmaceutical terms, the benzodiazepines are considered very safe drugs. Safety here refers to the concern whether an overdose will kill you. While the likelihood of dying from these drugs is small (much smaller than from the barbiturate drugs that had frequently been used to treat anxiety prior to the introduction of the benzodiazepines), we have become more aware of the negative side effects that suggest that the use of these drugs should be more limited.

Specifically, the benzodiazepines produce substantial cognitive deficits, including amnesia and associated impairment in learning and retention. Moreover, there is a suppression of one's ability to assess accurately one's level of mental and physical impairment. This is a particularly serious side effect because the benzodiazepines produce significant impairment of motor coordination. There are a number of studies (e.g., van Laar, Volkerts, & van Willigenburg, 1992) objectively demonstrating the impaired driving performance of persons under the influence of a benzodiazepine despite their subjective report of being unaffected mentally or motorically. This lack of self-awareness while taking these drugs is considered one of the drugs' most problematic features.

An additional problem with the benzodiazepines is their tolerance and dependence liabilities and difficulties surrounding withdrawal from them. There is a tendency for benzodiazepine users to develop tolerance, which over time means that larger doses of the drug are required to produce the same effect. Tolerance, however, is not nearly as serious a problem with the benzodiazepines as it is with drugs such as the barbiturates and alcohol. Of more concern is the fact that dependence develops with long-term use of benzodiazepines, and there is a significant withdrawal syndrome observed when use is discontinued. Withdrawal is initially characterized by a return of the symptoms, often in a more intense form, that the drug was originally prescribed to treat. For people suffering from anxiety this means that discontinuing drug treatment will lead to more acute levels of anxiety than existed before starting drug treatment.

Buspirone

Buspirone (BuSpar) is a new antianxiety agent that has received considerable attention because it is an effective antianxiety agent but seems to have fewer side effects then the benzodiazepines. Unlike the benzodiazepines, which affect the GABA neurotransmitter system, BuSpar's antianxiety effects seem to be due to its impact on the serotonin neurotransmitter system in the brain. BuSpar does not have the sedative effects of the benzodiazepines and is not reinforcing among those likely to abuse the benzodiazepines, namely those people who have a history of sedative drug abuse. Importantly, BuSpar does not induce physical dependency or result in withdrawal symptoms (Leccese, 1991). The amnesia and psychomotor impairment that characterizes the benzodiazepines do not occur with BuSpar. Unfortunately, even though objective measures reveal minimal cognitive and motor side effects from this drug, people taking this drug often report feeling lethargic and slowed both cognitively and motorically. Finally, another important feature of BuSpar is that its onset of action is much more gradual than that of the benzodiazepines, taking as much as two to three weeks to obtain maximal benefits.

Alcohol

As you know, alcohol is a nonprescription drug freely available to adults of legal age. It is a powerful central nervous system depressant, second only to caffeine as the most widely used psychoactive substance in the world (Julien, 1995). Alcohol has been used for centuries by many cultures because of its ability to reduce tension and divert people from their worries as well as for its other behavioral effects (Grilly, 1989). Interestingly, at low to moderate doses, alcohol can have a wide variety of behavioral effects, depending on the individual. Moderate levels of alcohol are associated with disinhibition, and some people react to the disinhibitory effects of alcohol with increased activity, excitement, and aggression (the rowdy or mean drunk). Others simply drink to "unwind" from a stressful day and find the behavioral effects of alcohol more in line with the sedative pharmacological effects of the drug (the "mellow" drunk). It turns out that the behavioral effects that one experiences with moderate doses of alcohol depend on one's expectancies or cognitive set (Critchlow, 1986; Hull & Bond, 1986). At high doses, however, cognitive set and expectancies have less influence on reaction to the drug because its sedative effects are overpowering.

Marijuana

Marijuana has traditionally been classified as a mild sedative-hypnotic drug with clinical effects resembling those of alcohol and the antianxiety drugs (Julien, 1995). In addition to these properties, marijuana also can produce euphoria and psychedelic effects. Typically, users report relaxation, relief from anxiety, increased sense of well-being, and mild euphoria (Julien, 1995). Between six and ten million Americans smoked marijuana at least once per week in 1990 (Julien, 1995). It is not clear how many people use marijuana primarily for its tension-anxiety-reducing properties.

Beta-Adrenergic Receptor Blockers

This long term actually translates fairly easily into English that you and I can understand. The word *adrenergic* refers to the norepinephrine neurotransmitter system, whereas the term *beta* refers to one specific type of adrenergic receptor. The prototypical beta-adrenergic receptor blocker is a drug called Inderal. Inderal and drugs like it decrease sympathetic nervous system activity (decrease sympathetic "tone") by blocking norepinephrine receptors of the beta subtype. As a result, they have a general dampening effect on the cardiovascular system, decreasing cardiac output, and decreasing total peripheral resistance. These drugs are extremely effective antihypertensives (reduce high blood pressure) but are sometimes misused, particularly by people in the performing arts who experience severe performance anxiety (stage fright). In controlled trials, beta-blockers have been shown to reduce heart rate and control tremor relative to a placebo (e.g., James & Savage, 1984). Presumably, people take these drugs to reduce the internal physiological sensations of anxiety (e.g., rapid heart rate) and thereby decrease their subjective sense of anxiety. Anecdotally, clients have described the effects of these drugs to the authors as follows: "If my body does not respond as if I am anxious, my mind doesn't know I am anxious, and so I am not anxious."

Antidepressants

It probably seems odd to have antidepressant drugs included in a list of antianxiety drugs. There are several different types of drugs that were first found to have antidepressant effects and that were later discovered to be effective in treating some types of anxiety. These drugs include the tricyclic antidepressants (e.g., Tofranil, Elavil) and the selective serotonin reuptake inhibitors (SSRIs) (e.g., Anafranil, Prozac). Basically, the tricyclics all share a similar molecular structure and work by prolonging the actions of the neurotransmitters norepinephrine and serotonin. The SSRIs all work by prolonging the activity of serotonin. These drugs seem to be effective antidepressant drugs because they correct an underlying insufficiency of norepinephrine and serotonin (serotonin seems to be the most important) in the depressed person's brain. Table 10–2 lists the generic and trade names of the tricyclic antidepressants and the "second generation" antidepressants, which include the SSRIs and other newly discovered compounds that are molecularly dissimilar to the tricyclics but are effective antidepressants.

It is important to note that the tricyclic antidepressants were labeled as antidepressant drugs simply because they were first used in the treatment of depression. If we had discovered that Tofranil (Imipramine) was useful in the treatment of agoraphobia before its antidepressant effect was discovered, this drug would have been called a tricyclic antiagoraphobia drug instead of a tricyclic antidepressant drug. The same holds for the selective serotonin reuptake inhibitors.

It was once thought that some of the antidepressants were effective in treating various anxiety disorders because the anxiety disorder really reflected a more fundamental problem with depression. This thinking has been largely discarded, because drugs that have proven antidepressant effects have failed to be effective in treating the anxiety disorders. People with certain types of anxiety benefit from these drugs not because they are depressed but because the drugs have more pervasive effects than were realized when the label *antidepressant* was attached to them. As we learn

TABLE 10–2. TRADE NAME AND GENERIC NAME FOR COMMONLY USED ANTIDEPRESSANTS

Trade Name	Generic Name
Tricyclic Compounds	
Trofanil*	Imipramine
Norpramin	Desipramine
Surmontil	Trimipramine
Vivactil	Protriptyline
Pamelor, Aventil	Nortriptyline
Elavil	Amitriptyline
Adapin, Sinequan	Doxepin
Second-Generation Compounds	
Asendin	Amoxapine
Ludiomil	Maprotiline
Desyrel	Trazodone
Prozac*	Fluoxetine
Wellbutrin	Bupropion
Zoloft*	Sertraline
Paxil*	Paroxetine
Anafranil*	Clomipramine
Effexor	Venlafaxine

*Drugs for which there is published research regarding the antianxiety effects of the drug.

more and more about the neurochemistry of the brain and its relationship to different mood disorders, we learn that traditional distinctions regarding what is classified as an antianxiety versus an antidepressant, or even antischizophrenic drug, are increasingly blurred. Some of the tricyclic antidepressants prove to be useful not only for depression and agoraphobia but also for such diverse disorders as migraine headaches and obsessive-compulsive disorders. Similarly, the second generation antianxiety drugs (e.g., BuSpar), which are drugs effective in the treatment of some types of anxiety but are not similar in structure or function to the benzodiazepines, are proving to be useful adjuncts in the treatment of a variety of mood and thought disorders as well. Prozac, which originally received FDA approval as an antidepressant, now is so widely prescribed for much less serious problems that its use has been labeled "cosmetic psychopharmacology" (Kramer, 1993).

With respect to their antianxiety effects, these "antidepressant" drugs have been studied most extensively with anxiety problems that are chronic and where the symptoms cluster to allow a specific diagnosis. Like any drug, these drugs can be misused and, some people believe, even abused (but not in the sense of a traditional addiction). These drugs have side-effects, including dry mouth, lethargy, and perceived weight gain that sometimes reduces a person's willingness to use the drug even when it is effective. The drugs that are useful in some anxiety disorders often take several weeks to exert their full antianxiety effects, although the negative side-effects begin immediately. Because of the length of time it takes to experience the antianxiety effect, coupled with the negative side-effects, many people who might profit from these drugs do not take them.

THE USE OF MEDICATION FOR FORMALLY DIAGNOSED ANXIETY DISORDERS

Prescription drugs are used to treat a variety of stress management problems, from formally diagnosed anxiety disorders to more transient anxiety states such as performance anxiety (e.g., "stage fright," test anxiety). In this section we focus on the anxiety disorders that pervasively affect a person's life across several spheres of functioning (work, social, family) and in which symptoms are severe enough to warrant a formal diagnosis. Sometimes prescription drugs alone are prescribed for anxiety problems, and/or a person attempts to self-medicate his or her anxiety and misuses drugs like alcohol or marijuana. As we alluded to in the previous section, there are prescription medications that are very effective in treating the formally diagnosed anxiety disorders that have very little potential for misuse and abuse. Often prescription drugs plus a structured psychological intervention will be a more effective treatment than either drugs or therapy alone. For prescription drugs used in the treatment of anxiety to be effective, they need to be prescribed by a knowledgeable physician who conducts a thorough assessment, arrives at the correct diagnosis, prescribes the appropriate medication, and provides follow-up care for the patient. Ideally, when dealing with a patient with an anxiety disorder, the physician would work with a psychologist to maximize a patient's outcomes.

The effectiveness of medication alone, of cognitive-behavior therapy alone, and of the combination of medication and therapy has been examined in carefully conducted treatment outcome studies for several of the anxiety disorders. In the sections that follow, the results of these studies are presented for three relatively common anxiety disorders: panic disorder, obsessive-compulsive disorder, and generalized anxiety disorder. A final section examines drug misuse and abuse across the various anxiety disorders.

Panic Disorder (PD) and Panic Disorder with Agoraphobia (PDA)

Sudden, largely unexpected bouts of extreme fear and anxiety are the hallmarks of PD. Agoraphobia refers to avoidance, or endurance with dread, of situations from which escape might be difficult or help unavailable in the event of a panic attack. According to Barlow and his colleagues (Craske & Barlow, 1993; Barlow, 1988), who treat a very select sample of patients with PD and PDA, about 50 percent of the clients who seek treatment at their psychology clinic report using a prescription antianxiety medication. Similarly, in a survey of nearly 800 volunteers participating in PD research, most had received an inadequate course of treatment prior to the study, and only 15 percent had received what the authors categorized as an adequate course of either pharmacological or psychological treatment (Taylor et al., 1989). Presumably, the rate of inadequate prescription medication usage is at least as high, if not higher, among clients seeking services at more general psychiatric or psychological services centers.

The two types of prescription medications most frequently prescribed for PD and PDA have been the benzodiazepines and the tricyclic drugs (Agras, 1993). In addition, the SSRI drug Prozac has received a great deal of attention for its putative antipanic (and other antianxiety effects) both in the popular press (Kramer, 1993; Breggin & Breggin, 1994) and scientific journals (Solyom, Solyom, & Ledwidge, 1991; Schneier, et al., 1990). We noted in the previous section that the benzodiazepines and "antidepressant" drugs (tricyclics and SSRIs) are two very different types of drugs and have quite different effects in the brain. It may be that the different types of drugs differentially affect the panic symptoms relative to the agoraphobia symptoms.

As noted in Chapter 4, the benzodiazepines seem to reduce anxiety by facilitating the effects of one of the naturally occurring brain chemicals, GABA. GABA is an inhibitory neurotransmitter, and the benzodiazepines therefore increase the inhibitory effects of GABA. Since GABA transmission is associated with a reduction in arousal both cortically and behaviorally, and the benzodiazepines facilitate GABA, then taking a benzodiazepine will work to reduce emotional arousal and decrease anxiety. The benzodiazepines therefore are probably exerting their most powerful effects in helping to manage the feelings of panic per se.

While the benzodiazepines seem to work well to help modulate the emotional aspects of PD, there has been some question as to whether they actually reduce the avoidant behavior that characterizes agoraphobia (Craske & Barlow, 1993). Others have reported that the short-acting, high-potency benzodiazepines (e.g., Xanax) are effective in treating both panic and the phobic avoidance behavior (agoraphobia) that often accompanies PD (Ballenger et al., 1988; Pollack et al., 1986). Despite some evidence of their usefulness, the use of benzodiazepines for PD and agoraphobia has proved controversial because of their side-effects and misuse and abuse potential. We will revisit this controversy at the end of this section, where the misuse and abuse of drugs in the treatment of the formal anxiety disorders are discussed.

A great deal of research has focused on the use of the tricyclic drugs in treating panic and agoraphobia. A series of studies by Mavissakalian and colleagues (Mavissakalian & Perel, 1985; Mavissakalian & Michelson, 1986; Mavissakalian, 1986; Mavissakalian, 1990) have focused on the use of the tricyclic Trofanil (Imipramine) alone and Trofanil (Imipramine) in combination with various graded exposure techniques. You might recall from an earlier chapter that graded exposure involves exposure to the feared situation in graded steps without opportunity to escape. The results of these studies and others suggest that PDA seems to be best treated with a combination of tricyclic drugs and graded exposure techniques (Agras, 1993; Craske & Barlow, 1993). Interestingly, a programmed practice manual for self-directed exposure may be a cost-effective alternative to therapist-assisted exposure sessions (Mavissakalian, 1990).

Obsessive Compulsive Disorder (OCD)

The key features in the diagnosis of OCD include the presence of obsessions or compulsions that cause substantial distress, that take more than an hour per day, or that interfere with functioning (American Psychiatric Association, 1994). Although most of us have been a bit obsessive-compulsive at times, few of us meet the criteria for a formal diagnosis. For the 2.5 percent of the population who receive this diagnosis at some point during the lifespan, effective pharmacological and cognitive-behavioral interventions are available. The use of prescription drugs in the treatment of OCD is relatively recent in the United States, although medication has been available in Europe for over forty years. The tricyclic drug Anafranil (Clominpramine) has been researched most thoroughly and has the best data documenting its beneficial effects for OCD clients. Prozac (an SSRI), which affects the brain in a similar manner as Anafranil (prolonging the effects of the brain neurotransmitter serotonin), has also been shown to be moderately effective in treating OCD. About 60 percent of the people who try one of these drugs obtain some relief, but the gains are usually moderate at best (McCarthy & Foa, 1990). Moreover, people relapse soon after discontinuing the drug, indicating that they will likely have to be on the medication for a lifetime if drug therapy alone is used in treating OCD. The data to date suggest that in terms of long-term outcomes, exposure-based therapies with or without medication are more effective than medication alone in treating OCD (Marks et al., 1980; Marks, Lelliot, Basoglu, & Noshirvani, 1988). There is growing evidence that medication, specifically medication that facilitates the action of serotonin in the brain, in conjunction with an exposure-based treatment, produces the most durable treatment effects (DeVeaugh-Geiss, 1993).

Generalized Anxiety Disorder (GAD)

Generalized anxiety disorder has been referred to as the "basic" anxiety disorder (Barlow, 1988) because the symptoms seem to represent the fundamental processes observed in all anxiety disorders; namely, the key feature of generalized anxiety disorder is anxious apprehension and worry (APA, 1994; see Chapter 1). Anxious apprehension is a component of the various formally defined anxiety disorders (e.g., OCD, PD) but is also an important component of less severe types of anxiety. Anxious apprehension and worry are experienced by most people in the course of day-to-day living. Like the other anxiety disorders discussed so far, whether the symptoms merit a formal diagnosis depends on how chronic the symptoms are and how severely they disrupt work, social, or family functioning.

For those people whose anxiety meets criteria for a formal diagnosis of GAD, treatment with the benzodiazepines without psychotherapy results in moderate relief (Barlow 1988; Brown, Hertz, & Barlow, 1992). In studies comparing the effects of the benzodiazepines and BuSpar, BuSpar has been found to be equally effective in relieving anxiety with fewer negative side-effects (Cohn & Rickels, 1989). When medication is used to treat GAD, BuSpar (or drugs like it) is considered the medication of choice (Julien, 1995). However, many medical and mental health practitioners urge that medication not be the treatment of first choice for GAD (Hunt & Singh, 1991; Barlow, Rapee, & Brown, 1992; Brown, O'Leary, & Barlow, 1993), primarily because of their dependence and relapse potential. Rather, anxiety management and general coping skills training are recommended (Hunt & Singh, 1991). In fact, in studies examining the effectiveness of psychological interventions, such as applied relaxation training or cognitive-behavioral interventions, one of the important measures of success is reduction in the use of antianxiety medications.

MISUSE AND ABUSE OF DRUGS
IN THE FORMAL ANXIETY DISORDERS

Clearly, there are medications that when used appropriately, can be useful adjuncts in the treatment of anxiety. The use of tricyclics or SSRIs in the treatment of PDA is the best example to date. These same drugs have demonstrated moderate success with OCD; but with both disorders, and particularly with OCD, the use of cognitive behavioral techniques such as graded exposure is necessary to prevent relapse. The use of medication with GAD is more equivocal, with many clinicians in the field recommending anxiety-management skills training as the first treatment option.

There is considerable misuse and abuse of both prescription and nonprescription drugs across all of the anxiety disorders. Prescription drug abuse can be initiated by either the patient or the physician and usually involves the benzodiazepine drugs. Sometimes patients pressure their physician to prescribe a particular drug, and it is easier for the physician to go along with the patient's request than to carefully assess the patient. Often a general practitioner does not know what questions to ask in order to arrive at an accurate diagnosis. Ideally, a physician might make a referral to a psychologist who could better determine which, if any, of the formal anxiety disorders the patient was suffering from. This would be useful information for selecting the appropriate medication and also to determine whether the patient's symptoms would be best treated with a combination of medication and psychotherapy. More typically, a benzodiazepine is prescribed for various types of anxiety without differential diagnosis of the exact type of anxiety, and often without systematic follow-up of the patient.

Misuse and abuse of nonprescription medications is also a frequent development among persons who suffer from a formal anxiety disorder. In a study assessing over 250 outpatients diagnosed with PDA, up to 20 percent also met criteria for alcoholism (Bibb & Chambless, 1986). Of the alcoholics, an overwhelming proportion reported using alcohol to reduce anxiety and control disturbing cognitions. Forty-three percent of subjects who did not meet criteria for alcoholism still reported using alcohol to self-medicate feelings of dysphoria. (Bibb & Chambless, 1986). A study examining the relationship between panic attacks and chemical dependencies in an inpatient population found similar results (Cox, Norton, Dorward, & Fergusson, 1989). Over 83 percent of the patients reporting panic attacks also reported using alcohol to self-medicate their panic attacks. Moreover, almost 75 percent of those who used alcohol to manage their panic attacks believed that alcohol did, in fact, prevent or reduce their panic attacks (Cox, Norton, Dorward, & Fergusson, 1989). Finally, in a study examining 103 subjects who met criteria for both PD and alcoholism, 54 percent of the subjects reported that their panic attacks preceded the use of alcohol (Malan, Norton, & Cox, 1993). Women in this study were more likely to report using drugs other than alcohol to self-medicate their anxiety.

The problems of alcohol and drug abuse among persons suffering from anxiety is thought by many to be pervasive, but it is difficult to obtain exact data on the problem. Most reviews simply indicate that it is a widespread problem or a potential problem that should be addressed whenever working with a person suffering from anxiety.

THE USE OF MEDICATION FOR ANXIETY ASSOCIATED
WITH SPECIFIC SITUATIONS OR STIMULI

There are many transient anxiety states that people experience in which the anxiety symptoms are not so serious that they meet criteria for one of the anxiety disorders previously described. Frequently, the situations for which people seek medication to manage their anxiety involve what is often referred to as performance anxiety or evaluation anxiety. In some cases, the anxiety may be severe enough to receive a formal diagnosis of social phobia or simple phobia. Common examples of this type of anxiety include test anxiety, speech anxiety, and anxiety among various types of public performers (musicians, singers, actors, and the like).

Everyone has experienced performance anxiety or evaluation anxiety at some time in life. Everything that you have learned from this text tells you that you can expect anxiety to emerge when the evaluation of your performance on some task by others is appraised as a threat to your self-esteem (this is Lazarus's primary appraisal process). Secondary appraisal processes relate to the balance between the perceived task demands (how difficult the task is, how much time it will take to prepare) and perceived self-resources (how much time do I have, how much energy do I have, do I have the skills or intellectual resources to handle the task). These appraisal processes relate to the implicit and explicit goals that we set for ourselves, with the difference between anxious and nonanxious performers relating to how rigidly these goals are set. If you believe you have to be perfect, then you are going to be anxious, and the only way to reduce anxiety is to attain complete mastery of the task or to give up completely and not try. There is some evidence that beliefs and goal setting might relate to the tendency to self-medicate when anxious.

Anxiety Among Professional Musicians

Performance anxiety is a serious problem among professional musicians. Survey data reveal that 24 percent of the over two thousand professional classical musicians surveyed report that performance anxiety or stage fright was a problem, and 16 percent reported that the problem was severe (Fishbein & Middlestadt's studies, cited in Clark & Agras, 1991). Twenty-seven percent of the musicians surveyed reported daily or occasional use of beta-blocking drugs. Seventy percent of the beta-blocker users reported occasional, nonprescription use of these drugs to control their performance anxiety, suggesting that the illicit use of beta-blockers among this population is substantial. However, when compared with a placebo, there is little empirical evidence that beta-blockers actually reduce subjective anxiety (James & Savage, 1984). A study of 97 musicians suffering from performance anxiety revealed that a substantial proportion (over 40 percent) used alcohol to help manage their symptoms (Clark and Agras, 1991). In this same study, 34 subjects elected to participate in a treatment program that tested the effectiveness of BuSpar alone, cognitive behavior therapy alone, cognitive behavior therapy with placebo, and placebo alone. Cognitive behavior therapy was associated with improvement on subjective measures of anxiety, whereas BuSpar was not. This study is limited by the relatively small number of subjects and by other problems (Chanel, 1992), but the fact that behavior therapy produced the most durable effects is consistent with its effectiveness with other types of anxiety disorders. For those who foresaw BuSpar as the emerging drug of choice for anxiety, the lack of effect in this study has been disappointing.

Test Anxiety

Of all the different forms of performance anxiety, test anxiety is among the most pervasive in a college population. If you are taking four courses per semester, you could easily be subjected to fourteen or more testing experiences during a semester. There is a good deal of evidence suggesting that the cognitive and emotional elements of both motivation and test anxiety exert considerable influence on student functioning and well-being.

We examine in this section the different types of test anxiety and the pattern of medication usage that seems to be associated with each type. While everyone has been test anxious at some point, there are forms of test anxiety that are more chronic and debilitating than those that most of us experience during our academic careers. A large study of over one thousand second- and third-year undergraduates revealed two different types of test anxious students (Depreeuw & De Neve, 1992), the Active Test Anxiety Student and the Passive Test Anxiety Student. Combined, these two groups represented only about 20 percent of all the students, but the profiles of these test anxious students were very different from those of the other students. For the active test anxiety student, failure was perceived as catastrophic (by both the students and their parents). These students reported that they were hard workers and were motivated, and they also reported relatively little avoidance behavior regarding test preparation. The passive test anxiety students reported being very anxious about testing but described themselves as being unmotivated for study. Though getting poor grades was perceived to be a very negative event, these students avoided engaging in study behavior. They had low self-esteem and lacked confidence in their skills and abilities. They tended to procrastinate more, attend class less, and study less than the active test anxiety student. In the opinion of the study's authors (Depreeuw & De Neve, 1992), these students were paralyzed by anxiety and therefore procrastinated and avoided studying. Surprisingly, both types of test anxious students consumed dramatically higher quantities of medical drugs. These medical drugs included those substances that produce antianxiety effects such as sleeping medications, tranquilizers (benzodiazepines), sedatives (barbiturates), as well as stimulants. These two types of test anxious students consumed more of these drugs than the rest of the student population both during exam time and during nonexam times. With respect to alcohol and caffeine, we find that the active anxiety student is actually less likely to consume alcohol or caffeine during the academic year relative to other students, and the passive anxiety student is more likely to consume caffeine during the exam period relative to other students.

An interesting study (James & James, 1973) assessed the effects of two different drugs and of a placebo (inert) drug on laboratory test performance of college undergraduates. The comparison of interest here is the performance of students receiving the antianxiety drug Librium (a benzodiazepine) versus the performance of students who received a placebo. Students were paid volunteers who were required to complete a digit symbol translation task under test conditions designed to create anxiety. The students were tested four times at weekly intervals. Results indicated that performance improved and anxiety decreased across testing sessions, but that the students who received the placebo drug performed significantly better and reported significantly *less* anxiety than the subjects who received Librium.

Taken together the results of the student survey study and the results of laboratory study suggest that medication is probably of little use in managing test anxiety, and in fact may have detrimental effects. This is particularly true when considering the use of alcohol or benzodiazepines, which are known to interfere with information processing and retention. It is possible that BuSpar may be a safe and more effective adjunct for test anxiety, but empirical reports have not been published regarding its utility with test anxiety.

CONTRAINDICATIONS FOR ANTIANXIETY MEDICATIONS

In discussing PDA and OCD, we found that medication, specifically the "antidepressants," were useful adjuncts to cognitive-behavioral interventions such as graded exposure. In later sections we discussed the relative lack of data supporting the use of medication for other types of anxiety disorders. In this section we will discuss both general and specific conditions under which the use of benzodiazepines and other antianxiety medications may actually hinder the effectiveness of other nonpharmacological types of stress management interventions. Some of the problems that antianxiety medications cause when used in conjunction with nonpharmacological interventions apply generally across the various nonpharmacological interventions. Other problems associated with medication use applies to their use in conjunction with specific therapeutic techniques, namely the exposure-based techniques discussed in Chapter 9. Both sets of concerns are discussed in the following sections.

General Concerns

The use of antianxiety medications in conjunction with psychotherapy has proved controversial (Klerman et al., 1994). Many psychotherapists, particularly those from the psychodynamic tradition, believe that when a person seeks therapy for an anxiety problem, it is important for him or her to feel anxious (i.e., uncomfortable) while in therapy, because anxiety serves as a motivator to change. A general concern of psychotherapists is thus that antianxiety medications, because they soothe aversive arousal and are often sedating, may decrease client motivation to invest the time and energy necessary to learn and practice new coping skills.

Another important drawback of antianxiety medication has to do with a person's perception of control. You have learned a great deal in previous chapters about how perceptions of control influence the stress response. When people take antianxiety medications in combination with therapy, they are much more likely to attribute their success to the drug rather than to their newly developed coping skills. The lack of perceived control may increase relapse potential when medication is withdrawn, or may contribute to maintenance of a medication regime under the assumption of its necessity (Agras, 1993; Craske & Barlow, 1993).

Specific Concerns

There are some psychotherapeutic techniques in which the use of antianxiety medications is clearly counterproductive. The various exposure techniques are the clearest example. They involve exposure to the feared stimulus, without the opportunity to escape but also without anything aversive or punishing actually happening, to facilitate extinction of the conditioned fear response. When an individual participates in exposure-based interventions while taking an antianxiety medication, the intervention has little chance of success because the patient does not get sufficiently aroused in the presence of the feared stimulus, and thus the fear response has no opportunity to extinguish. This is particularly true when the intervention includes exposure to feared physical sensations, such as in PD, and the medication prevents the person from experiencing the feared sensations.

Given that the exposure techniques are some of our most effective and frequently used interventions for anxiety conditions, it is important to be aware of how medication usage may hinder successful treatment. If you seek professional help for an anxiety or stress-related problem, it is important to talk to your therapist about any medications you may already be taking.

WHEN TO CONSIDER USING ANTIANXIETY MEDICATION

Overall, for most anxiety problems, some form of self-directed or therapist-assisted anxiety management training is more appropriate than medication. For some disorders such as PDA, the "antidepressants" have proven to be effective, but they are

MEDICAL CONDITIONS ASSOCIATED WITH INCREASED ANXIETY

Sometimes people suffer from anxiety that, unknowingly to them, is related to the foods, beverages, and drugs that they ingest. Similarly, sometimes anxiety is a manifestation of an undiagnosed medical condition. It is always sound advice to recommend a thorough physical if you suffer from unexplained anxiety. Certainly if anxiety persists despite your best attempts at the anxiety management techniques described in this book and in the workbook, you might consider visiting a health/mental health professional. The cognitive-behavioral anxiety management techniques are some of the most effective psychotherapeutic interventions that have been developed. Absence of relief after the systematic application of these techniques creates suspicion of a contributing medical condition. Some of the more common medical conditions associated with anxiety are listed and described below.

Respiratory Disorders. Hyperventilation and asthma are two fairly common respiratory disorders that have been linked to anxiety. In both disorders, anxiety can be a precipitate of the respiratory problem, a consequence, or both. During hyperventilation a person overbreathes (the person is usually unaware of doing so), causing a disruption of the normal balance between blood levels of oxygen and carbon dioxide. A frequent side-effect among people who suffer from hyperventilation syndrome (sustained or recurrent episodes of hyperventilation with no apparent organic cause) is anxiety. It has been estimated that hyperventilation is a contributing factor in as much as 60 percent of the patients diagnosed with an anxiety disorder. Hyperventilation is a contributing factor in 50 to 60 percent of persons diagnosed with panic disorder, and breathing retraining is a central component in treatment packages for the panic disorder patient. Moreover, a recent study suggests that hyperventilation is an independent contributor to the somatic complaints of psychophysiological symptoms associated with anxiety (Wientjes & Grossman, 1994). Overbreathing can occur in association with a variety of physical conditions (e.g., some types of drug poisoning, pregnancy, muscular exercise), which would in turn precipitate anxiety. Anxiety itself may precipitate an episode of hyperventilation and exacerbate an underlying anxiety state. It is interesting to note that when healthy volunteers hyperventilated, they reported the physical symptoms of light-headedness, tingling, and numbness in the extremities, but they did not report being anxious (Saltzman, Heyman, & Sieker, 1963). Because hyperventilation associated with anxiety usually occurs without the person's awareness, the physical symptoms that are evoked by hyperventilation are interpreted as more threatening and anxiety-provoking.

Cardiovascular Disorders. Obviously if you are having a heart attack, you are likely to feel quite anxious, but it is unlikely that anxiety management would be the first course of treatment that you or your physician would want to pursue. There are a variety of so-called "functional" cardiac disorders that straddle the divide between the somatoform disorders and psychophysiological disorders discussed in Chapter 5. Complaints of heart palpitations, chest pain, and increased cardiac awareness and anxiety that occur in the absence of demonstrable organic findings (other than overreactivity of the sympathetic nervous system) are all examples. Palpitations, either anxiety induced or occurring by chance, can initiate an upwardly spiraling cycle of palpitations>>>anxiety>>>increased palpitations>>>increased anxiety and so forth, with increased activation of the sympathetic nervous system at each upward turn in the spiral. Where there is no cardiac pathology per se, but rather an increased awareness and increased anxiety over these noticeable but objectively nonthreatening cardiac symptoms, then anxiety-management techniques would be the course of action to pursue. Even in the case of Mitral Valve Prolapse Syndrome, in which palpitations, chest pain, and subsequent anxiety can be traced to a documented abnormality in the mitral valve mechanism of the heart, anxiety management rather than medication is considered by many to be the most appropriate intervention. If you suffer from anxiety associated with palpitations and intermittent chest pain unrelated to exercise or emotion, you should consider a thorough workup from a cardiologist. Ask that mitral valve prolapse be assessed in addition to the standard cardiology workup. Do not be upset if the doctor cannot find anything wrong and gives your heart a clean bill of health. Be grateful. Not finding something "wrong" with your heart does not mean that your palpitations, light-headedness, or other symptoms

(continued)

are not "real." It simply means that they are probably triggered by increased activity of the sympathetic nervous system, possibly in conjunction with hyperventilation. Anxiety-management techniques teach you how to reduce your physiological arousal, reduce your symptoms, and help you live better with your symptoms.

Endocrine Disorders.   Hyperthyroidism refers to a condition in which there is an excessive supply of thyroid hormone in the tissue. The most frequent form of this disorder is known as Graves' disease, which is characterized by nervousness, restless agitation, fine tremor, sensitivity to heat, sweating (though the palms may remain dry), and weight loss (though appetite may increase). A specific sign of Graves' disease is localized changes in the skin in the lower legs or feet such that the skin is thick and raised and more deeply pigmented relative to the rest of the body skin. The anxiety reported with this disease takes the form of a restless agitation and lability of mood. Another endocrine example would be a tumor on the adrenal gland. This condition may be associated with an increased release of adrenaline, which would cause anxiety-like symptoms.

Drug-Related Anxiety.   Anxiety and panic-like symptoms can be expected with persons suffering from drug abuse. Anxiety is associated with a variety of drugs, including amphetamine and cocaine abuse, as well as during alcohol and benzodiazepine withdrawal.

more effective when combined with a graded exposure treatment. Otherwise, the long-term use of antianxiety medications (including the benzodiazepines, which bring rapid relief from anxiety) is of questionable utility. The beta-blockers are not effective antianxiety drugs, and their use without medical supervision can be dangerous. BuSpar and drugs like it are a safer alternative to anxiety management than chronic use of the other drugs covered in this chapter (benzodiazepines, alcohol, marijuana, or beta-blockers), but its efficacy for many types of anxiety problems has not yet been established. Placebos seem to be more effective than antianxiety medications (both benzodiazepines and BuSpar) in reducing different types of performance anxiety. The use of antianxiety medication even in coping with anxiety-provoking medical procedures has been questioned (Katz, Wilson, & Frazier, 1994).

If you are facing a relatively infrequent circumscribed stressor that does not require full motoric or intellectual processing on your part, then the use of a benzodiazepine to reduce anxiety is probably not harmful. For example, if your dreaded in-laws appear virtually unannounced once every blue moon, you might want to ask your doctor for some Librium next time they pop in. More seriously, if you are afraid of flying long distances but just won a free trip to Hawaii, there is little chance of harm in taking an antianxiety medication before you fly (of course it would be better for your self-efficacy beliefs and general coping repertoire to set aside enough time to proceed through a graded exposure or systematic desensitization program before you left). Or, if you object to taking medications, get a friend to slip you a placebo, because if you believe the pill is working, it probably will regardless of whether it is a sugar pill. The point here is that occasional use of antianxiety medication will probably not be associated with adverse consequences for most people, and there are certainly appropriate recreational and medical uses of antianxiety drugs. The problem arises when people use excessive quantities of antianxiety medications to mask severe distress (such as John in our opening vignette). The other problem arises when people gradually "slip" into a pattern of increasing dependence on medication such that it interferes with the quality of life. Finally, we put the emphasis back on learning new coping skills to deal with stress and anxiety in our lives. Wouldn't you rather have the skills and confidence to control your own emotional response than give that power to a pill?

𝒮UMMARY

1. The use of drugs to minimize the aversive arousal associated with anxiety is as old as recorded history. Any antianxiety drug (legal or illegal, prescription or nonprescription) has the potential to be abused. Distinguishing between appropriate and inappropriate drug use in anxiety is not always clear-cut, and a four-stage continuum approach for the classification of use and abuse of anxiety drugs is recommended. The four stages are (1) accepted medical or recreational use, (2) drug misuse, (3) compulsive abuse, and (4) addiction.

2. The most widely used types of antianxiety prescription drugs include the benzodiazepines, buspirone, alcohol, marijuana, beta-adrenergic receptor blockers, and the antidepressants. The benzodiazepines include drugs such as Valium and Librium, which primarily affect the GABA neurotransmitter system. In the last twenty-five years, the benzodiazepines have been some of the most frequently prescribed drugs in the United States. These drugs reduce feelings of anxiety quickly and are relatively safe in terms of likelihood of lethal overdose. Nevertheless, there are serious negative side-effects associated with the benzodiazepines, including loss of motor coordination and cognitive impairment. These drugs have substantial tolerance and dependence liabilities and withdrawal symptoms associated with their use.

3. Buspirone is a "second generation" antianxiety drug that primarily affects the serotonin neurotransmitter system. It takes several weeks to exert its antianxiety effects but has fewer negative side-effects than the benzodiazepines. Alcohol is a powerful central nervous system depressant that is second only to caffeine as the most widely used psychoactive substance in the world. It, like marijuana, is frequently used to self-medicate anxiety. The beta-adrenergic receptor blockers were developed primarily to treat hypertension, but some individuals with performance anxiety use these drugs because they decrease the physiological symptoms (e.g., rapid heart rate) of anxiety. Some drugs previously shown to be effective antidepressants (tricyclics and selective serotonin reuptake inhibitors) have proved to be effective in the treatment of various anxiety disorders.

4. Treatment outcome studies have evaluated the effectiveness of medication in the treatment of formally diagnosed anxiety disorders. The anxiety disorders that have received the most attention in this area are panic disorder (with or without agoraphobia), obsessive-compulsive disorder, and generalized anxiety disorder. Various drugs have been tried in the treatment of these disorders, including the benzodiazepines, tricyclics, and the selective serotonin reuptake inhibitors (e.g., Prozac). The best data to date suggest that cognitive-behavioral therapy, especially the exposure-based therapies, are often effective in treating these disorders and that the tricyclic drugs are often the most effective pharmacological adjunct to treatment. Panic disorder with agoraphobia can often be treated effectively with graded exposure techniques in combination with the tricyclic drug imipramine. The tricyclic clomipramine has been used effectively in the treatment of obsessive-compulsive disorder with exposure therapy. Effective medication in the treatment of generalized anxiety disorder has proved elusive, and many in the field recommend anxiety-management and coping-skills training exclusively for this disorder. Misuse and abuse of antianxiety drugs among those suffering from anxiety disorders is very prevalent.

5. The use and misuse of antianxiety drugs is also prevalent among those suffering from more transient, or situationally specific, anxieties. Stage fright among performers and test anxiety among students are common situations where one may either self-medicate or persuade a physician to prescribe an antianxiety medication. The range of medications include the benzodiazepines, beta-blockers, alcohol, and others. In a controlled test, Buspirone was found to be no more effective than placebo in moderating subjective anxiety. In general, there is little evidence that medication provides any enduring benefits beyond that obtained from a placebo in treating situational anxiety.

6. There are several concerns associated with the use of medication to manage anxiety. First, medication may decrease motivation to learn new skills and lead to a dependency on the drug. Second, individuals who take medication while learning anxiety-management skills often overattribute improvements that they make to the medication rather than to their learned skills. This lack of perceived control and self-efficacy can increase relapse potential when the drug is withdrawn. Finally, medications such as the benzodiazepines, when used in conjunction with the various exposure techniques, may reduce the effectiveness of these procedures.

 **KEY TERMS**

antidepressants   Several classes of drugs are included (e.g., tricyclics, serotonin uptake inhibitors), originally developed to treat depression, some of which are used to treat anxiety.

benzodiazepines   Commonly prescribed class of manufactured drugs designed to reduce anxiety; they are sometimes prescribed as muscle relaxants and sleeping medications.

beta-adrenergic receptor blockers   Class of drugs that have a dampening effect on the cardiovascular system by blocking beta-adrenergic receptors; they are typically prescribed for high blood pressure and are used by some people to self-medicate their anxiety.

Buspirone (BuSpar)   Relatively new antianxiety drug that has fewer side effects than benzodiazepines; there may be a feeling of lethargy associated with the drug, and symptom relief may take up to two or three weeks.

self-medication   Term used when one manages anxiety with alcohol or other drugs without professional help.

serotonin   Neurotransmitter implicated in the modulation of mood (e.g., depression, anxiety), sleep, and pain.

CHAPTER 11
Stress and the Workplace

My husband is one of the few left in his division. He hasn't seen our kids with their eyes open on a weekday for ages. He has yet to take the vacation time he's earned. He checks his voice mail all weekend and lugs his laptop everywhere. His car phone is always busy. He can't attend ballgames, dance recitals, school plays or even a 6:30 family dinner. He's not a workaholic—just a guy with a mortgage and family.

My husband and I both work for a huge conglomerate. We come home exhausted after putting in 12-hour days, drag ourselves behind lawn mowers and vacuum cleaners at 9 at night, miss our children's soccer games and school plays, and barely see each other. As for our sex life, there is neither the time nor the energy. Nobody dares quit a job these days. It's too risky. Please, Ann, tell corporate America that the stress is killing us.

In response to "Burnt Out" who survived a corporate downsizing but now feels overworked: I, too, had a terrific job and survived several downsizings. During the last layoff, my entire department was eliminated, and I was "downsized" out the door. I found a job in another field making 50 percent of my former salary, with fewer benefits, but I consider myself lucky. I can guarantee "Burnt Out" that any of the four people whose jobs he is doing would trade places with him. He should quit griping and count his blessings.

(Permission granted by Ann Landers and Creators Syndicate)

For most of us, work is not only a source of income, it is also an important source of self-esteem. Our occupation can bring us supportive social relationships, a sense of belonging to a group, a sense of optimism and of self-worth. Furthermore, a respected occupation represents status, which has been associated with lower disease levels and better mental health (Cohen, 1984). When the challenges of work are well matched to our available time and skills, we are said to enter a state of "flow" (Csikszentmihalyi, 1990) in which we are absorbed in activities because of their intrinsic interest. At its best, involvement in valued activities "is more fun than fun," observed playwright Noel Coward, and is one of the most important determinants of a subjective sense of happiness (Myers & Diener, 1995). However, as illustrated in the preceding vignettes, when work requirements exceed available time and skills, when working conditions become intolerable, or when we are deprived of the opportunity for meaningful work, the result can be unremitting and destructive levels of stress. High levels of job stress have been associated with employee theft, increased absenteeism, accidents, on-the-job illicit substance abuse, and reduced job performance (Jones & Boye, 1992).

One increasingly common reaction to stress and frustration on the job is violence. Usually this is in the form of a harmless tension releaser, as in humorist Dave Barry's "stress management" response to an office phone call telling him that the electric company had turned off his power: "I hung up the phone, took a deep breath, exhaled slowly, then punched my desk so hard that I could not make a fist for three days" (Barry, 1995, p. F1). Sometimes the effects are more profound as exemplified by a Pacific Bell employee in Riverside, California, who "became so distressed over the loss of his retirement benefits that he took hostages and destroyed $10 million worth of the company's telephone equipment." Another—an editor for Encyclopaedia Britannica in Chicago—"sought revenge for his dismissal by sabotaging the company's computer system and trying to rewrite history. Before he was caught, the man had substituted the names of Britannica employees for historical figures, and Allah for Jesus in numerous passages of the encyclopaedia" (Stress on the Job, 1988, p. 42).

Even more serious are incidents in which workers respond to perceived slights and inequities by attempting to kill or maim those whom they deem responsible for their problems. Workplace violence resulted in 1,071 Americans murdered on the job in 1994 and 160,000 physically assaulted, with 85 percent of assaults and 55 percent of homicides committed at retail trade or service industry sites (Elias, 1996). Elliott and Jarrett (1994) attribute the rising violence to increased competition for a shrinking pool of promotions, hostilities generated by intercultural conflicts, the influx of women into the workforce that has increased jealousy-based conflicts and sexual intimidation, and increased use of alcohol and other drugs that may disinhibit aggressive behavior.

Figure 11–1

Though stress has always been associated with work and the need to earn a liveli-hood, it took on a new dimension with the advent of the industrial revolution around the turn of the nineteenth century. In transforming Western civilization, the industrial revolution changed the nature of work, with the machine and the factory system now dictating the pace of work and producing an unremitting sense of time urgency. The dangers and abuses experienced by the typical factory worker were graphically depicted in the books of the "muckrakers," such as Upton Sinclair's *The Jungle* (1946/1971), and contributed to the growth of labor unions, which attempted to rectify these conditions. Though many positive changes were made through union influence, concern with stress-on-the-job continues at all levels of work. The cre-ation of the Occupational Safety and Health Administration (OSHA) in the Depart-ment of Labor, and the National Institute of Occupational Safety and Health (NIOSH), helped to formalize occupational stress as a field of study (Holt, 1993).

HOW WIDESPREAD IS OCCUPATIONAL STRESS?

According to Keita & Hurrell (1994, p. xi) "workers' compensation claims for psycho-logical disorders are at unprecedented levels"—resulting in "reduced productivity, increased absenteeism due to illness, and—decreased sense of personal well-being and effectiveness." Elaborating on the extent of the problem, Keita & Hurrell (pp. xii–xix) cite data from a Northwestern National Life Insurance Company survey (1991), noting that 13 percent of the claims that this company (which is a major un-derwriter for workers' compensation insurance) "indemnified in 1990 involved stress-related disorders, an increase of 6 percent from 1982." Also, "in a national sur-vey of American workers, Northwestern found that 72 percent of the workers sur-veyed experienced frequent stress-related physical or mental conditions that could increase health costs. Almost one half reported feeling that their jobs were very or extremely stressful, and over one fourth saw their jobs as the single greatest cause of stress in their lives." Both blood pressure and heart rate have consistently been found to be higher at work than on comparable nonwork days (Pieper, Warren, & Pickering, 1993; Steptoe, Roy, Evans, & Snashnall, 1995).

Why has work stress become such a pressing problem in the United States? Ac-cording to Keita & Hurrell (1994), the following are major factors:

1. An increasing number of workers are employed in service industries. These jobs seem to readily produce employee "burnout," at least in part because they require interpersonal skills, and frustrated workers are being inadequately trained in this area.
2. In the corporate world there is much restructuring, creating an atmosphere of uncertainty and loss of control for those at the mercy of unpredictable merg-ers, takeovers, downsizings, and bankruptcies.
3. Rapid advances in computer technology and in other areas have made some workers' competencies unmarketable and have increased the gap between needed and available worker skills.
4. Changes in employee demographics along the lines of more women, more eth-nic minorities, and more elderly people have caused problems in adjustment for many in these groups to the demands of the workplace.

WHICH JOBS ARE THE MOST STRESSFUL?

Though every person responds to circumstances in terms of what they mean to that person on an individual basis, some occupations seem to be more stressful than others. Table 11–1 represents the job stress ratings of over a hundred occupations

TABLE 11–1.   THE COOPER OCCUPATIONAL STRESS RATINGS[†]

1. Uniformed professions

Armed forces	4.7
Civil aviation (pilot)	7.5***
Merchant navy	4.8
Fire brigade	6.3**
Police force	7.7***
Prison service	7.5***
Ambulance service	6.3**
Average	6.4

2. Arts and communications

Art and design	4.2
Broadcasting	6.8**
Journalism	7.5***
Museum personnel	2.8
Photographer	4.6
Publishing	5.0*
Musician	6.3**
Acting	7.2***
Film production	6.5**
Professional sport	5.8*
Librarian	2.0
Average	5.3

3. Commerce/management

Advertising	7.3***
Management	5.8*
Marketing/export	5.8*
Market research	4.3
Personnel	6.0**
Public relations	5.8*
Purchasing and supply	4.5
Sales and retailing	5.7*
Secretary	4.7*
Company secretary	5.3*
Work study/O and M	3.6
Average	5.3

4. Industrial production

Ceramic technology	4.0
Food technology	4.0
Printing	5.6*
Plastics and rubber	4.5
Textiles/clothing technology	4.5
Timber/furniture technology	4.3
Leather/footwear technology	3.8
Mining	8.3***
Construction/building	7.5***
Brewing	4.0
Average	5.1

5. Caring professions

Nursery nursing	3.3
Social work	6.0**
Teaching	6.2**
Youth and community work	4.2
Church	3.5
Psychologist	5.2*
Average	4.7

6. Health

Chiropody	4.0
Dentistry	7.3***
Dietetics	3.4
Environmental health	4.6
Doctor	6.8**
Nursing/midwifery	6.5**
Occupational therapy	3.7
Optician	4.0
Osteopath	4.3
Pharmacist	4.5
Vet	4.5
Physiotherapy	4.2
Radiographer	4.0
Remedial gymnast	3.5
Speech therapy	4.0
Average	4.6

7. Personal service industries

Catering/hotel business, etc.	5.3*
Travel industry	4.8
Hairdressing	4.3
Beauty therapy	3.5
Average	4.5

8. Public service industries

Post and telecommunications	4.0
Gas	4.0
Electricity	4.6
Water	4.0
Public transport	5.4*
Average	4.5

(continued)

TABLE 11–1. *Continued*

9. Professional services		12. Environment	
Architect	4.0	Farming	4.8
Barrister	5.7*	Forestry	4.8
Solicitor	4.3	Horticulture	3.8
Surveyor	4.3	Nature conservancy	3.2
Estate agent	4.3	*Average*	3.9
Average	4.4		
		13. Technical specialties	
10. Public administration		Biologist	3.0
		Chemist	3.7
Civil service	4.4	Computer programmer	3.8
Diplomatic service	4.8	Engineer	4.3
Local government	4.3	Geologist	3.7
Town and country planning	4.0	Laboratory technician	3.8
Sports/recreation		Metallurgist	3.8
admin.	3.5	Operational researcher	3.8
Average	4.2	Packaging	3.8
		Patent work	4.2
11. Financial areas		Physicist	3.4
		Biochemist	3.6
Accountancy	4.3	Statistician	4.0
Banking	3.7	Linguist	3.6
Building societies	3.3	Astronomer	3.4
Insurance	3.8	*Average*	3.7
Actuary	3.3		
Stockbroker	5.5*		
Average	4.0		

[†]Six experienced stress researchers independently evaluated each job on a 10-point scale, from least stressful (1) to most stressful (10). Each score represents the mean average of these ratings. In order of the most stressful groups of jobs:

*** extremely stressful job

 ** very stressful job

  * above average stressful job

Source: Table 1. "The Cooper Occupational Stress Ratings" (pp 81–83) from *Living with Stress* by Cary L. Cooper, Rachel D. Cooper & Lynn H. Eaker (Penguin Books, 1988) copyright © Cary Cooper, Rachel Cooper, Lynn Eaker, 1988. Reproduced by permission of Penguin Books, Ltd.

(Professor Cooper was originally commissioned to carry out these ratings by the *Sunday Times*, and he would like to thank them for their support and encouragement.)

based on the judgments of six leading stress researchers, who evaluated each job on a ten-point scale from least stressful (1) to most stressful (10), taking into account available health findings in making their judgments.

Some observers contend that the most stressful occupation is still that of the working mother. According to Hancock (1995, p. 60), "Many women who are bringing home the bacon are still expected to fry and serve it, too. Even *unemployed* husbands do no more than 36 percent of the housework."

WHAT IS BURNOUT?

Burnout is a term that is used to signify the condition of an individual who, as a result of on-the-job stress, is completely drained and exhausted and can no longer function efficiently. Related terms include *brownout* ("when you are only part way there;" Greenberg, 1993) and *rustout* (Lawrence, 1975), which results from boredom

TABLE 11–2.	THREE STAGES OF BURNOUT AND THEIR ACCOMPANYING SYMPTOMS	
Emotional Exhaustion	**Depersonalization**	**Low Personal Accomplishment**
Feel drained by work	Have become calloused by job	Cannot deal with problems effectively
Feel fatigued in the morning	Treat people like objects	Am not having a positive influence on others
Feel burned out	Don't care what happens to people	Cannot understand others' problems
Frustrated	Feel others blame you for their problems	or empathize with them
Don't want to work with people		No longer feel exhilarated by job

From *Handbook of Organizational Stress Coping Strategies* by Amarjit Singh Sethi and Randall S. Schuler. Copyright © 1984 by Ballinger Publishing Company. Reprinted by permission of HarperCollins Publishers, Inc.

and low job challenge. Individuals experiencing rustout are underwhelmed by their work and feel that their capabilities are not being fully used. To experience burnout, on the other hand, one must have been "on fire" at one time (Danish, Arthur, & Conter, 1984).

Burnout has been used more specifically to refer to the stress reactions of highly motivated people who go into a career with high ideals and expectations but are subsequently disappointed when these expectations are not met (Pines, 1993). This aspect of burnout is most common among professionals who have invested much of the meaning in their lives in their work. When their emotional involvement and commitment are not rewarded as anticipated, signs of burnout appear. As measured by the Maslach Burnout Inventory (Maslach & Jackson, 1981), burnout consists of the following three dimensions: emotional exhaustion, depersonalization, and reduced personal accomplishments. The characteristics of these are presented in Table 11–2. Concern with burnout has led to studies examining the specific sources of stress in different occupations, particularly professionals.

SOURCES OF JOB STRESS IN PROFESSIONALS

There are some general factors that contribute to job stress in virtually all work situations. These are discussed in the next section. However, there are specific aspects of each work situation that are particularly problematic. It is useful to examine these because effective intervention programs must not only address stressors common to most work situations but must also respond to the needs specific to each.

As an example, we consider police work—a profession whose highly stressful nature is becoming increasingly recognized. Police work involves the constant threat of exposure to violence, the need to function within the context of a quasi-militaristic organizational environment with rigid policies, and continuing pressure from an often hostile public. As may be noted in Table 11–1, only mining received a higher score among the occupations rated for stressfulness. In a study of 210 Florida police officers who were asked to rate the amount of stress associated with job-related events on a 0 (low stress) to 100 (high stress) scale, Spielberger, Westbury, Greer, & Greenfield (1981) found the following ten events rated as most stressful:

1. Fellow officer killed in the line of duty, 89.3
2. Killing someone in the line of duty, 86.9
3. Exposure to battered or dead children, 79.3
4. Physical attack on one's person, 74.5
5. Situations requiring the use of force, 71.2
6. Inadequate salary, 70.2
7. Inadequate support by department, 70.1
8. Confrontation with aggressive crowds, 70.0
9. Ineffectiveness of the judicial system, 67.0
10. Inadequate support by supervisor, 66.4

The health care professions are another group of occupations that have been associated with high stress and burnout to the point of producing levels of emotional distress that can be debilitating to the individual and negatively affect delivery of services. Wolfgang (1988) compared the severity of sources of stress among three groups of health professionals: primary care physicians, nurses, and pharmacists. The overall job-related stress level, which was significantly different for the three groups, was found to be highest for nurses, followed by pharmacists, and then physicians. The greatest source of stress for physicians was "feeling ultimately responsible for patient outcomes," one of only just two areas in which they were higher than both nurses and pharmacists. The greatest concern of pharmacists was "being interrupted by phone calls or people while performing your job duties." Nurses cited "feeling that you are inadequately paid as a health professional" followed closely by "not having enough staff to adequately provide necessary services."

Turnage & Spielberger (1991) similarly examined sources of stress in three types of employees of the same firm and found differences in stress intensity and frequency in different areas as a function of job status. For example, meeting deadlines and working overtime were the most frequent stressors for managers and occurred frequently for professionals (largely engineers), though to a lesser degree, but were comparatively infrequent for clerical workers.

Thus, because occupations are structured differently, cover different task domains, and have different expectations, there are specific aspects to each that are particularly stressful. However, several general factors that are to some degree characteristic of most jobs have been identified as contributory to workplace stress.

GENERAL CAUSES OF OCCUPATIONAL STRESS

Factors Intrinsic to the Job

Cooper, Cooper, & Eaker (1988) list several factors intrinsic to the job itself that may contribute to work stress. Paramount among these are one's physical surroundings. Physically unpleasant working conditions, including those involving extremes of noise, unpleasant smells, temperature, lighting, and social isolation, produce increased stress and physical problems and lower job satisfaction. For example, a study of nurses working in intensive care units found that in addition to the "incessant routine nature" of many of their work activities in an environment of death and pain, they were confronted with overly bright artificial hospital lighting, unpleasant smells accentuated by poor ventilating systems, and a continuous high noise level. "Eventually the nurse begins to feel like a hamster on a tread mill" (Cooper et al., 1988, citing Hay & Oken, 1972).

Other factors include shift work (working rotating or staggered hours rather than a steady schedule) and long hours without sufficient breaks in work schedules. Inconsistent work schedules produce uncertainty and sometimes dangerous levels of fatigue. For example, one way that costs are controlled in the booming commuter airline industry in the United States is through longer hours for crews. One pilot noted that he recently spent long hours in the stuffy cockpit of the same plane after mechanical problems and thunderstorms kept delaying departures. "On his final leg most passengers were asleep. Up front, so was the crew. 'You think we were flying that airplane?—It was all we could do to get the airplane from point A to point B' (Hedges, Newman, & Cary, 1995, p. 33)."

Cooper et al. (1988) note that the following may also contribute to job stress: work overload (work assignments that cannot be completed in normal working hours either because there is too much work or because it is too difficult to master) and work underload (work that is repetitive, boring, and insufficiently challenging), facing physical risk and danger, and the need to adjust continuously to advances in technology.

Work overload has long been recognized as a source of stress that is associated with increased health problems (Repetti, 1993). Workaholism and work-related psychosomatic disorders have been a particular problem in Japan, especially among middle-aged males. Overwork-related death is sufficiently frequent in Japan that there is a term (karoshi) that refers to it. Because of this history of severe stress-related health problems linked to overwork, Japanese industry has made "antistress programs" a central part of the health care benefits provided to employees (Karaki, 1991; Nakagawa & Sugita, 1994).

Regarding physical danger, even when actual physical risks are low, the perception of risk surrounding a job may produce continuing apprehension. For example, although the risk of contracting HIV/AIDS is very low (.3 percent)—even in health-care-related occupations that involve exposure to HIV via blood and blood products—a relatively high proportion of workers (e.g., 48 percent of medical residency-program house officers) were found to be moderately or highly concerned about acquiring AIDS from patients even though they were aware of the very small actual chance of this happening (Quick, Murphy, Hurrell, & Orman, 1992).

Advances in technology have made some occupations obsolete because the job functions can be performed more efficiently by machines. For example, bank tellers are being replaced by ATMs, and some of the functions of telephone operators are being replaced by prerecorded voices. Although conventional wisdom says that technology always creates more jobs than it eliminates, Rifkin (1994) argues that the recent wave of technological progress is permanently cutting the number of available jobs because the new jobs created require highly specialized knowledge (e.g., writing computer software programs). Some advances require continuing adjustment and mastery of new skills. For many secretaries (and college professors), for example, the transition from typewriters to mastering computerized word processing programs was traumatic. As new programs are developed and older ones refined, continuing adjustments must be made. Technological advances that enhance efficiency have also added a source of stress related to how work performance is monitored. A study of workers in the telephone industry concluded that workers whose performance is tracked by computers and other electronic devices suffer more health problems, as well as psychological problems such as depression and anxiety, than those evaluated by human managers (Worker Stress, 1990).

Interpersonal Relations

The surest sign that you have a crisis at work is when no one tries to tell you how to do your job (Dickson, 1989).

The opportunity to discuss ideas or problems with colleagues, supervisors, and clients in a nonthreatening atmosphere goes a long way toward humanizing and making tolerable a work environment that would otherwise be unbearable. People who are unable to develop satisfying work relationships experience more stress and negative affect at work and are less satisfied with their jobs (Cooper & Marshall, 1976; House, 1981). A particular job-stress culprit is insensitive supervisors who stem the flow of communication in the name of short-term efficiency and profits (Repetti, 1993). Psychologist Robert Hogan identifies three particularly bad management styles: (a) "The arrogant manager. Know-it-all; beats up on workers; makes a sudden impact, then moves on. (b) The charmer. Highly likable, lazy, has no agenda, does no work; can't be fired—has no enemies. (c) The passive aggressive. Very smart, lots of social skills; seems nonhostile but strikes back sneakily when criticized" (Ubell, 1992, p. 8).

Sexual Harassment

Sexual harassment as a work stressor has recently come into the public spotlight with the Clarence Thomas–Anita Hill case. The fact that the female complainant in this case was a college law professor and the accused a U.S. Supreme Court nominee brought attention to the fact that sexual harassment at work is an issue at all status levels of the work environment. Crull (1984), describing the more typical situation of the average office worker, defines sexual harassment as "any attention of a sexual nature in the context of work which makes a woman uncomfortable, impedes her ability to do her work, or interferes with her employment opportunities." She adds, "We are not just talking about losing a job for not sleeping with the boss. We are talking about a whole range of attitudes from being expected to look sexy, to

Figure 11–2

From *The Wall Street Journal*, used with permission of Cartoon Features Syndicate.

"I'm sorry, but the only way I can deal with stress is by passing it on to others."

being turned into the butt of sexual jokes by customers or co-workers, to being co-erced into having an affair with a superior" (p. 179).

Sexual harassment in the workplace is of sufficient concern that organized measures have been undertaken to deal with it. These include the development of workshops by groups such as the Working Women's Institute to educate women how to head off sexual harassment, as well as how to deal with the economic and psychological repercussions of situations that they have been unable to prevent (Crull, 1984). Crull also notes that legal guidelines established via Title VII of the 1964 Civil Rights Act "put employers on notice that they are responsible for creating a workplace free of sexual harassment," and also that "many unions have begun to include sexual harassment in their contracts and have considered special grievance procedures for such cases (and) many employers have formulated policy statements condemning sexual harassment by their management and supervisory personnel" (p. 184).

High Task Demands, Low Control

Karasek & Theorell (1990) argue that the most important variables contributing to job stressfulness are the extent to which a job is perceived to be psychologically demanding, together with the extent to which the worker has latitude to make decisions and use different skills to do the job. The worst combination is a job with heavy psychological demands and little decision latitude (low control), resulting in "high strain" and debilitating stress symptoms. In support of this model, a number of studies have shown that high strain on the job is associated with a range of negative indicators including poor morale, depression, exhaustion, absenteeism, job dissatisfaction, lowered productivity, loss of self-esteem, elevated systolic blood pressure, and physical illness, in both men and women (Karasek & Theorell, 1990; Schnall, Landsbergis, & Baker, 1994). The studies note that although psychological demands do not differ significantly for men and women, men are far more likely to have high levels of control—especially in psychologically demanding jobs. Thus, there is a much higher proportion of high-strain jobs and a lower proportion of active jobs (high psychological demand, high control) for women versus men. Overall, high strain jobs represent a growing portion of available employment in industrial economies such as ours, producing unwanted outcomes for the economy as a whole and for companies, as well as for individual workers. Karasek & Theorell's classification of different occupations according to relative degree of psychological demands and decision latitude is presented in Figure 11–3. Their recommended solution to job strain is to increase worker control by decentralizing authority and increasing worker participation in decision-making. Companies that have done this have found lowered symptoms of coronary heart disease, lowered absenteeism, and decreased incidence of depression in workers (Karasek, 1990).

Role Ambiguity, Role Conflict

Role ambiguity refers both to a lack of clarity about a job's objectives and to expectations that supervisors and coworkers have regarding an individual's responsibilities in achieving objectives. "The first job, a promotion or transfer, a new boss, the first supervisory responsibility, a new company, or a change in the structure of the existing organization—all of these events, and others, may serve to create a temporary state of role ambiguity (Matteson & Ivancevich, 1987, p. 44)." Role ambiguity has been shown to produce a range of maladaptive outcomes, including lowered job satisfaction, decreased motivation, more job-related tension, depressed mood, and lowered self-esteem (Matteson & Ivancevich, 1987). *Role conflict* exists when job demands clash, when job functions do not appear to be consistent with how the job

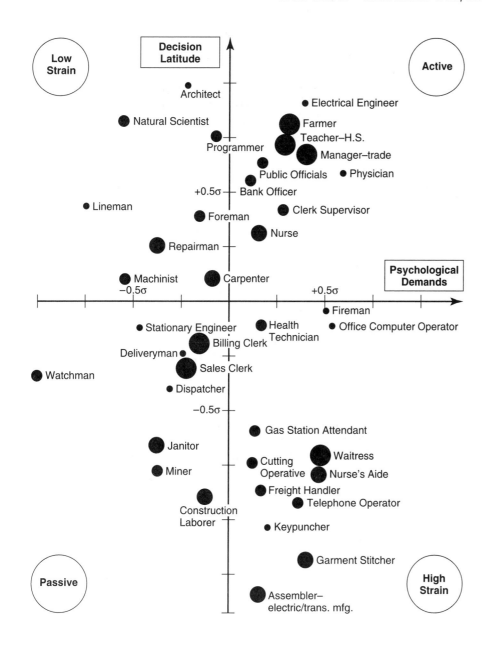

Low Strain

Active

Decision Latitude

Architect
● Electrical Engineer
● Natural Scientist
Farmer
Teacher–H.S.
Programmer
Manager–trade
Public Officials
● Physician
+0.5σ — Bank Officer
● Lineman
● Clerk Supervisor
● Foreman
Nurse
Repairman
Psychological Demands
● Machinist
● Carpenter
−0.5σ
+0.5σ
● Fireman
● Stationary Engineer
● Health Technician
● Office Computer Operator
Billing Clerk
Deliveryman ●
Sales Clerk
● Watchman
● Dispatcher
−0.5σ
● Gas Station Attendant
● Janitor
Waitress
● Cutting Operative
● Miner
Nurse's Aide
● Freight Handler
● Telephone Operator
Construction Laborer
● Keypuncher
Garment Stitcher
Passive
High Strain
Assembler– electric/trans. mfg.

Figure 11–3

The occupational distribution of psychological demands and decision latitude (U.S. males and females, N = 4,495). (From *International Journal of Health Services*, 1989, Robert Karasek, (Vol. 19:3), pp. 481–508. Used with permission of Baywood Publishing Co., Inc.)

has been defined, or when job tasks are viewed as undesirable (Cooper et al., 1988). Cooper, Mallinger, & Kahn (1978) found a high level of role conflict in dentists to be predictive of abnormally high levels of blood pressure. In these dentists, the conflict centered around the discrepancy between the idealized role of the dentist as caregiver and healer and the reality of being an "inflictor of pain."

INDIVIDUAL DIFFERENCES AND JOB STRESS

Are some people more prone to experience job-related stress? Ivancevich, Matteson, Freedman, & Phillips (1990) note that gender is a factor, with women more likely to experience stressors related to sex discrimination, including pay inequity and sexual harassment. They note that the data on ethnicity is less clear although there is suggestive evidence that John Henryism—"the tendency to cope actively with stressors and believe that one can control stressors through hard work and determination" (p. 259)—more effectively moderates stress among blacks than whites. Data from a recent study of 143 professionals (Light, Brownley, et al., 1995), however, conflict with this conclusion. It found that John Henryism was a common characteristic (observed in 71 percent) of black men and women (black and white) who had achieved high status jobs, and both of these groups (who traditionally have had less control in the workplace) were likely to have stress-related *high* blood pressure both when at work and when exposed to laboratory stressors. In contrast, John Henryism was seen in a minority (36 percent) of white men in high status jobs and was unrelated to increased blood pressure in this group. Another study found John Henryism predictive of *high* blood pressure in blacks, but not in whites (Somova, Connolly, & Diara, 1995). An earlier study suggests that the relationship between John Henryism and stress among black workers may be moderated by other work-related factors. James, Hartnett, & Kalsbeck (1983) found that among black male workers residing in a poor, rural community, those who were high in John Henryism and who felt that their race had hindered their chances of being successful had higher levels of diastolic blood pressure with increasing levels of job success. Elevated blood pressure levels were not observed among those who felt that being black had helped them.

Recent research indicates that age bears a U-shaped relationship to occupational stress, with people in their twenties and thirties reporting lower occupational well-being than younger or older workers (Warr, 1992).

Regarding personality dispositions, three interrelated traits have been shown to be useful predictors: external locus of control, high trait anxiety, and Type-A (versus Type-B) personality (Payne, 1988). Although locus of control and trait anxiety have been intensively studied as general predictors of stress reactions and coping (see Chapters 1 and 2), the Type-A behavior pattern has been the trait dimension most closely associated with occupational stress.

> Joe is an Assistant Professor at a major urban university. He is determined to become famous in his field, and he is willing to put everything else aside in order to achieve this goal. He works seven days most weeks. His pace is frenetic, and he is unable to delegate work to others. He is impatient with colleagues who do not measure up to his standards, and he is determined to get tenured and promoted in record time. He has an explosive temper and has had frequent run-ins with colleagues and even graduate students regarding work assignments and the issue of who should be listed as the senior author on professional articles and grant submissions. His incessant drive, competitive spirit, and uncompromising attitude make others anxious about the prospect of coming in conflict with him.

Joe is a classic Type-A person. As described in Chapter 4, these are aggressive, driven, highly achievement-oriented individuals who have great difficulty controlling their impatience and expressing their hostility in acceptable ways. Not only do they pose problems within the organizational setting, but also as individuals they are more prone to develop cardiovascular disease. Recent research suggests that the most "toxic" element of Type-A behavior is poor ability to control anger and hostility (Smith, 1992). The following suggestions for self-management of toxic hostility in Type A persons are based on research by Friedman & Ulmer (1984):

> 1. Announce to a close friend or spouse your intention to eliminate hostility. The friend or spouse could also be instructed to give a signal whenever he or she observes a sign of hostility or potential outburst.
> 2. Regularly express your appreciation to that helper for aiding you in reducing your hostility. Verbal expressions of sincere gratitude must become a habit.

3. Play to lose, at least some of the time. Type As play to win even when competing with an overmatched person.

4. Start smiling and laughing at yourself. By laughing and smiling, you begin to take yourself less seriously.

5. Do away with ideals. More often than not, Type As with a lot of free-floating hostility are idealists who have appointed themselves to be responsible for keeping everyone in line. As a result, they are often disappointed, since others rarely meet ideal standards. An ideal in the mind of a Type A is usually unrealistic and results in feelings of superiority over and contempt for others.

6. Develop a log of what makes you angry. Put details down in writing. Whenever you become upset or aggravated, jot down the time, situation, and people involved. At the end of a week or ten days, go over your list. Ask yourself whether the causes in each case warranted the wear and tear that you subjected your body, mind, and relationships to. Show your list to your helper and let him or her critique what is listed.

(Reprinted from Matteson & Ivancevich, 1987, pp. 235–236)

Figure 11–4 summarizes the stress process as it relates to the workplace. Under stressors, we have listed the major classes of events relevant to job stress. Under stress moderators, we list variables that may interact with stressors to affect the severity of the stress reaction. In addition to those discussed in the text, we list factors within the work setting (e.g., a fair reward and advancement system, an employee assistance program [EAP] that provides counseling and stress management) as well as outside factors (e.g., a supportive family) that may moderate a stress reaction. All of these factors affect one's cognitive appraisal of a situation and the coping strategies employed to manage situation outcomes, which in turn influence the severity of the stress reaction.

WORKSITE STRESS MANAGEMENT INTERVENTIONS

In enumerating the causes of job stress, we have noted some ways in which job stress may be moderated. In this section we elaborate on this area and include descriptions of more formalized programs that have been developed for this purpose. As may be noted in Figure 11–4, the causes of work stress are multiple and interac-

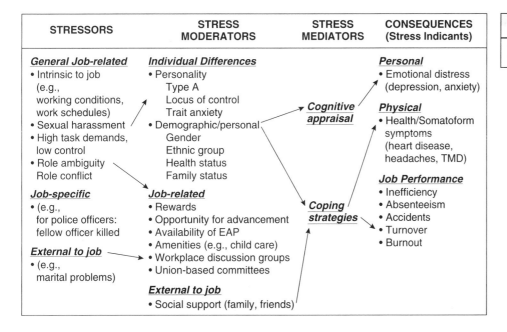

Figure 11–4

Job Stress Process.

tive. Given this complexity, a wide range of intervention targets are relevant. Appropriate targets include those at the organizational level (e.g., hiring, promotional, and layoff policies, plant closings, automation) and at the level of the work setting (e.g., design of work tasks, worker autonomy and participation in decision making, relations with coworkers and supervisors) including the physical environment (e.g., poor air or lighting, noise exposure) as well as those less directly associated with work but that affect job performance. The latter categories include interpersonal (e.g., marital/social, legal/financial difficulties), psychological (e.g., poor self-esteem, poor coping skills), and health-related (disease, disability) functioning. Worksite interventions are either directed toward helping individuals enhance their coping ability (usually by teaching them emotion-focused stress management techniques) so that they can deal more effectively with stressful work conditions, or (less frequently) take a problem-oriented approach and focus on changing features of the work environment that are inducing stress.

Next, we give examples of some specific ways in which stress management has been implemented in the work environment. Following the intervention model introduced in Chapter 6, we take a temporal approach to classifying interventions. They are categorized according to whether they are designed to (a) help new or prospective workers deal with stressors that they are likely to encounter in the workplace, (b) help workers cope effectively with stressors that they are currently encountering, or (c) help workers deal with the aftereffects of stressors already encountered.

Prestress (Preventive) Interventions

As in most other areas in which stress management programs are implemented, in the occupational field most programs are oriented toward responding to problems as they arise, with less emphasis on preventing potential problems. Thus, there are relatively few reports of programs that attempt to anticipate sources of worker stress and to do something about preparing the prospective employee, or which modify the work environment to minimize potential risk factors.

A good example of a program that helped workers anticipate and cope with future job stressors is Kramer's (1974) program of "anticipatory socialization" for nurses. The program was designed to prevent "reality shock" in nurses just entering the profession by preparing them (while still student nurses) for the stressors that they would actually encounter on the job. This program is based on the rationale that in nursing, as in many other professions, training programs foster idealized and unrealistic expectations in students about what really goes on in the work setting in terms of actual responsibilities that will be assumed and professional, personal, and bureaucratic conflicts that may arise. Kramer's philosophy is that prospective nurses need to be "immunized" by being exposed to the attitudes and values of practicing nurses who function effectively in the everyday world of nursing.

The three-year program consisted of four phases. Phase 1 was designed to produce some degree of reality shock by exposure to audiotape recordings of difficult job incidents experienced by working nurses that the novice nurse is not likely to anticipate. One example is that of a nurse describing an uncomfortable procedure (an open cardiac massage) performed on an elderly patient "just for practice." The instructor tried to moderate the young nurses' distress by presenting ways of viewing the incident that would help them put it in a meaningful context (e.g., "if the physician does not practice, how can the physician learn the necessary skills; if the nurse withdraws, doesn't this make things even worse for the patient?").

Phase 2 involved devising new solutions and helping students appreciate the wide range of reasons why less than ideal conditions exist in the work setting. The first two phases thus focused on nurses' expectations and their behavior as nurses. Phase 3 focused on teaching nurses about what others would expect of them. This involved exposure to input from physicians and nursing supervisors as well as from recent nursing graduates. Phase 4 emphasized teaching conflict resolution and negotiation skills with the underlying idea that nurses can affect the system and be change agents. They were taught ways in which they could deviate from "the prescribed nurse role" that would help them resolve conflicts constructively. Compared with a control group of nurses who did not participate in the program, the nurses who participated remained longer in their initial jobs and in nursing practice, were better able to develop strategies to use in managing conflict, were more empathic with patients, had fewer days of absence from work, and were rated as being happier, being more stimulated, and exerting more leadership on the job. Though specifically designed for nurses, this kind of preparatory program can serve as a model for any occupational group.

Kramer's (1974) program focuses on the individual and easing his or her transition to the work environment. Though most professions and companies fall short of the kind of systematic preventive programming that she developed, some large American companies have attempted to anticipate sources of stress and moderate them by providing a "progressive" workplace. For example, in one of its cellular telephone plants Motorola Corporation provides an on-site day care center and allows employees to have lunch and visit with their children, provides a flexible three- to four-day work week (11 hours per day) that allows the opportunity for second jobs as well as ongoing educational programs that offer upward mobility, and furnishes on-site amenities such as travel agencies, banks, dry cleaners, and snack shops. The company is making a concerted effort to remove the work situation as far as possible from the "doomy, gloomy" atmosphere of the typical early 1970s factory (Jones, 1995).

The recent increase in workplace violence has prompted businesses to find ways in which potentially violent persons may be identified and to implement organizational strategies that may be used to minimize the possibility of violence. Data on previous workplace murderers (Stuart, 1992b) indicate that they have been mostly middle-aged white males, loners who shy away from coworkers, have large gun collections, and are fascinated by exotic weapons. They are often angry, paranoid, and guarded, and though work history may be unstable, they get satisfactory work evaluations because they intimidate supervisors. Just as suicide committers often telegraph their intentions via "cries for help," workplace murderers often give direct verbal warnings of their intentions such as, "If you think what happened at the post office was bad, wait until you see what I do" (Stuart, 1992b, p. 74).

A difficulty with acting on such information is the high false positive rate—many people with these characteristics are not violent—and the meaning of warnings is not always clear. For example, in the wake of a rampage in which a laid-off technician set off two remote-controlled pipe bombs and shot out a switchboard before killing two executives of the Elgar Corporation in June 1991, it was remembered that the killer had previously said to his supervisor, "This is stressful—remember what happened at the Escondido post office." However, no one knew that he was referring to an incident in which an employee had shot and killed two coworkers and himself, and thus the remark was not interpreted as a threat (Stuart, 1992b, p. 84).

Organizational strategies for preventing workplace violence include the careful selection of employees to avoid the stress and frustration induced when individuals are mismatched with jobs, the use of the probationary period to carefully observe the employees' behavior to screen out potential troublemakers, the establishment of fair and unbiased grievance procedures to give employees an opportunity to vent their frustrations through established channels, and insuring that promotions, salary, and other rewards are dispensed on the basis of merit rather than favoritism or political pressure (Elliott & Jarrett, 1994). In the wake of six revenge killings that occurred in the U.S. Postal Service between 1985 and 1991 (leaving 28 people dead, mostly supervisors), the Postal Service estabished a national hot line that employees can call to report threats from past or current coworkers (Stuart, 1992a). Postal employees have also been notified that bringing a gun to work will result in dismissal (Postal employees, 1995).

Interventions for Ongoing Stress

The majority of work-site intervention programs are designed to deal with employees' ongoing stress-related problems. Most of the programs are in the form of organizationally sponsored stress management and health promotion programs, and many large U.S. companies (e.g., Equitable Life Assurance; Manuso, 1983) have made a commitment to such programs for their employees. This commitment has been motivated in large part by practical concerns. It is assumed that stress produces inefficiency, absenteeism, and turnover and that moderating employee stress will enhance productivity. In addition, employers pay approximately 80 percent of all private health insurance premiums, and workers' compensation laws usually include benefits for injuries resulting from worksite stress. In an increasing number of cases, employees in the United States have successfully sued their employers for psychological or physical injury due to stressful working conditions; thus, fear of employee litigation has become an important factor (Ivancevich et al., 1990; Reynolds & Briner, 1994). More idealistically, these programs are also thought to stem from the belief that an organization should take some responsibility for the welfare of its workers, who are their most valuable resource (Gebhardt & Crump, 1990). On the basis of survey data, among corporate health programs, stress management programs are far and away the top priority for both employers and employees (Pelletier & Lutz, 1988).

In the United States, in-house "fitness" or "wellness" programs are common in large companies. These employee assistance programs (EAPs) typically involve a range of stress management and health promotion activities, including dietary control, cardiovascular fitness, relaxation and exercise classes, stress education, and psychological counseling. These programs are designed to modify behavioral risk factors that lead to disease and poor health (Cooper & Cartwright, 1994). Often the major motivation for EAPs is the need to control spiraling substance abuse and mental health costs (Stuart, 1993). The effects of these broad-based programs are difficult to evaluate. Some companies have reported tremendous gains in terms of reductions in absenteeism and health care costs with savings-to-investments ratios up to 15:1. However, the lack of control groups and other methodological problems, along with difficulty in isolating which components of these multimodal programs (e.g., stress management versus physical health care) are accounting for positive changes, make it difficult to assess their true impact (Cooper & Cartwright, 1994).

A number of companies have offered self-contained preprogrammed stress-management packages to employees. These packages typically involve teaching workers one or a combination of emotion-focused techniques, such as meditation, autogenics, progressive muscle relaxation, or biofeedback. The small number of studies that have evaluated the impact of this training has generally found short-term reductions in physiological arousal and in self-reported anxiety and somatic symptoms in participants; some studies show increments in workers' performance ratings and work attitudes and decreased perceived stress at work (Murphy, 1984; 1987). However, as Murphy notes, there is a need to determine how to get people to continue to use the procedures. Also, most programs have been geared toward white-collar versus blue-collar workers, and there are few data on whether or how people actually apply learned relaxation skills to stressful encounters on the job. He argues that teaching relaxation skills without integrating this training into a broad-based occupational health strategy is of limited value.

One of the major criticisms of work-site interventions designed to deal with ongoing stress is that they are neither described operationally nor systematically evaluated. There have been scattered attempts in recent years, however, to design and evaluate problem-focused organizational and work setting-level interventions designed to reduce work stress (reviewed by Burke, 1993). For example, Wall & Clegg (1981) evaluated the effects of increasing worker autonomy in an organization where morale and motivation was low and productivity was poor. Autonomy was increased by giving work teams rather than supervisors the control over the rate of work, rest breaks, allocations of work assignments, and overtime. Participants showed increases in autonomy and task identity and significant reductions in emotional distress. Another research program showed that problem-solving seminars could be useful in reducing work-family conflict. Culbert & Crenshaw (1972) worked with employees whose job of field-testing products imposed a heavier than expected travel burden, resulting in disconnected family relationships and poor social life, as well as fatigue and depression about being absent from the home. The seminars concentrated on galvanizing the analytical and problem-solving skills of the husband-wife teams and on focusing them on coping with the separation and attendant problems. In contrast to controls, participants felt better able to cope with travel stresses and showed a decrease in an independent measure of travel stress. Burke concludes that work setting-level interventions such as these that are targeted at particular problems and that are systematically evaluated are the exception rather than the rule. He argues that there continues to be a gap between work-stress researchers and practitioners and that research findings have little impact on programs that are actually implemented in the workplace.

As noted before, sexual harassment is a major source of stress in the workplace, and extraorganizational and legal measures have been instituted to deal with it. Although there are few published research reports evaluating the effectiveness of the measures, many companies are committing resources to in-house programs designed to diminish sexual harassment. For example, the DuPont Company has developed a program that includes a twenty-four-hour confidential hot line, staffed by trained employees who carry beepers. The anonymity component helps potential complainants to understand what their options are and what decisions they will have to make prior to initiating any formal action (Solomon, 1991). Caudron (1995) notes that sexual harassment and diversity awareness programs may paradoxically have actually increased stress by polarizing the workforce—making men feel defensive and women victimized—resulting in less spontaneity and inhibiting communication between men and women. Men in particular feel victimized by these programs. They are portrayed as "the bad guys, the perpetrators, the oppressors—because of this they feel their needs go unrecognized (particularly regarding) family-friendly policies (which) are written as if only women are parents" (Caudron, 1995, p. 57). In response to these concerns, some companies are developing broader-based programs in which male and female employees air their concerns about such issues as quotas, gender differences in communication styles, and "how sexual harassment training and the forced 'reporting environment' has made everyone feel as if they were working in a fishbowl" (Caudron, 1995, p. 58).

Postvention: Dealing with the Aftermath of Workplace Stress

Although not a major part of many occupational stress management programs, there is growing realization in some settings of the need to provide support for employees who have experienced stressful transitions such as dismissal or those who have experienced traumatic events in the work setting. Some companies provide outplacement services for employees whom they lay off and provide counseling to help employees deal with the stress of job termination brought about by relocation, downsizing, or restructuring. Others have developed emergency plans for crisis situations including evacuation procedures, public relation policies, and contingency plans to protect against legal action (Braverman, 1992). But with the exception of high risk occupations in which emergencies occur fairly regularly (e.g., health care professions, law enforcement, firemen), businesses are usually not equipped to deal with the effects of traumatic workplace events on their employees' emotional well-being, morale, and adjustment at work.

When services are available to help employees deal with trauma, they have often been developed in response to particular events. For example one British financial services company, in the aftermath of a series of armed robberies, developed a program that provided immediate information and services to employee-victims, including critical-incident stress debriefing, counseling, peer support, and monitoring of emotional reactions (Richards, 1994). Each branch of the company contains a sealed "emergency pack" that is opened immediately following a robbery. This pack lists procedures, contains contact cards for peer supporters and counselors, and provides a leaflet that describes expected reactions to trauma and gives guidelines on what to do during the immediate postrobbery period. Support is provided both by local managers trained in "defusing" techniques and by ordinary staff volunteers trained in basic counseling skills.

In the wake of the 1991 shooting of two executives at the Elgar Corporation, management took a slightly different approach (Stuart, 1992b). They hired a professional trauma team, which instituted a short-term (two weeks) group and individual psychotherapy program working in close cooperation with management. The trauma team also worked with the families of employees and offered services to the wife of the murderer, who was also viewed as a victim. Special problems arose in working with employees who were immigrants from countries in Southeast Asia who were concerned that the "spirits of the dead" were still in the building. As a result, Buddhist monks were brought in to bless the building. Long-term changes instituted as a result of the traumatic murders (a mechanized employee identification card system and an emergency warning system) were primarily prevention-oriented and designed to make employees feel that the probability of such an event recurring had diminished.

In some work settings, traumatic events occur sufficiently frequently so that either a stress-debriefing program is continuously available on-site or critical-incident stress debriefing (CISD) teams are available on a standby basis. CISD teams typically consist of peer support personnel drawn from the ranks of emergency service organizations (e.g., police, fire, emergency medical services) combined with mental health professionals (Everly & Mitchell, 1995). It is estimated that there are approximately three hundred CISD teams in the U.S., providing assistance to a range of emergency personnel (Spitzer & Burke, 1993). In a not atypical situation involving a Henrico County, Virginia, police officer, the officer heard shots and then confronted a man who had emerged from a store that he had just robbed, pointing a gun at the officer. The officer shot the man twice. Though the officer stated that he did "what he had to do," the stress of the situation nonetheless affected him. For about four weeks, details of the incident would flash in front of him, most often when he was attempting to sleep, and his weight dropped because of poor appetite. CISD helped him in understanding that his response was to be expected and in putting the event in perspective. Some officers resist any kind of assistance having the connotation of mental health, asserting that they do not need to be told "how to feel." But practitioners assert that CISD helps reduce "guilt, finger pointing, and refusal to accept consequences" (Schermerhorn, 1989, p. 8).

In general, CISD is designed to provide a setting for trauma victims to interact, exchange information, and provide mutual support. It also helps identify those who may require formal psychological care (Everly & Mitchell, 1995). Spitzer & Burke (1993) describe an application of the CISD model developed by Mitchell (1983; Mitchell & Bray, 1990) to critical incidents in a hospital setting (e.g., an unexpected pediatric death during surgery). They view debriefing not as "situational critiques or psychotherapy but instead (as) opportunities to put traumatic experiences into perspective (p. 150)." The debriefing procedure consisted of progressive stages, culminating with identification of sources of follow-up assistance if needed (see Table 11–3).

**TABLE 11–3.   STAGES OF A FORMAL CRITICAL-INCIDENT
STRESS DEBRIEFING**

Introductory Phase
Debriefing staff are introduced.
Debriefing conduct rules are presented:
  1. Confidentiality is assured (unless suicide or homicide concerns exist);
     no disclosures will be made to superiors or press.
  2. There is no obligation to speak during the session.
  3. Disclosures are not used against attendees in any way.
  4. No pagers or premature departures are permitted.
  5. Participants are treated equally, regardless of rank.
  6. Debriefings are not situational critiques or performance appraisals. They
     allow emotional ventilation.

Fact Phase
Participants are requested to describe facts regarding themselves, the incident, and their activities during the incident. Participants are asked to state who they are, their rank, where they were, and what they experienced and did as they worked in and around the incident. Each person takes a turn adding details until the entire incident is re-created.

Thought Phase
Participants are requested to reveal the first thoughts they were aware of during the incident. This revelation helps the participants tap into the more personal aspects of the situation. This phase affirms that one's own thoughts are important and not to be hidden behind the facts of the incident.

Reaction Phase
Attention is turned to the participants' reactions during and subsequent to the incident. Participants are encouraged to discuss the effects not just on themselves, but on those around them (friends, colleagues, family, neighbors, spouse).

Teaching Phase
The facilitator identifies characteristic physical, emotional, and behavioral symptomatology associated with stress. Emphasis is placed on the normal expectation that personnel will experience stress in relation to their duties. Participants are advised on how to be aware of the signs of stress and taught techniques effective in reducing excessive stress.

Reentry Phase
This stage allows for questions, reassurances, and establishment of action plans. An overview is given of the debriefing, and encouragement is given to the participants. Additional referral resources are made available to health care workers who need follow-up counseling.

By permission of the National Association of Social Workers.

There are few reports objectively evaluating the effectiveness of CISDs or other programs designed to help employees deal with the aftermath of workplace stress. However, Stuart (1992b) states that the results of a study of two hundred people "suffering major psychic trauma during working hours" provides good business reasons to institute such programs. Compared with people who received delayed intervention (six to thirty months after the incident), those treated at a psychiatric clinic soon after the incident averaged faster recovery time before returning to work (twelve weeks versus forty-six weeks), and only 13 percent chose litigation (compared with 94 percent among the delayed treatment group).

*S*UMMARY

1. Analysis of workers' compensation claims for stress-related disorders and of worker surveys reveals that occupational stress is a serious and increasing problem in the United States.

2. Burnout refers to stress experienced by people who go into careers with high ideals but whose expectations are not met in the workplace.

3. Prominent causes of job stress include general factors intrinsic to the job itself (e.g., working conditions, work schedules, physical danger, work overload, work underload), stressful interpersonal relationships at work, sexual harassment, high task demands combined with low control, role ambiguity and role conflict, factors intrinsic to particular jobs (e.g., for pharmacists, being interrupted by phone calls), and factors external to the job.

4. The Type-A behavior pattern is the individual difference variable most closely associated with job stress. Its most toxic element is poor ability to control anger and hostility.

5. The extent to which job stress is experienced is a function of exposure to job stressors interacting with stress moderators (e.g., Type-A personality), producing cognitive appraisal of threat, and eliciting coping strategies that may be effective in moderating stress level or the conditions producing stress.

6. Worksite stress management interventions may be broadly classified into pre-stress (preventive) interventions, interventions for ongoing stress, and those (postvention programs) designed to help workers deal with stressors that have already been experienced.

7. Integrated prevention programs designed to prepare workers for specific jobs are relatively rare. However, some large companies have attempted to anticipate sources of workplace stress and defuse them by providing a "progressive" workplace. Because of the upsurge in workplace violence, some companies have also attempted to identify potentially violent persons and institute procedures designed to minimize the possibility of violence.

8. Most programs designed to deal with ongoing worker stress are organizationally sponsored, broad-based, on-site fitness or wellness programs of which stress management is one component. Although very popular, their effectiveness has not been definitively demonstrated with sound research. Some companies offer packaged stress management programs that primarily teach emotion-focused coping skills. These programs are generally effective in producing short-term changes in anxiety, but it is not clear whether the learned skills are applied by workers on the job. A few interventions have taught work-

ers problem-focused skills (e.g., controlling the rate of work) that have effectively moderated work-related stress. Programs designed to deal with sexual harassment in the workplace are being implemented in many large companies, although there are few published research reports documenting their effectiveness. Overall, ongoing stress-management programs have been criticized for taking a "band-aid" approach by assuming that stress is an inevitable fact of the work situation to which employees must adapt, rather than attempting to change stress-inducing aspects of the work situation to fit the needs of people (Cooper & Cartwright, 1994). Programs such as Wall & Clegg's (1981), in which worker autonomy on the job was increased, are the exception rather than the rule.

9. There has been increasing use of professional services designed to help employees deal with the aftereffects of exposure to trauma. For some emergency personnel (firefighters, paramedics, police) who experience trauma continually, critical-incident stress debriefing teams are available on a standby basis.

 **KEY TERMS**

anticipatory socialization   Process designed to help workers anticipate and therefore prepare for the stressors that they will face on the job.

burnout   Stress experienced in response to one's job situation; in particular, it refers to disappointment experienced by highly motivated individuals whose employment-related expectations are not met.

critical-incident stress debriefing   Defusing process in which peers and mental health professionals combine to provide a setting for victims of job-related traumatic stressors to share information and discuss their concerns.

employee assistance programs   Workplace-based programs that focus on promoting healthy lifestyles in employees and improving their stress management skills.

high task demands, low control   Reference to jobs that are psychologically demanding and that also provide little latitude to make important decisions; these job characteristics are said to produce job "strain."

intrinsic job stressors   Factors that are part of basic job tasks or of the work environment that are perceived as stressful (e.g., noise, social isolation).

John Henryism   Belief that the way to alleviate job stress is through hard work and determination to succeed.

karoshi   Overwork-related death (Japan).

role ambiguity   Lack of clarity about a job's objectives and expectations.

role conflict   Situation that occurs when there are inconsistencies between job demands and a worker's job expectancies.

sexual harassment   Attention or demands of a sexual nature that impede an individual's ability to function effectively and without undue stress on the job.

References

Abel, C. G., Blanchard, E. B., & Becker, J. V. (1976). An integrated treatment program for rapists. In R. Rada (Ed.), *Clinical aspects of the rapist* (pp. 161–214). New York: Grune & Stratton.

Adler, T. (1993, March). Bad mix: Combat stress, decisions. *APA Monitor, 24* (3), pp. 1, 15.

Agger, I., & Jensen, S. B. (1990). Testimony as ritual and evidence in psychotherapy for political refugees. *Journal of Traumatic Stress, 3,* 115–130.

Agras, W. S. (1993). The diagnosis and treatment of panic disorder. *Annual Review of Medicine, 44,* 39–51.

Agras, W. S., Sylvester, D., & Oliveau, D. (1969). The epidemiology of common fears and phobias. *Comprehensive Psychiatry, 10,* 151–156.

Aldag, R. J., & Fuller, S. R. (1993). Beyond fiasco: A reappraisal of the groupthink phenomenon and a new model of group decision processes. *Psychological Bulletin, 113,* 533–552.

Aldwin, C., & Stokols, D. (1988). The effects of environmental change on individuals and groups: Some neglected issues in stress research. *Journal of Environmental Psychology, 8,* 57–75.

Aldwin, C. M., Sutton, K. J., & Lachman, M. (1996). The development of coping resources in adulthood. *Journal of Personality, 64,* 837–872.

Alexander, C. N., Langer, E., Newman, R., Chandler, H., & Davies, J. (1989). Transcendental meditation, mindfulness, and longevity: An experimental study with the elderly. *Journal of Personality and Social Psychology, 57,* 950–964.

Al-Kubaisy, T., Marks, I. M., Logsdail, S., Marks, M. P., Lovell, K., Sungur, M., & Araya, R. (1992). Role of exposure homework in phobia reduction: A controlled study. *Behavior Therapy, 23,* 599–621.

Allman, W. F. (1985). Staying alive in the 20th century. *Science 85, 6(8),* 30–41.

Allred, K. D., & Smith, T. W. (1989). The hardy personality: Cognitive and physiological responses to evaluative threat. *Journal of Personality and Social Psychology, 56,* 257–266.

American Psychiatric Association (1994). *Diagnostic and statistical manual of mental disorders (DSM-IV)* (4th ed.). Washington, D.C.: Author.

Andrews, G., Tennat, C., Hewson, D., & Schonell, M. (1979). The relation of social factors to physical and psychiatric illness. *American Journal of Epidemiology, 109,* 186–204.

Aneshensel, C. S., & Gore, S. (1991). Development, stress, and role structuring: Social transitions of adolescence. In J. Eckenrode (Ed.), *The social context of coping* (pp. 55–77). New York: Plenum.

Antoni, M. H., Baggett, L., Ironson, G., & LaPerriere, A. (1991). Cognitive-behavioral stress management intervention buffers distress responses and immunologic changes following notification of HIV-1 seropositivity. *Journal of Consulting & Clinical Psychology, 59,* 906–915.

Antoni, M. H., Schneiderman, N., Fletcher, M. A., Goldstein, D. A., Ironson, G., & Laperriere, A. (1990). Psychoneuroimmunology and HIV-1. *Journal of Consulting and Clinical Psychology, 58,* 38–49.

Arkowitz, H., Hinton, R., Perl, J., & Himadi, W. (1978). Treatment strategies for dating anxiety in college men based on real life practice. *The Counseling Psychologist, 7,* 41–46.

Atkeson, B. M., Calhoun, K. S., Resick, P., & Ellis, E. M. (1982). Victims of rape: Repeated assessment of depressive symptoms. *Journal of Consulting and Clinical Psychology, 50,* 96–102.

Auerbach, S. M. (1973). Effects of orienting instructions, feedback-information, and trait anxiety level on state anxiety. *Psychological Reports, 33,* 779–786. (a)

Auerbach, S. M. (1973). Trait-state anxiety and adjustment to surgery. *Journal of Consulting and Clinical Psychology, 40,* 264–271. (b)

Auerbach, S. M. (1983). Crisis intervention research: Methodological considerations and some recent findings. In L. Cohen, W. Claiborn, & G. Specter (Eds.), *Crisis intervention* (2nd ed.) (pp. 191–211). New York: Human Sciences Press.

Auerbach, S. M. (1986). Assumptions of crisis theory and a temporal model of crisis intervention (pp 3–37). In S. M. Auerbach & A. L. Stolberg (Eds.), *Crisis intervention with children and families.* Washington, D.C.: Hemisphere.

Auerbach, S. M. (1989). Stress management and coping research in the health care setting: An overview and methodological commentary. *Journal of Consulting and Clinical Psychology, 57,* 388–395.

Auerbach, S. M. (1992). Temporal factors in stress and coping: Intervention implications. In B. N. Carpenter (Ed.), *Personal coping: Theory, research, and application* (pp. 133–147). Westport, Conn.: Praeger.

Auerbach, S. M., Kendall, P. C., Cuttler, H., & Levitt, N. R. (1976). Anxiety, locus of control, type of preparatory information, and adjustment to dental surgery. *Journal of Consulting and Clinical Psychology, 44,* 809–818.

Auerbach, S. M., & Kilmann, P. R. (1977). Crisis intervention: A review of outcome research. *Psychological Bulletin, 84,* 1189–1217.

Auerbach, S. M., Martelli, M., & Mercuri, L. G. (1983). Anxiety, information, interpersonal impacts, and adjustment to a stressful health care situation. *Journal of Personality and Social Psychology, 44,* 1284–1296.

Bailey, K. G. (1987). *Human paleopsychology: Applications to aggression and pathological processes.* Hillsdale, N.J.: Erlbaum.

Bailey, K. G. (1988). Psychological kinship: Implications for the helping professions. *Psychotherapy, 25,* 132–141.

Bailey, K. G. (1995, August). *Mismatch theory and the fourfold model of psychopathology.* Paper presented at the annual meeting of the Human Behavior and Evolution Society, Santa Barbara, Calif.

Ballenger, J. C., Burrows, G. D., DuPont, R. L., Lesser, I. M. (1988). Alprazolam in panic disorder and agoraphobia: Results from a multicenter trial: I. Efficacy in short-term treatment. *Archives of General Psychiatry, 45,* 413–422.

Band, E. B., & Weisz, J. R. (1988). How to feel better when it feels bad: Children's perspectives on coping with everyday stress. *Developmental Psychology, 24,* 247–253.

Bandura, A. (1977). Self-efficacy: Toward a unified theory of behavior change. *Psychological Review, 84,* 191–215.

Bandura, A. (1986). *Social foundations of thought and action: A social cognitive theory.* Englewood Cliffs, N.J.: Prentice-Hall.

Bandura, A. (1990). Conclusion: Reflections on nonability determinants of competence. In R. J. Sternberg & J. Kolligan (Eds.), *Competence considered* (pp. 315–362). New Haven: Yale University Press.

Bandura, A., Adams, N. E., Hardy, A. B., & Howells, G. N. (1980). Tests of the generality of self-efficacy theory. *Cognitive Therapy and Research, 4,* 39–66.

Banks, S., Salovey, P., Greener, S., Rothman, A. J., Moyer, A., Beauvais, & Epel, E. (1995). The effects of message framing on mammography utilization. *Health Psychology, 14,* 178–184.

Barlow, D. H., (1988). *Anxiety and its disorders: The nature and treatment of anxiety and panic.* New York: Guilford.

Barlow, D. H., Craske, M. G., Cerny, J. A., & Klosko, J. S. (1989). Behavioral treatment of panic disorder. *Behavior Therapy, 20,* 261–282.

Barlow, D. H., Rapee, R. M., & Brown, T. A. (1992). Behavioral treatment of generalized anxiety disorder. *Behavior Therapy, 23,* 551–570.

Baron, R., Byrne, D., & Kantowitz, B. (1978). *Psychology: Understanding behavior.* Philadelphia: W. B. Saunders.

Barry, D. (1995, July 16). Stress management: Don't get overwrought just because a few things go wrong. *Richmond Times-Dispatch,* p. F1.

Barsky, A. J. (1979). Patients who amplify bodily sensations. *Annals of Internal Medicine, 91,* 63–70.

Barsky, A. J., Goodson, J. D., Lane, R. S., & Cleary, P. D. (1988). The amplification of somatic symptoms. *Psychosomatic Medicine, 50,* 510–519.

Barsky, A. J., & Klerman, G. L. (1983). Overview: Hypochondriasis, bodily complaints, and somatic styles. *American Journal of Psychiatry, 140,* 273–283.

Barton, A. H. (1969). *Communities in disaster.* New York: Doubleday.

Bass, E., & Davis, L. (1988). *The courage to heal.* New York: Harper & Row.

Beatty, J. (1995). *Principles of behavioral neuroscience.* Chicago: Brown & Benchmark.

Beck, A. T., Brown, G., & Steer, R. A. (1989). Prediction of eventual suicide in psychiatric inpatients by clinical ratings of hopelessness. *Journal of Consulting and Clinical Psychology, 57,* 309–310.

Beck, A. T., Emery, G., & Greenberg, R. L. (1985). *Anxiety disorders and phobias.* New York: Basic Books.

Benner, P., Roskies, E., & Lazarus, R. S. (1980). Stress and coping under extreme conditions. In J. E. Dimsdale (Ed.), *Survivors, victims, and perpetrators: Essays on the Nazi Holocaust* (pp. 219–258). Washington, D.C.: Hemisphere.

Benson, H. (1975). *The relaxation response.* New York: Morrow.

Berger, P. B. (1996). Hope and caution: Report from the XI international conference on AIDS. *Canadian Medical Association Journal, 155,* 717–721.

Berger, S. M. (1962). Conditioning through vicarious instigation. *Psychological Review, 69,* 450–466.

Bernstein, D. A., & Borkovec, T. D. (1973). *Progressive relaxation training: A manual for the helping professions.* Champaign, Ill.: Research Press.

Bernstein, D. A., Borkovec, T. D., & Coles, M. G. H. (1986). Assessment of anxiety. In A. R. Cimenero, K. S. Calhoun, & H. E. Adams (Eds.), *Handbook of behavioral assessment,* (2nd ed.) (pp. 353–403). New York: Wiley.

Bernstein, D. A., & Carlson, C. R. (1993). Progressive relaxation: Abbreviated methods. In P. M. Lehrer & R. L. Woolfolk (Eds.), *Principles and practice of stress management*, (2nd ed.), (pp. 53–87). New York: Guilford.

Bettleheim, B. (1960). *The informed heart—autonomy in a massage*. New York: Free Press.

Bianchi, G. N. (1971). Origins of disease phobia. *Journal of Psychiatry, 5,* 241–257.

Bibb, J. L., & Chambless, D. L. (1986). Alcohol use and abuse among diagnosed agoraphobics. *Behavior Research & Therapy, 24,* 49–58.

Bierman, J. (1981). *Righteous gentile: The story of Raoul Wallenberg, missing hero of the Holocaust*. New York: Viking.

Bijou, S. W., & Baer, D. M. (1961). *Child development, Volume one: A systematic and empirical inquiry*. New York: Appleton-Century-Crofts.

Biran, M. W. (1990). Resourcefulness and successful treatment of agoraphobia. In M. Rosenbaum (Ed.), *Learned resourcefulness: On coping skills, self-control, and adaptive behavior* (pp. 182–201). New York: Springer.

Blanchard, E. B., & Epstein, L. H. (1978). *A biofeedback primer*. Reading, Mass.: Addison-Wesley.

Bloom, B. L. (1984). *Community mental health: A general introduction*. Monterey, Calif.: Brooks/Cole.

Bloom, J. R., Hayes, W. A., Saunders, F., & Flatt, S. (1987). Cancer awareness and secondary prevention practices in Black Americans: Implications for intervention. *Family and Community Health, 10,* 19–30.

Booth-Kewley, S., & Friedman, H. S. (1987). Psychological predictors of heart disease: A quantitative review. *Psychological Bulletin, 101,* 343–362.

Borysenko, M. (1987). The immune system: An overview. *Annals of Behavioral Medicine, 9,* 3–10.

Brady, J. V. (1958). Ulcers in "executive" monkeys. *Scientific American, 199,* 95–100.

Brady, J. V., Porter, R., Conrad, D., & Mason, J. (1958). Avoidance behavior and the development of gastroduodenal ulcers. *Journal of Experimental Analysis of Behavior, 1,* 69–72.

Braestrup, C., & Nielsen, M. (1993). Discovery of beta-carboline ligands for benzodiazepine receptors. *Psychopharmacological Serials, 11,* 1–6.

Braverman, M. (1992). Posttrauma crisis intervention in the workplace. In J. C. Quick, L. R. Murphy, & J. J. Hurrell, Jr. (Eds.) *Stress and well-being at work* (pp. 299–316). Washington, D.C.: American Psychological Association.

Brecher, E. J. (1994). *Schindler's legacy: True stories of the list survivors*. Harmondsworth, Middlesex, England: Penguin Books.

Breggin, P. R., & Breggin, G. R. (Eds.). (1994). *Talking back to Prozac*. New York: St. Martin's Press.

Brennan, S. C., Redd, W. H., Jacobsen, P. B., Schorr, O., Heelan, R. T., Sze, G. K., Krol, G., Peters, B. E., Morrissey, J. K. (1988). Anxiety and panic during magnetic resonance scans (letter). *Lancet, 2,* 512.

Brown, T. A., Hertz, R. M., & Barlow, D. H. (1992). New developments in cognitive-behavioral treatment of anxiety disorders. In A. Tasnman (Ed.), *American Psychiatric Press review of psychiatry* (Vol. 11, pp. 285–306). Washington, D.C.: American Psychiatric Press.

Brown, T. A., O'Leary, T. A., & Barlow, D. H. (1993). Generalized anxiety disorder. In D. H. Barlow (Ed.), *Clinical handbook of psychological disorders* (pp. 137–188). New York, N.Y.: Guilford Press.

Bryson, B. (1989, December). Life's little gambles. *Reader's Digest,* 61–62, 64.

Buckley, W. T. (1990, July). How to cope with crisis. *Reader's Digest,* 93–96.

Buda, M., & Tsuang, M. T. (1990). The epidemiology of suicide: Implications for clinical practice. In S. J. Blumenthal & D. J. Kupfer (Eds.), *Suicide over the life cycle: Risk fac-*

tors, assessment, and treatment of suicidal patients. Washington, D.C.: American Psychiatric Association.

Burger, J. M. (1989). Negative reactions to increases in perceived personal control. *Journal of Personality and Social Psychology, 56,* 246–256.

Burke, R. D. (1993). Organizational-level interventions to reduce occupational stressors. *Work and Stress, 7,* 77–87.

Burt, M. R. (1980). Cultural myths and supports for rape. *Journal of Personality and Social Psychology, 38,* 217–230.

Butcher, J. N., & Koss, M. P. (1978). Research on brief and crisis-oriented psychotherapies. In S. L. Garfield & A. E. Bergin (Eds.), *Handbook of psychotherapy and behavior change* (2nd ed.) (pp. 725–767). New York: Wiley.

Byrne, D. (1961). The repression-sensitization scale: Rationale, reliability, and validity. *Journal of Personality, 29,* 334–349.

Calhoun, K. S., & Resick, P. A. (1993). Post-traumatic stress disorder. In D. H. Barlow (Ed.), *Clinical handbook of psychological disorders* (2nd ed.) (pp. 48–98). New York: Guilford Press.

Caplan, G. (1964). *Principles of preventive psychiatry.* New York: Basic Books.

Caplan, G. (1974). *Support systems and community mental health.* New York: Behavioral Publications.

Carlson, C. R., & Hoyle, R. H. (1993). Efficacy of abbreviated progressive muscle relaxation training: A quantitative review of behavioral medicine research. *Journal of Consulting and Clinical Psychology, 61,* 1059–1067.

Carrington, P. (1993). Modern forms of meditation. In P. M. Lehrer & R. L. Woolfolk (Eds.), *Principles and practice of stress management* (2nd ed.) (pp. 139–168). New York: Guilford.

Cartwright, S., Cooper, C., & Barron, A. (1996). The company car driver: Occupational stress as a predictor of motor vehicle accident involvement. *Human Relations, 49,* 195–208.

Carver, C. S., Scheier, M. F., & Weintraub, J. K. (1989). Assessing coping strategies: A theoretically-based approach. *Journal of Personality and Social Psychology, 56,* 267–283.

Caudron, S. (1995). Sexual politics. *Personnel Journal, 74,* 50–61.

Chambless, D. L., & Gillis, M. M. (1993). Cognitive therapy of anxiety disorders. *Journal of Consulting and Clinical Psychology, 61,* 248–260.

Chanel, P. E. (1992). Performance anxiety. *American Journal of Psychiatry, 149,* 278.

Chapman, D. W. (1962). A brief introduction to contemporary disaster research. In G. W. Baker & D. W. Chapman (Eds.), *Man and society in disaster* (pp. 3–22). New York: Basic Books.

Charlesworth, E. A., & Nathan, R. G. (1982). *Stress management: A comprehensive guide to wellness.* Houston: Biobehavioral Press.

Chodoff, P. (1974). Psychiatric aspects of Nazi persecution. In S. Arieti (Ed.), *American handbook of psychiatry,* Vol. VI (2nd ed.) (pp. 932–946). New York: Basic Books.

Christensen, A., Arkowitz, H., & Anderson, J. (1975). Practice dating as treatment for college dating inhibitions. *Behaviour Research and Therapy, 13,* 321–331.

Christensen, A., & Jacobson, N. S. (1994). Who (or what) can do psychotherapy: The status and challenge of nonprofessional therapies. *Psychological Science, 5,* 8–14.

Christensen, A., Jacobson, N. S. & Babcock, J. C. (1995). Integrative behavioral couple therapy. In N. S. Jacobson & A. S. Gurman (Eds.), *Clinical handbook of couple therapy* (pp. 31–64). New York: Guilford.

Clark, D. B., & Agras, W. S. (1991). The assessment and treatment of performance anxiety in musicians. 143rd Annual Meeting of the American Psychiatric Association (1990, New York, New York). *American Journal of Psychiatry, 148,* 598–605.

Clarke, N. B., & Kardachi, B. J. (1977). The treatment of myofascial pain-dysfunction syndrome using the biofeedback principle. *Journal of Periodontology, 48,* 643–645.

Cleary, P. D. (1987). Why people take precautions against health risks. In N. Weinstein (Ed.), *Taking care: Understanding and encouraging self-protective behavior* (pp. 119–149). New York: Cambridge University Press.

Coates, T. J., Stall, R. D., Kegles, S. M., Lo, B., Morin, S. F., & McKusick, L. (1988). AIDS antibody testing. *American Psychologist, 43*, 859–864.

Coffey, P., Leitenberg, H., Henning, K., Turner, T., & Bennet, R. T. (1996). The relation between methods of coping during adulthood with a history of childhood sexual abuse and current psychological adjustment. *Journal of Consulting and Clinical Psychology, 64*, 1090–1093.

Cohen, B. G. F. (1984). Organizational factors affecting stress in the clerical worker. In B. G. F. Cohen (Ed.), *Human aspects in office automation* (pp. 33–42). Amsterdam: Elsevier.

Cohen, S., & Edwards, J. F. (1989). Personality characteristics as moderators of the relationship between stress and disorder. In R. Neufeld (Ed.), *Advances in the investigation of psychological stress* (pp. 235–283). New York: Wiley.

Cohen, S., & Wills, T. A. (1985). Stress, social support, and the buffering hypothesis. *Psychological Bulletin, 98*, 310–357.

Cohler, B. J. (1987). Adversity, resilience, and the study of lives. In E. J. Anthony & B. J. Cohler (Eds.), *The invulnerable child* (pp. 363–424). New York: Guilford.

Cohn, J. B., & Rickels, K. (1989). A pooled, double-blind comparison of the effects of buspirone, diazepam and placebo in women with chronic anxiety. *Current Medical Research and Opinion, 11*, 304–320.

Columbia Area Mental Health Center (1974). Plan for minimizing psychiatric casualties in a disaster. *Hospital and Community Psychiatry, 25*, 665–668.

Compas, B. E., Malcarne, V. L., & Fondacaro, K. M. (1988). Coping with stressful events in older children and young adolescents. *Journal of Consulting and Clinical Psychology, 56*, 405–411.

Cooper, C. L., & Cartwright, S. (1994). Healthy mind, healthy organization—A proactive approach to occupational stress. *Human Relations, 47*, 455–471.

Cooper, C. L., Cooper, R. D., & Eaker, L. H. (1988). *Living with stress*. London: Penguin.

Cooper, C. L. & Faragher, E. B. (1993). Psychosocial stress and breast cancer: The inter-relationship between stress events, coping strategies and personality. *Psychological Medicine, 23*, 653–662.

Cooper, C. L., Mallinger, M., & Kahn, R. (1978). Identifying sources of occupational stress amongst dentists. *Journal of Occupational Psychology, 51*, 227–234.

Cooper, C. J., & Marshall, J. (1976). Occupational sources of stress: A review of the literature relating to coronary heart disease and mental ill health. *Journal of Occupational Psychology, 49*, 11–28.

Costa, P. T., & McCrae, R. R. (1986). Personality stability and its implications for clinical psychology. *Clinical Psychology Review, 6*, 407–423.

Cousins, N. (1976). Anatomy of an illness (as perceived by the patient). *New England Journal of Medicine, 295*, 1458–1463.

Cox, B. J., Norton, G. R., Dorward, J., & Fergusson, P. A. (1989). The relationship between panic attacks and chemical dependencies. *Addictive Behaviors, 14*, 53–60.

Craske, M. G., & Barlow, D. H. (1993). Panic disorder and agoraphobia. In D. H. Barlow (Ed.), *Clinical handbook of psychological disorders* (pp. 1–47). New York: Guilford Press.

Critchlow, B. (1986). The powers of John Barleycorn: Beliefs about the effects of alcohol on social behavior. *American Psychologist, 41*, 751–763.

Crook, C. E., & Jones, S. D. (1989). Educating women about the importance of breast screenings: The nurse's role. *Cancer Nursing, 12*, 161–164.

Crowe, M. J., Marks, J. M., Agras, W. S., & Leitenberg, H. (1972). Time limited desensitization, implosion, and shaping for phobic patients: A crossover study. *Behaviour Research and Therapy, 10*, 319–328.

Crull, P. (1984). The stress effects of sexual harassment in the office. In B. G. F. Cohen (Ed.), *Human aspects in office automation* (pp. 177–186). Amsterdam: Elsevier.

Culbert, S. A., & Crenshaw, J. R. (1972). Coping with the stresses of travel as an opportunity for improving the quality of work and family life. *Family Process, 11,* 321–337.

Curran, J. P. (1977). *Social skills training manual.* Unpublished manuscript. Providence, R.I.: Brown University School/Veterans Administration Hospital.

Curran, J. P., Monti, P. M., & Corriveau, D. P. (1977). *Social skills therapist training manual.* Unpublished manuscript. Providence, R.I: Brown University School/Veterans Administration Hospital.

Curran, J. P., Wallander, J. L., & Farrell, A. D. (1985). Heterosocial skills training. In L. L'Abate & M. A. Milan (Eds.), *Handbook of social skills training and research* (pp. 136–169). New York: Wiley.

Curry, S. L., & Russ, S. W. (1985). Identifying coping strategies in children. *Journal of Child Clinical Psychology, 14,* 61–69.

Csikszentmihalyi, M. (1990). *Flow: The psychology of optimal experience.* New York: Harper & Row.

Danish, S., Arthur, J., & Conter, J. J. (1984). Understanding and intervening in burnout: Strategies for enhancing work satisfaction. Unpublished manuscript, Pennsylvania State University.

Dantzer, R. (1989). Neuroendocrine correlates of control and coping. In A. Steptoe and A. Appels (Eds.), *Stress, personal control and health* (pp. 277–294). Luxembourg, Brussels: Wiley & Sons, Ltd.

Davey, G. C. L. (1992). Classical conditioning and the acquisition of human fears and phobias: A review and synthesis of the literature. *Advances in Behaviour Research and Therapy, 14,* 29–66.

Dawes, R. M. (1991). Biases of retrospection. *Issues in Child Abuse Accusations, 1, (3),* 25–28.

Deffenbacher, J. L., & Suinn, R. M. (1988). Systematic desensitization and the reduction of anxiety. *The Counseling Psychologist, 16,* 9–30.

De Jongh, A., Muris, P., Ter Horst, G., Van Zuuren, F., Schoenmakers, N., & Makkes, P. (1995). One session cognitive treatment of dental phobia: Preparing dental phobics for treatment by restructing cognitions. *Behaviour Research and Therapy, 33,* 947–954.

DeLong, R. D. (1970). Individual differences in patterns of anxiety arousal, stress-relevant information and recovery from surgery. Doctoral dissertation, University of California, Los Angeles.

Depreeuw, E., & De Neve, H. (1992). Test anxiety can harm your health: Some conclusions based on a student typology. In D. G. Forgays, T. Sosnowski, & K. Wrzesniewski (Eds.). *Anxiety: Recent developments in cognitive, psychophysiological, and health research* (pp. 211–228). Washington, D.C.: Taylor & Francis.

DeVeaugh-Geiss, J. (1993). Diagnosis and treatment of obsessive compulsive disorder. *Annual Review of Medicine, 44,* 53–61.

DiCara, L. V., & Miller, N. E. (1968). Instrumental learning of vasomotor responses by rats: Learning to respond differentially in the two ears. *Science, 159,* 1485–1486.

Dickson, P. (1991, March). Rules that explain almost everything. *Readers Digest,* 110–111.

Diekstra, R. F. W. (1989). Suicide and attempted suicide: An international perspective. *Acta Psychiatrica Scandinavica,* 80 (Supplement 354):1.

Dise-Lewis, J. (1988). The Life Events and Coping Inventory: An assessment of stress in children. *Psychosomatic Medicine, 50,* 484–499.

Dixon, P. (1989). *The new official rules.* Reading, MA.: Addison-Wesley.

Dohrenwend, B. S., & Dohrenwend, B. P. (Eds.) (1981). *Stressful life events and their contexts.* New York: Prodist.

D'Zurilla, T. J. (1986). *Problem-solving therapy: A social competence approach to clinical intervention.* New York: Springer.

D'Zurilla, T. J., & Goldfried, M. R. (1971). Problem-solving and behavior modification. *Journal of Abnormal Psychology, 78*, 107–126.

D'Zurilla, T. J., & Nezu, A. M. (1989). Clinical stress management. In A. N. Nezu & C. M. Nezu (Eds.), *Clinical decision making in behavior therapy: A problem-solving perspective* (pp. 371–400). Champaign, Ill.: Research Press.

D'Zurilla, T. J., & Sheedy, C. F. (1991). Relation between social problem-solving ability and subsequent level of psychological stress in college students. *Journal of Personality and Social Psychology, 61*, 841–846.

Ebata, A. T., & Moos, R. H. (1991). Coping and adjustment in distressed and healthy adolescents. *Journal of Applied Developmental Psychology, 12*, 33–54.

Ebata, A. T., & Moos, R. H. (1994). Personal, situational, and contextual correlates of coping in adolescence. *Journal of Research on Adolescence, 4*, 99–125.

Eisenberg, D. M., Kessler, R. C., Foster, C. Norlock, F. E., Calkins, D. R., & Delbanco, T. L. (1993). Unconventional medicine in the United States: Prevalence, costs, and patterns of use. *New England Journal of Medicine, 328*, 246–252.

Eitinger, L. (1980). The concentration camp syndrome and its late sequelae. In J. E. Dimsdale (Ed.), *Survivors, victims, and perpetrators: Essays on the Nazi Holocaust* (pp. 127–162) Washington, D.C.: Hemisphere.

Ekman, P., & Friesen, W. V. (1975). *Unmasking the face.* Englewood Cliffs, N.J.: Prentice-Hall.

Elias, M. (1996, July 8). Epidemic of violence on the job at an all-time high. *USA Today,* p. A1.

Elkins, M. (1971). *Forged in fury.* New York: Ballantine Books.

Elliott, T. R. (1992). Problem-solving appraisal, oral contraceptive use, and menstrual pain. *Journal of Applied Social Psychology, 22*, 286–297.

Elliott, T. R., Godshall, F. J., Herrick, S. & Witty, T. E. (1991). Problem-solving appraisal and psychological adjustment following spinal cord injury. *Cognitive Therapy and Research, 15*, 387–398.

Elliott, T. R., Godshall, F., Shrout, J. R., & Witty, T. E. (1990). Problem-solving appraisal, self-reported study habits, and performance of academically at-risk students. *Journal of Counseling Psychology, 37*, 203–207.

Elliott, R. H., & Jarrett, D. T. (1994). Violence in the workplace: The role of human resource management. *Public Personnel Management, 23*, 287–299.

Ellis, A. (1971). *Growth through reason.* Palo Alto: Science and Behavior Books.

Ellis, A., & Bernard, M. E. (1985). What is rational-emotive therapy (RET)? In A. Ellis & M. E. Bernard (Eds.), *Clinical applications of rational-emotive therapy* (pp. 1–30). New York: Plenum.

Ellis, A. E., & Harper, R. (1975). A *new guide to rational living.* North Hollywood, Calif.: Wilshire Books.

Ellis, A. E., & Whitely, J. M. (1979). *Theoretical and empirical foundations of rational-emotive therapy.* Monterey, Calif.: Brooks/Cole.

Ellis, E. M. (1983). A review of empirical rape research: Victim reactions and response to treatment. *Clinical Psychology Review, 3*, 473–490.

Ellison, J. M., Hughes, D. H., & White, K. A. (1989). An emergency psychiatry update. *Hospital and Community Psychiatry, 40*, 250–260.

Emery, P. E., Emery, V. O., & Berry, N. (1993). Trauma psychology: A psychoanalytic model and application. *Journal of Social Behavior and Personality, 8*, 29–48.

Endler, N. S., & Parker, J. D. A. (1990). Multidimensional assessment of coping: A critical evaluation. *Journal of Personality and Social Psychology, 58*, 844–854.

Engels, G. I., Garnefski, N., & Diekstra, R. F. (1993). Efficacy of rational-emotive therapy: A quantitative analysis. *Journal of Consulting and Clinical Psychology, 61*, 1083–1090.

Esterling, B. A., Antoni, M. H., Fletcher, M. A., Margulies, S., & Schneiderman, N. (1994). Emotional disclosure through writing or speaking modulates blatant

Epstein-Barr Virus Antibody titers. *Journal of Consulting and Clinical Psychology, 62,* 130–140.

Evans, G. W., & Cohen, S. (1987). Environmental stress. In D. Stokols & I. Altman (Eds.), *Handbook of Environmental Psychology, Volume 1* (pp. 571–610). New York: Wiley.

Everly, G. S., & Mitchell, J. T. (1995). Prevention of work-related posttraumatic stress: The Critical Incident Stress Debriefing Process. In L. R. Murphy, J. H. Hurrell, S. L. Sauter, & G. P. Keita (Eds.), *Job stress interventions* (pp. 173–183). Washington, D.C.: American Psychological Association.

Eysenck, H. J. (1990). The prediction of death from cancer by means of personality/stress questionnaire: too good to be true? *Perceptual and Motor Skills, 71,* 216–218.

Eysenck, H. J. (1991). *Smoking, personality, and stress: Psychosocial factors in the prevention of cancer and coronary heart disease.* New York: Springer-Verlag.

Fairbank, J. A., Schlenger, W. E., Caddell, J. M., & Woods, G. M. (1993). Posttraumatic stress disorder. In P. B. Sutker & H. E. Adams (Eds.), *Comprehensive handbook of psychopathology* (2nd ed.) (pp. 145–165). New York: Plenum.

Farberow, N. L. (1974). *Suicide.* Morristown, N. J.: General Learning Press.

Farberow, N. L., Heilig, S. M., Litman, R. E. (No date). Training manual for evaluation and emergency management of suicidal persons. Unpublished manuscript, Suicide Prevention Center, Los Angeles.

Felsman, J. K., Vaillant, G. E. (1987). Resilient children as adults: A 40-year study. In E. J. Anthony & B. J. Cohler (Eds.), *The invulnerable child* (pp. 289–314). New York: Guilford.

Fenz, W. D. (1975). Strategies for coping with stress. In I. G. Sarason & C. D. Spielberger (Eds.), *Stress and anxiety,* (Volume 2) (pp. 305–336). Washington, D.C.: Hemisphere.

Fenz, W. D., & Epstein, S. (1967). Gradients of physiological arousal in parachutists as a function of an approaching jump. *Psychosomatic Medicine, 29,* 33–51.

Feurstein, M., Labbe, E. E., & Kuczmierczyk, A. R. (1986). *Health psychology: A psychobiological perspective.* New York: Raven Press.

Field, T. (1991). Stress and coping from pregnancy through the postnatal period. In E. M. Cummings, A. L. Greene, & K. H. Karraker (Eds.), *Life-span developmental psychology: Perspectives on stress and coping* (pp. 45–59). Hillsdale, N.J.: Lawrence Erlbaum.

Fields-Meyer, T. (1995, September 11). Death in a crowded place. *People,* pp. 99–103.

Finkelhor, D., & Hotaling, G. (1983). Sexual abuse in the National Incidence Study of Child Abuse and Neglect (Final Report, National Center on Child Abuse, Grant 90-CA840/01). Durham, N.H. Family Violence Research Program, University of New Hampshire.

Flanders, J. P. (1976). *Practical psychology.* New York: Harper & Row.

Flor, H., & Turk, D. C. (1989). Psychophysiology of chronic pain: Do chronic pain patients exhibit symptom-specific psychophysiological responses? *Psychological Bulletin, 105,* 215–259.

Flynn, T. M., Taylor, P., & Pollard, C. A. (1992). Use of mobile phones in the behavioral treatment of driving phobias. *Journal of Behavior Therapy and Experimental Psychiatry, 23,* 299–302.

Foa, E. B., Hearst-Ikeda, D., & Perry, K. J. (1995). Evaluation of a brief cognitive-behavioral program for the prevention of chronic PTSD in recent assault victims. *Journal of Consulting and Clinical Psychology, 63,* 948–955.

Foa, E. B., & Kozak, M. J. (1986). Emotional processing of fear: Exposure to corrective information. *Psychological Bulletin, 99,* 20–35.

Foa, E. B., Riggs, D. S., Massie, E. D., & Yarczower, M. (1995). The impact of fear activation and anger on the efficacy of exposure treatment for posttraumatic stress disorder. *Behavior Therapy, 26,* 487–499.

Foa, E. B., Rothbaum, B. O., Riggs, D. S., & Murdock, T. B. (1991). Treatment of post-traumatic stress disorder in rape victims: A comparison between cognitive-behavioral procedures and counseling. *Journal of Consulting and Clinical Psychology, 59,* 715–723.

Foa, E. B., Rothbaum, B. O., & Steketee, G. S. (1993). Treatment of rape victims. *Journal of Interpersonal Violence, 8,* 256–276.

Folkman, S., & Lazarus, R. S. (1985). If it changes it must be a process: Study of emotion and coping during three stages of a college examination. *Journal of Personality and Social Psychology, 48,* 150–170.

Folkman, S., Lazarus, R. S., Dunkel-Schetter, C., DeLongis, A., & Gruen, R. J. (1986). Dynamics of a stressful encounter: Cognitive appraisal, coping, and encounter outcomes. *Journal of Personality and Social Psychology, 50,* 992–1003.

Forceful hostage hard on self, others. (1991, December 8). *Richmond Times-Dispatch,* p. A–2.

Ford, C. V. (1986). The somatizing disorders. 32nd Annual Meeting of the Academy of Psychosomatic Medicine. *Psychosomatics, 27,* 327–337.

Ford, C. V. (1995). Dimensions of somatization and hypochondriasis. Special issue: Malingering and conversion reactions. *Neurologic Clinics, 13,* 241–253.

Forsythe, C. J., & Compas, B. E. (1987). Interaction of cognitive appraisals of stressful events and coping: Testing the goodness of fit hypothesis. *Cognitive Therapy and Research, 11,* 473–485.

Frank, E., Anderson, B., Stewart, B. D., & Dancu, C. (1988). Efficacy of cognitive behavior therapy and systematic desensitization in the treatment of rape trauma. *Behavior Therapy, 19,* 403–420.

Freud, S. (1936). *The problem of anxiety.* New York: Norton.

Friedman, M., & Rosenman, R. H. (1974). *Type A behavior and your heart.* New York: Knopf.

Friedman, M., & Ulmer, D. (1984). *Treating Type A behavior and your heart.* New York: Knopf.

Fritz, C. E., & Marks, E. S. (1954). The NORC studies of human behavior in disaster. *Journal of Social Issues, 10,* 26–41.

Frueh, B. C., Turner, S. M., Beidel, D. C., Mirabella, R. F., & Jones, W. J. (1996). Trauma Management Therapy: A preliminary evaluation of a multicomponent behavioral treatment for chronic combat-related PTSD. *Behaviour Research and Therapy, 34,* 533–543.

Galassi, J. P., Galassi, M. D., & Fulkerson, K. (1984). *Assertion training in theory and practice: An update.* In C. M. Franks (Ed.), *New developments in behavior therapy: From research to clinical application* (pp. 319–376). New York: Haworth Press.

Galassi, M. D., & Galassi, J. P. (1977). *Assert yourself: How to be your own person.* New York: Human Sciences Press.

Gale, E. N. (1986). Behavioral approaches to temporomandibular disorder. *The Society of Behavioral Medicine, 8,* 11–16.

Gale, E. N., & Carlsson, S. G. (1978). Frustration and temporomandibular joint pain. *Oral Surgery, 45,* 39.

Garmezy, N., & Rutter, M. (1985). Acute reactions to stress. In M. Rutter & L. Hersov (Eds.), *Child psychiatry: Modern approaches,* 2nd ed. (pp. 152–176). Oxford: Blackwell Scientific.

Gebhardt, D. L., & Crump, C. E. (1990). Employee fitness and wellness programs in the workplace. *American Psychologist, 45,* 262–272.

Girdano, D. A., Everly, G. S., & Dusek, D. E. (1990). *Controlling stress and tension: A holistic approach.* Englewood Cliffs, N.J.: Prentice-Hall.

Glaser, R., & Kiecolt-Glaser, J. K. (1987). Stress-associated depression in cellular immunity: implications for acquired immune deficiency syndrome (AIDS). *Brain, Behavior & Immunity, 1,* 107–112

Gleser, G. C., & Ihilevich, D. (1969). An objective instrument for measuring defense mechanisms. *Journal of Consulting and Clinical Psychology, 33,* 51–60.

Glick, I. O., Weiss, R. S., & Parkes, C. M. (1974). *First year of bereavement.* New York: Wiley.

Glyshaw, K., Cohen, L., & Towbes, L. (1989). Coping strategies and psychological distress: Prospective analyses of early and middle adolescents. *American Journal of Community Psychology, 17,* 607–623.

Goldfried, M. (1971). Systematic desensitization as training in self-control. *Journal of Consulting and Clinical Psychology, 37,* 228–234.

Goldhagen, D. J. (1996). *Hitler's willing executioners: Ordinary Germans and the Holocaust.* New York: Alfred A. Knopf.

Goldiamond, I. (1965). Self-control procedures in personal behavior problems. *Psychological Reports, 17,* 851–868.

Gore, S. (1978). The effect of social support in moderating the health consequences of unemployment. *Journal of Health and Social Behavior, 19,* 157–165.

Gorman, J. M., Kertzner, Cooper, T., Goetz, R. R., Logomasino, I., Novacenko, H., Williams, J. B., Stern, Y., Mayeux, R., & Ehrhardt, A. A. (1991). Glucocorticoid level and neuropsychiatric symptoms in homosexual men with HIV infection. *American Journal of Psychiatry, 148,* 41–45.

Gorman, J. M., Warne, P. A., Begg, M. D., & Cooper, T. B., Novacenko, H., Williams, J. B., Rabkin, J. Stern, Y. Ehrhardt, A. A. (1992). Serum prolactin levels in homosexual and bisexual men with HIV infection. *American Journal of Psychiatry, 149,* 367–370.

Gramling, S. E., & Auerbach, S. M. (1998). *Stress management workbook: Techniques and self-assessment procedures.* Englewood Cliffs, N.J.: Prentice-Hall.

Gramling, S. E., Clawson, E. P., & McDonald, M. K. (1996). Perceptual and cognitive abnormality model of hypochondriasis: Amplification and physiological reactivity in women. *Psychosomatic Medicine, 58,* 423–431.

Gramling, S. E., Grayson, R. L., Sullivan, T. N. & Schwartz, S. (1996). Schedule-induced masseter EMG in facial pain subjects versus no-pain controls. *Physiology and Behavior, 61,* 1–9.

Gramling, S. E., Neblett, J., Grayson, R., & Townsend, D. (1996). Temporomandibular disorder: Efficacy of an oral habit reversal treatment program. *Journal of Behavior Therapy and Experimental Psychiatry, 27,* 212–218.

Grassick, P. (1990). The fear behind the fear: A case study of apparent simple injection phobia. *Journal of Behavior Therapy and Experimental Psychiatry, 21,* 281–287.

Gray, J. A. (1987). *The psychology of fear and stress..* Cambridge, England: Cambridge University Press.

Greenberg, J. S. (1993). *Comprehensive stress management.* Dubuque, IA.: Brown & Benchmark.

Greene, C. S., Olson, R. E., & Laskin, D. M. (1982). Psychological factors in the etiology, progression and treatment of myofacial pain syndrome. *Journal of the American Dental Association, 105,* 443–448.

Gregorius, H. H., & Smith, T. S. (1991). The adolescent mentally ill chemical abusers: Special considerations in dual diagnosis. *Journal of Adolescent Chemical Dependency, 1,* 79–113.

Greist, J. H. (1990). Treatment of obsessive-compulsive disorder: Psychotherapies, drugs, and other somatic treatments. *Journal of Clinical Psychiatry, 51,* 44–55.

Grilly, D. M. (Ed.) (1989). *Drugs and human behavior.* Needham, Mass.: Allyn and Bacon.

Gross, L. (1988). *The last Jews in Berlin.* New York: Simon & Schuster.

Grossarth-Maticek, R., Bastiaans, J., & Kanazir, D. T. (1985). Psychosocial factors as strong predictors of mortality from cancer, ischaemic heart disease and stroke: The Yugoslav prospective study. *Journal of Psychosomatic Research, 29,* 167–176.

Guard held hostage says prayer helped pass time. (1991, September 21). *Richmond Times-Dispatch,* p. A–2.

Gullick, E. L. (1973). Behavioral contracting: A controlled study. Unpublished doctoral dissertation, University of Georgia.

Haaga, D. A., & Davison, G. C. (1993). An appraisal of rational-emotive therapy. *Journal of Consulting and Clinical Psychology, 61*, 215–220.

Haber, J. D., Moss, R. A., Kuczmierczyk, A. R., & Garrett, J. C. (1983). Assessment and treatment of stress in myofascial pain-dysfunction syndrome: A model for analysis. *Journal of Oral Rehabilitation, 10*, 187–196.

Hamilton, M., & Yee, J. (1990). Rape knowledge and propensity to rape. *Journal of Research in Personality, 24*, 111–122.

Hanback, J. W. & Revelle, W. (1978). Arousal and perceptual sensitivity in hypochondriacs. *Journal of Abnormal Psychology, 87*, 523–530.

Hancock, L. (1995, March 6). Breaking point. *Newsweek*, pp. 56–61.

Hanson, C. L., Cigrang, J., Harris, M., Carle, D., Relyea, G., & Burghen, G. (1989). Coping styles in youths with insulin-dependent diabetes mellitus. *Journal of Consulting and Clinical Psychology, 57*, 644–651.

Harvey, P., Forehand, R., Brown, C., & Holmes, T. (1988). The prevention of sexual abuse: Examination of the effectiveness of a program with kindergarten-age children. *Behavior Therapy, 19*, 429–435.

Hatton, C. L., Valente, S. M., & Rink, A. (1977). Assessment of suicide risk. In C. L. Hatton, S. M. Valente, & A. Rink (Eds.), *Suicide assessment and intervention*. New York: Appleton-Century-Crofts.

Hay, D., & Oken, D. (1972). The psychological stresses of intensive care nursing. *Psychosomatic Medicine, 34*, 109–118.

Hedges, S. J., Newman, R. J., & Cary, P. (1995, June 26). What's wrong with the FAA? *U.S. News and World Report, 118(25)*, 28–37.

Heide, F. J., & Borkovec, T. D. (1983). Relaxation-induced anxiety: Paradoxical anxiety enhancement due to relaxation training. *Journal of Consulting and Clinical Psychology, 51*, 171–182.

Heinrich, H. W. (1931). *Industrial accident prevention: A scientific approach by H. W. Heinrich.* New York: McGraw-Hill.

Henbeck, J. W., & Revelle, W. (1978). Arousal and perceptual sensitivity in hypochrondriasis. *Journal of Abnormal Psychology, 87*, 523–530.

Heppner, P. P., Baumgardner, A. H., & Jackson, J. (1982, August). *Problem-solving styles, depression, and attribution styles: Are they related?* Paper presented at American Psychological Association Meeting, Washington, D.C.

Heppner, P. P., Reeder, B. L., & Larson, L. M. (1983). Cognitive variables associated with personal problem-solving appraisal: Implications for counseling. *Journal of Counseling Psychology, 30*, 537–545.

Hilberg, R. (1980). The nature of the process. In J. E. Dimsdale (Ed.), *Survivors, victims, and perpetrators: Essays on the Nazi Holocaust* (pp. 5–54). Washington, D.C.: Hemisphere.

Hodges, W. F., & Spielberger, C. D. (1966). The effects of threat of shock on heart rate for subjects who differ in manifest anxiety and fear of shock. *Psychophysiology, 2*, 287–294.

Hogan, R. A. (1968). The implosive technique. *Behaviour Research and Therapy, 6*, 423–431.

Holmes, D. S. (1984). Meditation and somatic arousal reduction: A review of the evidence. *American Psychologist, 39*, 1–10.

Holmes, D. S. (1985). To meditate or rest? The answer is rest. *American Psychologist, 40*, 728–731.

Holmes , T. H., & Rahe, R. H. (1967). The Social Readjustment Rating Scale. *Journal of Psychosomatic Research, 11*, 213–218.

Holohan, C. J., & Moos, R. H. (1987). Personal and contextual determinants of coping strategies. *Journal of Personality and Social Psychology, 52*, 946–955.

Holt, R. R. (1993). Occupational stress. In L. Goldberger & S. Breznitz (Eds.), *Handbook of stress: Theoretical and clinical aspects, Second edition* (pp. 342–367). New York: Free Press.

Horne, R. L., & Picard, R. S. (1979). Psychosocial risk factors for lung cancer. *Psychosomatic Medicine, 41,* 503–514.

Horowitz, M. (1984). Short-term therapeutic interventions in stress-related disorders. In M. R. Zales (Ed.), *Stress in health and disease* (pp. 189–205). New York: Bruner/Mazel.

House, J. A. (1981). *Work stress and social support.* Reading, Mass.: Addison-Wesley.

Hull, J. G., & Bond, C. F. (1986). Social and behavioral consequences of alcohol consumption and expectancy: A meta-analysis. *Psychological Bulletin, 99,* 347–359.

Hunt, C., & Singh, M. (1991). Generalized anxiety disorder. *International Review of Psychiatry, 3,* 215–229.

Hytten, K., Jensen, A., & Skauli, G. (1990). Stress inoculation training for smoke divers and free fall lifeboat passengers. *Aviation, Space, and Environmental Medicine, 61,* 983–988.

Ivancevich, J. M., Matteson, M. T., Freedman, S. M., & Phillips, J. S. (1990). Worksite stress management interventions. *American Psychologist, 45,* 252–261.

Jackson, S. E. (1984). Organizational practices for preventing burnout. In A. S. Sethi & R. S. Schuler (Eds.), *Handbook of organizational stress coping strategies* (pp. 89–111). Cambridge, Mass.: Ballinger.

Jacobs, D. (1983). Evaluation and management of the violent patient in emergency settings. *Psychiatric Clinics of North America, 6,* 259–269.

Jacobs, T. J., & Charles, E. (1980). Life events and the occurrence of cancer in children. *Psychosomatic Medicine, 42,* 11–24.

Jacobson, E. (1924). The technic of progressive relaxation. *Journal of Nervous and Mental Disease, 60,* 568–578.

Jacobson, E. (1938). *Progressive relaxation* (2nd ed.). Chicago: University of Chicago Press.

Jacobson, P. B. (1991). Treating a man with a needle phobia who requires daily injections of medication. *Hospital and Community Psychiatry, 42,* 877–878.

James, B., & James, N. M. (1973). Tranquilizers and examination stress. *Journal of the American College Health Association, 21,* 241–243.

James, I., & Savage, I. (1984). Beneficial effect of nadolol on anxiety-induced disturbances of performance in musicians: A comparison with diazepam and placebo. *American Heart Journal, 4,* 1150–1155.

James, S. A., Hartnett, S. A., & Kalsbeck, W. D. (1983). John Henryism and blood pressure differences among Black men. *Journal of Behavioral Medicine, 6,* 259–275.

Janis, I. L. (1958). *Psychological stress.* New York: Wiley.

Janis, I. L. (1972). *Victims of groupthink.* Boston: Houghton Mifflin.

Janis, I. L. (1982). Decision making under stress. In L. Goldberger & S. Bresnitz (Eds.). *Handbook of stress: Theoretical and clinical aspects* (pp. 68–87). New York: Free Press.

Janis, I. L., Mahl, G. F, Kagan, J., & Holt, R. R. (1969). *Personality: Dynamics, development, and assessment.* New York: Harcourt, Brace & World.

Janis, I. L., & Mann, L. (1977). *Decision making: A psychological analysis of conflict, choice, and commitment.* New York: Free Press.

Janoff-Bulman, R. (1989). The benefits of illusions, the threat of disillusionment, and the limitations of accuracy. *Journal of Social and Clinical Psychology, 8,* 158–177.

Jason, L. A., Curran, T., Goodman, D., & Smith, M. (1989). A media-based stress management intervention. *Journal of Community Psychology, 17,* 155–165.

Jeffrey, R. W. (1989). Risk behaviors and health: Contrasting individual and population perspectives. *American Psychologist, 44,* 1194–1202.

Jelinek, J. M., & Williams, T. (1984). Post-traumatic stress disorder and substance abuse in Vietnam combat veterans: Treatment problems, strategies and recommendations. *Journal of Substance Abuse Treatment, 1,* 87–97.

Jenkins, C. D., Rosenman, R. H., & Friedman, M. (1967). Development of an objective psychological test for the determination of the coronary prone behavior pattern in employed men. *Journal of Chronic Diseases, 20,* 371–379.

Jensen, J. A. (1994). An investigation of eye movement desensitization (EMD/R) as a treatment for posttraumatic stress disorder (PTSD) symptoms of Vietnam combat veterans. *Behavior Therapy, 25,* 311–325.

Johnson, B. K., & Kenkel, M. B. (1991). Stress, coping, and adjustment in female adolescent incest victims. *Child Abuse and Neglect, 15,* 293–305.

Jones, C. (1995, July 23). Benefits a big deal to Motorola workers. *Richmond Times Dispatch,* pp. A1, A14.

Jones, J. W., & Boye, M. W. (1992). Job stress and employee counterproductivity. In J. C. Quick, L. R. Murphy, J. J. Hurrell, Jr. (Eds.), *Stress and well-being at work* (pp. 239–251). Washington, D.C.: American Psychological Association.

Julien, R. M. (Ed.) (1995). *A primer of drug action: A concise, nontechnical guide to the actions, uses, and side effects of psychoactive drugs* (7th ed.). New York: W. H. Freeman and Company.

Kagan, J. (1983). Stress and coping in early development. In N. Garmezy & M. Rutter (Eds.), *Stress, coping, and development in children* (pp. 191–216). New York: McGraw-Hill.

Kagan, J., Snidman, N., & Arcus, D. M. (1993). Initial reactions to unfamiliarity. *Current Directions in Psychological Science, 1,* 171–174.

Kapel, L., Glaros, A. G., & McGlynn, D. (1989). Psychophysiological responses to stress in patients with myofascial pain-dysfunction. *Journal of Behavioral Medicine, 12,* 397–406.

Kaplan, H. I., & Sadock, B. J. (1996). *Pocket handbook of clinical psychiatry* (2nd ed.). Baltimore: Williams & Wilkins.

Karaki, M. (1991). Work and stress in workers in Tokyo: Its actual state, and anti-stress countermeasures taken by employers. *Journal of Human Ergology, 20,* 137–145.

Karasek, R. (1990). Lower health risk with increased job control among white collar workers. *Journal of Organizational Behavior, 11,* 171–185.

Karasek, R., & Theorell, T. (1990). *Healthy work: Stress, productivity and working life.* New York: Basic Books.

Karniol, R., & Ross, M. (1996). The motivational impact of temporal focus: Thinking about the future and the past. In J. T. Spence, J. M. Darley, & D. J. Foss (Eds.), *Annual review of psychology, Volume 47, 1996.* Palo Alto, Calif.: Annual Reviews.

Karraker, K. H., & Lake, M. A. (1991). Normative stress and coping processes in infancy. In E. M. Cummings, A. L. Greene, & K. H. Karraker (Eds.), *Life-span developmental psychology: Perspectives on stress and coping* (pp. 85–108). Hillsdale, N.J.: Lawrence Erlbaum.

Katkin, E. S. (1971). *Instrumental autonomic conditioning.* Morristown, N. J.: General Learning Press.

Katz, J. O., & Rugh, J. D. (1986). Psychophysiological aspects of oral disorders. *Annals of Behavioral Medicine, 8,* 3–9.

Katz, R. C., Wilson, L., & Frazer, N. (1994). Anxiety and its determinants in patients undergoing magnetic resonance imaging. *Journal of Behavior Therapy & Experimental Psychiatry, 25,* 131–134.

Kazdin, A. (1976). Developing assertive behavior through covert modeling. In J. D. Krumboltz & C. E. Thorenson (Eds.), *Counseling methods* (pp. 475–486). New York: Holt, Rinehart, & Winston.

Keefe, T. (1988). Stress-coping skills: An ounce of prevention in direct practice. *Social Casework, 69,* 475–482.

Keicolt-Glaser, J. K., & Glaser, R. (1987). Psychosocial moderators of immune function. *Annals of Behavioral Medicine, 9,* 16–19.

Keita, G. P., & Hurrell, J. J., Jr. (Eds.) (1994). *Job stress in a changing workforce.* Washington, D.C.: American Psychological Association.

Keller, F. S., & Schoenfeld, W. N. (1950). *Principles of psychology.* New York: Appleton-Century-Crofts.

Kellner, R. (1990). Somatization: Theories and research. *Journal of Nervous & Mental Disease, 178,* 150–160.

Kendall, P. C. (1993). Cognitive-behavioral therapy with youth: Guiding theory, current status, and emerging developments. *Journal of Consulting and Clinical Psychology, 61,* 235–247.

Kendall, P. C., & Bemis, K. M. (1983). Thought and action in psychotherapy: The cognitive-behavioral approaches. In M. Hersen, A. E. Kazdin, & A. E. Bellack (Eds.), *The Clinical Psychology Handbook* (pp. 565–592). New York: Pergamon.

Keneally, T. (1982). *Schindler's ark (Schindler's list).* London: Hodder & Stoughton.

Kertzner, R., Goetz, R., Todak, G., Cooper T., Lin, S., Reddy, M., Novacenko, H., Williams, J. B., Ehrhardt, A. A., Gorman, J. M. (1993). Cortisol levels, immune status, and mood in homosexual men with and without HIV infection. *American Journal of Psychiatry, 150,* 1674–1678.

Khantzian, E. J. (1985). Self-regulation and self-medication factors in alcoholism and the addictions. Similarities and differences. *Recent Developments in Alcoholism, 8,* 255–271.

Khantzian, E. J. (1985). The self medication hypothesis of addictive disorders: Focus on heroin and cocaine dependence. *American Journal of Psychiatry, 142,* 1259–1264.

Kihlstrom, J. F. (1987). The cognitive unconscious. *Science, 237,* 1445–1452.

Kilpatrick, D. G., & Calhoun, K. S. (1988). Early behavioral treatment for rape trauma: Efficacy or artifact? *Behavior Therapy, 19,* 421–427.

Kilpatrick, D. G., & Veronen, L. J. (1983). Treatment for rape-related problems: Crisis intervention is not enough. In L. Cohen, W. Claiborn, & G. A. Specter (Eds.), *Crisis Intervention* (2nd ed.) (pp. 165–185). New York: Human Sciences Press.

Kimble, G. A. (1961). *Hilgard and Marquis' conditioning and learning.* New York: Appleton-Century-Crofts.

King, N. J., & Gullone, E. (1990). Acceptability of fear reduction procedures with children. *Journal of Behavior Therapy and Experimental Psychiatry, 21,* 1–8.

King, N. J., Hamilton, O. I., & Ollendick, T. H. (1988). *Children's phobias: A behavioural perspective.* Chichester: Wiley.

Kleber, H. D. (1990). The nosology of abuse and dependence. *Journal of Psychiatric Research, 24 Suppl.2,* 57–64.

Kleiman, R. (1977). The bereavement crisis: A review of the literature with implications for intervention. *Crisis Intervention, 8,* 126–145.

Klerman, G. L., Weissman, M. M., Markowitz, J., Glick, I., Wilner, P. J., Mason, B., Shear, M. K. (1994). Medication and psychotherapy. In A. H. Bergin & S. L. Garfield (Eds.), *Handbook of psychotherapy and behavior change* (pp. 734–782). John Wiley & Sons.

Klorman, R., Weerts, T. C., Hastings, J. E., Melamed, B. G., & Lang, P. J. (1974). Psychometric description of some specific-fear questionnaires. *Behavior Therapy, 5,* 401–409.

Klusman, L. E., Moulton, J. M., Hornbostel, L. K., & Picano, J. J. (1991). Neuropsychological abnormalities in asymptomatic HIV seropositive military personnel. *Journal of Neuropsychiatry & Clinical Neurosciences, 3,* 422–428.

Kobasa, S. C. (1982). The hardy personality: Toward a social psychology of stress and health. In G. Sanders & J. Suls (Eds.), *Social psychology of health and illness* (pp. 3–32). Hillsdale, N.J.: Erlbaum.

Kolko, D. J., & Milan, M. A. (1985). Conceptual and methodological issues in the behavioral assessment of heterosocial skills. In L. L'Abate & M. A. Milan (Eds.), *Handbook of social skills training and research* (pp. 50–73). New York: Wiley.

Konner, M. (1990). *Why the reckless survive*. New York: Viking.

Koop, E. (1986). *The health consequences of involuntary smoking*. Washington, D.C.: U.S. Government Printing Office.

Kramer, M. (1974). *Reality shock: Why nurses leave nursing*. St. Louis: Mosby.

Kramer, P. D. (Ed.). (1993). *Listening to Prozac: A psychiatrist explores antidepressant drugs and the remaking of the self*. New York, N.Y.: Penguin Books.

Krantz, D. S., Baum, A., & Wideman, M. (1980). Assessment of preferences for self-treatment and information in health-care. *Journal of Personality and Social Psychology, 39*, 977–990.

Krop, H., & Krause, S. (1976). The elimination of a shark phobia by self-administered systematic desensitization. *Journal of Behavior Therapy and Experimental Psychiatry, 7*, 293–294.

Kurdek, L. A., & Sinclair, R. J. (1988). Adjustment of adolescents in two-parent nuclear, stepfather, and mother-custody families. *Journal of Consulting and Clinical Psychology, 56*, 91–96.

Kvale, S., & Bruce, B. (1992). Family-based desensitization of an MRI phobia. Unpublished manuscript, Mayo Clinic, Rochester, Minnesota.

L'Abate, L., & Milan, M. A. (Eds.) (1985). *Handbook of social skills training and research*. New York: Wiley.

Lamb, D. H. (1969). The effects of public speaking on self-report, physiological, and behavioral measures of anxiety. Doctoral dissertation, Florida State University.

Lang, P. J. (1979). A bio-informational theory of emotional imagery. *Psychophysiology, 6*, 495–511.

LaPerriere, A., Antoni, M., Schneiderman, N., Ironson, G., Klimas, N., Caralis, P., Fletcher, M.A. (1990). Exercise intervention attenuates emotional distress and natural killer cell decrements following notification of positive serologic status for HIV-1. *Biofeedback & Self-Regulation, 15*, 229–242.

LaPerriere, A., Fletcher, M., Antoni, M., Klimas, N., Ironson, G., & Schneiderman, N. (1991). Aerobic exercise training in an AIDS risk group. *International Journal of Sports Medicine, 12*, s53–s57.

LaPerriere, A., Ironson, G., Antoni, M., Schneiderman, N., Klimas, N., & Fletcher, M. (1994). Exercise and psychoneuroimmunology. *Medical Science and Sports Exercise, 26*, 182–190.

Laskin, D. M. (1969). Etiology of pain-dysfunction syndrome. *Journal of the American Dental Association, 79*, 147–153.

Laskin, D. M., & Block, S. (1986). Diagnosis and treatment of myofacial pain-dysfunction (MPD) syndrome. *Journal of Prosthetic Dentistry, 56*, 75–84.

Latane, B., & Rodin, J. (1977). A lady in distress: Inhibiting effects of friends and strangers on bystander intervention. In A. Aronson (Ed.), *Readings about the social animal* (pp. 28–41). San Francisco: W. H. Freeman.

The latest head trip: Virtual-reality technology may be a cost-effective therapy. (1996, February 12). U.S. *News and World Report*, p. 55.

Lavin, N. I., Thorpe, J. G., Barker, J. G., Blakemore, C. B., & Conway, C. G. (1961). Behavior therapy in a case of transvestism. *Journal of Nervous and Mental Disease, 133*, 346–353.

Lawrence, P. R. (1975). Individual differences in the world of work. In E. L. Cass & F. G. Zimmer (Eds.), *Man and work in society* (pp. 19–29). New York: Van Nostrand Reinhold.

Lazarus, R. S. (1983). The costs and benefits of denial. in S. Bresnitz (Ed.), *The denial of stress* (pp. 1–32). New York: International Universities Press.

Lazarus, R. S., & Folkman, S. (1984). *Stress, appraisal, and coping*. New York: Springer.

Leccese, A. P. (Ed.) (1991). *Drugs and society: Behavioral medicines and abusable drugs*. Englewood Cliffs, N.J.: Prentice-Hall.

Lehman, D. R., Ellard, J. H., & Wortman, C. B. (1986). Social support for the bereaved: Recipients' and providers' perspectives on what is helpful. *Journal of Consulting and Clinical Psychology, 54*, 438–446.

Lehman, D. R., Wortman, C. B., & Williams, A. F. (1987). Long-term effects of losing a spouse or child in a motor vehicle crash. *Journal of Personality and Social Psychology, 52*, 218–231.

Lehrer, P. M., & Woolfolk, R. L. (1993). Research on clinical issues in stress management. In P. M. Lehrer & R. L. Woolfolk (Eds.), *Principles and practice of stress management* (2nd ed.) (pp. 521–538). New York: Guilford.

Leitenberg, H., Greenwald, E., & Cado, S. (1992). A retrospective study of long-term methods of coping with having been sexually abused during childhood. *Child Abuse and Neglect, 16*, 399–407.

Lemonick, M. D., & Dorfman, A. (1990, January 29). An overblown asbestos scare? *Time*, p. 65.

Leon, G. R., Butcher, J. N., Kleinman, M., Goldberg, A., & Almagor, M. (1981). Survivors of the Holocaust and their children: Current status and adjustment. *Journal of Personality and Social Psychology, 41*, 503–516.

Levenson, M. R. (1990). Risk taking and personality. *Journal of Personality and Social Psychology, 58*, 1073–1080.

Leventhal, H., Meyer, D., & Nerenz, D. (1980). The common sense representation of illness behavior. In S. Rachman (Ed.), *Medical Psychology, Vol. 2* (pp. 7–30). New York: Pergamon.

Levine, B. A., & Wolpe, J. A. (1980). *In vivo* desensitization of a severe driving phobia through radio contact. *Journal of Behavior Therapy and Experimental Psychiatry, 11*, 282–282.

Levine, P. (1986). Stress. In M. H. G. Coles, E. Donchin, & S. W. Porges (Eds.), *Psychophysiology: Systems, processes, and applications* (pp. 331–353). New York, NY: Guilford Press.

Levine, S. (1971). Stress and behavior. *Scientific American, 224*, 26–31.

Levis, D. J. (1980). Implementing the technique of implosive therapy. In A. Goldstein & E. B. Foa (Eds.), *Handbook of behavioral interventions: A clinical guide* (pp. 92–151). New York: Wiley.

Levis, D. J. (1991). A clinician's plea for a return to the development of nonhuman models of psychopathology: New clinical observations in need of laboratory study. In M. R. Denny (Ed.), *Fear, avoidance, and phobias: A fundamental analysis* (pp. 395–427). Hillsdale, N.J.: Erlbaum.

Levis, D. J. (1995). Decoding traumatic memory: Implosive theory of psychopathology. In W. O'Donohoe & L. Krasner (Eds.), *Theories of behavior therapy: Exploring behavior change* (pp. 173–207). Washington, D.C.: American Psychological Association.

Levis, D. J., & Hare, N. (1977). A review of the theoretical rationale and empirical support for the extinction approach of implosive (flooding) therapy. In M. Hersen, R. M. Eisler, & P. M. Miller (Eds.), *Progress in behavior modification Vol. 4* (pp. 299–376). New York: Academic Press.

Lewinsohn, P. M., & Alexander, C. (1990). Learned resourcefulness and depression. In M. Rosenbaum (Ed.), *Learned resourcefulness: On coping skills, self-control, and adaptive behavior* (pp. 202–217). New York: Springer.

Lichstein, K. L. (1988). *Clinical relaxation strategies*. New York: Wiley.

Liddell, H. (1949). The role of vigilance in the development of animal neurosis. In P. Hoch & J. Zubin (Eds.), *Anxiety*. New York: Grune & Stratton.

Lifton, R. J., & Olson, E. (1976). Human meaning of total disaster. *Psychiatry, 101*, 141–148.

Light, K. C., Brownley, K. A., Turner, J. R., Hinterliter, A. L., Girdler, S. S., Sherwood,

A., & Anderson, N. B. (1995). Job status and high-effort coping influence work blood pressure in women and blacks. *Hypertension, 25,* 554–559.

Linden, W. (1993). The autogenic training method of J. H. Schultz. In P. M. Lehrer & R. L. Woolfolk (Eds.), *Principles and practice of stress management* (2nd ed.) (pp. 205–229). New York: Guilford.

Lindquist, C. W., Framer, J. A., McGrath, R. A., MacDonald, M. L., & Rhyne, L. D. (1975). Social skills training: Dating skills treatment manual. *JSAS Catalogue of Selected Documents in Psychology, 5,* 279.

Linehan, M. M., Brown, S. H., Nielsen, S. L., Olney, K., & McFall, R. M. (1980, November). *The effectiveness of seven styles of assertion.* Paper presented at the annual convention of the Association for the Advancement of Behavior Therapy, New York.

Lipovsky, J. A. (1991). Posttraumatic stress disorder in children. *Family and Community Health, 14,* 42–51.

Lipsett, L. (1983). Stress in infancy: Toward understanding the origins of coping behavior. In N. Garmezy & M. Rutter (Eds.), *Stress, coping, and development in children* (pp. 161–190). New York: McGraw-Hill.

Loftus, E. F. (1992). The reality of repressed memories. Unpublished manuscript, University of Washington, Seattle. (Expanded version of address presented at the American Psychological Association Meeting, Washington, D.C., August 1992).

Loftus, E. F. (1993). The reality of repressed memories. *American Psychologist, 48,* 518–537.

Loftus, E. F., & Klinger, M. R. (1992). Is the unconscious smart or dumb? *American Psychologist, 47,* 761–765.

Lohr, J. M. (1996). Eye movement desensitization and reprocessing: Three views; Analysis by analogy for the mental health clinician. *Contemporary Psychology, 41,* 879–880.

Lourens, P. (1990). Theoretical perspectives on error analysis and traffic behavior. *Ergonomics, 33,* 1251–1263.

Lundeen, T. F., Sturdevant, J. R., & George, J. M. (1987). Stress as a factor in muscle and temporomandibular joint pain. *Journal of Oral Rehabilitation, 14,* 447–456.

Lushene, R. E. (1970). The effects of physical and psychological threat on the autonomic, motoric, and ideational components of state anxiety. Doctoral dissertation, Florida State University.

Lutgendorf, S. K., Antoni, M. H., Ironson, G., Klimas, N., Kumar, M., Starr, K., McCabe, P., Cleven, K., Fletcher, M. A., & Schneiderman, N. (1997). Cognitive-behavioral stress management decreases dysphoric mood and herpes simplex virus-type 2 antibody titers in symptomatic HIV-seropositive gay men. *Journal of Consulting and Clinical Psychology, 65,* 31–43.

Luthe, W. (1983). Stress and autogenic therapy. In H. Selye (Ed.), *Selye's guide to stress research,* Vol. 2 (pp. 146–213). New York: Scientific and Academic Editions.

Lydiard, R. B., Roy-Byrne, P. P., & Ballenger, J. C. (1988). Recent advances in the psychopharmacological treatment of anxiety disorders. *Hospital and Community Psychiatry, 39,* 1157–1165.

Lyons, J. A., & Keane, T. M. (1989). Implosive therapy for the treatment of combat-related PTSD. *Journal of Traumatic Stress, 2,* 137–152.

MacLean, P. (1990). *The triune brain in evolution: Role in paleocerebral functions.* New York: Plenum Press.

MacNair, R. R., & Elliott, T. R. (1992). Self-perceived problem-solving ability, stress appraisal, and coping over time. *Journal of Research in Personality, 26,* 150–164.

Malan, J. R., Norton, G. R., & Cox, B. J. (1993). Panic attacks and alcoholism: Primacy and frequency of attacks. *Alcoholism Treatment Quarterly, 10,* 95–105.

Manuso, J. (1983). The Equitable Life Assurance Society program. *Preventive Medicine, 12,* 658–662.

Marbach, J. J., Lennon, M. C., & Dohrenwend, B. P. (1988). Candidate risk factors for temporomandibular pain and dysfunction syndrome: Psychosocial, health behavior, physical illness and injury. *Pain, 34,* 139–151.

Marks, I. M. (1978). *Living with fear.* New York: McGraw-Hill.

Marks, I. M. (1987). *Fears, phobias, and rituals.* New York: Oxford University Press.

Marks, I. M., Grey, S., Cohen, S. D., Hill, R., Mawson, D., Ramm, E., & Stern, R. (1983). Imipramine and brief therapist-aided exposure in agoraphobics having self-exposure homework: A controlled trial. *Archives of General Psychiatry, 40,* 153–162.

Marks, I. M., Lelliot, P. T., Basoglu, M., & Noshirvani, H. (1988). Clomipramine, self-exposure and therapist-aided exposure for obsessive-compulsive rituals. *British Journal of Psychiatry, 152,* 522–534.

Marks, I. M., Stern, R. S., Mawson, D., Cobb, J., & McDonald, R. (1980). Anafranil and exposure for obsessive-compulsive rituals-I. *British Journal of Psychiatry, 131,* 1–25.

Marquis, J. N. (1991). A report on seventy-eight cases treated by eye movement desensitization. *Journal of Behaviour Therapy and Experimental Psychiatry, 22,* 187–192.

Marquis, J. N. (1977). Orgasmic reconditioning: Changing sexual object choice through controlling masturbation fantasies. In J. Fischer & H. L. Gochros (Eds.), *Handbook of behavior therapy with sexual problems, Vol. I* (pp. 120–130). New York: Pergamon.

Marshall, W. L. (1977). Flooding therapy: Effectiveness, stimulus characteristics, and the value of brief in vivo exposure. *Behaviour Research and Therapy, 15,* 79–97.

Martelli, M. F., Auerbach, S. M., Alexander, J., & Mercuri, L. G. (1987). Stress management in the health care setting: Matching interventions with patient coping styles: *Journal of Consulting and Clinical Psychology, 55,* 201–207.

Martinez-Urrutia, A. (1975). Anxiety and pain in surgical patients. *Journal of Consulting and Clinical Psychology, 43,* 437–442.

Marzuk, P. M. (1991). Suicidal behavior and HIV illnesses. *International Review of Psychiatry, 3,* 365–371.

Maslach, C., & Jackson, M. E. (1981). The measurement of experienced burnout. *Journal of Occupational Behavior, 2,* 99–113.

Masters, J. C., Burish, T. G., Hollon, S. D., & Rimm, D. (1987). *Behavior therapy: Techniques and empirical findings.* New York: Harcourt Brace Jovanovich.

Matheny, K. B., Aycock, D. W., Pugh, J. L., Curlette, W. L., & Cannella, K. A. (1986). Stress coping: A qualitative and quantitative synthesis with implications for treatment. *The Counseling Psychologist, 14,* 499–549.

Matteo, S. (1988). The risk of multiple addictions. Guidelines for assessing a woman's alcohol and drug use. *The Western Journal of Medicine, 149,* 741–745.

Matteson, M. T., & Ivancevich, J. M. (1987). *Controlling work stress.* San Francisco: Josey-Bass.

Matthews, K. A. (1988). Coronary heart disease and Type A behaviors: Update on and alternative to the Booth-Kewley and Friedman (1987) quantitative review. *Psychological Bulletin, 104,* 373–380.

Mavissakalian, M. (1986). Imipramine in agoraphobia. *Comprehensive Psychiatry, 27,* 401–406.

Mavissakalian, M. (1990). Sequential combination of imipramine and self-directed exposure in the treatment of panic disorder with agoraphobia. *Journal of Clinical Psychiatry, 51,* 184–188.

Mavissakalian, M., & Hamman, M. (1987). DSM-III personality disorder in agoraphobia II. Changes with treatment. *Comprehensive Psychiatry, 28,* 356–361.

Mavissakalian, M., Jones, B., Olson, S. C., & Perel, J. M. (1990). The relationship of plasma Anafranil and N-desmethylclomipramine to response in obsessive-compulsive disorder. 29th Annual Meeting of the New Clinical Drug Evaluation Unit (1989, Key Biscayne, Florida). *Psychopharmacology Bulletin, 26,* 119–122.

Mavissakalian, M., & Michelson, L. (1986). Agoraphobia: Relative and combined effectiveness of therapist-assisted in vivo exposure and imipramine. *Journal of Clinical Psychiatry, 47,* 117–122. (a)

Mavissakalian, M., & Michelson, L. (1986). Two-year follow-up of exposure and imipramine treatment of agoraphobia. *American Journal of Psychiatry, 143,* 1106–1112. (b)

Mavissakalian, M., Michelson, L., & Dealy, R. (1983). Pharmacological treatment of agoraphobia: Imipramine versus imipramine with programmed practice. *British Journal of Psychiatry, 143,* 348–355.

Mavissakalian, M., Perel, J. (1985). Imipramine in the treatment of agoraphobia: Dose-response relationships. *American Journal of Psychiatry, 142,* 1032–1036.

May, R. (1950). *The meaning of anxiety.* New York: Ronald Press.

May, R. (1958). Contributions of existential psychotherapy. In R. May, E. Angel, & H. F. Ellenberger (Eds.), *Existence* (pp. 37–91). New York: Basic Books.

McCarthy, P., & Foa, E. B. (1990). Treatment interventions for obsessive-compulsive disorder. In M. Thase, B. Edelstein, & M. Hersen (Eds.), *Handbook of outpatient treatment of adults.* New York: Plenum Press.

McEwan, S. (1983). Isn't it time to leave minimal daters alone? *The Behavior Therapist, 6,* 101.

McGee, R. K. (1974). *Crisis intervention in the community.* Baltimore: University Park Press.

McGuigan, F. J. (1993). Progressive relaxation: Origins, principles, and clinical applications. In P. M. Lehrer & R. L. Woolfolk (Eds.), *Principles and practice of stress management* (2nd ed.) (pp. 17–52). New York: Guilford.

McNally, R. J. (1987). Preparedness and phobias. *Psychological Bulletin, 101,* 283–303.

McNamee, G., O'Sullivan, G., Lelliot, P., & Marks, I. (1989). Telephone-guided treatment for housebound agoraphobics with panic disorder: Exposure vs. relaxation. *Behavior Therapy, 20,* 491–497.

McNeill, C., Moh., N. D., Rugh, J. D., & Tanaka, T. T. (1990). Temporomandibular disorders: Diagnosis, management, education, and research. *Journal of the American Dental Association, 120,* 253–263.

Meichenbaum, D. (1985). *Stress inoculation training.* New York: Pergamon.

Meichenbaum, D. (1993). Stress inoculation training: A 20-year update. In P. M. Lehrer & R. L. Woolfolk (Eds.), *Principles and practice of stress management* (2nd ed.) (pp. 373–406). New York: Guilford.

Meichenbaum, D. (1996). Stress inoculation training for coping with stressors. *The Clinical Psychologist, 49(4),* 4–7.

Mellstrom, M., Cicala, G. A., & Zuckerman, M. (1976). General versus specific trait anxiety measures in the prediction of fear of snakes, heights, and darkness. *Journal of Consulting and Clinical Psychology, 44,* 83–91.

Menzies, R. G., & Clarke, J. C. (1995). The etiology of phobias: A nonassociative account. *Clinical Psychology Review, 15,* 23–48.

Mercuri, L. G., Olson, R. E., & Laskin, D. M. (1979). The specificity of response to experimental stress in patients with myofascial pain dysfunction syndrome. *Journal of Dental Research, 58,* 1866–1871.

Meyerowitz, B. (1996, September). Cited in Azur, B., Scientists examine cancer patients' fears. *APA Monitor, 27 (9),* 32.

Milan, M. A., & Kolko, D. J. (1985). Social skills training and complementary strategies in anger control and the treatment of aggressive behavior. In L. L'Abate & M. A. Milan (eds.), *Handbook of social skills training and research* (pp. 101–135). New York: Wiley.

Miles, C. (1977). Conditions predisposing to suicide: A review. *Journal of Nervous and Mental Disease, 164,* 231.

Miller, S. M. (1987). Monitoring and blunting: Validation of a questionnaire to assess styles of information seeking under threat. *Journal of Personality and Social Psychology, 52,* 345–353.

Miller, S. M., Brody, D. S., & Summerton, J. (1988). Styles of coping with threat: Implications for health. *Journal of Personality and Social Psychology, 54,* 142–148.

Miller, S. M., & Mangan, C. E. (1983). Interacting effects of information and coping style in adapting to gynecologic stress: Should the doctor tell all? *Journal of Personality and Social Psychology, 45,* 223–236.

Mitchell, J. T. (1983). When disaster strikes: The critical incident stress debriefing process. *Journal of Emergency Medical Services, 8,* 36–39.

Mitchell, J. T., & Bray, G. (1990). *Emergency services stress: Guidelines for preserving the health and careers of emergency service personnel.* Englewood Cliffs, N.J.: Prentice Hall.

Moos, R. H., & Billings, A. G. (1982). Conceptualizing and measuring coping resources and coping processes. In L. Goldberger & S. Bresnitz (Eds.), *Handbook of stress: Theoretical and clinical aspects* (pp. 212–230). New York: Free Press.

Moss, R. A., & Adams, H. E. (1984). Physiological reactions to stress in subjects with and without myofascial pain dysfunction symptoms. *Journal of Oral Rehabilitation, 11,* 219–232.

Moss, R. A., Garrett, J., & Chiodo, J. F. (1982). Temporomandibular joint dysfunction and myofascial pain dysfunction syndromes: Parameters, etiology, and treatment. *Psychological Bulletin, 92,* 331–346.

Mossman, B. T., Bignon, J., Corn, M., Seaton, A., & Gee, J. B. L. (1990). Asbestos: Scientific developments and implications for public policy. *Science, 244,* 294–301.

Mucha, T. F., & Reinhardt, R. F. (1970). Conversion reactions in student aviators. *American Journal of Psychiatry, 127,* 493–497.

Murphy, L. R. (1984). A comparison of worksite relaxation methods. In B. G. F. Cohen (Ed.), *Human aspects in office automation* (pp. 257–265). Amsterdam: Elsevier.

Murphy, L. R. (1987). A review of organizational stress management research: Methodological considerations. In J. M. Ivancevich & D.C. Ganster (Eds.), *Job stress: From theory to suggestions* (pp. 215–227). New York: Haworth Press.

Murray, E. J., & Jacobson, L. I. (1971). The nature of learning in traditional and behavioral psychotherapy. In A. Bergin & S. Garfield, *Handbook of psychotherapy and behavior change* (pp. 709–747). New York: Wiley.

Myers, D. G., & Diener, E. (1995). Who is happy? *Psychological Science, 6,* 10–19.

Nakagawa. T., & Sugita, M. (1994). Life style changes and psychosomatic problems in Japan. *Homeostasis in Health and Disease, 35,* 180–189.

Neal, G. W., & Heppner, P. P. (1982, March). *Personality correlates of perceived effective personal problem solving.* Paper presented at American Personnel and Guidance Association Meeting, Detroit.

Nezu, A. M., & D'Zurilla, T. J. (1989). Social problem solving and negative affective conditions. In P. C. Kendall & D. Watson (Eds.), *Anxiety and depression: Distinctive and overlapping features* (pp. 285–315). New York: Academic Press.

Nicholson, T., Duncan, D. F., Hawkins, W., Belcastro, P. A., & Gold, R. (1988). Stress treatment: Two aspirins, fluids, and one more workshop. *Professional Psychology: Research and Practice, 19,* 637–641.

Nietzel, M., Bernstein, D. A., & Russell, R. L. (1988). Assessment of anxiety and fear. In A. S. Bellak & M. Hersen (Eds.), *Behavioral assessment: A practical handbook* (3rd ed.) (pp. 280–312). New York: Pergamon.

Nomikos, M. S., Opton, E., Averill, J. R., & Lazarus, R. S. (1968). Surprise versus suspense in the production of stress reaction. *Journal of Personality and Social Psychology, 8,* 204–208.

Northwestern National Life Insurance Company. (1991). *Employee burnout: America's newest epidemic.* Minneapolis, Minn: Author.

Obrist, P. A., Light, K. C., Langer, A. W., & Koepke, J. P. (1986). Psychosomatics. In C. Michael, E. Donchin, & D. Porges (Eds.), *Psychophysiology systems, processes, and applications* (pp. 626–645). New York, London: The Guilford Press.

O'Connell, D. F. (1989). Treating the high risk adolescent: A survey of effective programs and interventions. In P. B. Henry (Ed.), *Practical approaches in treating adolescent chemical dependency: A guide to clinical assessment and intervention* (pp. 49–69). New York: Haworth.

Ohman, A. (1986). Face the beast and fear the face: Animal and social fears as prototypes for evolutionary analyses of emotion. *Psychophysiology, 23,* 123–145.

O'Leary, A., Ozer, E., Parker, L., & Wiedenfeld, S. (1994). Efficacy: For Albert Bandura. *The Behavior Therapist, 17,* 127.

Oliner, S. P., & Oliner, P. M. (1988). *The altruistic personality: Rescuers of Jews in Nazi Europe.* New York: Free Press.

Orr, E., & Westman, M. (1990). Does hardiness moderate stress, and how?: A review. In M. Rosenbaum (Ed.), *Learned resourcefulness: On coping skills, self-control, and adaptive behavior* (pp. 64–94). New York: Springer.

Ost, L-G. (1987). Applied relaxation: Description of a coping technique and review of controlled studies. *Behaviour Research and Therapy, 25,* 397–409.

Ost, L-G., Salskovskis, P. M., & Hellstrom, K. (1991). One-session therapist-directed exposure vs. self-exposure in the treatment of spider phobia. *Behavior Therapy, 22,* 407–422.

Ozer, E. M., & Bandura, A. (1990). Mechanisms governing empowerment effects: A self-efficacy analysis. *Journal of Personality and Social Psychology, 58,* 472–486.

Parker, M. W. (1990). A dynamic model of etiology in temporomandibular disorder. *Journal of the American Dental Association, 120,* 283–290.

Parkes, K. (1984). Locus of control, cognitive appraisal, and coping in stressful episodes. *Journal of Personality and Social Psychology, 46,* 655–668.

Pato, M. T., Zohar-Kadouch, R., Zohar, J., & Murphy, D. L. (1988). Return of symptoms after discontinuation of Anafranil in patients with obsessive-compulsive disorder. *American Journal of Psychiatry, 145,* 1521–1525.

Payne, R. (1988). Individual differences in the study of occupational stress. In C. L. Cooper & R. L. Payne (Eds.), *Causes, coping, and consequences of stress at work,* (pp. 209–232). Chichester: Wiley.

Pelissolo, A. (1995). The benzodiazepine receptor: The enigma of the endogenous ligand. *Encephale, 21,* 133–140.

Pelletier, K. R., & Lutz, R. (1988). Healthy people—healthy business: A review of stress management programs in the workplace. *American Journal of Health Promotion, 2,* 5–12, 19.

Pennebaker, J. W. (1989). Confession, inhibition, and disease. In L. Berkowitz (Ed.), *Advances in experimental social psychology,* Vol. *22* (pp. 211–244). Orlando, Fl.: Academic Press.

Pennebaker, J. W. (1990). *Opening up: The healing powers of confiding in others.* New York: Morrow.

Perry, R. W., & Lindell, M. K. (1978). The psychological consequences of natural disaster: A review of research on American communities. *Mass Emergencies, 3,* 105–115.

Petersen, D. (1984). *Human-error reduction and safety management.* Deer Park, New York: Aloray.

Petronko, M. (1996). The lighter side of behavior therapy: Be prepared. *The Behavior Therapist, 19(2),* 23.

Pieper, C., Warren, K., & Pickering, T. G. (1993). A comparison of ambulatory blood pressure and heart rate at home and work on work and non-work days. *Journal of Hypertension, 11,* 177–183.

Pikoff, H. (1984). A critical review of autogenic training in America. *Clinical Psychology Review, 4,* 619–639.

Pines, A. M. (1993). Burnout. In L. Goldberger & S. Breznitz (Eds.), *Handbook of stress: Theoretical and clinical aspects* (2nd ed.) (pp. 386–402). New York: Free Press.

Pollack, M. H., Tesar, G. E., Rosenbaum, J. F., Spier, S. A., (1986). Clonazepam in the treatment of panic disorder and agoraphobia: A one year follow-up. *Journal of Clinical Psychopharmacology, 6,* 302–304.

Postal employees warned on guns in the workplace (1995, August 2). *Richmond Times-Dispatch,* p. A2.

Quick, J. C., Murphy, L. R., Hurrell, J. J., Jr., Orman, D. (1992). The value of work, the risk of distress, and the power of prevention. In J. C. Quick, L. R. Murphy, & J. J. Hurrell, Jr. (Eds.), *Stress and well-being at work* (pp. 3–13). Washington, D.C.: American Psychological Association.

Rabin, B. S., Cohen, S., Ganguli, R. Lysle, D. T., & Cunnick, J. E. (1989). Bidirectional interaction between the central nervous system and the immune system. *Critical Review of Immunology, 9,* 279–312.

Rachman, S. (1980). Emotional reprocessing. *Behaviour Research & Therapy, 18,* 51–60.

Rapee, R. M., & Barlow, D. H. (1993). Generalized anxiety disorder, panic disorder, and the phobias. In P. B. Sutker & H. E. Adams (Eds.). *Comprehensive handbook of psychopathology* (2nd ed.) (pp. 109–127). New York: Plenum.

Raymond, M., & Moser, R. (1995). Aviators at risk. *Aviation, Space, & Environmental Medicine, 66,* 35–39.

Redlemier, D. A., & Tibshirani, R. J. (1997). Association between cellular-telephone calls and motor vehicle collisions. *New England Journal of Medicine, 336,* 453–458.

Remembering "repressed" abuse (1992). APS *Observer, 5(4),* 6–7.

Repetti, R. L. (1993). The effects of workload and the social environment at work on health. In L. Goldberger & S. Bresnitz (Eds.), *Handbook of stress* (pp. 368–385). New York: Free Press.

Resick, P. A. (1993). The psychological impact of rape. *Journal of Interpersonal Violence, 8,* 223–255.

Resick, P. A., Calhoun, K. S., Atkeson, B. M., & Ellis, E. M. (1981). Social adjustment in victims of sexual assault. *Journal of Consulting and Clinical Psychology, 49,* 705–712.

Resick, P. A., & Schnicke, M. K. (1992). Cognitive processing therapy for sexual assault victims. *Journal of Consulting and Clinical Psychology, 60,* 748–756.

Resnik, H. L. P. (1980). Suicide. In H. I. Kaplan, A. M. Freedman, & B. J. Sadock (Eds.), *Comprehensive textbook of psychiatry,* Vol. 2 (3d ed.) (pp. 2085–2097). Baltimore, Md: Williams & Wilkins.

Reynolds, S., & Briner, R. B. (1994). Stress management at work: With whom, for whom and to what ends? *British Journal of Guidance and Counselling, 22,* 75–89.

Rice, M. E., Helzel, M. F., Varney, G. W., & Quinsey, V. L. (1985). Crisis intervention and prevention training for psychiatric staff. *American Journal of Community Psychology, 13,* 289–304.

Richards, D. (1994). Traumatic stress at work: A public health model. *British Journal of Guidance and Counselling, 22,* 51–64.

Rickels, K., Fox, I. L., Greenblatt, D. J., & Sandler, K. R. (1988). Clorazepate and lorazepam: Clinical improvement and rebound anxiety. *American Journal of Psychiatry, 145,* 312–317.

Rifkin, J. (1994). *The end of work.* New York: Putnam.

Riggs, D. S., & Foa, E. B. (1993). Obsessive compulsive disorder. In D. H. Barlow (Ed.), *Clinical handbook of psychological disorders* (pp. 189–239). New York, N.Y.: Guilford Press.

Roberts, A. H. (1985). Biofeedback: Research, training, and clinical roles. *American Psychologist, 40,* 938–941.

Roberts, R. J. (1989). Passenger fear of flying: Behavioural treatment with extensive in-vivo exposure and group support. *Aviation, Space, and Environmental Medicine, 60,* 342–348.

Robinson, D. (1990, July 22). Stressbusters. *Parade,* pp. 12, 13.

Rodin, J. (1980). Managing the stress of aging: The role of coping, In S. Levine & H. Ursin (Eds.), *Coping and health* (pp. 171–202). New York: Plenum.

Rosen, G. (1996). Level II training for EMDR: One commentator's view. *The Behavior Therapist, 19,* 76–77.

Rosenbaum, M. (1990). Role of learned resourcefulness in self-control of health behavior. In M. Rosenbaum (Ed.), *Learned resourcefulness: On coping skills, self-control, and adaptive behavior* (pp. 3–30). New York: Springer.

Rosenbaum, M., & Merbaum, M. (1984). Self-control of anxiety and depression: An evaluative review of treatments. In C. M. Franks (Ed.), *New developments in behavior therapy: From research to clinical application* (pp. 105–154). New York: Haworth Press.

Rosenthal, T. L. (1993). To soothe the savage breast. *Behaviour Research and Therapy, 31,* 439–462.

Rothbaum, B. O., & Foa, E. B. (1992). Exposure therapy for rape victims with post-traumatic stress disorder. *The Behavior Therapist, 15,* 291–222.

Rothbaum, B. O., Hodges, L. F., Kooper, R., Opduke, D., Williford, J. S., & North, M. (1995). Effectiveness of computer-generated (virtual reality) graded exposure in the treatment of acrophobia. *American Journal of Psychiatry, 152,* 626–628.

Rothman, A. J., Salovey, P., Antone, C., Keough, K., & Martin, C. (1993). The influence of message framing on health behavior. *Journal of Experimental Social Psychology, 29,* 408–433.

Rothman, A. J., Salovey, P., Turvey, C., & Fishkin, S. A. (1993). Attributions of responsibility and persuasion: Increasing mammography utilization among women over 40 with an internally oriented message. *Health Psychology, 12,* 39–47.

Rotter, J. B. (1966). Generalized expectancies for internal versus external control of reinforcement. *Psychological Monographs, 80* (1, Whole No. 609).

Rudestam, K., & Bedrosian, R. (1977). An investigation of the effectiveness of desensitization and flooding with two types of phobias. *Behaviour Research and Therapy, 15,* 23–30.

Rutter, M. (1990). Psychosocial resilience and protective mechanisms. In J. Rolf, A. S., Masten, D. Cicchetti, K. H. Neuchterlein, & S. Weintraub (Eds.), *Risk and protective factors in the development of psychopathology* (pp. 181–214). New York: Cambridge University Press.

Ryan, M. (1991, Fall). Trying to will a miracle. *People Extra: Amazing American,* pp. 88–93.

Sagan, C. (1993, March 7). What's really going on? *Parade,* pp. 4–6.

Saigh, P. A. (1989). The use of an in vitro flooding package in the treatment of traumatized adolescents. *Journal of Developmental and Behavioral Pediatrics, 10,* 17–21.

Salter, M. W., Brooke, R. I., & Merskey, H. (1986). Temporomandibular pain and dysfunction syndrome: The relationship of clinical and psychological data to outcome. *Journal of Behavioral Medicine, 9,* 97–109.

Saltzman, H. A., Heyman, A., Sieker, H. O. (1963). Correlation of clinical and physiologic manifestations of sustained hyperventilation. *New England Journal of Medicine, 268,* 1431–1436.

Sapolsky, R. M. (1994). *Why zebras don't get ulcers: A guide to stress, stress-related diseases, and coping.* New York: W. H. Freeman.

Sarason, B. R., Sarason, I. G., & Pierce, G. R. (1990). Traditional views of social support and their impact on assessment. In B. R. Sarason, I. G. Sarason, & G. R. Pierce (Eds.), *Social support: An interactional view* (pp. 9–25). New York: Wiley.

Scheier, M. F., & Carver, C. S. (1985). Optimism, coping, and health: Assessment and implications of generalized outcome expectancies. *Health Psychology, 4,* 219–247.

Scheier, M. F., Mathews, K. A., Owens, J. F. & Magovern, G. J. (1989). Dispositional optimism and recovery from coronary artery bypass surgery: The beneficial effects on physical and psychological well-being. *Journal of Personality and Social Psychology, 57,* 1024–1040

Scheier, M. F., Weintraub, J. K., & Carver, C. S. (1986). Coping with stress: Divergent strategies of optimists and pessimists. *Journal of Personality and Social Psychology, 51,* 1257–1264.

Schermerhorn, W. (1989, 12, April). Stress: Sometimes, rescue workers need help, too. *Richmond Times-Dispatch-Henrico/Hanover PLUS,* p. 8.

Schewe, P., & O'Donohue, W. (1993). Rape prevention: Methodological problems and new directions. *Clinical Psychology Review, 13,* 667–682.

Schmolling, P. (1984). Human reactions to the Nazi concentration camps: A summing up. *Journal of Human Stress, 10,* 108–120.

Schnall, P. L., Landsbergis, P. A., & Baker, D. (1994). Job strain and cardiovascular disease. *Annual Review of Public Health, 15,* 381–411.

Schneier, F. R., Martin, L. Y., Liebowitz, M. R., & Gorman, J. M. (1990). Alcohol abuse in social phobia. *Journal of Anxiety Disorders, 3,* 15–23.

Schulz, R., & Decker, S. (1985). Long-term adjustment to physical disability. *Journal of Personality and Social Psychology, 48,* 1162–1172.

Schuster, R. (1993, August 3). 76ers' pick Bradley: Man on a mission. *USA Today,* pp. 1–2.

Schwartz, M. A., and Associates, (Eds.). (1995). *Biofeedback: A practitioner's guide* (2nd ed). New York, London: The Guilford Press.

Schwartz, R. M. (1982). Cognitive-behavior modification: A review. *Clinical Psychology Review, 2,* 267–295.

Schwartz, S., & Gramling, S. E. (1993). Integration of the adjunctive behavior paradigm with etiological models of Myofascial Pain Disorder. *The Mississippi Psychologist, 49,* 3–7.

Schwartz, S., Gramling, S. E., & Mancini, A. (1994). The influence of life stress, personality, and learning history on illness behavior. *Journal of Behavior Therapy and Experimental Psychiatry, 25,* 135–142.

Scott, D. S. (1981). Myofascial pain-dysfunction syndrome: A psychobiological perspective. *Journal of Behavioral Medicine, 4,* 451–465.

Seligman, M. E. P. (1971). Phobias and preparedness. *Behavior Therapy, 2,* 307–320.

Seligman, M. E. P. (1975). *Helplessness: On depression, development, and death.* San Francisco: Freeman.

Seligman, M. E. P. (1991). *Learned optimism.* New York: Alfred A. Knopf.

Selye, H. (1956). *The stress of life.* New York: McGraw-Hill.

Shader, R. I., & Greenblatt, D. J. (1993). Use of benzodiazepines in anxiety disorders. *New England Journal of Medicine, 328,* 1398–1405.

Shaffer, J. W., Graves, P. L., Swank, R. T., & Pearson, T. A. (1987). Clustering of personality traits in youth and the subsequent development of cancer among physicians. *Journal of Behavioral Medicine, 10,* 441–447.

Shapiro, F. (1989). Efficacy of the eye movement desensitization procedure in the treatment of traumatic memories. *Journal of Traumatic Stress, 2,* 199–223.

Shapiro, F. (1994). EMDR: In the eye of a paradigm shift. *Behavior Therapist, 17,* 153–156.

Shapiro, F. (1995). *Eye movement desensitization and reprocessing: Basic principles, protocols and procedures.* New York: Guilford.

Shavit, Y., & Martin, F. C. (1987). Opiates, stress, and immunity: Animal studies. *Annals of Behavioral Medicine, 9,* 11–15.

Shavit, Y., Martin, F. C., Yirmiya, R., & Ben-Eliyahu, S. (1987). Effects of a single administration of morphine or footshock stress on natural killer cell cytotoxicity. *Brain, Behavior, & Immunity, 1,* 318–328.

Shearn, D. W. (1962). Operant conditioning of heart rate. *Science, 137,* 530–531.

Shweder, R. (1997, February 2). Stress (the word) is American's all purpose, global export. *Richmond Times-Dispatch,* G5.

Siegman, A. W. (1982). Nonverbal correlates of anxiety and stress. In L. Goldberger &

S. Bresnitz, *Handbook of stress: Theoretical and clinical aspects* (pp. 306–319). New York: Free Press.

Silver, R. L., & Wortman, C. B. (1980). Coping with undesirable life events. In J. Garber & M. E. P. Seligman (Eds.), *Human helplessness: Theory and applications* (pp. 279–340). New York: Academic Press.

Silverman, P. (1974). *Helping each other in widowhood.* New York: Health Sciences Press.

Simon, F., & Corbett, C. (1996). Road traffic offending, stress, age, and accident history among male and female drivers. *Ergonomics, 39,* 757–780.

Sinclair, U. (1946/1971). *The jungle.* Cambridge, Mass.: R. Bentley.

Skinner, E. A., & Wellborn, J. G. (1994). Coping during childhood and adolescence. In D. L. Featherman, R. M. Lerner & M. Perlmutter (Eds.), *Life-span development and behavior, Vol. 12* (pp. 91–133). Hillsdale, N.J.: Lawrence Erlbaum.

Slaikeu, K. A. (1990). *Crisis intervention: A handbook for practice and research.* Boston: Allyn and Bacon.

Slovic, P., Fischoff, B., & Lichtenstein, S. (1979). Rating the risks. *Environment, 21*(3), 14–20, 36–39.

Smith, J. C. (1986). Meditation, biofeedback, and the relaxation controversy: A cognitive-behavioral perspective. *American Psychologist, 41,* 1007–1009.

Smith, J. C. (1993). *Understanding stress and coping.* New York: MacMillan.

Smith, M. C. (Ed.) (1991). *A social history of the minor tranquilizers: The quest for small comfort in the age of anxiety.* Birmingham, N.Y.: Haworth Press.

Smith, R. E., & Nye, S. L. (1973). A comparison of implosive therapy and systematic desensitization in the treatment of test anxiety. *Journal of Consulting and Clinical Psychology, 41,* 37–42.

Smith, T. W. (1992). Hostility and health: Current status of a psychosomatic hypothesis. *Health Psychology, 11,* 139–150.

Snyder, S. H. (Ed.) (1986). *Drugs and the brain.* New York, N.Y.: Scientific American Books.

Solberg, W. D., Woo, M. W., & Houston, J. B. (1979). Prevalence of mandibular dysfunction in young adults. *Journal of the American Dental Association, 98,* 25–34.

Solomon, C. M. (1991). Sexual harassment after the Thomas hearings. *Personnel Journal, 70,* 33–37.

Solyom, L., Solyom, C., & Ledwidge, B. (1991). Fluoxetine treatment of obsessive-compulsive disorder. *Canadian Journal of Psychiatry, 36,* 723–727.

Sommers-Flanagan, J., & Sommers-Flanagan, R. (1995). Intake interviewing with suicidal patients: A systematic approach. *Professional Psychology: Research and Practice, 26,* 41–47.

Somova, L. I., Connolly, C., & Diara, K. (1995). Psychosocial predictors of hypertension in Black and white Africans. *Journal of Hypertension, 13,* 193–199.

Sorenson, J. H., & Mileti, D. S. (1987). Programs that encourage the adoption of precautions against natural hazards: Review and evaluation. In N. Weinstein (Ed.), *Taking care: Understanding and encouraging self-protective behavior* (pp. 208–230). New York: Cambridge University Press.

Spacapan, S., & Cohen, S. (1983). Effects and aftereffects of stressor expectation. *Journal of Personality and Social Psychology, 45,* 1243–1254.

Spence, D. (1982). Verbal indicators of stress. In L. Goldberger & S. Bresnitz, *Handbook of Stress: Theoretical and Clinical Aspects* (pp. 295–305). New York: Free Press.

Spielberger, C. D. (1966). The effects of anxiety on complex learning and academic achievement. In C. D. Spielberger (Eds.), *Anxiety and behavior* (pp. 361–397). New York: Academic Press.

Spielberger, C. D. (1972). Current trends in theory and research on anxiety. In C. D. Spielberger (Ed.), *Anxiety: Current trends in theory and research, Vol. 1* (pp. 3–19). New York: Academic Press.

Spielberger, C. D., Gorsuch, R. L., & Lushene, R. E., Vagg, P. R., & Jacobs, G. A.

(1983). *State-Trait Anxiety Inventory (Form Y).* Palo Alto, Calif.: Consulting Psychologists Press.

Spielberger, C. D., Westbury, L. G., Greer, K. S., & Greenfield, G. (1981). *The police stress survey: Sources of stress in law enforcement.* Human Resources Institute, Monograph Series Three, No. 6, College of Social and Behavioral Sciences, University of South Florida, Tampa, Florida.

Spitzer, W. J., & Burke, L. (1993). A critical-incident stress debriefing program for hospital-based health care personnel. *Health and Social Work, 18,* 149–156.

Sreenivasan, U., Manocha, S. N., & Jain, V. K. (1979). Treatment of severe dog phobia in childhood by flooding: A case report. *Journal of Child Psychiatry and Psychology and Allied Disciplines, 20,* 255–260.

Stampfl, T. G., & Levis, D. J. (1967). Essentials of implosive therapy: A learning theory based psychodynamic behavioral therapy. *Journal of Abnormal Psychology, 72,* 496–503.

Steffy, B. D. Jones, J. W., Murphy, L. R., & Kunz, L. (1986). A demonstration of the impact of stress abatement reducing employees' accidents and their costs. *American Journal of Health Promotion, 1,* 25–32.

Steptoe, A., Roy, M. P., Evans, O., & Snashall, D. (1995). Cardiovascular stress reactivity and job strain as determinants of ambulatory blood pressure at work. *Journal of Hypertension, 13,* 201–210.

St. Lawrence, J. S., & Kelly, J. A. (1989). AIDS prevention: Community and behavioral interventions. In M. Hersen, R. M. Eisler, & P. M. Miller (Eds.), *Progress in behavior modification, Vol. 24* (pp. 11–59). Newbury Park, Calif.: Sage Publications.

Stone, A. A. (1987). Event content in a daily survey is differentially associated with current mood. *Journal of Personality and Social Psychology, 52,* 56–58.

Stone, A. A., Reed, B. R., & Neale, J. M. (1987). Changes in daily event frequency precede episodes of physical symptoms. *Journal of Human Stress, 13,* 70–74.

Strentz, T. (1996). *Hostage survival handbook.* Manuscript in preparation.

Strentz, T., & Auerbach, S. M. (1988). Adjustment to the stress of simulated captivity: Effects of emotion-focused vs. problem-focused preparation on hostages differing in locus of control. *Journal of Personality and Social Psychology, 55,* 652–650.

Stress on the job. *Newsweek,* April 25, 1988, pp. 40–45.

Stuart, P. (1992). Murder at work. *Personnel Journal, 71,* 27. (a)

Stuart, P. (1992). Murder on the job. *Personnel Journal, 71,* 72–84. (b)

Stuart, P. (1993). Investments in EAPs pay off. *Personnel Journal, 72,* 45–54.

Sturgis, E. T. (1993). Obsessive-compulsive disorders. In P. B. Sutker & H. E. Adams (Eds.), *Comprehensive handbook of psychopathology* (2nd ed.) (pp. 129–144). New York: Plenum.

Sturgis, E. T., & Gramling, S. E. (in press). Psychophysiological assessment. In A. S. Bellack & M. Hersen (Eds.), *Behavioral assessment: A practical handbook* (4th ed.). New York: Pergamon Press.

Suarez, Y., Adams, H. E., & McCutcheon, B. A. (1976). Flooding and systematic desensitization: Efficacy in subclinical phobics as a function of arousal. *Journal of Consulting and Clinical Psychology, 44,* 872.

Suinn, R. N., & Deffenbacher, J. L. (1988). Anxiety management training. *The Counseling Psychologist, 16,* 31–49.

Suinn, R. N. & Richardson, F. (1971). Anxiety management training: A nonspecific behavior therapy program for anxiety control. *Behavior Therapy, 2,* 498–510.

Suls, J., & Fletcher, B. (1985). The relative efficacy of avoidant and nonavoidant coping strategies. *Health Psychology, 4,* 249–288.

Suokas, J., & Lonnqvist, S. J. (1991). Outcome of attempted suicide and psychiatric consultation: Risk factors and suicide mortality during a five year follow-up. *Acta Psychiatica Scandinavica, 84,* 545.

Suomi, S. J. (1991). Early stress and adult emotional reactivity in rhesus monkeys. In

G. R. Bock & J. Whelan (Eds.), *The childhood environment and adult disease* (pp. 171–188). Chichester, England: Wiley.

Sutton, S. R. (1982). Fear arousing communications: A critical examination of theory and research. In J. R. Eiser (Ed.), *Social psychology and behavioral medicine* (pp. 303–337). New York: Wiley.

Swift, C. F. (1986). Community intervention in sexual child abuse. In S. M. Auerbach & A. L. Stolberg (Eds.), *Crisis intervention with children and families* (pp. 149–172). Washington, D.C.: Hemisphere.

Swinson, R. P., & Kuch, K. (1989). Behavioral psychotherapy of agoraphobia/panic disorder. *International Review of Psychiatry, 1,* 195–205.

Tallis, F., & Smith, E. (1994). Does rapid eye movement desensitization facilitate emotional processing? *Behaviour Research and Therapy, 32,* 459–461.

Taylor, C. B., King, R., Margraf, J., Ehlers, A., & Telch, M. (1989). Use of medication and in vivo exposure in volunteers for panic disorder research. *American Journal of Psychiatry, 146,* 1423–1426.

Taylor, S. E. (1995). *Health psychology* (3rd ed.) New York: McGraw-Hill.

Taylor, S. E., & Brown, J. D. (1988). Illusion and well-being: A social psychological perspective on mental health. *Psychological Bulletin, 103,* 193–210.

Taylor, S. E., Kemeny, M. E., Aspinwall, L. G., Schneider, S. G., Rodriguez, R., & Herbert, M. (1992). Optimism, coping, psychological distress, and high-risk sexual behavior among men at risk for Acquired Immunodeficiency Syndrome (AIDS). *Journal of Personality and Social Psychology, 63,* 460–473.

Taylor, V. A., Ross, G. A., & Quarentelli, E. L. (1976). *Delivery of mental health services in disasters: The Xenia tornado and some implications.* Disaster Research Center, Ohio State University, Book and Monograph Series No. 11.

Temoshock L. & Dreher, H. (1992). *The Type C connection: Behavioral links to cancer and your health.* New York: Random House.

Thoits, P. (1986). Social support as coping assistance. *Journal of Consulting and Clinical Psychology, 54,* 416–423.

Thomas, L. J., Tiber, N., & Schireson, S. (1973). The effects of anxiety and frustration on muscular tension related to temporomandibular joint syndrome. *Oral Surgery, 36,* 763–768.

Thomas, R. M. (1977). The crisis of rape and implications for counseling: A review of the literature. Part I. *Crisis Intervention, 8,* 105–116.

Tinbergen, J. (1951). *Econometrics; translated from the Dutch by* H. Rijkenvan Olst. Philadelphia: Blakiston.

Tobach, E., & Bloch, H. (1958). Effects of stress by crowding prior to and following tuberculous infection. *American Journal of Physiology, 187,* 399–402.

Tuckman, J., & Youngman, W. F. (1968). Assessment of suicidal risk in attempted suicide. In H. L. P. Resnik (Ed.), *Suicidal behaviors.* Boston: Little, Brown, & Company.

Turnage, J. J., & Spielberger, C. D. (1991). Job stress in managers, professionals, and clerical workers. *Work and Stress, 5,* 165–176.

Turner, S. M., Beidel, D.C., Cooley, M. R., Woody, S. R., & Messer, S. C. (1994). A multicomponent behavioral treatment for social phobia. *Behaviour Research and Therapy, 32,* 381–390.

Twentyman, C. T., & McFall, R. M. (1975). Behavioral training of social skills in shy males. *Journal of Consulting and Clinical Psychology, 43,* 384–395.

Tyrer, P., Lee, I., & Alexander, J. (1980). Awareness of cardiac function in anxious, phobic and hypochondriacal patients. *Psychological Medicine, 10,* 171–174.

Ubell, E. (1992, May 10). Is your job good for you? *Parade Magazine,* pp. 8–9.

VandeCreek, L., & Knapp, S. (1993). *Tarasoff and beyond.* Sarasota, Fla.: Professional Resource Press.

Van Laar, M. W., Volkerts, E. R., & van Willigenburg, A. P. (1992). Therapeutic effects and effects on actual driving performance of chronically administered buspirone and diazepam in anxious outpatients. *Journal of Clinical Psychopharmacology, 12,* 86–95.

Violanti, J., & Marshall, J. (1996). Cellular phones and traffic accidents: An epidemiological approach. *Accident Analysis and Prevention, 28,* 265–270.

Wagner, B. M. (1997). Family risk factors for child and adolescent suicidal behavior. *Psychological Bulletin, 121,* 246–298.

Wagner, B. M., & Compas, B. E. (1990). Gender, instrumentality, and expressivity: Moderators of the relation between stress and psychological symptoms during adolescence. *American Journal of Community Psychology, 18,* 383–406.

Walk, R. D. (1956). Self-ratings of fear in a fear-invoking situation. *Journal of Abnormal and Social Psychology, 52,* 171–178.

Walker, J. G., Johnson, S., Manion, I., & Cloutier, P. (1996). Emotionally focused marital intervention for couples with chronically ill children. *Journal of Consulting and Clinical Psychology, 64,* 1029–1036.

Wall, T. O., & Clegg, C. W. (1981). A longitudinal study of group work redesign. *Journal of Occupational Behavior, 2,* 31–49.

Wanderer, Z., & Ingram, B. L. (1991). Therapeutic use of tape-recorded repetitions of flooding stimuli. *Journal of Behavior Therapy and Experimental Psychiatry, 22,* 31–35.

Warr, P. (1992). Age and occupational well-being. *Psychology and Aging, 7,* 37–45.

Warwick, H. M. C., & Salkovskis, P. M. (1990). Hypochondriasis. *Behaviour Research and Therapy, 28,* 105–117.

Watanabe, T. (1995). Japan's Schindler. In T. Fensch (Ed.), *Oskar Schindler and his list* (pp. 243–246). Forest Dale, Vt.: Paul S. Eriksson.

Watson, C. G., & Tilleskjor, C. (1983). Interrelationships of conversion, psychogenic pain, and dissociative disorder symptoms. *Journal of Consulting and Clinical Psychology, 51,* 788–789.

Watson, D. L., & Tharpe, R. G. (1993). *Self-directed behavior: Self-modification for personal adjustment.* Pacific Grove, Calif.: Brooks/Cole.

Watson, J. B., & Rayner, R. (1920). Conditioned emotional reactions. *Journal of Experimental Psychology, 3,* 1–14.

Weinberger, A., & Englehart, R. S. (1976). Three group treatments for reduction of speech anxiety among students. *Perceptual and Motor Skills, 43,* 1317–1318.

Weiss, J. M. (1971). Effects of coping behavior in different warning signal conditions on stress pathology in rats. *Journal of Comparative & Physiological Psychology, 77,* 1–13. (a)

Weiss, J. M. (1971). Effects of coping behavior with and without a feedback signal on stress pathology in rats. *Journal of Comparative & Physiological Psychology, 77,* 22–30. (b)

Weiss, J. M. (1971). Effects of punishing the coping responses (conflict) on stress pathology in rats. *Journal of Comparative & Physiological Psychology, 77,* 14–21. (c)

Weiss, J. M. (1977). Psychological and behavioral influences on gastrointestinal lesions in animal models. In J. Maser & M. Seligman (Eds.), *Psychopathology: Experimental models* (pp. 232–269). San Francisco: W. H. Freeman.

Weiss, R. D. (1991). The role of psychopathology in the transition from drug use to abuse to dependence. In M. Glantz & R. Pickens (Eds.), *Vulnerability to Drug Abuse.* Washington, D.C.: American Psychological Association.

Wells, J. K., Howard, G. S., Nowlin, W. F., & Vargas, M. J. (1986). Presurgical anxiety and postsurgical pain and adjustment: Effects of a stress inoculation procedure. *Journal of Consulting and Clinical Psychology, 54,* 831–835.

Wenger, D. E. (1978). Community response to disaster: Functional and structural alterations. In E. L. Quarantelli (Ed.), *Disasters: Theory and Research* (pp. 17–47). Beverly Hills, Calif.: Sage.

Wertlieb, D., Wiegel, C., & Feldstein, M. (1987). Measuring children's coping. *American Journal of Orthopsychiatry, 57,* 548–560.

West, B. L., Goethe, K. E., & Kallman, W. M. (1980). Heterosocial skills training: A behavioral-cognitive approach. In D. Upper & S. M. Ross (Eds.), *Behavioral group therapy*, 1980: *An annual review*. Champaign, Ill.: Research Press.

Wetzler, S. (1992, October 12). Sugarcoated hostility. *Newsweek*, p. 14.

Wiebe, D. J. (1991). Hardiness and stress moderation: A test of proposed mechanisms. *Journal of Personality and Social Psychology, 60,* 89–99.

Wientjes, C. J. E., & Grossman, P. (1994). Overactivity of the psyche or the soma? Interindividual associations between psychosomatic symptoms, anxiety, heart rate, and end-tidal partial carbon dioxide pressure. *Psychosomatic Medicine, 56,* 533–540.

Wilson, S. A., Becker, L. A., & Tinker, R. H. (1995). Eye movement desensitization and reprocessing (EMDR) treatment for psychologically traumatized individuals. *Journal of Consulting and Clinical Psychology, 63,* 928–937.

Wolfgang, A. P. (1988). Job stress in the health professions: A study of physicians, nurses, and pharmacists. *Behavioral Medicine, 14,* 43–47.

Wolpe, J. (1990). *The practice of behavior therapy.* New York: Pergamon.

Wolpe, J., & Abrams, J. (1991). Post traumatic stress disorder overcome by eye movement desensitization: A case report. *Journal of Behavior Therapy and Experimental Psychiatry, 22,* 39–43.

Wolpe, J., & Lazarus, A. A. (1966). *Behavior therapy techniques.* New York: Pergamon.

Wooley, S. C., Blackwell, B., & Winget, C. (1978). A learning theory model of chronic illness behavior: Theory, treatment and research. *Psychosomatic Medicine, 40,* 379–401.

Worchel, S., & Shebilske, W. (1986). *Psychology: Principles and applications, Second edition.* Englewood Cliffs, N.J.: Prentice-Hall.

Worker stress. *Richmond Times-Dispatch.* October 5, 1990, p. A–5.

Wortman, C. B., & Lehman, D. R. (1985). Reactions to victims of life crises: Support attempts that fail. In I. G. Sarason & B. G. Sarason (Eds.). *Social support: Theory, research, and applications.* Dodrecht Martinus: Nijhoff, Netherlands.

Wortman, C. B., & Silver , R. C. (1989). The myths of coping with loss. *Journal of Consulting and Clinical Psychology, 57,* 349–357.

Wurtele, S. K. Saslawsky, D. A., Miller, C. L., Marrs, S. R., & Britcher, J. C. (1986). Teaching personal safety skills for potential prevention of sexual abuse: A comparison of treatments. *Journal of Consulting and Clinical Psychology, 54,* 688–692.

Ziedonis, D. M. (1995). Psychiatric patients. In R. H. Coombs & D. M. Ziedonis (Eds.), *Handbook on Drug Abuse Prevention* (pp. 445–469). Needham, Mass.: Allyn & Bacon.

Zois, C. (1992). *Think like a shrink.* New York: Warner.

Zuckerman, M. (1979). *Sensation seeking: Beyond the optimal level of arousal.* Hillsdale, N.J.: Lawrence Erlbaum.

Zuckerman, M., Buchsbaum, M. S., & Murphy, D. L. (1980). Sensation seeking and its biological correlates. *Psychological Bulletin, 88,* 187–214.

Author and Subject Indexes

SUBJECT INDEX